All the Fun's in

How You Say

a Thing

Also by Timothy Steele

Uncertainties and Rest

Sapphics against Anger and Other Poems

Missing Measures: Modern Poetry and the Revolt against Meter

The Color Wheel

Sapphics and Uncertainties: Poems 1970–1986

The Poems of J. V. Cunningham (editor)

All the Fun's in

AN EXPLANATION OF

How You Say

METER AND VERSIFICATION

a Thing

TIMOTHY STEELE

OHIO UNIVERSITY PRESS

ATHENS

Ohio University Press, Athens, Ohio 45701
© 1999 by Timothy Steele
Printed in the United States of America
All rights reserved

Ohio University Press books are printed on acid-free paper ⊗ ™

10 09 08 07   7 6 5

Notices of permission to reprint excerpts from published sources
are provided in the section titled "Permissions and Copyrights"

Library of Congress Cataloging-in-Publication Data
Steele, Timothy.
    All the fun's in how you say a thing : an explanation of meter and
versification / Timothy Steele.
      p.   cm.
    Includes bibliographical references (p.   ) and index.
    ISBN 0-8214-1259-0 (cloth : acid-free paper). — ISBN
0-8214-1260-4 (paper : acid-free paper)
    1. English language—Versification. 2. English language—Rhythm.
3. Poetry—Authorship. 4. Poetics. I. Title.
PE1505.S73 1999
821.009—dc21
                                               98-43612
                                                  CIP

For Mark Salzman

Contents

Part Two: Other Matters, Other Meters

However minute the employment may appear, of analysing lines into syllables, and whatever ridicule may be incurred by a solemn deliberation upon accents and pauses, it is certain, that without this petty knowledge no man can be a poet; and that from the proper disposition of single sounds results that harmony that adds force to reason, and gives grace to sublimity; that shackles attention, and governs passion.

Samuel Johnson, Rambler no. 88

"Warm in December, cold in June, you say?"

"I don't suppose the water's changed at all.
You and I know enough to know it's warm
Compared with cold, and cold compared with warm.
But all the fun's in how you say a thing."

Robert Frost, "The Mountain," 100–104

Acknowledgments

In the writing of this book, I have been sustained by the kindness of many people. Ruben Quintero, Terry Santos, Helen Pinkerton Trimpi, and my wife, Victoria, have been especially and repeatedly generous with their sympathy and encouragement. Others who have provided valuable assistance include Robert L. Barth, Edgar Bowers, Peter Brier, Turner Cassity, Wendy Cope, the late Henri Coulette, Dick Davis, Kevin Durkin, Lelde Gilman, Patricia Gilmore-Jaffe, the late Charles Gullans, Jack Hagstrom, Dolores Hayden, Debra Hotaling, Martin Huld, Richard Janko, X. J. Kennedy, Robert Mezey, Leslie Monsour, Paul G. Naiditch, Joshua Odell, Anthony Olcott, Nancy Packer, Tom Peterson, John Ridland, Vikram Seth, Donald G. Sheehy, Wesley Trimpi, Bruce Whiteman, and Richard Wilbur. A version of the first chapter of the book appeared in the Fall 1990 issue of *Hellas,* and a version of the fifth chapter appeared in the Winter 1997 issue of the *Michigan Quarterly Review.* In addition, certain ideas developed here were initially explored in articles that I contributed to the Summer 1992 issue of *Brandeis Review* and to David Baker's *Meter in English: A Critical Engagement* (Fayetteville: The University of Arkansas Press, 1996). Thanks are due to Mr. Baker, as well as to Gerald Harnett, the editor of *Hellas,* to Brenda Marder, formerly the editor of *Brandeis Review,* and to Laurence Goldstein, the editor of the *Michigan Quarterly Review.* I am grateful as well to Nancy Basmajian of Swallow Press/Ohio University Press for her sensitive and insightful copyediting of the complete manuscript.

Finally, I wish to thank Mark Salzman, who read this book in draft form and who kept assuring me that it would one day be finished, however much I at times doubted that eventuality.

All the Fun's in

How You Say

a Thing

Introduction

> Here lies the preacher, judge, and poet, Peter,
> Who broke the laws of God, and man, and metre.

FRANCIS JEFFREY'S SATIRICAL EPITAPH on Peter Robinson reflects a long-standing assumption about poets and their work. Just as ministers are concerned with divine law, and judges with human law, so poets are concerned with metrical law, with meter. ("Meter" is the older of the alternative spellings of the word and is preferred in the United States; "metre," an Anglicized version of the French *mètre*, is preferred in Britain. Both countries use the older form in compounds indicating particular meters, such as "pentameter" and "tetrameter." The word ultimately derives from the Greek *metron*, "measure.") To be sure, poetry involves much more than meter. Good poems offer us liveliness of wit, sincerity of feeling, depth of intelligence, apt metaphor, illuminating imagery, engrossing storytelling, or some combination of these and other qualities. Yet throughout literary history, metrical practice has provided a unifying basis of craft for the great diversity of people who have composed poetry. Though the subject matter may have changed from age to age and poet to poet, the manner of presentation has retained its link with the concept of metrical arrangement. Even in the past one hundred years or so, when many writers have challenged the efficacy or legitimacy of traditional versification, meter has remained an instrument of undiminished value and has been brilliantly employed by a wide range of modern and contemporary poets.

This book offers an explanation of English meter. It describes and illustrates the principles of versification according to which most of the major poetry in our language has been written. More specifically, it examines the ways that poets reconcile the expressive and variable rhythms of living speech with the fixed units of meter. The book shows how poets maintain meter while at the same time modulating it, so that, even as it preserves its underlying regularity, it accommodates a limitless wealth of grammatical structures and sentence forms.

If one idea guides my analysis, it is that form and individuation harmonize in versification no less than in other pursuits and states of being. Just as, for instance, virtually all people have the same basic skeletal structure, the same basic arrangement of limbs and organs, and the same basic emotional and perceptual capacities, so all verse lines in a certain meter correspond to the same fundamental pattern. Yet just as each specific person embodies, in an utterly individual way, the general properties of our common humanity, so every actual verse line is a unique realization of its metrical paradigm. Universal type and particular manifestation coexist simultaneously and inextricably.

I hope that my remarks will provide pleasure and profit for anyone interested in poetry, but this book is designed first and foremost for younger readers, especially students who may for the first time be examining the corpus of verse in English. One can, admittedly, read poems with no regard for their meters. Nevertheless, the effect of a fine poem, be it an epic like John Milton's *Paradise Lost* or a lyric by Thomas Hardy, is intimately connected with its metrical element. Unless one recognizes and hears the verse, unless one feels the ways in which the words and phrases are adjusted to and are riding across the metrical pattern, much of the force or beauty of the poem will be lost. What is more, the meanings of lines, not infrequently, are clarified by the meter. Where ambiguity exists as to the correct rhetorical interpretation of a line, the meter can guide us to the right reading. Conversely, ignorance of metrical structure may confuse our sense of a poem, as anyone who has attended a poor performance of a Shakespeare play can testify. When ill-informed actors and actresses misdeliver the verse, they not only drain it of energy but also garble sentence structures so that whole passages become unintelligible.

I hope as well that this study will be of interest to aspiring poets, particularly those looking to achieve that special blend of vivacity and order characteristic of excellent metrical composition. Skillfully employed, meter can give language a rare elegance and tension and can make a singular appeal to the ear, mind, and memory of readers or listeners. Working together, the idiosyncratic personal voice and the normative metrical pattern continually transform and are transformed by each other. The metrical pattern gives the personal voice a resistant grace and solidity, while the voice infuses the pattern, in itself merely an abstract schema, with vigor and suppleness. Meter can, moreover, provide a writer with the opportunity to render perceptions with a precision unattainable by other means. Against the ground bass of a meter, shades of accent may be more sensitively registered than is possible in nonmetrical media, and the relative weight and speed of words and phrases may be more acutely felt. Also, because meter operates concurrently with grammar, the poet can regulate the relationship between the two in interesting ways. For example, by making lines end at and coincide with grammatical junctures, the poet can highlight or emphasize meaning. Conversely, by running sentence structure on over the end of a line—by setting metrical units at variance with syntactical ones—the poet can shift and shade sense. Finally, meter can help poets manage and move between different levels of style. Meter can give staying power and rhythmical interest to lower-keyed passages; and its steady undercurrent may help support and sustain a more elevated tone. Even a poet who ultimately adopts one of the many modes of free verse that have flourished in recent times will be better off for knowing meter. Knowledge of meter will promote a surer ear for rhythm and will alert one to useful arrangements of sound and speech.

We can best begin our consideration of meter by defining it and supplying a preliminary demonstration of its nature and function.

Meter is *organized rhythm*. The adjective in this definition is as important as the noun. Most speech is to some degree rhythmical. Common devices of sentence structure, such as antithesis and parallelism, impose rhythm on language. But meter is rhythm ordered in a conscious, specific manner. The metrical unit repeats, and once we feel or recognize, in reading a poem, this scheme of repetition, we can anticipate its continuance as a kind of pulse in the verse.

The opening stanza of John Keats's "To Autumn" illustrates this point.

> Season of mists and mellow fruitfulness,
> > Close bosom-friend of the maturing sun;
> Conspiring with him how to load and bless
> > With fruit the vines that round the thatch-eaves run;
> To bend with apples the moss'd cottage-trees,

And fill all fruit with ripeness to the core;
　　To swell the gourd, and plump the hazel shells
　With a sweet kernel; to set budding more,
And still more, later flowers for the bees,
Until they think warm days shall never cease,
　　For summer has o'er-brimm'd their clammy cells.

The stanza consists of a single sentence or, to be more exact, a long introductory phrase punctuated as a sentence. (The main clause is actually the first line of stanza 2, "Who hath not seen thee oft amid thy store?") The rhythmical integrity of the sentence is in part established by parallelism. The opening address to autumn features two parallel elements that characterize it ("Season of mists . . . / Close bosom-friend"), and the activities and powers of the sun-assisted autumn are set forth by means of parallel infinitives ("to load and bless," "To bend . . . / And fill," "To swell . . . and plump," "to set budding"). These correspondences create aural weight and direction, and are reinforced by alliteration (i.e., the device of beginning with the same sound two or more syllables in a related group of words, as in "_m_ists and _m_ellow," "_r_ound . . . _r_un," "_f_ill all _f_ruit") and consonance (i.e., the device of reiterating the same consonantal sound in a related group of words, as with the _m_s and _r_s of "su_mm_e_r_ has o'e_r_-b_r_i_mm_'d thei_r_ cla_mm_y").

Yet one might find such elements in prose as well as in poetry. Indeed, an ability to manage grammatical structure, and a sensitivity to the cooperative capacities of words, are as characteristic of accomplished prose writers as they are of expert writers of verse. What, then, distinguishes the rhythms of Keats's lines from the rhythms of prose? Are there additional factors— and from the standpoint of versification even more significant factors— that contribute to the well-knit texture of Keats's verse but would not occur in prose?

There are. And scrutinizing the stanza, we may perceive them. For one thing, we may note that each of Keats's lines has ten syllables. Now if only two or three successive lines had this characteristic, we might dismiss it as coincidental. However, their being all the same in this respect indicates that the poet has designed them to be this way. For another thing, we may notice that the word stress in each line tends to follow a pattern of alternating lighter and heavier syllables. This alternation, we should note, is not absolute: it is not invariably very light, very heavy, very light, very heavy, and so on, but rather involves a more relative lighter-to-heavier fluctuation that is at some points quite marked and at other points less emphatic. In addition, Keats makes use, in his first and eighth lines, of a liberty historically allowed in this type of verse: he begins these lines with two syllables whose rhythm is heavy-light rather than light-heavy.

Still, the lines consistently feature ten syllables and, generally, a pattern of alternating offbeats and beats. Observing these qualities, we may, if we know something of verse terminology, recognize that Keats is writing in the most familiar of English meters, iambic pentameter. And if we wish to analyze more closely the structure of an individual line, we can "scan" it. We can break it down into "feet"—a foot being the most elementary metrical component or building block of the line—and assign a metrical value to each syllable in each foot. Using a vertical bar to mark the boundaries between feet, an "x" to indicate a metrically unaccented syllable, and a slanting stroke to note a metrically accented syllable, we may scan, for example, line 7 of "To Autumn" thus:

$$\text{x} \quad / \quad \text{x} \quad / \quad \text{x} \quad / \quad \quad \text{x} \quad / \quad \text{x} \quad /$$
To swell | the gourd, | and plump | the ha | zel shells

This shows us the structure of the line and helps explain why it is called iambic pentameter. "Iambic" refers to the rhythm according to which the line is organized, "iambic" being the term that denotes the alternating lighter-heavier pattern. The basic unit of that pattern is an "iamb," a foot consisting of a metrically unaccented syllable followed by a metrically accented one. And the meter of the complete line, having five such feet, is called pentameter, *penta-* being the Greek prefix meaning five.

It is this organization of rhythm that makes Keats's composition metrical. It is this that makes it, in the traditional sense, verse as opposed to prose. (That the lines are pointed by "end rhyme" also contributes to the effect of the poem, but rhyme is a topic we must set aside for the present. We must also defer for now discussion of line indentation, which Keats and other poets sometimes employ to highlight stanzaic arrangements and rhyme pairings.)

To clarify the distinction between the organized rhythms of meter and the looser rhythms of prose, we can examine a prose passage that treats the same subject as "To Autumn." The passage occurs in chapter 10 of Jane Austen's novel *Persuasion*, published in 1818, just a year before Keats wrote his poem. At this point in the novel, the heroine, Anne Elliot, has joined several other people for a walk in the autumn countryside. Included in the party are Anne's onetime suitor, Captain Wentworth, and the two Musgrove sisters, who have designs on the Captain's affections and who use the walk as an pretext to engage his attention. Anne, however, refuses to enter into competition with them, and Austen writes of her:

> Her *pleasure* in the walk must arise from the exercise and the day, from the view of the last smiles of the year upon the tawny leaves and withered hedges, and from repeating to herself some few of the thousand poetical descriptions extant of autumn, that season of peculiar and inexhaustible influence on the mind of taste and tenderness, that season which has drawn from every poet, worthy of being read, some attempt at description, or some lines of feeling.

This passage, like Keats's stanza, consists of a long sentence sustained by parallelism ("from the exercise and the day . . . from the view . . . from repeating to herself;" "that season of peculiar and inexhaustible influence . . . that season which has drawn;" "some attempt at description, or some lines of feeling"). Austen also employs alliteration, more sparingly than Keats does, but in her own quiet manner (e.g., "inexhaustible influence . . . taste and tenderness"). In addition, the two pieces of writing are of roughly the same length: Keats's runs to eighty-five words, Austen's to eighty, though the latter occupies barely eight lines of text in the Signet Classic edition of *Persuasion* from which I have cited, whereas the stanza of verse, regardless of the edition, occupies eleven lines, thanks to the typographical custom of lineating metric units rather than laying them out continuously from margin to margin as would be done with prose.

Lastly, Austen's passage contains elements that, taken out of context, might appear to be verse lines. This is not as surprising as it may initially seem. Because meters are generally abstractions from or models of common patterns of speech, we often utter (or write in prose) sequences of words that fall, without our being aware of it, into meters or fragments of them. For instance, these phrases from the Austen passage scan as iambic pentameters, the first and third having a "feminine ending"—an extra unaccented syllable at the close:

```
  x  /   x  /  x  /    x   /   x    / (x)
  upon the tawny leaves and withered hedges

  x  /   x  /  x  /   x    /  x  /
  upon the mind of taste and tenderness

    x  / x    /   x   /    x  / x  /(x)
  that season which has drawn from every poet
```

Nevertheless, however much it resembles the Keats selection, Austen's passage is not verse. While some parts fall into measure, others do not, and it would take a fair amount of revision to bring them into sync with those that do. And though one could divide the passage into ten-syllable segments to produce the appearance of verse (and though poets in English have occasionally experimented with verse based on syllable count alone), the segmentalized version would not possess the rhythmical correspondences characteristic of verse. Rather than being consistently shaped by sound and sense, the lines would seem arbitrary, hacked to closure after every tenth syllable:

> Her *pleasure* in the walk must arise from
> The exercise and the day, from the view
> Of the last smiles of the year upon the
> Tawny leaves and withered hedges, and from
> Repeating to herself some few of the
> Thousand of the poetical descrip-
> Tions extant of autumn, that season of
> Inexhaustible influence on the . . .

Nor would we produce verse by resolving the passage into syntactical constituents and lineating them:

> Her *pleasure* in the walk must arise
> From the exercise and the day,
> From the view of the last smiles of the year
> Upon the tawny leaves and withered hedges,
> And from repeating to herself
> Some few of the thousand of the poetical descriptions
> Extant of autumn,
> That season of inexhaustible influence . . .

Though the passage has grace and weight, though Austen's dexterous manipulation of sentence structure gives it a thoughtful cadential flow, no pattern of rhythm emerges.

These remarks are not intended to disparage Austen. Her novels are among the greatest treasures of our language. Neither do I mean to suggest that verse is better than prose. Each has virtues. Good verse has an exceptional liveliness and memorability. Prose is freer and more capacious and may allow an author to present subjects in greater circumstantial detail than could be done in verse. To say that verse is traditionally written with meter, and prose without it, is not to make a value judgment, but simply to note that the media are different.

It is important, however, to note this difference, since many current texts skirt, blur, or ignore it, or imply that meter and rhythm are the same. They are not. They are related, in that meter is a special kind of rhythm. It is, to recur to our definition, organized rhythm.

To be effective, meters must suit the languages they serve, and nowhere is this truer than in English. People who do not understand versification sometimes say that it is unnatural to write in iambic measures, the chief measures of English poetry, because we do not speak in them. But, as was suggested a moment ago, we frequently do speak in them. For instance, the following extracts from actual or possible conversations are iambic trimeters —lines consisting of three iambic feet or, to put it another way, six syllables falling into an alternating lighter-to-heavier pattern. (The last sentence has a feminine ending, and its final word refers to the name of a family in northeastern Vermont, and not to a cucumber preserved in brine.)

> I always care too much.
> Perhaps he doesn't know.
> Who says that she can't pay?
> Her mother was a Pickle.

These are iambic tetrameters—lines consisting of four iambic feet:

> The air conditioner just died.
> I couldn't find a parking place.
> How many questions did I miss?
> He says he loves me for my mind.

And these are iambic pentameters:

> Let's get a cup of coffee after class.
> Whatever you decide is fine with me.
> I can't believe that I forgot my keys.
> You haven't kissed me since we got engaged.

Some might ask why iambic rhythm so naturally suits English. Three factors are crucial. The first concerns our tendency to space stresses at roughly equal intervals and to distinguish, for purposes of clear articulation, between stress levels of adjacent syllables. As linguists have observed, we "promote" a light syllable—give it slightly greater emphasis than we would otherwise —when it is flanked, fore and aft, by other light syllables. When we speak a run of three light syllables, their intelligibility increases if we raise the middle one a bit. In the following line, for instance,

And gnaw the frozen turnip to the ground

(John Clare, "Sheep in Winter," 3)

```
   x     /    x   /  x   /   x  /   x    /
And gnaw | the fro | zen tur | nip to | the ground
```

we stress, in the fourth foot, the preposition "to" a touch more than we might normally. The word is still comparatively light. But since it follows the even lighter second syllable of "turnip" and precedes the light article "the," it carries more weight than it would if it appeared in the vicinity of heavy syllables, as in phrases like "a train to catch" or "a call to arms."

Conversely, we "demote" a weighty syllable sandwiched between other weighty syllables. An obstructive effect results if we try to say several consecutive syllables with the same degree of heavy stress. In the following verse,

The mules that angels ride come slowly down

(Wallace Stevens, "Le Monocle de Mon Oncle," 67)

```
   x    /    x   /  x   /   x      /    x   /
The mules | that an | gels ride | come slow | ly down
```

we slightly de-emphasize "come" since it appears after the weighty syllable "ride" and before the heavy syllable "slow-." Generally, monosyllabic verbs like "come" are heavy, both in speech and verse; and here the word is, notwithstanding its demotion, fairly weighty. Yet it is not as emphatic as it would be if it were surrounded by lighter syllables, as in constructions like "They come and go" or "Your cousins come tomorrow."

Promotion and demotion are important to our prosody because they facilitate the integration, into iambic rhythm, of adjacent syllables of approximately the same stress qualities. Iambic verse requires of poets only that they maintain the basic lighter-to-heavier fluctuation of the line. The degree of fluctuation is, in strictly metrical terms, immaterial. Similarly, the only requirement of an iambic foot is that its second syllable be heavier than its first. How much heavier does not, for purposes of scansion, matter. To return to the examples above, "The mules" is an iamb, an iamb in which there is a marked difference of stress level between the two syllables. But "-y of" and "come slow-" also are iambs, though in the first case, both syllables are relatively light and in the second case, both are relatively heavy.

The shape (or "morphology") of English words is the second factor that makes our language so suitable to iambic rhythm. As Noam Chomsky and

Morris Halle demonstrate in their *Sound Pattern of English,* most English words of more than one syllable have alternating stress. By no means always does this alternation entail rhythm that rises iambically from lighter to heavier syllables. Though such words as "reverse," "surprising," "philosopher," and "procrastination" are configured so that the odd-numbered syllables are lighter and the even-numbered syllables are heavier, many other words are trochaically contoured, with the odd-numbered syllables having the most weight. ("Trochaic" refers to rhythm that falls from heavy to light syllables; and a "trochee" is a foot consisting of a metrically accented syllable followed by a metrically unaccented one.) Consider in this regard "purple," "idolize," "celebration," and "immortality," in each of which the odd-numbered syllables are heavier and the even-numbered lighter. Yet regardless of whether the rhythm of this or that word rises or falls, the alternation contributes, in conjunction with the third and final factor, to the prevalence of iambic meters.

This third factor is the comparatively uninflected or "analytic" character of our language. In more compressed, "synthetic" languages, inflectional suffixes are frequently added to the stems of words to indicate their grammatical functions and relationships. The classical Indo-European languages of Sanskrit, Greek, and Latin are all of this type, as is Old English, and when we study them we are struck by the complexity of their verb conjugations and of their declensions of nouns and adjectives. Middle and Modern English, in contrast, mainly convey meaning not by word ending but by word order. They entail arranging words in such significant sequences as adjective-noun and subject-verb-object, and make liberal use of particles (i.e., articles, conjunctions, prepositions, and the like) and of pronouns to indicate grammatical connections between different words, phrases, and clauses. Particles and pronominals are usually weakly stressed, and many of the most common, including *the, a, and, or, his, you, she, it, to, of,* and *in,* are monosyllabic. And the mixing of these words with lexically weightier words like nouns and verbs inclines English toward iambic rhythm. Even if the chief words of clauses and sentences are not in themselves iambic (and in English, monosyllabic words and trochaically contoured words far outnumber iambically shaped words), they may nevertheless be swept up into iambic rhythm, on account of being introduced or connected by particles and pronominals.

We can appreciate the cooperation in iambic verse of these three factors —the demotion-promotion phenomenon, the alternating stress of most English words of two or more syllables, and our frequent use of particles—

by examining two iambic pentameters from the first stanza of William Butler Yeats's "Among School Children":

> The children learn to cipher and to sing,
> To study reading-books and history

No one word here is in itself iambic. Indeed, the major words are heavy monosyllables ("learn," "sing"), fore-stressed disyllables ("children," "cipher," "study"), or trisyllables with a light middle syllable ("reading-books," "history"). Yet the words blend smoothly into the meter. "Children" blends because it is introduced by the definite article. "Learn" fits since it follows the light syllable of "children." (This transition indicates how words with a falling rhythm can contribute to iambics. It does not matter, in the context of Yeats's line, that "children" runs heavy-light. Its alternating stress is the thing that counts; and, having itself been incorporated, with the help of "the," into the iambic rhythm, its unaccented second syllable, "-dren," assists in integrating another uniambic word into the meter.) And though "cipher" is fore-stressed, and though "sing" is a heavy monosyllable, both are infinitive and preceded by the proposition "to"; and the infinitives are coordinated by "and," which is promoted to a metrical accent as a result of appearing between the light second syllable of "cipher" and the light preposition "to."

>   x   / x   /   x / x /   x /
> The children learn to cipher and to sing,

As for the second line, even though the verb and its two objects seem to countervail iambic rhythm, they mesh with the meter, because "study" is introduced by "to," because "reading-books" is preceded by the unaccented second syllable of "study," and because "reading-books" and "history" are coordinated by "and."

>   x   / x / x   /   x   / x /
> To study reading-books and history

(Some readers may note that "and" was promoted to a metrical accent in the previous line, but is metrically unaccented in this one; in the next chapter we will examine the ways in which the metrical nature of syllables in English may alter according to phrasal and rhetorical context.)

What is more, neither Yeats nor any other experienced poet needs to strain to integrate, into iambic rhythm, such disparate verbal material. Once poets acquire an ear for writing in measure, the structure and customs of the language work with them.

These circumstances not only explain why iambic rhythm is so prevalent in English poetry; they also suggest why our iambic meters emerged when they did, to wit, in the thirteenth and fourteenth centuries. Students of Middle English verse have often remarked that rhyme became easier in our poetry after the breakdown of the inflectional system of Old English and after English had become grammatically less compressed. This process—which resulted partly from developments within Old English and partly from the transforming fusion of English with French after the Norman Conquest—contributed as well to the emergence of iambic verse. The rhythm of Old English verse is roughly trochaic. In a seminal essay, "Old Germanic Metrics and Old English Metrics," Eduard Sievers identifies five types of half-lines as comprising the Old English poet's metrical armory; and the type most commonly used, both overall and especially to begin the line, runs *beat, offbeat, beat, offbeat.* By the thirteenth and fourteenth centuries, however, Middle English poets are writing in rhythms that tend to rise from lighter to heavier syllables. This is equally true of a poet like William Langland, who works with a modified version of the old Anglo-Saxon four-beat alliterative mode, and of poets like John Gower and Geoffrey Chaucer, who work in the newer iambic mode that will become the staple of poets in Modern English. As English relies less on flexional elements and more on relational words—as it becomes a language that communicates more by word order than by word ending—it tilts toward iambic rhythm.

Iambics can result from linguistic conditions other than those described above. Iambic meters appear in the poetries of a number of Indo-European languages. Indeed, some metrists have theorized that iambic is a sort of universal meter. The brain itself, according to this theory, relishes binary patterns and finds iambic rhythm congenial. Though I lack the competence in neurology to evaluate such speculations, they should be, I believe, approached with caution. Many prosodic systems, including those of French, Persian, and Chinese, do not involve iambic measures.

Further, diverse practices exist among languages that have employed iambics. For example, in ancient Greek, the iambic trimeter is an important measure, and Aristotle comments on several occasions (*Rhetoric* 1404a30, 1408b34; *Poetics* 1449a25) on the speechlike naturalness of iambics. But the principles of the Greek trimeter differ from those of English iambic meters. Ancient Greek verse arranges syllables according to their durations rather than their stress properties. Poets compose their lines in patterns of short and long syllables rather than unaccented and accented ones. Then, too, because the Greeks consider iambic a swift rhythm, they regard iambic lines not in terms of disyllabic feet, but in terms of four-syllable groups. These groups—or, as they are sometimes called, *metra*—are arranged according to the sequence, anceps-long-short-long. (An "anceps" position is one that can be can be long or short at the poet's discretion.) Finally, in ancient Greek verse, iambic is not as predominant a rhythm as it is in English poetry. Equally important, for example, is the dactylic-spondaic rhythm that ancient poets use in hexametric verse.

What is clear is merely that English—in its grammatical structure, its vocabulary, and its accentuation—well suits iambic rhythm.

As an aside, we should observe that it was the Greeks who coined the word "iamb" (*iambos*). One guess about the term's origin concerns the fact that, in ancient Greece, iambic verse was associated with the cult of Demeter and was initially employed for satire. Apollodorus (*Bibliotheca*, 1.5.1ff.) reports that after the kidnapping of her daughter Persephone by Hades, Demeter searched everywhere for her child, rejecting rest and consolation until, coming to the palace of Celeus in Eleusis, she laughed at an off-color joke, cracked by an old crone named Iambe. In honor of this woman who had coaxed the goddess from her grief, the Greeks applied "iambic" to humorous or mocking verse. And because such verse usually alternated between short and long syllables, "iambic" came to denote this pattern. (The orthographic and phonic resemblance between "iamb" and a measure that in English might suggest an *I am I am I am* movement is coincidental.)

Since languages differ structurally from one another, poets in different languages treat, as metrically significant, different aspects of speech. To return to the root meaning of "meter," poets "measure" those elements of their language that are most essential to its nature and structure. For example, pitch is crucial in Chinese, and in classical Chinese verse, lines are arranged not only according to the number of characters (each character being a single syllable), but also according to the tone levels of the characters. Syllabic length or "quantity" is a distinguishing feature of ancient Sanskrit, Greek, and Latin, and poets in those languages dispose their verses in patterns of long and short syllables. Italian and French poets measure their lines principally in terms of the number of syllables; accentuation, which is relatively faint in those languages, plays a subsidiary role.

Since the fourteenth century, English poets have chiefly measured two things: first, the number of syllables per line; second, the number and arrangement of accents per line. When people call English meter "accentual-syllabic," they are indicating that our verse lines have, as their norm, a fixed number and pattern of accents and a fixed number of syllables. As we have seen in Keats's "To Autumn," the norm of the iambic pentameter is ten syllables, with metrical accents falling on the five even-numbered syllables.

For the remainder of this introduction, I should like to explain a few of the considerations that have determined the arrangement of this book and its treatment of its subject matter.

First, because most of the major poetry in our language is iambic, this book focuses on iambic verse. I do not mean to slight the other rhythms English poets have explored. Indeed, I shall devote a chapter to accentual-syllabic meters other than iambic, as well as a chapter to the alternatives to accentual-syllabic that poets have practiced or proposed at one time or another. But these additional forms are historically secondary. In any case, to appreciate them, and the achievements of those who have worked with them, we need a solid grounding in the iambic tradition. The aim here is to chart the main stream of English verse practice. Once oriented, students can investigate tributaries that catch their curiosity.

In illustrating iambic versification, this book looks primarily to the pentameter. One reason for this approach is that the pentameter is the most capacious line commonly used in English and thus has the greatest potential for modulation. Other meters have considerable capacities for modulation, too. The resources of the iambic tetrameter have received estimable discussion in Vladimir Nabokov's *Notes on Prosody*. Yet the pentameter illuminates the rhythmical range of English-language verse more fully than the shorter lines do. One can learn more about metrical practice from it than from any other line.

A related reason for concentrating on pentameter is that the line is the hardest of the common measures to hear and write. The shorter lines can be more readily grasped. In the case of younger readers, this is so partly because of their having grown up with pop songs, whose lyrics are frequently in tetrameters or trimeters. It may also be easier for us to hear the tetrameter, on account of the residual influence of the old four-beat alliterative line of the Germanic tradition. If there is such a thing as a collective memory, it may contain that line's thumping pattern. In any event, it is relatively easy to learn to hear and write correct tetrameters or correct stanzas in "ballad meter" and "common meter"—those quatrain forms that involve alternating tetrameters and trimeters. As we acquaint ourselves with these short lines, we may read them stiffly. When first we try to write them, we may produce verses in which the rhythm is wooden and the diction hackneyed. But we can usually get a handle on the measures.

The pentameter, however, is more flexible than the shorter lines. It is not just a matter of its being longer. The line has as well a wonderfully fluid asymmetry. Even when a pentameter falls into two five-syllable sections, separated by a grammatic pause or "caesura" (marked below as < >), the first half has only two metrical beats, whereas the second has three:

```
  x  / x  / x      / x  / x  /
The broken soldier, < > kindly bade to stay
```
(Oliver Goldsmith, "The Deserted Village," 155)

And while the pentameter is a long line, it has no obligatory caesural division. It is not conventionally partitioned into more manageable subsections, as are long lines in some other poetries. Poets composing in traditional French alexandrines customarily pause after the sixth syllable; poets writing in the old Germanic alliterative line divide it after the word bearing the second metrical beat; poets working in ancient hexameters usually have a break between words (and often a grammatical pause as well) in the third foot; less frequently this break comes in the fourth foot. In contrast, poets writing English pentameters are free to pause or not to pause anywhere in the line and may divide the line in any number of ways:

A hand that taught what might be said in rhyme
(Henry Howard, Earl of Surrey, "Tribute to Wyatt," 13)

Imposture, witchcraft, charms, or blasphemy
(Ben Jonson, "An Execration upon Vulcan," 16)

And—"What a world I never want!" he cries
(Thomas Parnell, "An Elegy to an Old Beauty," 64)

A heavy heart, Belovèd, have I borne
(Elizabeth Barrett Browning, Sonnets from the Portuguese, 25.1)

The stacks, like blunt impassive temples, rise
(Frances Cornford, "Cambridgeshire," 1)

And there, a field rat, startled, squealing bleeds
(Jean Toomer, "Reapers," 6)

Though this flexibility makes the pentameter inexhaustibly exciting for the experienced poet, it takes a while for younger readers and writers to develop an intuitive familiarity with it.

A final recommendation for concentrating on iambic pentameter is that so much of our most significant poetry is written in the measure. An immense amount of outstanding work has been done in other lines; I shall cite from this work as time and space permit. However, the pentameter is the vehicle for Chaucer's *Canterbury Tales,* Shakespeare's plays and sonnets, Milton's *Paradise Lost,* the satires of John Dryden and Alexander Pope, not to mention some of the greatest poems of the Romantics and Victorians, as well such moderns as Yeats and Robert Frost. Consequently, studying the line will assist us in appreciating many of the principal achievements of English-language poetry.

Mention should also be made as to why this book employs conventional (sometimes called "traditional," "standard," or "classical") scansion. Many students of poetry have regretted our system of metrical analysis. They have noted that it derives from ancient Greek and Latin prosody and have rightly argued that the conceptual basis and nomenclature of ancient prosody have never entirely suited the principles of English speech and verse. And various scholars have proposed alternative systems of metrical notation and terminology. Some of these alternatives are enlightening. However, they introduce as many problems as they resolve, and they are almost always, in the number and the application of their diagrammatic and diacritical devices, more complicated than the system they would replace. I sympathize with the complaints about conventional scansion. Yet I believe that this method remains the best. As a teacher, I have found it useful to supplement scansion with concepts developed by modern linguists and with visual aids of my own devising. Such supplements will figure in this study. But conventional scansion, rightly grasped, is a valuable tool. Whatever its flaws, it communicates certain fundamentals of English versification better than any other scheme.

Moreover, many critics of conventional scansion condemn it for failing to fulfill purposes for which it was never designed. For example, a number of twentieth-century critics have attacked the concept of the foot and of foot division, on the grounds that feet do not necessarily record or reflect those phrasal and clausal elements of speech essential to verbal communication, poetic and otherwise. Such critics, that is, adduce lines like the following made-up iambic pentameter,

The cherry table, loaded heavily

The cher | ry ta | ble, load | ed heav | ily

and point out that its five feet—"The cher-," "-ry ta-," "-ble, load-," "-ed heav-," and "-ily"—are in and of themselves nonsensical. And, say the critics, so far as foot division focuses attention on these syllabic snippets instead of on the phrases and clauses, it violates or confuses our actual experience of lines of poetry. As Otto Jespersen puts it, the conventional system "can only delude the reader into 'scanning' lines with artificial pauses between the feet—often in the middle of words and in other most unnatural places."

Such criticisms of scansion seem misguided. Scansion does not aim to account for the infinite complexities of verbal and grammatical structure, but simply tries to refer such complexities to basic patterns. *Feet do not mark units of sense, but units of rhythm.* To be sure, poets writing iambic verse do not cobble lines together two syllables at a time, but instead shape them by means of larger phrases and clauses. So, too, readers apprehend lines not foot by foot, but rather in terms of larger segments of speech, such as "The cherry table" and "loaded heavily." I appreciate these points and am myself, as this study will show, keenly interested in the ways that words, phrases, and clauses of different lengths and shapes mesh with metrical patterns. However, when those phrases and clauses are arranged according to a recurrent sequence of light and heavy syllables, it is only natural to think of the basic element of that sequence as a light and heavy syllable. Foot division enables us to see the pattern of the line, to see how often the basic element repeats, and to investigate metrical variations in the line, if such exist. As long as we remember that scansion is concerned with rhythm and not semantics, there is no cause for confusion.

While on the subject of scansion, I should add that this book follows the time-honored custom of placing scansion marks over the vowel element of the syllable to which they refer, whether this element is a single vocalic letter (as in the *i* of "light"), a vocalic digraph (as in the *ea* in "seat"), a diphthong (as in the *oi* in "toil"), or vocalic consonant or semivowel (as in the *m* in "prism"). However, this procedure, derived from the metrical analysis of ancient verse, produces occasional oddities in English because of the vagaries of our spelling. For instance, when we scan,

The glory of the castle he admires

(Anne Bradstreet, *The Four Monarchies,* 1979)

<pre>
  x   /   x /   x   /   x /   x   /
</pre>
The glor | y of | the cas | tle he | admires

the metrically unaccented syllable of the fourth foot resists accurate description. Though the second syllable of "castle" is spelled "-tle," it is pronounced "-el" or (to use a schwa, the upside-down-and-backwards *e* that dictionaries employ to indicate reduced vowels) "əl." And it may seem quirky to set the scansion mark after the *l*, since in speech the vowel precedes rather than follows the consonant. On the other hand, placing the scansion mark over the *t* or *l* makes little sense. While the *t* is sounded in the Latin *castellum* and the Old English *castel*, it is silent in Modern English. And while some lexicographers treat *l* as a semivowel, here it does not appear to be independently syllabic; it really seems to be preceded by a vocalic element. In light of these circumstances, it is best to set the scansion mark over the vowel, as peculiar as this looks from a phonetic standpoint.

Orthography can also bedevil foot division. *X*, as the double consonant *ks*, can cause special problems. How should we divide, for example, the third from the fourth foot of this iambic pentameter?

The wise for cure on exercise depend

(John Dryden, "To John Driden of Chesterton," 94)

It would look strange to set the bar right down through the *x*, though that is where the syllable boundary lies. It would look scarcely less strange to spell the first two syllables of "exercise" phonetically and then make the foot division:

The wise | for cure | on ek | sercise | depend

The least distracting course, then, is to place the vertical bar after the *x*,

The wise | for cure | on ex | ercise | depend

though Henry Higgins might rap our knuckles for doing so.

We should note an additional point about syllable division. Most of the time, determining the number of syllables in words is easy. (Exceptions to this situation will be examined in chapter 4.) However, it is not always clear where boundaries between syllables lie. Few would disagree that "traipsing" has two syllables, but a grammarian, eyeing the root of the word, will divide it and may pronounce it "traips • ing," whereas many of the rest of us, following an instinct to separate consonants for syllabic balance, will say "traip • sing." Similarly, "children" (which we encountered in one of the lines cited from Yeats) can be divided "child • ren" or "chil • dren." We should acknowledge such quandaries, so far as their existence may occasionally make syllable divisions in our scansions look arbitrary. But since scansion aims to illuminate verse structure rather than to register minute phonetic discriminations, we need not further concern ourselves with the matter.

The vocabulary of metrical analysis has long suffered from sponginess, and this book may at points partake of this shortcoming. In describing versification, I speak of "weakly stressed" syllables and "heavily stressed" ones, of "unaccented" and "accented" ones, of "light" and "weighty" ones, and of "offbeat" and "beat." All such paired terms indicate the contrasting character of the different syllables in a metrical foot. (For other purposes, I draw, in the first chapter, a distinction between "metrical accent" and "speech stress.") If my terms overlap somewhat, I promise to keep their meanings clear in context. Also, I would point out that even specialists are not always consistent in this area. For instance, whereas some phoneticians treat "accent" as a synonym for "stress," others regard it as signifying pitch acuity alone. As long as I do not violate common sense and understanding, I hope that I will be granted a degree of terminological flexibility.

On the subject of terminology, I should note as well that earlier poets and readers sometimes characterize metrical phenomena differently than we do. Today, for example, we reasonably describe George Gascoigne's "Lullaby of a Lover" as "accentual-syllabic": Gascoigne writes his poem in iambic tetrameter, each line having eight syllables and four metrical accents, with the accents generally falling on the second, fourth, sixth, and eighth syllables. In Gascoigne's day, however, English phonemics and phonetics were poorly understood, and prosodic discussion was powerfully influenced by the vocabulary of ancient prosody, which is, as has been observed, governed by syllabic length rather than syllabic accent. Hence in a treatise he wrote on versification, Gascoigne speaks of English syllables more often as long or short than as accented or unaccented, even though length is less determinate in English than accent and even though Gascoigne's actual poetic practice makes clear that he disposes words and syllables by accent, however much he talks, as a theoretician, of length and mixes together the qualities of length and accent.

We would be remiss if we did not bear in mind that our vocabulary differs from his and from that of many of our other predecessors. But if our terms justly characterize their objects, it is not only reasonable but necessary that we use them. This book would be unreadable if, whenever we introduced a line of verse from an earlier period of our poetry, we had to stop to specify the state of linguistic description then current.

Two words merit special explanation. These are "metrics" and "prosody." They are often employed interchangeably; I so employ them in the present work. Yet though they are nearly synonymous, "prosody" has a somewhat broader application than "metrics," as can be inferred from the definitions for the words in *The Random House Dictionary of the English Language*. "Metrics" is characterized as "the science of meter." "Prosody" (from the Greek *prosôidia*, "tone or accent, modulation of voice, song sung to music") is described as "the science or study of poetic meters and versification." In other words, prosody suggests not only the topic of meter, but also such related topics as stanzaic structure and rhyme. Moreover, until the development of modern linguistics, prosody was treated as one of the four parts of grammar, along with orthography, etymology, and syntax. As such, prosody comprised what linguists today call "phonology"—the study of speech sounds—and included training in pronunciation. Knowing how words are pronounced is important to all oral and written communication, but is indispensable to the appreciation of poetry. False accentuation may spoil its rhythms. Mistaken rendering of vowels or consonants may spoil its rhymes. Because both metrics and prosody concern meter, and because prosody has lost its former associations with grammar and elocution, it would be unnecessarily pedantic to draw fine distinctions between the two terms throughout this book. Yet we may find it helpful to be aware of their different histories and connotations, especially when we encounter in an earlier text, such as Thomas Carlyle's *History of the French Revolution,* a sentence like, "She expressed herself with a purity, with a harmony and prosody that made her language like music."

This book implies a historical coherence in the accentual-syllabic tradition of English versification. This coherence, however, should never be confused with stasis or monotony. Changes in practices and preferences are always occurring within the tradition, and these reflect all sorts of personal, aesthetic, social, moral, political, and religious outlooks. From age to age, views vary regarding the rhythmical modulations desirable or permissible in different meters. Further, particular verse forms, such as the sonnet, the heroic couplet, and the ballad, are constantly coming into or going out of fashion. Yet the underlying metrical structures have remained and accommodated the transformations in diction, tone, and taste that have occurred throughout our literary history. Even the dialect confusions and linguistic shifts in English in the fifteenth century only temporarily obscured, without fundamentally altering, the development of our prosody.

We can appreciate this situation if we examine examples of blank verse (i.e., unrhymed iambic pentameter) from the Renaissance down to our time. The blank verse of Ben Jonson's plays, with its careful syntactical divisions and its resolute avoidance of melodic effect, sounds completely unlike the tumblingly run-on, look-out-below blank verse of Milton's *Paradise Lost.* By the same token, the quiet and contemplative blank verse of William Wordsworth's "Tintern Abbey" is light-years from Milton's practice, and the colloquial ease and gravity of Frost's "Black Cottage" is something else again. Yet the basic pentametric pattern is the same in each case.

Likewise, if early masters of our poetry could be teleported to the twentieth century and could hear fine metrical verse of our time, they would recognize its forms. Hearing Richard Wilbur's "A Finished Man," Chaucer would appreciate that it, like his own "Wife of Bath's Tale," was written in heroic couplets. (Heroic couplets are iambic pentameters that rhyme in pairs.) Hearing W. H. Auden's *Letter to Lord Byron,* Robert Henryson would be able to tell that it was structured by means of the same rhyme royal stanzas in which he had written *The Testament of Cresseid.* (The rhyme royal stanza consists of seven lines of iambic pentameter, the first line rhyming with the third, the second rhyming with the fourth and fifth, and the sixth rhyming with the seventh.) It might take the earlier poets a little listening to adjust from Middle English and Middle Scots to Modern English. The twentieth-century locutions and modulations would differ from theirs. But once adjustments were made, they would be able to follow the measures of their modern counterparts.

Some critics appear to believe that dramatic revolutions in meter occur every couple of generations or so, but in truth our poetry has undergone only one metrical revolution, and it happened gradually and quietly between the eleventh and thirteenth centuries, when English itself underwent that great structural shift from being a largely synthetic language to being a relatively analytic one. Many and valuable are the revolutions in style and idiom that have transpired since the fourteenth century. God willing, many more such revolutions will periodically transform and reinvigorate our poetry. But these are another matter. Meters derive from and depend on the languages within which they operate; our metrical system is unlikely to alter radically until English grammar and syntax again change as they did in the Middle Ages.

Because some readers may be wondering where free verse fits into this picture, I should probably add that, though I greatly admire many poems in that medium, it is not metrical, at least not in the sense that the word has been understood for three thousand years. And while twentieth-century free verse certainly represents a revolution in poetry, and a fascinating one, it is a revolution *away* from meter, not *of* or *in* meter.

This book can take readers only so far. I hope that it helpfully explains and illustrates metrical principles, but in the final analysis great poets themselves offer the most valuable instruction about versification. Once we have some understanding of the subject, the best and most pleasurable way to enrich our knowledge is to read poems, lots of poems, and to learn to hear their lines, whether we read them silently or aloud. Reading enables us to absorb, by a sort of rhythmical osmosis, a sense of different lines and forms and of different ways they may be managed.

Moreover, though this book concerns technique, there is more to poetry, as I suggested earlier, than its technical aspects. In every fine poem, there is a quality of genius—of vital spirit working through material of interest. This spirit can be felt in the nervous, self-interrupting energy of Philip Sidney, in the scrupulous understatement of Christina Rossetti, or in the satirical precision of J. V. Cunningham. If I talk little about this spirit, it is only because it takes as many forms as there are fine poets and because it cannot be imparted by teaching. It is a gift from a divine agency or basic life-force. Technique, on the other hand, can be explained and analyzed. Its rules can be imparted logically. It is even possible to indicate ways in which those rules support and fuse with the more elusive property of genius. And if it is true that technique without genius is arid, it is no less the case that genius without technique is often unfocused, diffuse, and self-defeating. Finally, the very fact that there are qualities of eloquence beyond the reach of technique can only be learned, as Longinus remarks (*On the Sublime,* 2.3), by a study of technique.

While I shall in this book analyze technical effects, I do not wish to imply that poets always produce these consciously. Rational thought and training play key roles in the poet's education, but writing poems involves highly intuitive processes. In this respect, gifted poets are like gifted athletes. In practice sessions, athletes may deliberately work on maneuvers. Calculatedly moving from one position to another on a court or field, they may take certain numbers of certain kinds of shots or strokes. In a real game or match, however, they will react viscerally to the flow of play. The skills acquired by conscious practice will inform every move, but the moves themselves will reflect an immediate sensitivity to an immediate context. In the same manner, a poet absorbed in composition may be drawing on years of study and on years of purposively learning how to reconcile to measure various types of phrasing and rhythm. But since each new poem presents new situations and challenges, as it unfolds the poet will respond instinctively to its conditions.

Though I have spared this text footnotes, in hopes of making it as readable as possible, I have included a general endnote for each chapter, in order to acknowledge my debts to earlier writers on versification and to indicate materials that particularly illuminate metrical questions. And while I have tried in the text to define technical terms when I introduce them, a glossary at the back of the book provides a readily accessible and alphabetized instrument for checking the meaning of, for instance, the name of a foot or a stanza or a type of rhyme.

My greatest hope is that this book will communicate the insight and joy that verse can bring us. The masterpieces of our poetry are an enduring resource. They have a singular power to instruct, elevate, console, move, and civilize, particularly if we experience them in the spirit in which they were written, hearing and internalizing their rhythms of thought and sensibility. Reading and writing can help us relish the beauty of the world, appreciate its sanctity, fight against its evils, and bear its vicissitudes and sorrows. Because of their measures, fine poems can serve us as models of intelligence, eloquence, and wit. Because of its metaphoric element, poetry can reveal and make intelligible connections between experiences or phenomena that might otherwise seem disparate and confusing. Lines of poems we memorize when we are young may in later years rise unbidden to mind and, in a flash, illuminate our entire experience. And whether we write or read them, verse measures can help us to a vision of existence more coherent and comprehensive than our own lives provide, and can fortify us and encourage us to fuller and truer ways of acting and being. In Louise Bogan's words ("Single Sonnet," 13–14) on this subject:

> Staunch meter, great song, it is yours, at length,
> To prove how stronger you are than my strength.

ONE

Iambic Verse

I

Metrical Norm and Rhythmical Modulation

VERSIFICATION INVOLVES A continual reconciliation of two apparently opposed elements. One is rhythm, in the sense of the fluid and shifting movements of live speech. The other is meter, in the sense of a fixed, abstract pattern according to which those movements are organized. And this steady and ongoing reconciliation between meter and rhythm is almost like a loving relationship between two people. There exists a harmony that is stable and constant and, at the same time, ever-changing and lively. The two elements are engaged in a spirited dialectic that is always expressing itself in new ways and is always expanding and enriching the relationship without breaking it. Furthermore, just as every vital interpersonal relationship has its own character—no two being quite the same—so in the work of every excellent poet, the interplay between meter and rhythm will have special traits and vivacities.

This chapter will explore the relationship of meter and rhythm. So fundamental is this relationship to verse practice that I wish to examine it even before discussing scansion, a topic often considered to be the proper basis and starting point of any study of versification. The central point of the chapter is that poets achieve variety in traditional verse not by "breaking" or "departing from" metrical pattern, but rather by using the variable rhythms of speech to modulate the pattern from within.

Before proceeding, however, we should remind ourselves of a couple of points.

First, English verse, like English speech, is distinguished by the dynamic stress of its syllables—by the relative force they receive when uttered. All syllables have at least a little stress; otherwise they would be inaudible. But any time we speak normally, some syllables are more prominent than others.

Stress is a complex phenomenon and can be produced by a number of factors. Notably stressed syllables may be characterized by rising pitch, or they may be louder than other syllables in their vicinity. So, too, their duration and vowel quality may be particularly marked or conspicuous. For instance, when we say "desert," signifying an arid landscape, the first syllable has strong stress, partly because it is closed and because its vowel is more fully realized ("déz • ərt"). In contrast, when we say "desert," meaning "to abandon," the first syllable is weakly stressed, partly because its vowel is reduced and because it is open (i.e., not closed and lengthened by a consonant —"di • súrt"). Similar analysis could be directed at the word's second syllable.

The Oxford Companion to the English Language notes three major types of stress. One is "word stress." In words of two or more syllables, one of the syllables usually takes primary stress. In "person," for example, the first syllable is the more prominent. In "envision" the second syllable is the most emphatic. In "congregation" the third is the weightiest. Longer words may have, in addition to a primarily stressed syllable, a syllable or syllables with notable secondary stress. The initial syllable of "congregation," for instance, falls into this category. Most dictionaries, when they syllabify a word, will place a dark accent mark over or before syllables with primary stress and a lighter accent mark over or before syllables with secondary stress. Occasionally, a word will have alternative accentuations, which differentiate sense, as in "désert" and "desért," or which distinguish parts of speech, as in "cóntest," the noun meaning "a struggle," and "contést," the verb meaning "to struggle."

A second type of stress is "sentence stress" or "lexical stress." Information-carrying words, such as nouns, verbs, adjectives, and adverbs, usually receive more stress than do words or syllables whose function is merely relational, such as articles, conjunctions, prepositions, and affixes. Consider the sentence, "The child was trying hard to please." The noun "child," the root verb "try," the adverb "hard," and the verb "please" communicate meaning and are strongly stressed. In contrast, weak stress characterizes the article "the," the auxiliary verb "was," the flexional "-ing," and the preposition "to." These latter words or syllables are grammatically important, but they do not have the expressive significance of the other sentence elements.

The third kind of stress noted by *The Oxford Companion* is "contrastive stress." Such stress derives not from the intrinsic property of a word or syllable, but rather from a rhetorical context that requires us to emphasize a word or syllable that does not normally receive heavy stress. For instance, though customarily we do not stress prepositions, attributive adjectives, or prefixes, we might stress them if we said, "Are you suggesting that we ride *on* the jet rather than *in* the jet?" or "I wanted you to adopt *her* cat, not *my* cat," or "He never managed the company, he *mis*managed it."

Other qualities and circumstances influence stress. We will examine these in this and other chapters. For now it will suffice to note the importance of stress and to repeat an observation made in the introduction: iambic measures are so prevalent in our verse precisely because they flexibly accommodate the structure and stress patterns of English.

Another point to keep in mind throughout this chapter and book is that metrical practice is more complex than metrical description. Actual versification involves rhythmical nuances and subtleties that can be only roughly indicated by scansion. Conventional metrical description postulates merely two values, unaccentedness and accentedness, whereas metrical practice— the real writing of verse lines—entails the much broader spectrum of stress values of spoken language. To say that a poem is in iambic pentameter is just to refer its verses to a general model involving an alternation of metrically unaccented and metrically accented syllables. This does not necessarily mean, however, that all the odd-numbered syllables in the line are very weak and that all the even-numbered syllables in the line are very strong. Nor does it mean that all the odd-numbered syllables are equally weak and that all the even-numbered syllables are equally strong.

To put the matter another way, versification involves the concurrent but distinguishable phenomena of meter and rhythm. Meter is the basic norm or paradigm of the line. It is an analytical abstraction. In the case of the iambic pentameter, for example, the norm is:

one **two**, one **two**, one **two**, one **two**, one **two**

Rhythm, on the other hand, is the realization in speech of this pattern. On rare occasions, poets will write pentameters in which the realization virtually coincides with the paradigm. They will write lines consisting of five successive two-syllable, rear-stressed phrasal or verbal units:

But we, alas! are chased, and you, my friends

(Christopher Marlowe, *Edward II*, 4.6.22)

The earth, the seas, the light, the days, the skies

(Thomas Traherne, "The Salutation," 29)

Above, below, without, within, around

(Pope, "The Temple of Fame," 458)

More frequently, the rhythm may involve an alternation of weak and strong syllables that approximates the norm fairly closely:

That **blond**reth **forth** and **peril cast**eth **noon**
That blunders forth and gives no consideration to peril

(Chaucer, *The Canterbury Tales*, G 1414 ["The Canon Yeoman's Tale"])

Al**though** the **course** be **turned** some **oth**er **way**

(Walter Ralegh, "The Ocean's Love to Cynthia," 82)

And **here** we **dwell** to**gether**, **side** by **side**

(Mary Coleridge, "We never said farewell," 5)

Per**haps**, if **summer ever came** to **rest**

(Stevens, "The Man Whose Pharynx Was Bad," 10)

However, most pentameters do not feature such uniform fluctuations. Though the type with five obvious offbeats and beats is the most common, it can claim only a smallish plurality in our verse. In his entry for "Meter" in *The New Princeton Encyclopedia of Poetry and Poetics*, T. V. F. Brogan plausibly suggests the figure of 25 percent. Poets write not only in feet, but also in phrases, clauses, and sentences. And because these have all sorts of different lengths and shapes and stress-shadings, most iambic lines exhibit a fluctuation between lighter and heavier that is not absolutely regular, but is instead sometimes more emphatic, sometimes less. Many pentameters have fewer than five strong syllables. The pentameters below, for example, have four, three, and two, respectively:

The **pen**ance, and the **woeful pride** you **keep**

(Edwin Arlington Robinson, "Captain Craig," 199)

The **bos**om of his **Fath**er and his **God**

(Thomas Gray, "Elegy Written in a Country Churchyard," 128)

The repu**ta**tion of Ti**epo**lo

(Anthony Hecht, "The Venetian Vespers," 6.94)

Many pentameters have more than five strong syllables. These, for instance, have six, seven, eight, and nine, respectively:

No **selfish wish** the **moon's bright glance** confines

(Jones Very, "The Absent," 7)

Kind pity chokes my **spleen; brave scorn** for**bids**

(John Donne, "Satire III," 1)

True thoughts, good thoughts, thoughts fit to **treasure up**

(Robert Browning, "Transcendentalism," 5)

Milk hands, rose cheeks, or **lips more sweet, more red**

(Sidney, *Astrophel and Stella*, 91.7)

Yet, however different their rhythms, all these verses realize the same metrical paradigm. Even Robert Browning's line, which reiterates a word consecutively in the fourth and fifth syllable positions, maintains the basic iambic fluctuation.

In this respect, we might think of iambic lines as mountain ranges. Peaks and valleys alternate. But not every peak is an Everest, nor is every valley a Grand Canyon. Sometimes one of the peaks is not as high as the others:

The penance, and the woeful pride you keep

Sometimes, one of the valleys is not as deep as the others:

No selfish wish the moon's bright glance confines

In addition, iambic verse allows for a number of conventional variations. These we shall examine in the next chapter. The most common include feminine endings and substitutions of inverted (i.e., trochaic) feet, especially at line beginnings or after mid-line pauses. But the key thing in English iambic verse is the fluctuation of the strength of the stresses. And the practice of traditional iambic meter involves the poet's taking this basic alternating norm and modulating it internally. The poet works within and conforms to the one pattern, but does so in many and continually different ways.

We can better examine rhythmical modulations of lines by supplementing the conventional two-level system of scansion with a four-level numerical register that Jespersen and other linguists have employed. That is, in addition to marking syllables as metrically unaccented or accented, we can speak of them as (1) weak, (2) semiweak, (3) semistrong, or (4) strong. According to this procedure, we can use the conventional minimal-maximal signs to indicate the basic meter of, for example, Robinson's and Very's lines,

```
  x   /   x    /    x   /   x   /    x   /
The pen | ance, and | the woe | ful pride | you keep
  x  /  x   /    x   /    x   /    x   /
No self | ish wish | the moon's | bright glance | confines
```

and can employ the numerical register to suggest the rhythmical modulations of the lines:

```
  1   4   1    2    1   4   1   4    1   4
The pen | ance, and | the woe | ful pride | you keep
  1   4   1   4    1   4    3   4    1   4
No self | ish wish | the moon's | bright glance | confines
```

The four-level numerical register should be regarded as merely a *supplement* to the conventional system of scansion. As was mentioned in the introduction, traditional foot division and metrical notation are, whatever their limitations, the most useful procedures we have for metrical description. Moreover, we must not mistake the numerical register for a high-precision instrument. It simplifies, scarcely less than the two-level system does, the endless variabilities of live speech. The four numbers are approximations, much as the two scansion marks are approximations. Someone with an ear as acute as Apollo's might hear the second foot of Robinson's line not as 1–2 but as 1.16–1.83 and the fourth foot of Very's line not as 3–4 but as 3.11–3.94. Further, especially in cases involving intermediate stress, different readers may differently shade a syllable. And though it is for practical purposes permissible to treat all heavily stressed syllable as 4s, any complete articulation in English has only one primary stress; hence it is wrong, in strict linguistic description, to suggest that a phrase like "and the woeful pride you keep" has three 4s. Because the speaker of the line is criticizing the sour sense of superiority that can lurk behind conventional piety, "pride" is probably the phrase's pivotal point, and for most readers that word will be a true 4, whereas "woe-" and "keep" will be a little lower.

Still, as long as we remember that the four-level register deals with approximations, it provides a helpful way of showing that, for the practicing poet, the iambic pentameter is not so much a single rhythm, consisting of five minimally and five maximally stressed syllables, as it is a general model that can be realized in many ways, by many different syntactical arrangements.

If it is important to distinguish between a line's meter and its rhythm, it may also be helpful to distinguish, in terms of its individual syllables, between "metrical accent" and "speech stress." By metrical accent, I refer to the character of a syllable when it is considered simply according to the offbeat-beat system of scansion. If it receives more emphasis than the other syllable or syllables of the foot in which it appears, it is metrically accented. If it receives less emphasis, it is metrically unaccented. By speech stress, I refer to the character of the syllable when it is actually spoken. Speech stress involves the emphasis that a syllable carries not merely in the foot in which it figures, but also in the larger phrasal or clausal environment of which it may be part. Metrical accent and speech stress are related, just as the light-heavy paradigm and the internal modulations of it in actual lines of verse are related. But the two are not inevitably or exactly the same. To return to Robinson's line,

<pre>
    x   /   x   /   x   /   x   /   x   /
The pen | ance, and | the woe | ful pride | you keep
</pre>

the second, sixth, eighth, and tenth syllables are metrically accented and also carry notable speech stress. However, the fourth syllable, though bearing a metrical accent (on account of being stronger than the syllable with which it shares its foot), does not have much speech stress. And in Very's line,

<pre>
    x / x   /   x   /   x   /   x   /
No self | ish wish | the moon's | bright glance | confines
</pre>

the first, third, fifth, and ninth syllables are metrically unaccented and weakly stressed. But the seventh syllable, though metrically unaccented (being weaker than the syllable with which it shares its foot), has notable speech stress.

Often in English verse, a metrically unaccented syllable at one point in the line actually carries more speech stress than a metrically accented syllable at another point. Consider, for example, these lines:

Old Elm that murmured in our chimney top

(Clare, "To a Fallen Elm," 1)

And makes my thought take cover in the facts

(Wilbur, "On the Marginal Way," 34)

Even as they embody interesting modulations, these lines remain conventional iambic pentameters. All the feet are iambic. All exhibit a weaker-to-stronger relationship, and the line itself follows the lighter-to-heavier fluctuation. To return once more to our figure of the mountain range, the peaks are still peaks and the valleys are still valleys:

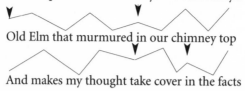

Old Elm that murmured in our chimney top

And makes my thought take cover in the facts

But the metrically unaccented syllable of the first foot of Clare's line ("Old") has more speech stress than the metrically accented syllable of the third foot ("in"). And in Wilbur's line the third foot's metrically unaccented syllable ("take") has more speech stress than the metrically accented syllable of the fourth foot ("in").

From time to time in iambic verse, we will encounter two adjacent feet whose four syllables represent four rising degrees of stress. This occurs in the first two feet of the opening line of one of Sidney's sonnets (*Astrophel and Stella,* 31):

> 1   2   3 4
> With how | sad steps, | O moon, | thou climb'st | the skies

The same phenomenon appears in the second and third feet of this line,

>   1 2   3   4
> The pal | lor of | girls' brows | shall be | their pall
>
>   (Wilfred Owen, "Anthem for Doomed Youth," 12)

and in the third and fourth feet of this one,

>   1   2   3   4
> They drive, | and squan | der the | huge Bel | gian fleet
>
>   (Dryden, *Annus Mirabilis,* 266)

and in the fourth and fifth feet of this one,

>   1 2   3 4
> One's glance | could cross | the bor | ders of | three states
>
>   (Hart Crane, "Quaker Hill," 26)

Strictly speaking, the feet of such lines remain iambic, since the second syllable in each foot is stronger than the first. However, because we have a light iamb followed by a heavy iamb, the overall rise-and-fall of the line is suspended in favor of continuous ascent. (In Sidney's line the ascent is notably expressive: the climbing rhythm of "With how sad steps" suggests the moon's rising in the sky.)

Once we have observed this phenomenon, there is little to say about it. It appears in Chaucer and in the Scottish Chaucerians:

1 2   3   4

How myght | y and | how greet | a lord | is he!

(Chaucer, *Canterbury Tales* A 1786 ["The Knight's Tale"])

1   2   3   4

And quhat | distres | scho thoil | lit, and | quhat deid
And what distress she suffered, and [of] what [she] died

(Robert Henryson, *The Testament of Cresseid*, 70)

And it is common in Modern English iambic verse from the sixteenth century down to the present.

If light iambs are sometimes followed by heavy ones, the combination of a heavy iamb followed by a light one is almost as common. This other juxtaposition occurs in the earlier-cited Richard Wilbur line, reprinted here with two more instances:

3   4   1 2
x   /   x /

And makes | my thought | take cov | er in | the facts

3   4   1   2
x   /   x   /

Expect | things great | er than | thy larg | est hopes

(Ben Jonson, *Sejanus*, 1.2.102)

3   4   1   2
x   /   x   /

The day | becomes | more sol | emn and | serene

(Percy Bysshe Shelley, "Hymn to Intellectual Beauty," 73)

Once in a while, a line will feature both kinds of juxtaposition. That is, the heavy-plus-light-foot combination will overlap with the light-plus-heavy combination. In the following line, for instance, the first and third feet are heavy and the second is light, with the result that the relationship between the first and second feet is heavy-to-light and the relationship between the second and third feet is light-to-heavy:

```
  3   4   1   2    3   4
```
Slow an | ger to | hard an | swers in | a glance

(Helen Pinkerton, "Elegy at Beaverhead County, Montana," 14)

And here the fourth foot is also light, in consequence of which the heavy-and-light foot pattern introduced at the beginning of the line is echoed subsequently:

```
  3   4   1   2
```
Slow an | ger to

```
  3   4    1   2
```
hard an | swers in

Something similar happens in a line in the pentametric "What thou lov'st well" passage of Ezra Pound's eighty-first Canto, although this line has the added wrinkle of concluding with a heavy foot and of thus exhibiting an alternation of heavy and light feet across the entire line:

```
   3    4    1   2    3   4   1   2    3   4
```
Made cour | age, or | made or | der, or | made grace

We have, twice repeated, both a 3–4–1–2 pattern and a 1–2–3–4 pattern, and the patterns interlock across the line.

If counterpoints and contrasts of light and heavy feet can exist within a line, so rhythms involving such feet can echo from one line to another. In Frost's "Death of the Hired Man," for example, Mary's comment about Silas's plight provides, in successive lines (100–101), four degrees of rising stress over the second and third feet; and in both cases a light foot follows, so that the lines have a 3–4–1–2 pattern, too:

```
  1     4  1   2   3    4   1   2   1    4
```
And nothing to look backward to with pride

```
  1     4  1   2   3    4   1   2   1    4
```
And nothing to look forward to with hope

It might be added that the twin risings through the second and third feet—and the falling-offs to a light fourth foot—throw into rhythmic relief the words "backward" and "forward" and throw into thematic relief Silas's desolate past and empty future.

One need not, in reading, note consciously such subtleties of rhythm as Pinkerton's, Pound's, or Frost's. To the trained and appreciative ear, they will carry across subliminally. The advantage of analyzing verses like these is that they suggest some of the more unusual possibilities for rhythmical modulation and counterpoint within the conventional pentameter. They also indicate how incredibly complex metrical practice is in comparison to metrical description.

Observations made thus far with respect to iambic pentameter could be made with regard to other meters. Reading poems in iambic tetrameter, for example, we on rare occasions find lines in which the metrical norm and the speech rhythm are the same. We find, that is, lines composed in phrasal units of two syllables each, with stress on the second syllable:

> Now swift, now slow, now tame, now wild;
> Now hot, now cold, now fierce, now mild
>
> > (Ben Jonson, "Come, let us here enjoy the shade," 14–15)

> My joy, my grief, my hope, my love
>
> > (Edmund Waller, "On a Girdle," 7)

> But ah, my foes, and oh, my friends
>
> > (Edna St. Vincent Millay, "First Fig," 3)

More often, tetrameters feature four stress peaks coinciding with the line's even-numbered syllables:

> The **pres**ent **mom**ent's **all** my **lot**
>
> > (John Wilmot, Earl of Rochester, "Life and Love," 8)

> In **trem**bling **zeal** he **seiz'd** his **hair**
>
> > (William Blake, "A Little Boy Lost," 10)

Yet some tetrameters have five, six, or seven speech stresses:

> We **smile**, but, **O great Christ**, our **cries**
>
> > (Paul Laurence Dunbar, "We Wear the Mask," 10)

> **Bob Hope**, **John Wayne**, and **Mar**tha **Raye**
>
> > (R. L. Barth, "Movie Stars," 1)

> **Haud up** thy **han'**, **Deil**!* **ance, twice, thrice**!   *Devil, Lucifer
>
> > (Robert Burns, "Scotch Drink," 117)

And some have only three, two, or one:

> When **first** we **prac**tice to de**ceive**
>
> > (Walter Scott, *Marmion*, 6.17.28)

His existentialists de**clare**

(Auden, "Under Which Lyre," 124)

But individu**al**ity

(Vikram Seth, *The Golden Gate*, 2.2.7)

In addition, in some tetrameters we find two successive feet exhibiting four degrees of rising stress. And, as was the case with pentameters, this phenomenon may occur at any point in the line—early, middle, or late:

```
1     2     3     4
```
And your quaint honor turn to dust

(Andrew Marvell, "To his Coy Mistress," 29)

```
      1     2   3     4
```
the eye of that young awkward girl

(Gwen Harwood, "Wind," 5)

```
        1     2   3     4
```
To darken me and my sad Clime

(Henry King, "The Exequy," 40)

Also, we may find tetrameters in which one of the metrically unaccented syllables receives more speech stress than one of the metrically accented syllables. In the mountain range of the line, one of the valleys may prove higher than one of the peaks:

The dumb grows strangely talkative

(Winthrop Mackworth Praed, *A Love*, Preface, 30)

Old warder of these buried bones

(Alfred Tennyson, *In Memoriam*, 39.1)

Tennyson's line offers as well an instance where a light iamb follows a heavy one:

```
3      4    1  2
x      /    x  /
```
Old ward | er of | these bur | ied bones

Here we should make an additional observation about the relationship between the metrical norm and the rhythmical modulation of it in living lines of verse. For purposes of analysis, we can differentiate between the comprehensive pattern and the individual realizations of it. But in practice the two things are inseparable. The general metrical essence and the particular rhythmical manifestation occur and are experienced simultaneously. If we have an ear for the pentameter, when we read we will simply recognize, without reflection, that lines are metrical,

> Unseen, preserved beneath dark velvet, lie
> Pale water-colours fugitive to light

(Dick Davis, "Fräulein X," 1–2)

or (as in these made-up decasyllabics) that lines are unmetrical,

> It rains almost always when I visit;
> Such humidity is hard on my joints.

We perceive the pentameter pattern in the rhythmical modulation of the lines themselves, or we perceive that the rhythm does not correspond to the pattern. We do not hear the abstract norm and then recognize the modulation, or hear the modulation and then realize it agrees with the norm. Both happen at once.

If we grasp the relationship between metrical description and metrical practice—if we comprehend the interplay and concurrence of the abstract norm of a line and the different possible modulations of it in living verse—we will understand that the chief sources of variation in metrical composition reside *within* the norm itself. Indeed, modulation is possible only so long as the meter is respected. Only by adhering to the basic structure of the line can the poet achieve, within it, arresting or pleasing rhythms that point meaning and tone.

Many authorities on prosody, however, fail to grasp the relationship between meter and modulation. Such authorities suggest that rhythmical variation in English poetry is secured principally by the frequent use of variant feet or through outright violations of the metrical pattern. It is these confusions that we should now consider. In this regard, attention should first be directed at pyrrhics and at spondees and at discussions of versification that suggest that these feet occur often in English poems.

Pyrrhics and spondees are derived, as are the other feet we use in metrical description, from the terminology of Greek and Latin prosody. Ancient meter measures syllable duration rather than syllable stress, and a pyrrhic consists of two metrically short syllables and a spondee of two metrically long ones. By analogy an English pyrrhic is considered to have two metrically unaccented syllables and a spondee two metrically accented ones.

Pyrrhics and spondees are natural in Greek and Latin prosody, since length in those languages can be determined by phonemics and phonetics. If the vowel in a syllable is long or a diphthong, the syllable is long; if the vowel is short, but is "closed" by a consonant, the syllable is also long. Otherwise, the syllable is short. (Some meters feature "anceps" positions, positions that admit either a long or a short syllable. There are also certain anceps syllables, but these mostly occur in words that admit of alternative syllabifications, and the metrical nature of such syllables can thus be recognized phonetically. For example, the second syllable of *volucris,* a Latin word for a flying insect or bird, is long when the word is syllabified *vo · luc · ris,* but is short when the word is treated as *vo · lu · cris.*)

In English, however, we cannot abstractly categorize the metrical values of syllables to the degree that the ancients could in Greek and Latin. English meter measures stress, which depends not only on phonemics and phonetics, but also on verbal, grammatical, and rhetorical context. To determine metrical values, we must look at more than the intrinsic nature of the syllable.

To address a more specific aspect of this matter, all our monosyllabic words can, given the right context, serve as either metrical beats or metrical offbeats. Admittedly, light monosyllabic articles, prepositions, and conjunctions are most often metrically unaccented, but it is not uncommon for them to appear in metrically accented positions, as "and" does in the fourth foot of this line:

x /

Prepared to scrub the en | try and | the stairs

(Jonathan Swift, "A Description of the Morning," 8)

And though monosyllabic verbs and nouns tend to appear in metrically accented positions, frequently they turn up in metrically unaccented ones, as "fetch" does in the first foot of the following verse:

x   /

Fetch wa | ter, dripping, over desert miles

(James David Corrothers, "The Negro Singer," 10)

The versatility of English monosyllables manifests itself even more clearly in lines in which the same monosyllabic word appears in both metrically unaccented and accented positions. This can occur when the monosyllables involved are in adjacent feet,

x / x   /

Doth teach | *that* ease | and *that* | repose | to say

(Shakespeare, Sonnet 50, 3)

or even when they are side by side, as in the Robert Browning line cited earlier:

<pre>
                   x   /   x   /
True thoughts, | good *thoughts*, | *thoughts* fit | to trea | sure up
</pre>

A line may even feature a repeated pair of monosyllabic words whose metric natures shift in the course of the line:

<pre>
   x   /   x   /   x   /
Up roos | the sonne | and *up* | *roos* Em | elyë
</pre>

(Chaucer, Canterbury Tales, A 2273 ["The Knight's Tale"])

<pre>
   x   /   x   /   x   /
All men | think *all* | *men* mor | tal, but | themselves
</pre>

(Edward Young, Night Thoughts, 1.424)

For that matter, a monosyllabic word may begin with one metrical identity, switch to the other, and then return to its original form. Here "so" goes from an offbeat to a beat and then back to an offbeat:

<pre>
              x   /   x   /   x   /
She was | *so* han | dy, *so* | discreet, | *so* nice
</pre>

(George Crabbe, "The Wife and the Widow," 102)

"Is" undergoes the same transformations in a line (1.294) in Pope's *Essay on Man,* and Pope uses majuscules to help us hear the shifting stress relative to the word:

<pre>
   x   / x   /   x / x / x /
One truth is clear, "Whatever IS, is RIGHT."
</pre>

And in this line, "what" goes from a beat to an offbeat and then back to a beat:

<pre>
   x   / x   /   x / x   /   x   /
Of what he was, what is, and what must be
</pre>

(Milton, Paradise Lost, 4.25)

A poet may, moreover, volley a syllable about in a way that reminds me of what my sister does with the ball when we play tennis. She repeatedly hits shots in one direction and, just when I have been lulled into thinking that she intends to continue this arrangement indefinitely, she rifles the ball to the opposite and undefended side of the court. In the tenth line of "Shakespeare," Matthew Arnold hits, so to speak, the combining word "self-" into metrically unaccented positions three times and then fires it the other way the fourth time around:

```
   x      /    x     /     x    / x     / x /
Self-school'd, self-scann'd, self-honor'd, self-secure
```

These examples suggest that English iambic versification has greatly benefited from the historical tendency toward monosyllabism in our language. English is of course not purely monosyllabic, nor has its tendency toward monosyllabism gone unchecked by countervailing influences. English has tens of thousands of words of more than one syllable, and particularly in the Middle English and Early Modern English periods, it plentifully imports relatively long words from French and Latin. Yet English has, more so than its cognate languages, an abundance of frequently used monosyllabic words, and one reason is that, over the centuries, many Old English words have reduced to shorter Modern English versions. To mention just a few cases of fore-stressed disyllables that have evolved into monosyllables, "cyning" has become "king," "lætan" "let," "buton" "but," "siththan" "since," "cuman" "come," and "feower" "four." Not only did this development—along with the factors mentioned in the introduction—nudge English away from the falling rhythm of the Old Germanic tradition; the increasing number of common monosyllabic words also helped to give the accentual-syllabic mode its great flexibility.

To be sure, early students of Modern English worried that our monosyllables would impoverish our verse. Trained in classical languages, and interested in the possibilities of appropriating for English the measures of classical versification, such students appreciated the importance of polysyllabic words to the textures of ancient meters, especially to the dactylic hexameter. For instance, in his *Schoolmaster* (published 1570), Roger Ascham writes: "[O]ur English tong, hauing in vse chiefly wordes of one syllable which commonly be long, doth not well receiue the nature of *Carmen Heroicum* [Epic Poetry], bicause *dactylus*, the aptest foote for that verse, conteining one long and two short, is seldom therefore found in English; and doth also rather stumble than stand vpon *Monasyllabis.*" Similarly, Thomas Campion remarks in his *Observations in the Art of English Poesie* (composed circa 1591, published 1602) that one reason dactylic rhythm does not work well in our language is that "the concurse of our monasillables make our verses unapt to slide"; and while praising the pithiness of English, William Camden in his *Remains Concerning Britain* (1614) suggests that the monosyllabic tendencies in the language ill suit poetry: "As for the Monosyllables so rife in our tongue which were not so originally, . . . they are unfitting for verses and measures."

But concerns about monosyllables soon subside. The durational and proportional correspondences of classical verse prove irrelevant to our stress-based meters; and though subsequent poets caution against an over-reliance on monosyllables—Pope especially in his comment, "And ten low words oft creep in one dull line" (*Essay on Criticism*, 347)—monosyllabic words are wonderfully handy. Indeed, Gascoigne makes this point in his pioneering 1575 treatise, *Certain Notes of Instruction Concerning the Making of Verse or Rhyme in English*. After extolling monosyllables as "the most ancient English words," Gascoigne recommends them for their metrical versatility: "Also words of many syllables do cloy a verse and make it unpleasant, whereas words of one syllable will more easily fall to be short or long as occasion requireth."

Shifts in the metrical nature of monosyllabic words can be caused by several factors. One is verbal or phrasal context, especially as it relates to the phenomena of promotion and demotion that we explored in the introduction. As we observed, light syllables receive slightly greater emphasis when flanked by other light syllables. In the following line, for instance, "a" would seem to be promoted the second time that it appears:

x / x /

Our birth | is but | *a* sleep | and *a* | forgetting

(Wordsworth, "Ode: Intimations of Immortality
from Recollections of Early Childhood," 58)

That is, the first time "a" occurs it is metrically unaccented not only because it is unemphatic to begin with, but also because it stands between two comparatively heavy syllables. When it next turns up, however, it serves as a metrical accent: it stands between a light conjunction and the light first syllable of "forgetting," and receives a little more weight than it would normally.

Conversely, heavy syllables are demoted if flanked by other heavy syllables, a circumstance that explains the metrical properties of this line:

x / x /

And des | tined *Man* | himself | to judge | *Man* fall'n

(Milton, *Paradise Lost*, 10.62)

The first time "Man" appears it is metrically accented not only because it is a fairly heavy and significant word to begin with, but also because it falls between two light syllables. The second time it appears it is still fairly weighty, but is less emphatic on account of being sandwiched between two other weighty and significant words.

Rhetorical context is another major factor that produces metrical shifts. Indeed, poets can focus meaning by shuttling words between metrically accented and unaccented positions. This technique can be seen in a couplet from William Cartwright's tetrametric "To Chloe Who Wished Herself Young Enough For Me" (17–18), a poem which celebrates love and in which the poet asserts that love restores youth to those who are aging and maintains youth in those who are young. In the first line of the couplet, Cartwright indicates love's restorative power by the setting of "young" in a metrically accented position; in the second line, he highlights the element of maintenance by metrically subordinating the adjective to verbs and an adverb.

<pre>
x   /   x   /   x   /   x   /
Love makes those young whom age doth chill

x   / x /   x   /   x   /
And whom he finds young, keeps young still.
</pre>

(The metrical and rhythmical nature of "whom" also shifts, as the focus switches from Love, in the first line, to, in the second line, the person *whom* love affects.)

So, too, when in *Paradise Lost* (10.832) Adam laments that the blame for the corruption of humankind falls

<pre>
x   /   x /
On me, | me on | ly, as | the source | and spring
</pre>

it is natural as well as metrical that "me" should be accented in the first foot and subordinated in the second. In the first case, Adam terribly perceives that he bears responsibility (on **me**) for the catastrophe. In the second he realizes—what is yet more terrible—that he alone (me **only**) is responsible.

Rhetorical shifts also explain one of the most fascinating phenomena of our prosody: two monosyllabic words may share a foot on two different occasions, and may switch metrical roles from the first occasion to the next. A good example of this occurs in Shakespeare's comment (Sonnet 129, 13–14) about the destructive consequences of yielding to illicit sexual passion. (Though I shall focus on the first of the lines below, I should mention with regard to the second that, in Shakespeare's time, "heaven" was said as a monosyllable and could be treated metrically as a monosyllable or a disyllable. Hence, though the last line seems for us to have an extra syllable, for Shakespeare it does not.)

> All this | the world | well knows, | yet none | knows well
> To shun the heaven that leads men to this hell

Here the third foot of the divided line consists of the adverb "well" plus the verb "knows"; then, two feet later, Shakespeare gives us another foot with the same words, but transposed. And, paradoxically, both feet are iambs. Shakespeare initially perceives that everyone *knows* that lust is wrong, and then sadly adds that such knowledge is not always *sufficient* to prevent dishonorable conduct:

> All this | the world |well *knows,* | yet none | knows *well*

Once in a while, an iamb will consist of a single but repeated monosyllabic word, whose second occurrence has greater rhetorical weight than the first. Such a situation arises when Frost, at the end of "Acceptance" (13–14), suggests that the bird who has just found a perch for the night is resigned to whatever the future may bring. Frost pictures the bird as thinking that it does not wish

> ... to see
> Into the future. Let what will be, be.

"Be" supplies both the offbeat and the beat of the final foot of the last line. The first time the word appears, it follows "will," which not only is the metrically accented syllable of the fourth foot, but also is conceptually crucial, indicating the futurity with which the bird and poem are concerned—what *will* be. Hence the voice drops when it moves from "will" to the first "be." Yet the voice gives prominence to the second "be," since here the focus shifts from the sense of future to the very order of existence and the bird's acceptance of it. The second "be" also receives weight because it is the culminating word of the sentence (and the poem) and because it is the line's rhyme-syllable.

> x / x /
> Into | the fu | ture. Let | what will | be, be.

A similar case—though this one involves grammatical more than rhetorical context—appears in Frost's description of a railroad-hating man who regrets not having sabotaged some track when he had the chance:

> He wished when he had had the track alone
> He had attacked it with a club or stone
>
> ("The Egg and the Machine," 5–6)

"Had" changes its metrical nature in the third foot of the first line of the couplet because the poet is writing in the past perfect tense. The first "had" is merely auxiliary, whereas the second "had"—the past participle of "have" —is the main verb:

                  x   /

He wished | when he | had had | the track | alone
He had attacked it with a club or stone

(In the couplet's second line, the auxiliary "had" is promoted to a metrical beat because it is preceded by the light pronoun "He" and is followed by a past participle, "attacked," whose word accent is not on its first but its second syllable.)

The expressive variability we have been exploring comprises a beauty peculiar to English versification, as opposed to ancient versification, in which metrical identities are less susceptible to manipulation. However, the variability also indicates the danger of imagining that syllabic stress is as inherently determinable in modern prosody as length was in ancient metrics.

To put this issue in pedestrian terms, we might say that the principle of less *and* greater—the principle of iambics, trochees, dactyls, amphibrachs, anapests—was adaptable to English from Greek and Latin, since the principle is as characteristic of our stress-based metrical feet as it was of the corresponding length-based ancient feet. However, *equivalence*—the principle of the pyrrhic and spondee—is not for the most part characteristic of English meter or speech.

True spondees and pyrrhics perhaps appear in English in only two cases. The first is when the rhythm of a poem or passage is so close to the metrical norm that a foot with two relatively weighty syllables, or two relatively light ones, really does stand out as unusual. The second is when the syllables are spoken with the same degree of emphasis, as in the first feet of the impatient exclamations in the bitter exchange in the closet scene from *Hamlet* (3.4.12–13):

QUEEN
Come, come, you answer with an idle tongue.

HAMLET
Go, go, you question with a wicked tongue.

Despite the rarity of true pyrrhics and spondees in English verse, many authorities introduce them almost willy-nilly into accounts of poems in conventional iambic measure. For instance, one text examines the opening of the second stanza of Yeats's "Sailing to Byzantium" and, hearing a light third foot in lines 1 and 2, scans those feet as pyrrhics:

```
 x  /  x   /  x x  x /   x  /
An ag | ed man | is but | a pal | try thing, |

 x /  x    /   x x  x /   x  /
A tat | tered coat | upon | a stick, | unless |
```

The same text finds spondees in the following lines from Pope (*Eloisa to Abelard*, 251; *Epistle to Dr. Arbuthnot*, 182):

```
 x  /  x  /   /   /   x  /   x  /
Thy life | a long | dead calm | of fixed | repose; |

                   /       /      /    /
And strains from hard- | bound brains, | eight lines | a year.
```

A second text illustrates spondaic substitution with a line from Pope (*Essay on Criticism*, 369) and pyrrhic substitution with a line in Keats (*The Eve of St. Agnes*, 7):

```
 x   /    /   /   x   /   x / x  /
The hoarse | rough verse | should like | the tor | rent roar

 x  / x /  x    x   x /   x  /
Like pi | ous in | cense from | a cen | ser old
```

Such scansions are commendable to the extent that they reflect an awareness of genuine rhythmical variations in the lines. But the scansions contradict what we hear in English speech. Of the four spondees discovered by the authorities, three consist of a monosyllabic adjective followed by a monosyllabic noun. When we utter this construction, we usually subordinate the adjective to its noun, except when we wish to emphasize, rhetorically or contrastively, the adjective rather than the noun—as in this reworking of one of the Pope lines:

He strains out *nine* lines every year, not *eight.*

Or a poet may stress the adjective to produce a comic effect, as when Samuel Taylor Coleridge, in his poem "Metrical Feet," rhymes his name ("Cóle • ridge") with "whóle ridge."

Similar remarks could be made about the pyrrhics discovered in the lines above. Consider, for example, the second line of Yeats's poem and the supposedly pyrrhic "upon." Our dictionary tells us that "upon" is accented on its second syllable; "on" may not be as heavily stressed as "coat" in the overall context of the line, but it takes more stress than the "up-" with which it shares the line's third foot. The third foot of Yeats's first line is more complicated, but it, too, would appear to be an iamb. Emphasis drops after the noun "man" and rises on the word "but," which is a word important to the sense of the line: Yeats is saying, An aged man is *nothing more than* a paltry thing. (That he later qualifies the statement does not alter the tonality of this particular line.) As for Keats's line with the incense simile, the third foot is light. Nevertheless, "from" initiates the prepositional phrase that occupies the second half of the line, and the word takes more stress than the weak second syllable of "incense."

With the two-value system of notation, we can scan only the meter of a line; we cannot scan its rhythm. We can refer the line to its general type. We can also note clear divergences from it, such as feminine endings and substitutions of trochees for iambs. But scansion involves a certain comprehensiveness and abstraction from the endless variabilities of living language. It is this comprehensiveness that enables us to use scansion to demonstrate metrical patterns and to relate individual lines of verse to them. If we attempt to force scansion to record rhythmical subtleties, we are likely to muddle matters and even to lose hold of the distinction between meter and rhythm.

I do not wish to seem spondicidal or pyrrhicidal. Neither do I want to insist too much on my opinion, since the writers whose scansions I have criticized are gifted and thoughtful scholars, and many others feel, as they do, that spondees and pyrrhics are common in English verse. However, if we want to distinguish an iamb involving something like the words "eight lines" from an iamb involving something like "a scratch," perhaps it would be preferable to speak, as I did earlier, of a "heavy foot" or "heavy iamb." Likewise, we might use, for a foot in which both syllables are comparatively unemphatic, the term "light foot" or "light iamb." But as for scansions that mark syllables as unaccented or accented, the best course is to treat as an iamb any foot whose second syllable is heavier than its first syllable. The degree of difference much affects the rhythm of a line, but is irrelevant to the meter.

Be it noted as well that there are practical problems with regularly scanning pyrrhics and spondees into English verse. Feet whose syllables are relatively close in their stress level occur all the time in flexibly written iambics and are, regardless of how we construe them, absorbed into the prevailing pattern. As Robert Bridges once suggested, when we are reading *Paradise Lost* and are sweeping along with the continually and inventively shifting modulations of Milton's verse, even a line as solemn and impeded as 2.621,

> Rocks, caves, lakes, fens, bogs, dens, and shades of death

does not feel like a novel spondaic interjection into the iambic rhythm. And even reading the line in isolation, we may have a hard time giving the first six words exactly the same amount of stress, unless we drain expressive color from the voice and render the words as though they were items on a grocery list. Similarly, even disyllabic compounds whose syllables are equal or nearly so (e.g., "full-tilt," "star-crossed") usually fall in with the predominant rhythm, especially when metrical accent falls on the compound's first syllable and reinforces our general inclination in English to move stress to the front of words:

> From forth the fatal loins of these two foes
>
> x / x / x / x / x /
> A pair of star-crossed lovers take their life

> (Shakespeare, *Romeo and Juliet,* Prologue, 5–6)

If we start marking every heavy or light foot as a spondee or a pyrrhic, our scansions may bewilder readers, especially those who are young and unfamiliar with verse. They may wonder why iambic pentameters and tetrameters are so named, since so few of them will appear to conform to the pattern they ostensibly embody. Moreover, scansions full of pyrrhics and spondees may lead young poets to think that any and all substitutions have always been permitted at any point in the line. Such scansions suggest as well that poets who wish to write conventional iambic pentameters are thereby doomed to construct lines according to the two-syllables-per-phrase model or are at least obliged to construct lines in which the maximal-minimal pattern is closely followed.

This suggestion is made explicit in the second of the texts cited a few paragraphs back. Introducing a discussion of "Variation of Meter in Iambic Feet," the authors state: "Very few poets keep strictly to normal iambic meter (or any other meter). The verse would become intolerably monotonous if they did!" If, by "normal iambic meter," the authors mean the minimal-maximal pattern, they have confused the theoretical structure of the line—the analytical abstraction, the line conceived of as a comprehensive type—with its actual manifestations in practice. Very few poets keep strictly to "normal iambic meter," in the sense that the authors use the term, not only because the procedure is monotonous, but also because it is well-nigh impossible.

This may seem like a small confusion, but it can lead to, or can reinforce, a much bigger one, to wit, that meter is most vital when violated. This notion is famously expressed by T. S. Eliot in his "Reflections on *Vers Libre*":

> [T]he most interesting verse which has yet been written in our language has been done either by taking a very simple form, like the iambic pentameter, and constantly withdrawing from it, or taking no form at all, and constantly approximating to a very simple one.

Eliot made great contributions to our poetry, and he never consciously intended to harm the art; but probably no notion has been more destructive to modern verse practice than this one. And whatever one feels about Eliot's effect on subsequent writing, it is important to observe that, as historical description, the view he advances is mistaken. It has not been by taking a form and withdrawing from it, or by taking no form and approximating a form, that poets have produced "the most interesting verse which has yet been written in our language," unless Eliot means to exclude from this category the verse of Chaucer, Shakespeare, Milton, Pope, Keats, and Emily Dickinson and to reserve laurels exclusively for certain Jacobean dramatists —and then only in certain passages—and for modern vers-libristes. Historically, the masters of our poetry have achieved their expressive effects principally by modulating metrical forms internally rather than by withdrawing from them.

That Eliot really means "withdrawing" rather than "modulating" is clear, I should add, from the two examples that he offers shortly after making his pronouncement. The first is T. E. Hulme's "Embankment," whose seven lines run from three to twelve syllables; the second is the final seven lines of Ezra Pound's "Near Perigord," lines which are mostly iambic but which run from eight to eleven syllables. Of these examples, Eliot says: "It is obvious that the charm of these lines could not be, without the constant suggestion and the skilful evasion of iambic pentameter."

The unhappiest consequence of the idea that meter is most interesting when violated is that it may seduce poets into making a virtue of clumsiness. If the conventional line is thought to be monotonous, and if departures from it are viewed as beneficial, poets may come to see their inability to control the medium as an indication of technical subtlety. Regardless of any initial allegiance they may feel to verse form, they may think themselves at liberty to break its rules when doing so suits their convenience, and may see the results of these infractions as exceptional felicities. It is as if basketball players were to ask to be credited with scoring not only when they put the ball through the hoop, but also when they dribbled it off a foot or threw it out of bounds. Indeed, it is as if players were to ask for extra points in these latter cases—or were to ask for two points when they made a shot and for four points when they missed.

It is perfectly permissible to put meter and rhythm into, as Frost once said, "strained relation"—to test and explore the possible correspondences and counterpoints between the abstract measure and the intonations of living speech. It is quite another thing to divorce rhythm from meter—to sacrifice measure to personal rhythm or to use measure merely as a reference point about which rhythm may hover intermittently.

But to return to the main point of this chapter, in successful versification fixed form and personal rhythm operate in harmony. The chief source of variety in poetry in English is the internal modulation of the metrical line.

2

Scansion and Metrical Variation

1. Principles of Scansion

SCANSION IS A SIMPLE MATTER as long as we remember two points. Though we have touched on them already, they merit repetition and additional illustration.

First, scansion records units of rhythm, not units of sense. Scansion treats verse lines as rows of discrete syllables, and it divides lines into feet without reference to the ways in which the syllables may be clustered into words. Hence foot division and word division do not always coincide. In the following iambic pentameter couplet, for example, the foot boundaries in the first line lie between words, whereas in the second line "temples" and "tapers" cross foot boundaries:

> One thought | of thee | puts all | the pomp | to flight,
> Priests, tap | ers, temp | les, swim | before | my sight

(Pope, *Eloisa to Abelard*, 273–74)

By the same token, phrases and clauses sometimes terminate at the ends of feet, sometimes within them. Both pentameters below consists of two distinct syntactical elements. However, in the first line, the elements fall on either side of the boundary between the second and third feet, while in the second line, they divide in the middle of the third foot:

> Once in | a dream <|> (for once | I dreamed | of you)
> We stood | togeth | er <> in | an op | en field

(Christina Rossetti, "A Dream," 1–2)

The second point is that, in scanning, we determine if a syllable is metrically accented by comparing it with the other syllable or syllables of the foot in which it appears. We do not assess its metrical value by weighing it against all the other syllables in the line. A syllable lightly stressed in speech may, if it appears in a foot in which the other syllable receives even less stress, take a metrical accent. This happens in the second foot of this pentameter:

x / x / x / x / x /
No long | er by | these streams, | but far | away

(William Cullen Bryant, "The Prairies," 93)

Though "by" is light, the unaccented second syllable of "longer" is even lighter, in consequence of which "by" bears metrical accent. Conversely, a syllable with considerable speech stress may, if it appears in a foot in which the other syllable is even weightier, be metrically unaccented. We meet this situation in the third foot of the tenth line of Keats's "To Autumn":

x / x / x / x / x /
Until | they think | warm days | will nev | er cease

"Warm" receives a good deal of speech stress. Nevertheless, "days" is heavier, so "warm" is metrically unaccented.

It follows that we should, in scanning, refrain from imposing convoluted readings on lines that admit of straightforward interpretation. If we come across a slightly unusual line like Bryant's or Keats's, we should not jump to the conclusion that the poet has suddenly plunged into an experiment with exotic feet or rhythms. Rather, we should first check to see if the line can be reconciled with the prevailing metrical pattern. If it can, we should assume that the poet is modulating rather than altering the meter.

To scan a line is not to insist that everyone must or will read it exactly alike. Though we may all read a line according to the same fundamental scheme, we may individually shade syllables and phrases, depending upon our feeling for the poet's words. Consider, for example, this line, which describes an old man casting a horseshoe at a peg:

He swings, and weight once more inhabits space

(X. J. Kennedy, "Old Men Pitching Horseshoes," 8)

Most of us will treat this line as an iambic pentameter, entailing an alternation, five times repeated, between weaker and stronger syllables. But variations may occur in our renderings of the line's last eight syllables. These make up a clause that we can speak continuously. And because any complete articulation has only one primary stress, we likely will emphasize one of the clause's four metrically accented syllables more than the others. But which syllable will we favor? The clause has three arresting ideas, expressed by the subject, verb, and direct object, respectively. "Weight" is arresting in that it involves the force of gravity. There is the literal gravity of the toss, arc, and fall of the horseshoe. There is the figurative gravity—the dignity—of the old man. There is also the gravity—the seriousness—of the grave, towards which the old man is drawn ever closer, even as he plays horseshoes. "Inhabits" is a striking word, too. It reminds us that the activities of living beings give character to what otherwise would be mere emptiness. Lastly, "space" is interesting, since it surrounds those who play the game, and the planet on which they play it. Space is the universal medium in which matter and life occur. (Though the adverbial phrase "once more" is important, too, it is not as semantically essential as the subject, verb, or object.)

Yet regardless of the reading we give the line—whether we emphasize "weight," the middle syllable of "inhabits," or "space"—we will maintain some version of the iambic fluctuation between weaker and stronger syllables. Our interpretation will affect the line's rhythm. Metrically, however, our choice is irrelevant: each reading will adhere to the iambic pentameter paradigm. Regardless of the subtle differences in our inflections of the line, we will scan it,

```
  x    /    x    /    x    /   x  /  x    /
He swings, | and weight | once more | inhab | its space
```

Occasionally, a foot will admit of more than one metrical interpretation. One person, that is, will metrically accent one of the syllables of the foot, whereas another person will accent the other syllable (or, in the case of verse in trisyllabic feet, one of the others). We will discuss this matter at the close of this chapter.

2. The Principal Iambic Meters

As was mentioned in the introduction, English verse is in the main "accentual-syllabic," a term that indicates that the poetic line has a certain number and pattern of accents and a certain number of syllables. If the line is the essential unit of versification, the basic component of the line is the foot. A foot consists of either two or three syllables, one and only one of which bears a metrical accent. For practical purposes, English versification involves five feet:

the iamb:	x /
the trochee:	/ x
the anapest:	x x /
the dactyl:	/ x x
the amphibrach:	x / x

Because our poets have written chiefly in iambics—and because we will be examining, in a later chapter, meters involving trochaic and trisyllabic feet—we can best proceed by examining poems that exemplify the principal iambic meters. For now I will neither divide the lines into feet nor mark syllables as metrically unaccented and accented. At this point, we should concentrate on perceiving the general structure of the lines: prosodic notation might prove distracting.

Names for verse lines denote both the characteristic foot in the line and the number of such feet that the line contains. For instance, a poem in *iambic monometer* has one *(mono-)* foot per measure and that foot is an iamb, as in Ogden Nash's "Geographical Reflection":

> The Bronx?
> No, thonks!

A longer poem in this measure is Robert Herrick's "Upon His Departure Hence."

> Thus I
> Pass by
> And die:
> As One
> Unknown
> And gone:
> I'm made
> A shade
> And laid
> I'th' grave:
> There have
> My cave,
> Where tell,
> I dwell.
> *Farewell.*

Poems in iambic monometer are rare. Though the measure is deftly employed by Herrick and Nash, it does not encourage complexity of argument or rhythmical invention. Slightly more common are works in *iambic dimeter,* a line of two iambic feet. Philip Larkin's poem on the fiftieth anniversary of the Brynmor Jones Library at the University of Hull illustrates this measure:

> New eyes each year
> Find old books here,
> And new books, too,
> Old eyes renew;
> So youth and age
> Like ink and page
> In this house join,
> Minting new coin.

A poem in *iambic trimeter* has three iambic feet as the norm, as in Dick Davis's "Touring a Past," which compares an out-of-the-way and little-visited archeological site to the ruins of an unhappy love affair:

> Even from here I see
> How stagnant and unused
> The brackish waters lie,
> As if the bank had oozed
> This stream that sluggishly
> Reflects the idle sky.
>
> There is no boat to cross
> From that ill-favored shore
> To where the clashing reeds
> Complete the work of war
> Together with the grass,
> And nesting birds, and weeds.
>
> I read that now there is
> Almost no evidence—
> No walls or pottery—
> Of what I know were once
> The walks and palaces
> Love lent to you and me.

A poem in *iambic tetrameter* has lines of four iambic feet, as in Anne Finch's "Song," a trenchant analysis of alcoholism:

The nymph in vain bestows her pains
That seeks to thrive where Bacchus reigns;
In vain are charms, or smiles, or frowns,
All images his torrent drowns.

Flames to the head he may impart,
But makes an island of the heart,
So inaccessible and cold,
That to be his is to be old.

And Richard Wilbur's "Transit" exemplifies *iambic pentameter,* a line consisting of five iambic feet:

A woman I have never seen before
Steps from the darkness of her town-house door
At just that crux of time when she is made
So beautiful that she or time must fade.

What use to claim that as she tugs her gloves
A phantom heraldry of all the loves
Blares from the lintel? That the staggered sun
Forgets, in his confusion, how to run?

Still, nothing changes as her perfect feet
Click down the walk that issues in the street,
Leaving the stations of her body there
As a whip maps the countries of the air.

The pentameter is the longest line commonly used in English, but poets have experimented with more extended measures, including the iambic hexameter and the iambic heptameter. The heptameter—or "fourteener," as the seven-foot iambic line is also called—may be set aside until we examine stanzaic verse. It may, however, be well to speak here about the hexameter.

Consisting of six iambs, the iambic hexameter is sometimes referred to as an "alexandrine," after the twelve-syllable measure of French poetry. However, applying this term to the English line is misleading, since the French alexandrines neither are iambic nor have six beats. To the extent that the French alexandrine reflects stress order, it generally follows one of two arrangements. The first, characteristic of the Neoclassical period, involves a medially divided line with four accents. The second and fourth accents fall on the sixth and twelfth syllables respectively; the other two accents are variably disposed in the interior of the half-lines, often falling on syllables 3 and 9:

$$\overset{\text{/}}{\text{Je n'escris}} \mid \overset{\text{/}}{\text{de plaisir,}} \mid \overset{\text{/}}{\text{me trouvant}} \mid \overset{\text{/}}{\text{douloureux}}$$

I don't write of pleasure, finding myself sad

(Joachim Du Bellay, Les Regrets, 79.4)

The second pattern, more characteristic of the Romantic period, avoids the medial caesura and involves three rhythmical units:

$$\overset{\text{/}}{\text{Le Christ immense}} \mid \overset{\text{/}}{\text{ouvrant ses bras}} \mid \overset{\text{/}}{\text{au genre humain}}$$

The great Christ opening his arms to humankind

(Victor Hugo, L'Aigle du Casque, 337)

The French speak of the first type of alexandrine as a *tétramètre* and the second as a *trimètre*. In either form, the line is swifter and more lithe than our alexandrine, which tends to lumber and break down into (or sound like) two iambic trimeters.

This lumbering quality may be illustrated by Michael Drayton's *Polyolbion*. This poem's title means "having many blessings," and the poem itself provides a versified survey of England, discussing the topography, legends, history, and commerce of the country's districts. The tone is mostly encomiastic, though in the passage below (3.111–20) the plain of Salisbury, having erupted into speech, criticizes the darkness and clamminess of forests:

> Away ye barb'rous woods, however ye be plac'd
> On mountains or in dales, or happily be grac'd
> With floods or marshy fells, with pasture or with earth
> By nature made to till, that by the yearly birth
> The large-bay'd barn doth fill, yea though the fruitfulst ground.
> For, in respect of plains, what pleasures can be found
> In dark and sleepy shades? where mists and rotten fogs
> Hang in the gloomy thicks, and make unstedfast bogs,
> By dropping from the boughs, the o'er-grown trees among,
> With caterpillar kells, and dusky cobwebs hung.

Though Drayton is a gifted poet, here his versification is monotonous. Sedulous to maintain the unwieldy measure, he lays down the beats with obvious regularity and pauses heavily after the sixth syllable of each line. Perusing such verse is like riding a mechanical seesaw: up we go to syllable 6, down we go to syllable 12, up we go to syllable 6, down we go to syllable 12. Relineating the passage as trimeters might make it seem more readable.

(It also might make it seem twice as long.) But relineation would not lend the lines the rhythmical alertness that we find in the trimeters of Davis's "Touring a Past" or—to mention other excellent poems in trimeters—Louise Bogan's "Song for a Lyre" and Richard Moore's "In Praise of Old Wives."

Despite its unwieldiness, the iambic hexameter has served as the vehicle for a number of fine poems. Relatively early specimens include Surrey's paraphrase of the fifty-fifth Psalm and the opening sonnet of Sidney's *Astrophel and Stella*. In more recent poetry, A. E. Housman uses the line admirably in the forty-eighth poem of *The Shropshire Lad* ("Be still, my soul, be still"), as does Yeats in such poems as "Fallen Majesty," "Cold Heaven," and "The Magi."

Mostly, however, English-language poets have used the iambic hexameter not as a measure for entire poems, but as a variant in poems in iambic pentameter. For instance, the great satirists of the seventeenth and eighteenth century employ the hexameter to diversify poems in heroic couplets. Sometimes the hexameter supplies the second line of the couplet, as in Pope's censure of the measure (*An Essay on Criticism*, 356–57):

> A needless Alexandrine ends the song,
> That like a wounded snake, drags its slow length along.

At other times, the hexameter further counterpoints the pentametric-couplet pattern by appearing as the concluding unit of a triplet. This procedure is illustrated by George Crabbe's account (*The Borough*, 21.47–57) of an old man who, after a lifetime of piety, is converted by degenerate young associates to a halting, timid hedonism:

> For Abel enter'd in his bold career,
> Like boys on ice, with pleasure and with fear;
> Lingering, yet longing for the joy, he went,
> Repenting now, now dreading to repent;
> With awkward pace, and with himself at war,
> Far gone, yet frighten'd that he went so far;
> Oft for his efforts he'd solicit praise,
> And then proceed with blunders and delays.
> The young more aptly passion's calls pursue,
> But age and weakness start at scenes so new,
> And tremble when they've done, for all they dared to do.

When a hexameter appears in heroic-couplet verse, it usually serves, as it does in this example, not merely as the concluding line of the couplet or triplet in which it figures, but also as the climax of a passage of narrative or argument.

Hexameters have served as variant lines in other metrical contexts. Edmund Spenser employs the hexameter as the concluding line of the nine-line stanza (the first eight lines being pentameters) that he invented for *The Fairie Queene*. This stanza is also familiar to us from such later poems as James Thomson's "Castle of Indolence," Byron's *Childe Harold's Pilgrimage*, Keats's "Eve of St. Agnes," and Shelley's "Adonais." Milton closes with a hexameter the rhyme-royal stanzas of the prefatory section of his "On the Morning of Christ's Nativity." Wordsworth does the same in the rhyme-royal stanzas of his "Resolution and Independence"; and he ends with a hexameter the eight-line stanzas of the otherwise tetrametric "Ode to Duty."

Alexandrines appear, too, as variants in the blank-verse plays of the Renaissance dramatists. Shakespeare, for example, introduces an alexandrine into that passage in *Measure for Measure* (2.4.116–19) where Isabella, pleading with Angelo for her brother's life, says that she does so not because she thinks little of his transgression, but because she loves him so much:

> O, pardon me, my lord. It oft falls out
> To have | what we | would have, | we speak | not what | we mean.
> I something do excuse the thing I hate
> For his advantage that I dearly love.

Alexandrines also occasionally appear in nondramatic blank verse. Of the 166 lines of Frost's "Death of the Hired Man," for example, four (1, 78, 106, and 132) are hexameters. The last of these occurs during Mary's assurance to Warren that if they have to nurse Silas for the long term, she will appeal to Silas's banker-brother to assume some responsibility in the case:

> I think his brother ought to help, of course.
> I'll see | to that | if there | is need. | He ought | of right
> To take him in, and might be willing to—
> He may be better than appearances.

3. The Three Common Metrical Variations in Iambic Verse: The Trochaic Substitution in the First Foot, the Mid-line Trochaic Substitution, and the Feminine Ending

Under certain conditions a different foot may be "substituted" for the prevailing foot in a line. The most common substitution in iambic verse is a trochee-for-iamb switch in the first foot of the line. We see this switch in these lines from the Larkin, Davis, Finch, and Wilbur poems, cited in full above:

> / x   x   /
> Minting | new coin

> / x   x   /   x /
> Even | from here | I see

> /   x   x   /   x   /   x   /
> Flames to | the head | he may | impart

> / x   x /   x   /   x /   x   /
> Leaving | the sta | tions of | her bod | y there´

So common is this substitution—it occurs in upwards of 10 percent of all iambic lines in English—that certain metrists do not consider it a variant. Such metrists speak of the foot "inverted" rather than "trochaic," on the grounds that the latter term suggests an alteration or disruption of rhythm that does not actually occur. I have no preference in this matter.

Here are other instances of trochaic or inverted first feet:

> /   x   x / x /   x   / x /
> Look to my little babes, my dear remains

(Anne Bradstreet, "Before the Birth of One of Her Children," 22)

> /   x   x   /   x / x / x   /
> Daughters of Time, the hypocritic Days

> /   x x   /   x   /   x   / x /
> Muffled and dumb like barefoot dervishes

(Ralph Waldo Emerson, "Days," 1–2)

> / x   x   /   x   / x   / x /
> Motionless torrents! silent cataracts

(Coleridge, "Hymn before Sunrise," 53)

```
/ x  x / x  / x    / x  /
```
Nevertheless, a message from the dawn

(Frost, "The Tuft of Flowers," 30)

```
/ x  x / x  /    x    / x  /
```
Savonarola looks more grim to-day

(Max Beerbohm, Savonarola Brown, 1.1.1)

As these examples show, an inverted first foot may result from various verbal configurations. These include a heavy monosyllable followed by a light monosyllable ("Look to") or a forestressed disyllable ("Daughters," "Muffled"). Another possibility involves a trisyllabic word with strong stress on the first syllable and intermediate stress on the third ("Motionless"). In this case the iambic tread is restored by the line's fourth syllable's having sufficient weight to take precedence over the third syllable. An additional arrangement involves a four-syllable word ("Nevertheless") with significant stress on the first and fourth syllables, and weaker stress on the second and third. Still another possibility is a five-syllable word ("Savonarola") with considerable stress on syllables 1 and 4, and light stress on syllables 2, 3, and 5.

Novices in prosody must be cognizant of the convention of the inverted first foot. They must discern not only when such inversions occur, but also how the line recovers iambic rhythm after the inversion. Beginning students may seize upon the concept of alternating stress and, finding a heavy-light syllable group at the opening of a line, tramp trochaically through the rest of it, producing scansions like the following:

```
/    x  / x  / x    / x   / x
```
Look to my little babes, my dear remains

Such a scansion distorts normal pronunciation, obliging us to say "little" and "remains" as if their stress contours were the same as "hotel" and "lemons." The scansion also requires emphasizing the "my's" to an extent that would make an egotist blush.

A less common, but still relatively frequent, substitution is a trochee-for-iamb switch in the middle of the line—in the third or fourth foot in the pentameter and in the third foot in the tetrameter. Usually, a grammatical pause precedes the mid-line inversion. However, the pause may be unpunctuated, as is the case in the third example below:

```
     x / x    /       / x  x   / x   /
The joyous birds, | shrouded | in cheerful shade
```

(Spenser, The Fairie Queene, 2.12.71.1)

```
     x    /     x / x  /      / x    x   /
What though the sea be calm? | Trust to | the shore
```

(Herrick, "Safety on the Shore," 1)

```
  x / x       / x   /     / x  x    /
In silence through a wood | gloomy | and still
```

(Wordsworth, The Prelude, 4.447)

```
  x  /   x  /    / x  x   / x   /
To laugh or fail, | diffi | dent, wonder-starred
```

(Gwendolyn Brooks, "The Children of the Poor," 1.8)

As with the inverted first foot, the mid-line trochee may result from different verbal situations. These include a heavy monosyllable followed by a light one ("Trust to"), a fore-stressed disyllable ("shrouded," "gloomy"), or a trisyllabic word with primary stress on its first syllable ("diffident"). In this last case, a strongly stressed syllable will follow the word's final (and intermediately stressed) syllable and, taking accentual precedence over it, will resume the line's iambic tread.

The final common variation in iambic verse is an extra unaccented syllable at the close of a line. Such a syllable (sometimes called "hypermetrical") produces a "feminine ending." This term derives from French prosody. In French the mute *e* is a common feminine suffix. For instance, if we wish to refer to "a black sky," we write *un ciel noir*, since the noun is masculine; but if we wish to refer to "a black dress" we write *une robe noire*, since the noun is feminine. And as *robe* reminds us, many feminine substantives in French conclude with a mute *e*. Words of this type include—to mention only several that relate to poetry—*la poésie, l'épigramme, la rime, la mesure, la metaphore, la Muse, la cadence, la grâce, la satire*. In traditional French verse, the mute *e* at the end of a word is sounded, unless elided on account of being followed by a word beginning with a vowel or silent *h*. A mute *e*, or an unaccented syllable containing a mute *e*, that appears at the end of a line is allowed as an extra syllable that does not count metrically; and two-syllable rhymes in which the second syllable is or contains an unaccented *e* are called "feminine rhymes." Though our inflectional system differs from that of French, we have adopted the term "feminine" to describe a line ending that features an extra unaccented syllable. We also use in English the term "feminine rhyme" to indicate two-syllable rhymes in which accent falls on the penultimate syllable rather than on the final one.

The iambic pentameters below illustrate the convention of the unaccented extra syllable. When scanning such lines, some metrists treat the extra syllable as entailing the substitution of an amphibrach for an iamb. Yet it is more logical to parenthesize the scansion mark over the syllable. This makes clear that the syllable is, literally, "hypermetrical"—"beyond" or "over" the boundary of the meter.

```
  x   /   x   /     x   /    x   /   x  / (x)
I'll not | be pleased | with less | than Cle | opatra
```

(Dryden, All for Love, 2.1.446)

```
  x   /    x    /    x  /    x . /   x    /  (x)
She woke | sometimes | to feel | the day | light coming
```

(Adrienne Rich, "Living in Sin," 26)

```
 x /   x   / x / x  /    x / (x)
The age | of mir | acles | is gone | forever
```

(Charles Martin, "Easter Sunday, 1985," 7)

```
  x    /   x  /   x  /   x  /    x   /  (x)
What would | it take, | a mag | ic word | to free you
```

(Robert B. Shaw, "Narcissus," 23)

As these lines indicate, feminine endings—like inverted first feet and mid-line inversions—may involve constructions of various types. Feminine endings most often result from the poet's placing at the end of a line, as Rich does, a fore-stressed disyllable like "coming." Yet a feminine ending may also consist of a light monosyllabic word, such as the pronoun "you" which concludes Shaw's line. Or a feminine ending may consist of the last syllable of a trisyllabic word with the stress on the middle syllable, as in the example from Martin. Or the hypermetrical element may consist of the final unaccented syllable of a polysyllabic word such as "Cleopatra."

Occasionally, a line may feature two hypermetrical syllables. In blank verse, it is not always clear whether the extra syllables are hypermetrical or instead constitute an additional foot. For instance, when the Ghost of Hamlet's father summarizes (1.5.80) his feelings about being poisoned by his brother, we can treat the line either as a pentameter with two extra unaccented syllables or as an alexandrine:

```
x   / x  / x  / x  /   x   / (x) (x)
```
O, horrible! O, horrible! Most horrible!

```
x   / x  / x  / x  /   x   / x  /
```
O, horrible! O, horrible! Most horrible!

If this line appeared in a passage of rhymed verse, and the Ghost went on to say,

> And Gertrude thinks the villain is adorable!

we could tell that the tenth syllable is the last metrically accented one, since the main rhyme syllable in rhymed verse marks the metrical end of the line:

```
x     / x    /    x / x  / x  / (x) (x)
```
And Gertrude thinks the villain is adorable!

But the matter is less clear in rhymeless verse, since the last two syllables of "horrible" can serve as a light iamb when placed elsewhere in the line, as happens when the word runs from syllables 2 to 4 and 6 to 8 in the Ghost's exclamation.

A line may feature both an inverted first foot and a feminine ending. This occurs frequently in Chaucer. In Middle English more words conclude with *e* than they do in Modern English; and in Middle English, the final *e*, whether intrinsically part of the word or an inflectional ending, is conventionally sounded at the close of line (as it is elsewhere when the meter requires it):

```
/   x x / x  /   x  / x   / (x)
```
Right as an aspes leef she gan to quakë

(Troilus and Criseyde, 3.1200)

```
/ x x  / x  /   x  / x  / (x)
```
Redy to wenden on my pilgrymagë

(Canterbury Tales, A 21 ["General Prologue"])

```
/  x   x /    x   /  x / x  / (x)
```
Help and releeve, thou mighti debonayrë*   *gracious person

("An ABC," 6)

Here are additional lines with both inverted first feet and feminine endings:

```
/  x x /  x   / x  / x  /   (x)
```
Dante is hard, and few can understand him

(Ben Jonson, Volpone, 3.4.95)

```
/  x  x  /    x  /  x    /    x  /  (x)
```
Often rebuk'd, yet always back returning

(Emily Brontë, "Stanzas," 1)

Pentameters may also feature both line-beginning and mid-line trochees:

```
/   x   x /   x   /    /    x  x  /
```
Nothing beside remains. Round the decay

(Shelley, "Ozymandias," 12)

```
/ x x   /   /  x  x  / x   /
```
Hero or saint, coward or guttersnipe

(Charles Gullans, "John Wilkes," 23)

This verse has both an inverted foot after a mid-line pause and a feminine ending:

```
x   /   x   /   / x  x  /   x   /  (x)
```
Good night, good night! Parting is such sweet sorrow

(Shakespeare, *Romeo and Juliet*, 2.2.185)

And in these lines, the initial inversion, the mid-line inversion, and the feminine ending all appear:

```
/ x   x  / x   /    /   x   x  /  (x)
```
Writ in my cousin's hand, stol'n from her pocket

(Shakespeare, *Much Ado about Nothing*, 5.4.89)

```
/   x  x   /  x /  /  x  x   /  (x)
```
Sleepless as Prospero back in his bedroom

(Gjertrud Schnackenberg, "Darwin in 1881," 1)

Similar variations occur in iambic tetrameters. Here, for instance, is a tetrameter with an inverted first foot:

```
/   x   x   /   x   /  x  /
```
Crushing the world with such a light

(Allen Tate, "The Cross," 5)

This tetrameter has a feminine ending:

```
x   /   x  /   x   /   x  /  (x)
```
A theme for all the world's attention

(William Cowper, "The Retired Cat," 102)

This has an inverted first foot and a mid-line inversion:

```
/ x    x   /   / x   x  /
```
Lilies without, roses within

(Marvell, "The Nymph Complaining for the Death of her Fawn," 92)

Here I should pause to put in an opinion (no book on versification would be complete without one) about Marvell's much debated line,

To a green thought, in a green shade

("The Garden," 48)

I hear this as a light trochee, a heavy iamb, a light trochee, a heavy iamb. The line features, incidentally, one of the two common syntactical patterns in which we clearly hear the four degrees of stress of which linguists speak. We hear weak, semiweak, semistrong, and strong stresses when they rise, in 1–2–3–4 pattern continuously over two feet, as in Sidney's "With how sad steps." And we hear the four degrees, in 2–1–3–4 pattern, in prepositional phrases with a monosyllabic preposition, monosyllabic article, monosyllabic object, and a monosyllabic adjective modifying it. Examples include "In a cool night," "On a wet lawn," "Up the steep slope," or, to return to Marvell's line and its parallel prepositional phrases,

```
 2  1   3       4      2  1   3      4
```
To a green thought, in a green shade

To return to our illustrations, this iambic tetrameter has an inverted first foot and a feminine ending,

```
 / x    x    / x    /   x    /  (x)
```
Nothing but chaff, and straws, and feathers

(Swift, "Cadenus and Vanessa," 56)

and this has an inverted first foot, a mid-line inversion, and a feminine ending:

```
 /   x x   /    /   x x / (x)
```
Let me explain, Phil, my position

(Seth, *The Golden Gate*, 5.9.9)

Why have these three conventional variations—the feminine ending, the line-opening inversion, and the inversion after a mid-line pause—emerged and established themselves in English iambic verse? There are a couple of answers to this question.

One concerns phonology. At line and phrase boundaries, the ear toler-ates metrical modifications more readily than it does elsewhere. Following a pause between lines or phrases, the rhythm is temporarily suspended. At such junctures, an inverted foot is less disruptive than it would be if it ap-peared in the midst of a developing segment of rhythm. Discussing in-verted feet at linear and syntactical divisions, Roman Jakobson has observed: "This license . . . is entirely explainable by the particular import of the relation between an upbeat [i.e., unstressed syllable] and the immedi-ately preceding downbeat [i.e., stressed syllable]. Where such an immediate precedence is impeded by an inserted pause, the upbeat becomes a kind of *syllaba ancep* [i.e., an undecided syllable, a syllable that may be either light or heavy]."

A related argument might explain the convention of the feminine end-ing. An extra unstressed syllable that follows the final beat of an iambic line is not felt as a break in the prevailing pattern. Indeed, in iambic verse, the feminine ending continues the fluctuation between light and heavy sylla-bles. Especially in blank verse, in which there is no rhyme to draw attention to the additional syllable, feminine endings largely pass unnoticed. (It is for this reason that they are so much more common in blank verse than in rhymed verse.) Nor does a feminine ending, succeeded by an iamb at the head of the next line [(x) | x /], produce the impression of an anapest, since the line break suspends the rhythm after the hypermetrical syllable and be-fore the iamb that opens the next line.

The shapes and stress properties of English words also account, I believe, for the existence of the conventional variations in iambic verse. This point is especially pertinent to the line-opening trochee and the feminine ending. Many English words of two or more syllables start with a heavy syllable or end with a light one. Though such words can be integrated into the middle of the iambic line, it is useful also to have the option of setting them at the head or at the end of the line. The conventions of the inverted first foot and of the feminine ending vouchsafe poets these alternative placements.

Consider the following line (115) from Frost's "Generations of Men":

Making allowance, making due allowance

This line twice features the fore-stressed disyllabic word "making" and the middle-stressed trisyllabic word "allowance." The second time "making" appears, it is integrated iambically into the interior of the line; however, the convention of the trochaic first foot lets Frost position the word at the line beginning as well. When "allowance" first appears, Frost merges it into the iambic rhythm of the line's interior; but the convention of the feminine ending permits Frost to employ the word at the line ending, too:

/ x   x /   x   /   x   /   x / (x)
Making | allow | ance, mak | ing due | allowance

Frost, incidentally, may be having a little joke here. This line, about making allowance, makes use of the two most common allowances of English verse.

Similarly, in this line (507) from Frost's *Masque of Mercy,*

Failure is failure, but success is failure

the conventions of the inverted first foot and of the feminine ending enable the poet to use "failure" in three different metrical manners. The word initially figures as a trochaic first foot, then is integrated into the line's overall iambic rhythm, and finally serves to produce a feminine ending:

/ x   x /   x   /   x /   x / (x)
Failure | is fail | ure, but | success | is failure

Nor is this phenomenon rare. We often find Shakespeare using, in his plays, the conventional licenses to situate fore-stressed disyllabic character names in different parts of the line. For example, in this line (*Troilus and Cressida,* 5.5.47) he successively employs "Hector," as Frost does "failure," as an inverted first foot, an element of iambic rhythm, and an element figuring in a feminine ending:

/ x   x   / x / x   /   x   / (x)
Hector! Where's Hector? I will none but Hector.

The first-foot inversion can also enable poets to use weighty monosyllabic words more versatilely than they otherwise could. This point is illustrated by the Duke's summary couplet (5.1.412–13) near the end of *Measure for Measure.* Here Shakespeare uses "haste" and "like" first in trochees and then in iambs. (He also integrates "leisure" and "measure" into the iambic interior of the line and then places them at the end, where they produce hypermetrical syllables.)

/   x x   /   x   / x   /   x   / (x)
Haste still pays haste, and leisure answers leisure;
/   x   x /   x   / x   /   x   / (x)
Like doth quit like, and Measure still for Measure

Shakespeare likes the rhythm and rhetoric of this construction, and we find it elsewhere in his work, as in (*Richard II,* 2.3.86),

```
/   x  x  /   x  /  x  / x  / (x)
Grace me no grace, nor uncle me no uncle
```

The mid-line inversion gives poets similar latitude. For instance, in the following epigram by Cunningham, "naked" serves not only as an inverted first foot, but also as a mid-line trochaic substitution. The word appears as well, in the epigram's second line, integrated into the iambic texture of the verse.

```
/ x   x  /     / x  x /     x  /
Naked | I came, | naked | I leave | the scene,
x   /  x  /   x  /  x  /  x   /
And nak | ed was | my pas | time in | between.
```

Thanks to the convention of the first-foot inversion, poets can also use, relatively freely, trisyllabic words whose first syllable is strongly stressed, whose second is weakly stressed, and whose third is somewhere in the in-termediate range. Robert Browning is particularly fond of laying such words across the frame of the pentameter so that they figure first in line-opening trochees and then in the rising, iambic rhythm:

```
/ x x  /    x  /  x  / x /
Vanity, saith the preacher, vanity
```

> ("The Bishop Orders His Tomb at Saint Praxed's Church," 1)

```
/ x x   / x / x  /  x      /
Quietly, quietly the evening through
```

> ("Andrea del Sarto," 17)

```
/ x  x   / x /  x    / x /
Setebos, Setebos, and Setebos
```

> ("Caliban upon Setebos," 24)

The feminine ending also enables poets to place at line endings polysyl-labic words accented on the penultimate syllable. Though poets usually in-tegrate into the metrical grid such words as "consideration,"

```
x  / x / x   /  x  / x  /
Consideration like an angel came
```

> (Shakespeare, *Henry V,* 1.1.28)

the allowance of the hypermetrical syllable permits words of this type to be set at the end of the line:

```
x    /  x  /   x   /   x  / x / (x)
And his disguise with due consideration
```

(Byron, Don Juan, 6.790)

Finally, the conventions we have been examining enable poets to handle variously a number of common syntactical patterns. One involves clauses that feature a transitive verb followed by a lightly stressed direct-object pronoun. When, for instance, Almeria cries out (2.2.38) to Leonora in the crypt scene of William Congreve's *Mourning Bride,*

```
 /   x   x   /   x   /   x   /   x   /   (x)
Comfort me, help me, hold me, hide me, hide me
```

the convention of the feminine ending allows Congreve to set the verb-object phrase, "hide me," not only in the interior of the pentameter, but also at its end.

In the same manner, when Almeria, on the brink of being forced into an unwelcome bigamous marriage, pleads (3.1.269) with her disguised and imprisoned husband, Alphonso,

```
 /   x   x   /   x   /   x   /   x   /
Kill me, then kill me, dash me with thy chains
```

the allowance of the inverted first foot permits Almeria to say, "Kill me" at the head of the pentameter as well in the middle of it. (It warms a metrist's heart that, when all else fails Almeria, prosodic convention staunchly supports her, accommodating her every passionate outburst and despairing lament. Happily, she survives her crises and, in the fifth act, is triumphantly reunited with a liberated Alphonso.)

In sum, given the three common metrical variations that we have been examining, skillful poets can flexibly handle, in regular iambic verse, pretty much any and all of the verbal and syntactical resources of English.

The variations have additional advantages. For one thing, from time to time it may be beneficial, merely in terms of sound, to begin iambic verses trochaically. Not only may the variety be welcome, but the forceful opening cadence may prove expressive. Illustrative in this regard is Robinson's "The Clerks," a sonnet which is regularly iambic until we encounter the inverted first feet of the final three lines. (The word "alnage" in the last line refers to the measurement of woolen cloth by the ell, a unit of measure roughly corresponding to the length of a man's arm.) I shall add italics to highlight the inverted feet.

> I did not think that I should find them there
> When I came back again; but there they stood
> As in the days they dreamed of when young blood
> Was in their cheeks and women called them fair.
> Be sure, they met me with an ancient air,—
> And yes, there was a shop-worn brotherhood
> About them; but the men were just as good,
> And just as human as they ever were.
>
> And you that ache so much to be sublime,
> And you that feed yourselves with your descent,
> What comes of all your visions and your fears?
> *Poets* and kings are but the clerks of Time,
> *Tiering* the same dull webs of discontent,
> *Clipping* the same sad alnage of the years.

No matter how often I read this poem, I am startled and moved by its conclusion, and I believe that the change in rhythm contributes to this effect. Robinson's respect for people who live decent if modest lives suddenly acquires an impressive weight, a weight almost inexplicable in a poem whose language is so direct and plain. Doubtless the dignity and humanity of the poet is chiefly responsible. The quiet firmness of statement about the vanity of human pride doubtless also plays a role. Yet the inverted feet are a factor, too. They convey a heartfelt emphasis that drives home the point.

Lines that open with trochees can also arrestingly counterpoint standard iambic lines. Such counterpoint appears in these tetrameter couplets (60–63) from Matthew Arnold's "Memorial Verses," an elegy for Wordsworth that Arnold wrote in April 1850, the month of the older poet's death:

> Time may restore us in his course
> Goethe's sage mind and Byron's force;
> But where will Europe's latter hour
> Again find Wordsworth's healing power?

Each line of the first couplet begins with a trochaic foot, and these inversions communicate an assertive solemnity. (In the first line, we could accent the auxiliary verb "may" at the expense of "Time," but favoring "Time" is more natural, since it is lexically and thematically such an important word.)

The lines of the second couplet, however, open iambically and flow more lyrically. And this rhythmical contrast reinforces a larger and more poignant human contrast. In the first couplet, Arnold speaks of losses that may, though sorrowful, find compensation. In the second, he speaks of an irredeemable loss.

Mid-line inversions can also produce expressive effects. Such an effect appears in Milton's *Paradise Lost,* when Satan, newly arrived in Hell, bitterly resolves (1.159) to persist in his jealous defiance of truth and virtue:

> To do ought good | never | will be our task

Here "never," by constituting an inverted foot, carries special and disruptive emphasis, and highlights the speaker's destructive and misplaced vigor.

Beginning a line with a trochee may also help the poet create a countercurrent to the iambic rhythm. When the middle or later stages of the line feature a di-, tri-, or polysyllabic word or words with falling rhythm, an initial trochee can give us a sense that a trochaic movement exists simultaneously with the prevailing iambic current. When Yeats, for example, opens the second section of "The Second Coming" with the lines,

> Surely some revelation is at hand;
> Surely the Second Coming is at hand

it is as if "revelation," and "Second Coming"—though incorporated into the rising rhythm of the lines—have taken up the trochaic motif of "Surely."

Like inverted feet, feminine endings not only can serve the poet's convenience, but also can provide expressive effects. Such an effect appears in Mary Wortley Montagu's epigram in response to Lord Lyttleton's "Advice to a Lady," an effort notorious for such gems as:

> Seek to be good, but aim not to be great;
> A woman's noblest station is retreat. (51–52)

It seems no accident, that is, that Montagu's neatly caustic rejoinder, "Summary of Lord Lyttelton's *Advice to a Lady,"*

> Be plain in dress and sober in your diet;
> In short, my deary, kiss me, and be quiet.

features feminine rhymes. They give an added fillip to her irritation with Lyttelton's patronizing poem.

So, too, it may be significant that Dorothy Parker delivers her rueful comment ("Sonnet for the End of a Sequence," 4),

```
 / x  x /    x  /   x  / x / (x)
```
Ever she longed for peace, but was a woman

in a pentameter in which the very word "woman" produces a feminine ending. The first-foot trochee may also give the line extra punch.

4. Less Common Trochaic Substitutions and Trochees That Maybe Are Not Trochees

As we have noted, when trochees appear in iambic pentameters, it is most often in the first foot and less frequently in the third or fourth foot following a grammatical pause. Second-foot trochees are comparatively rare in pentametric verse, fifth-foot inversions rarer still. In theory a poet may substitute one type of foot for another at any point in the line, such substitutions being permissible as long as they are not so frequent that they undermine the line's metrical integrity. However, the pentameter is so flexible that adding or shifting syllables about, unless there is a line or sense break, can prove destabilizing. Second-foot inversions, it is sometimes said, tend to disrupt the line's developing rhythm. And fifth-foot trochees may create metrical confusion at that very place in the line where the ear expects conclusive and predictable rhythm.

Yet second-foot trochees can be effective in pentameter lines, especially if introduced after a pause following the first foot. In such cases, we are likely to hear, notwithstanding the unusual inversion, five beats and are thus likely to be able to retain a sense of the meter.

In addition, second-foot trochees can create expressive effects appropriate to certain subjects or situations. When, for example, Helen Pinkerton speaks ("On Breughel the Elder's 'The Harvesters' in the Metropolitan Museum," 5) of people whose lives are sacrificed to hard physical labor,

```
 x /   / x x /    x    / x   /
```
Fatigue, deep as disease, maims mind and bone

her inversion of the second foot produces a sense of heaviness and curtailment that perfectly and sadly accords with the exhaustion that she is describing.

Second-foot trochees may prove as well effective when the initial foot is also inverted, as we can see in the opening line of the first of Donne's *Holy Sonnets:*

```
 /   x     /   x   x    /    x   /    x  /
Thou hast | made me, | and shall | thy work | decay?
```

As does Pinkerton, Donne sustains clarity of beat count: since we still hear two strong stresses in the first two feet, the ear can navigate the unusual rhythm. And, as was the case with Pinkerton's line, the rhythm of this line suits its context: with his characteristically aggressive piety, Donne is reminding God of His responsibility and stake in the salvation of the being He has created. And the opening trochees communicate the urgency of the poet's request for attention and mercy. (Some might speculate that Donne wants us to strain for an iambic reading of the two feet, or at least of the second one—Thou *hast* made *me* or Thou hast made *me*—but I believe that the two-trochee reading is more plausible.)

Another expressive use of the first-foot plus second-foot inversion appears in this pentameter, a pentameter that beautifully suggests the tug-and-catch movement of a bee extricating itself from the stigma of flower.

```
  /   x    /   x   x   /   x   /   x   /
Eager | quickly | to free | its stic | ky foot
```

(Louise Bogan, "Animal, Vegetable and Mineral," 26)

Once in a blue moon, a poet will invert a fifth foot:

```
 x /   x     /    x  /  x     /      /  x
Ela | tions when | the for | est blooms; | gusty
Emotions on wet roads on autumn nights
```

(Stevens, "Sunday Morning," 26–27)

Even here, certain metrists would argue that the pause after the semicolon is in essence a phantom unstressed syllable and would mark it with a caret. This procedure restores the conventional iambic character of Stevens's line, transforming "gusty" from a ninth-to-tenth-position trochee to a tenth-to-eleventh-position feminine ending:

```
 x /   x     /    x  /  x     /     ^  /  (x)
Ela | tions when | the for | est blooms; | gusty
```

Since we do not generally count pauses as phantom syllables, and since phantom syllables are not syllables at all, this interpretation is dubious. But it indicates how unusual inverted final feet are. When they occur, people regard them as aberrational and try to explain them away.

Other apparently inverted final feet occur in *Paradise Lost*. Most of these, however, upon inspection turn out to consist of compounds or Latinate disyllables which, though fore-stressed today, may have been regarded by Milton as allowing stress on the second syllable. In some current editions of the epic (e.g., Scott Elledge's Norton Critical Edition) these words carry accent marks to indicate their evidently heterodox pronunciation. The following line (6.841) illustrates this matter:

```
x    /    x    /   x  / x  /    x   /
Of Thrones and mighty Seraphim prostráte
```

Similar considerations may be relevant to the first of these lines from Algernon Charles Swinburne ("Laus Veneris," 339, 343):

```
x   /  x   /   x   /   x    /   ?  ?
And ate like fire mine eyes and mine eyesight . . .
Seen where men's eyes look through the day to night.
```

Today, "eyesight" is fore-stressed. Yet the fact that Swinburne is rhyming the word with "night"—and the fact that he follows, throughout "Laus Veneris," the custom of rhyming on the line's last accented syllable—suggests that for him "eyesight" was stressed on the second syllable or at least that the word's two syllables were closer in accentuation for him than they are for us.

A related question arises with regard to the final foot in the first line of this couplet (1.313–14) in Keats's *Endymion*:

```
x    /  x /   /  x  x /   ?  ?
Young companies nimbly began dancing
To the swift treble pipe, and humming string.
```

It seems only logical to scan "dancing," as an inverted final foot. However, Keats may want us to wrench accent, so as to place the stress on the second syllable of the final word of the first line: "dancíng." Otherwise, the line does not rhyme securely. Keats himself called *Endymion* "slip-shod" after it was published. Given the poem's outstanding descriptive details, this judgment is too harsh; but possibly he had in mind couplets like this one, which do not feature the skill characteristic of his best work. (Keats's often cited line, "How many bards gild the lapses of time," is perhaps another iffy metrical moment, though the line can be scanned as two iambs, two trochees, and an iamb; and if we pause, as is not unnatural, after "bards," we hear five beats unambiguously.)

If some feet that initially look trochaic prove, when scrutinized, to be doubtful, other apparent trochees will prove to be downright illusory. For example, seeing in isolation constructions like "strike out" and "yield up," we might assume that the verb would take precedence over the preposition and that if the contructions appeared in a disyllabic foot the foot would be a trochee. However, phrasally connected, the two words are of almost equal lexical importance, and can be fit into an iambic foot without any disruption of rhythm:

```
x    /    x    /    x    /  x  /  x  /
My pride struck out new sparkles of her own
```

(Dryden, *The Hind and the Panther*, 1.75)

```
x   / x    /   x  /   x    /   x  /
Till parted waves of song yield up the shore
```

(Dante Gabriel Rossetti, *The House of Life*, 1.1.5.3 ["Heart's Hope"])

Another type of illusory trochee involves Chaucer. In Chaucer's day, England was still bilingual, trilingual if Latin is counted, and when Chaucer was a boy English schoolchildren were still taught in French. Not until 1362 and the Statute of Pleading did English supplant French as the language in which the laws of the land were written; not until that same year was English rather than French used to open Parliament. (Gower, Chaucer's great friend, was so unsure of his country's linguistic future that, spreading his bets to win literary immortality, he wrote his three major poems—*Mirour de l'Omme, Vox Clemantis,* and *Confessio Amantis*—in French, Latin, and English respectively.) During this period, the Anglo-Germanic tendency to stress the beginnings of words coexisted with the French tendency to place accent on the last syllable. In consequence, many words, especially disyllables derived from French (e.g., "labor," "nature," "service," "comfort"), admitted of both rear-stressed, Romanic pronunciation and fore-stressed Teutonic pronunciation. And Chaucer switches back and forth, according to metrical context, between alternative pronunciations. For instance, when introducing (A 411–13) the doctor in his General Prologue to *The Canterbury Tales,* Chaucer gives "physic" (from the Old French *fisique,* "medicine, the study of medicine") rear-stressed Romanic pronunciation in one line and then fore-stressed Teutonic pronunciation a couple of lines later:

```
x   /  x   / x  /  x    /   x /
With us ther was a DOCTOUR OF PHISIK;
In al this world ne was ther noon hym lik
x    /   x   / x  /   x   / x  /(x)
To speke of phisik and of surgeryë,
```

Unless we are aware of such shifting pronunciations, we may mistakenly read trochaic substitutions into regularly iambic lines by Chaucer.

Dual pronunciations last (often more as a matter of literary convention than as a reflection of actual speech practice) into the seventeenth century. For instance, Ben Jonson, in the forty-fifth of his sequence of epigrams, rear-stresses "envy" in accordance with its older pronunciation and accentuation and its French derivation *(envie, envier):*

> O, I could lose all father now! For why
>
> x / x / x / x / x /
> Will man lament the state he should envy?

("On My First Son," 5–6)

Yet ten epigrams later, in his mini-tribute to Francis Beaumont, Jonson says the word in conventional fore-stressed Modern English fashion:

> When even there where thou most praisest me
>
> x / x / x / x / x /
> For writing better, I must envy thee.

("To Francis Beaumont," 9–10)

It may be noteworthy that in the 1616 Folio edition of Jonson's *Works,* in which these epigrams were first published, "envy" is spelled in the French fashion, with *-ie* rather than *-y* at the end of the word. (Though *-ie* appears, in the Renaissance, widely as an alternative rendering of word-ending *-y*, it is especially common in words derived from French, such as "melodie," "harmonie," and "poesie.") It is also interesting that, according to the *OED,* the older pronunciation of "envy" survives in the Modern Scottish dialect.

Occasionally, we will encounter within a line an apparent trochaic substitution that is not preceded by a grammatical pause. Such cases usually concern a foot-straddling disyllabic compound like "foretaste":

> x / x / ? ? x / x /
> With all the foretaste of a pleasant day

(Crabbe, *Tales of the Hall,* 8.30 ["The Sisters"])

Or they concern a foot-straddling combination of monosyllabic adjective and monosyllabic noun like "white pink"—"pink" in this case being the name for a flower of the genus *dianthus:*

> x / ? ? x / x / x /
> The white pink, and the pansy freak'd with jet

(Milton, "Lycidas," 144)

In light of logic, the feet in question are trochaic. Though "foretaste" takes primary stress on its first syllable, some dictionaries (e.g., *The Random House Dictionary of the English Language*) give "-taste" secondary stress, and the syllable looks in any case more prominent than "of." Likewise, "pink" would seem obviously to bear more stress than "and."

The ear, however, may hesitate to accept this judgment. A residual sense of iambic pattern persists. One reason may be that a slight pause occurs immediately before the light words that follow the second syllables of "foretaste" and "white pink." Jespersen suggests, "[A] pause . . . covers and hides away metrical irregularities," and certainly the pauses here prevent our comparing the syllables of the questionable feet as closely as we might otherwise. The feet may well be trochaic, but they are not as emphatic as the trochees in the examples adduced in the previous section of this chapter.

Some might suggest that the pulse of the verse may also contribute to bringing these feet into conformity with iambic rhythm, though I am reluctant to accord meter independent power to override natural speech stress. Anyone who has written verse knows how easy it is to justify all kinds of sloppy writing, once you convince yourself that meter has this capacity. Rather than struggling faithfully to correct a faulty line or refractory passage, you rationalize that because you have been driving along smoothly up to this point, you can bang your way through a couple of potholes without tossing the reader off the tailgate. Nevertheless, the lines above from Crabbe and Milton do suggest that, as a poem develops, meter may assume a power, albeit very limited, to mold speech stress.

5. Loose Iambic—Iambic Verse with Anapestic Substitutions

Prior to 1800, English poets do not usually admit into the interior of the iambic line extra syllables, unless they can be elided—metrically contracted or slurred away in speech. (An exception to this rule is verse drama, which is accorded greater metrical license, on account of the exigencies of theatrical presentation.) However, the nineteenth and early twentieth centuries witness a growing interest in what Frost calls "loose iambic" verse. Loose iambic lines feature extra unaccented syllables that produce, or can most conveniently be scanned as, anapests. Such verse appears in earlier periods in, for example, the old border ballads, the February and May Eclogues of Spenser's *Shepherd's Calendar*, and Renaissance songs like Ralegh's lovely "Walsingham" ("As you came from the holy land"). But only in the nineteenth century does loose iambic come into its own.

Loose iambics have been used mostly in rhymed verse in short measures. In such measures, the identity of the line can be maintained by the rhyme, by the regular beat count, and by the tight compass in which both are operating. Hardy's "The Wound," which has an iambic dimeter base, exemplifies the loose iambic mode:

```
x   /       x  x   /
I climbed | to the crest,
          x     /   x  /
          And, fog- | festooned,
    x  /   x   /
The sun | lay west
          x   x   /   x     /
          Like a crim | son wound:
  x    x   /     x   /
Like that wound | of mine
          x    /    x      /
          Of which | none knew,
  x x   /   x  x  /
For I'd giv | en no sign
          x x   /       x    /
          That it pierced | me through.
```

Though six of this poem's sixteen feet are anapests, the iambic current is clear. Just as important, because the ear can easily locate the two metrical beats in each line, and because rhymes point the line endings, the additional unaccented syllables do not obscure the measure. Reading this poem, we can also see the great practical advantage of the looser mode: even as Hardy is confining himself to tight dimeters, the allowance of extra syllables provides him with additional space in which to maneuver.

A more complex poem in loose iambics is Frost's "Neither Out Far Nor In Deep," which is written in trimeter. This poem examines our fascination with the unknown, exploring its theme by means of a contrast in which the sea symbolizes the unknown and the land represents the known.

The people along the sand
All turn and look one way.
They turn their back on the land.
They look at the sea all day.

As long as it takes to pass
A ship keeps raising its hull;
The wetter ground like glass
Reflects a standing gull.

The land may vary more;
But wherever the truth may be—
The water comes ashore,
And the people look at the sea.

They cannot look out far.
They cannot look in deep.
But when was that ever a bar
To any watch they keep?

In this poem, as in Hardy's, a fair number of feet (eleven feet out of forty-eight) are anapests instead of iambs.

```
   x  /    x x /    x  /
The peo | ple along | the sand
 x   /   x    /   x    /
All turn | and look | one way.
   x  /    x   /   x  x /
They turn | their back | on the land.
   x  /   x  x  / x   /
They look | at the sea | all day.
 x  /    x x /    x  /
As long | as it takes | to pass
 x   /   x    /  x  x  /
A ship | keeps rais | ing its hull;
  x  / x   /    x    /
The wet | ter ground | like glass
  x  /  x   /   x   /
Reflects | a stand | ing gull.
  x  /    x  /  x  /
The land | may var | y more;
 x   x /  x  x  /    x  /
But wherev | er the truth | may be—
  x  / x  /    x  /
The wa | ter comes | ashore,
```

```
  x    x   /   x  /   x  x  /
And the peo | ple look | at the sea.

   x   /   x   /   x   /
They can | not look | out far.

   x   /   x   /   x   /
They can | not look | in deep.

   x    /    x   x  /   x x  /
But when | was that ev | er a bar

  x /  x  /      x   /
To an | y watch | they keep?
```

Yet the beat count is clear, and—again, as with Hardy's "The Wound"—the rhymes help us hear the line endings distinctly.

Loose iambic has distinctive expressive capacities, some of which can be observed in "Neither Out Far Nor In Deep." Particularly interesting is the way Frost coordinates his intermittently lilting rhythm with his theme. For example, in each of the first two lines of the second stanza he introduces an anapest, and these suggest the instability of the sea and the rocking of the passing vessel on the horizon:

```
  x   /    x x  /    x  /
As long | as it takes | to pass

  x   /   x    /  x   x   /
A ship | keeps rais | ing its hull;
```

Then in the stanza's third and fourth lines, Frost returns to regular iambics to suggest the stability of the land:

```
  x   /  x    /    x    /
The wet | ter ground | like glass

  x /  x   /    x    /
Reflects | a stand | ing gull.
```

A related effect appears in the final stanza. The first two lines are not only iambic. Their regularity is metronomic. The light syllables are very light, the heavy ones very heavy. And this is appropriate. Frost is making an emphatic statement. Oceans—literal and figurative—lie out far and in deep in the universe. They are beyond our knowing and our hope of knowing. Of their mysteries, people can get only distant views and incomplete glimpses.

```
 x   /    x   /    x   /
They can | not look | out far.

 x   /    x   /    x   /
They can | not look | in deep.
```

Yet this does not diminish their curiosity or their desire to probe the unknown. And when Frost, in the stanza's third line, expresses this counter-idea
—"But when was that ever a bar . . . "—the rhythm shifts away from the
straightforward regularity of the previous lines, almost in defiance of them
and the truth they express:

```
 x    /    x   x  /  x x  /
But when | was that ev | er a bar
```

It is an exquisite touch, and sets up the return to the norm in the final line:

```
 x  / x  /      x    /
To an | y watch | they keep?
```

Because of their lilting quality, loose iambics have a limited capacity for
modulation. Neither does loose iambic have the generic versatility that the
conventional iambic line does. Whereas a fine poet can use the iambic pentameter to write a satirical epigram, a love sonnet, a comedy such as *As You
Like It,* or an epic like *Paradise Lost,* loose iambic is principally a lyric mode.
(Indeed, the rise of loose iambic in the nineteenth century partly reflects
the elevation of lyric over all other types of poetry in that period and the
coincident belief that an indefinite and suggestive rhythm is particularly
appropriate to lyric verse.) Nonetheless, in the hands of masters like Frost,
the mode is a wonderful one.

Other outstanding poems in loose iambic dimeter include Louise
Bogan's "Knowledge" and Mark Van Doren's "Good Night." Fine poems in
loose iambic trimeter include Hardy's "Transformations," Yeats's "Fiddler of
Dooney," and Wilbur's "The Ride." Excellent poems in loose iambic tetrameter poems include Robert Browning's "Meeting at Night" and "Parting at
Morning," Hardy's "The Roman Gravemounds," Yeats's "The Song of the
Old Mother," Frost's "Need of Being Versed in Country Things," and Janet
Lewis's "No-Winter Country." Loose iambic poems that mix lines of different length include Scott's "Proud Maisie" (trimeters and dimeters), Elizabeth Barrett Browning's "A Musical Instrument" (tetrameters and
trimeters), Hardy's "The Oxen" (tetrameters and trimeters), and Gavin

Ewart's amusing "2001: The Tennyson/Hardy Poem" (tetrameters and dimeters).

In the nineteenth and early twentieth centuries, poets increasingly allow an extra syllable now and then into the conventional pentameter; we will explore this development in our fourth chapter. But generally extra syllables do not so much make the pentameter lilt as wilt. The line is so flexible to begin with that accessory elements may cause it to sag. Still, loose iambic pentameters are put to interesting use by Frost in "Mowing," "On Looking Up by Chance at the Constellations," and "Willful Homing." And Hardy's extraordinary "Afterwards" features a cross-rhyming quatrain whose first and third lines are loose iambic hexameters and whose second and fourth lines are loose iambic pentameters.

6. Other Variants: Divided Lines, Clipped Lines, Broken-Backed Lines, and Feminine Caesuras

It would be impossible to discuss every variant in the history of English metrical practice. However, I should like to mention some of the more unusual ones, including three associated with Middle English verse.

One of these is the "feminine caesura," which consists of an extra metrically unaccented syllable before a mid-line pause. The feminine caesura appears in medieval French verse, from which it is adopted by Middle English poets. Chaucer's work supplies a number of instances of this variant:

```
   x    /      x  /(x) x / x  /      x    /
And forth | we riden | a lit | el moore | than paas
   And forth we rode, at little more than walking speed
```

(*The Canterbury Tales*, A 825 ["The General Prologue"])

```
   x  /      x  /(x)   x  /    x  /   x /
That oon | Puella, | that ooth | er Ru | beus
```

(*The Canterbury Tales*, A 2045 ["The Knight's Tale"])

Some metrists, including George Saintsbury, treat feminine caesuras (and feet involving elisions) as conventional trisyllabic substitutions. As I shall explain in chapter 4, I sympathize with this position, but believe that the effects of feminine caesuras and elisions are different from those produced by the trisyllabic feet we find in Hardy's "The Wound" or Frost's "Neither Out Far Nor In Deep."

Another Middle English variant is the unhappily named "broken-backed" pentameter. Broken-backed pentameters lack a metrically unaccented syllable in the middle of the line. Generally, the missing syllable is the fifth (i.e., the line's third offbeat). This variant is associated chiefly with John Lydgate, the prolific fifteenth-century poet, two of whose broken-backed lines appear below:

```
x    /   x   /  ^  /  x / x   /
And seyth for him, shortly in a clause
```

("On the Departing of Thomas Chaucer," 55)

```
x   /  x    /   ^/x   /   x   /
And for her trouth, if I shal not lie
```

(Temple of Glass, 73)

Various attempts have been made to explain this and other curiosities in Lydgate's versification. Lydgate often divides his pentameters, as medieval French poets divide their decasyllabic lines, into sections of four syllables and six syllables. Possibly Lydgate felt that the pause after the fourth syllable could supply the offbeat, though this is not a feature of French practice. Possibly at least some of his broken-backed lines result from textual corruptions.

The third and final Middle English variant is the "clipped" (also called "truncated," "headless," or "acephalous") pentameter we at times find in Chaucer:

```
^   /   x    / x /   x   /x /
   We, that weren in prosperite
```

(The Legend of Good Women, 1030)

```
^   /    x / x  / x  /    x    /  (x)
   Next the foulë netle, rough and thikkë
```

(Troilus and Criseyde, 1.948)

Thomas Tyrwhitt, the great eighteenth-century editor of Chaucer, considered clipped lines to be the result of scribal errors, and some scholars still hold the Tyrwhittian view. Textual transmission was dicey in Chaucer's time, and the surviving early manuscripts of his work, with their many small inconsistencies, do not inspire confidence in the accuracy of those who copied them and passed them on to posterity. Chaucer himself begs his secretary ("Chaucer's Wordes Unto Adam, His Owne Scriveyn," 4) to "wryte more trewe." Likewise, at the end of *Troilus and Criseyde,* the poet alludes to the instabilities of the English of his day and to its welter of dialects, and worries (5.1793–96) that copyists will "mismeter" the poem, will foul up the versification. Addressing his poem ("the" = "thee, you"), he says:

> And for ther is so gret diversite
> In Englissh and in writyng of oure tongë,
> So I prey God that non myswritë the,
> Ne the mysmetre for defaute of tongë

The woolly nature of the clipped-line question is reflected in William Walter Skeat's edition (1894–97) of Chaucer. It was Skeat who, in his introduction to *The Legend of Good Women,* made the definitive case for the existence of clipped pentameters in Chaucer. Yet Skeat read what has become Chaucer's best-known clipped line not as

> ^   /   x /   x /   x /   x / (x)
> Whan | that Ap | rill with | his shou | res sootë

> (*The Canterbury Tales,* A 1 ["The General Prologue"])

but as a conventional pentameter, in accordance with the form and pronunciation of the Latin *aprilis:*

> x   /   x / x /   x /   x / (x)
> Whan that | April | lë with | his shou | res sootë

Most editors have opted for the clipped version, ever since its adoption by John M. Manly and Edith Rickert in their 1940 edition of *The Canterbury Tales;* but Skeat's reading has retained distinguished supporters, including Robert O. Evans, who, however, suggests that the first foot is trochaic ("Whán that") rather than iambic.

Such observations notwithstanding, the arguments for clipped Chaucerian pentameters are strong. Chaucer sometimes drops the unstressed first syllable from his iambic tetrameters, and, in his tetrametric *House of Fame* (1098), he apologizes that "som vers fayle in a sillable." Having admitted this license with regard to the first syllable of his octosyllabic lines, Chaucer may have allowed it for his decasyllabic lines as well. Further, though Chaucer's clipped pentameters are relatively rare, too many of them seem to be sprinkled here and there in his verse to be dismissed simply as glitches of puzzled or negligent copyists.

These three variants—the feminine caesura, the broken-backed line, and the clipped line—are not characteristic of Modern English pentametric verse. Yet though they are rare in lyrical and narrative verse after Thomas Wyatt's time, they appear in sixteenth- and seventeenth-century plays. Feminine caesuras occur, for instance, in Shakespeare's dramatic verse. When they appear, it is usually in the middle of lines that are not complete units of thought, but that consist of the conclusion of one sentence or clause and the beginning of another:

<pre>
   x /   x /   (x)   x / x / x   / (x)
That is | the madman; | the lov | er, all | as frantic
</pre>

(A Midsummer Night's Dream, 5.1.10)

<pre>
 x   / x / x /   (x)   x /   x /
And by | oppos | ing end them. | To die, | to sleep
</pre>

(Hamlet, 3.1.60)

Also, broken-backed and clipped pentameters have recently enjoyed a resurgence, a circumstance that may reflect the loosening of versification in the twentieth century. Lydgatian broken-backed pentameters—pentameters in which the third foot (or vertebra) is snapped—appear often in Larkin's work:

<pre>
 x / x   /   ^ / x   /   x   /
Another church: matting, seats, and stone
</pre>

("Church Going," 3)

<pre>
 x / x / ^ / x   /   x /
I fell asleep, waking at the fumes
</pre>

("Dockery and Son," 20)

And here are clipped pentameters by two distinguished contemporary poets:

<pre>
 ^ / x /   x   /   x / x   /
Underneath your wheels, another we
</pre>

(Turner Cassity, "A Descent from San Simeon," 11)

<pre>
 ^   / x / x   /   x / x   /
Harry Nason writes the boy's name, Steve
</pre>

(Thomas Carper, "The Solemn Son," 2)

If poets write broken-backed or clipped pentameters, they should probably follow the example of Larkin, Cassity, and Carper: they should probably, in the case of headless verses, place a strong beat at the head of the line, and, in the case of broken-backed verses, start with a strong beat after the missing syllable. Otherwise, the line will skip and sound not like a pentameter minus an unaccented syllable, but like a tetrameter with an extra unaccented syllable. For example, in these made-up headless and broken-backed lines,

> In the night the boy wrote headless lines
> This line is short, by a syllable

many of us will hear an anapest

> ```
>   x    x   /
> ```
> In the night the boy wrote headless lines
> ```
>        x x  /
> ```
> This line is short, by a syllable

where we are supposed to hear two iambs, the first of which is missing its offbeat:

> ```
>  ^ /    x  /
> ```
> In the night the boy wrote headless lines
> ```
>        ^  / x  /
> ```
> This line is short, by a syllable

Clipped lines are less problematical in tetrametric verse than they are in pentametric verse. As Saintsbury once observed, no instantly familiar meter lurks short of the tetrameter in the way that it lurks short of the pentameter. And unlike clipped pentameters, clipped tetrameters are common in our verse, as we shall see in our seventh chapter, from Chaucer on. (Clipped lines also sometimes appear in poems in iambic trimeter and dimeter.)

Verse dramas may feature divided lines—lines which break in their midst, so as to mark a change of speaker. For instance, in Shakespeare's *Winter's Tale* (3.2.145–47) when Queen Hermione faints at the news of her son's death, her friend Paulina and her husband, King Leontes, share not only alarm, but an iambic pentameter in which they express it. In the second of the lines below, Paulina speaks the first three and a half feet, Leontes the final foot and a half:

> PAULINA
> This news is mortal to the queen—look down
> ```
>   x    /    x   /   x  /x
> ```
> And see what death is doing.

/   x   /

Take her hence;
Her heart is but o'ercharged, she will recover.

When a speech ends within a line, Shakespeare may leave the line incomplete and begin at the left-hand margin the next speaker's words; and
incomplete lines appear as well, if less frequently, within speeches. The
number of such lines increases from the earlier to the later plays, and thus
represents a developing stylistic trait. However, some of the incomplete
lines result from patch-up adjustments to dialogue made during rehearsals
or stage-runs of the plays, as can be inferred from Ben Jonson's discussion
of his friend and rival:

> His wit was in his own power; would the rule of it had been so too. Many
> times he fell into those things, could not escape laughter: as when he said
> in the person of Caesar, one speaking to him, "Caesar, thou dost me wrong";
> he replied, "Caesar did never wrong, but with just cause"; and such like:
> which were ridiculous. But he redeemed his vices with his virtues. There
> was ever more in him to be praised than to be pardoned.

In other words, in the original working script of *Julius Caesar,* the final line
(3.1.47) of the speech in which Caesar rejects Metellus's petition on behalf
of his banished brother seems to have read,

> Caesar did never wrong, but with just cause.

The line was a regular pentameter with an inverted first foot. When, however, the play was finally first published in the Folio edition of 1623, the text
ran:

> Know, Caesar doth not wrong, nor without cause
> Will he be satisfied.

As Jonson suggests, the original line was overly compressed or unwittingly
paradoxical. How does one justly do wrong or injury? At some juncture,
Jonson or someone else apparently pointed this out to Shakespeare, and he
corrected the defect. (That Jonson also alludes in his own play, *The Staple of
News* [Induction, 35–37], to the line may indicate that it was part of *Julius
Caesar* long enough to acquire a certain notoriety among theatergoers.) The
process of emendation, however, generated an additional line, "Will he be
satisfied," that is short two feet and that sticks out in the passage in which it
appears. All the other lines in the vicinity are complete pentameters. Evi-

dently, Shakespeare had not the time nor the inclination, when making the correction, to bring the spillover line into sync with the decasyllabic norm. Nor would this have seemed a crucial matter: Shakespeare's text was designed for stage performance, not for the private reader perusing a printed page in his or her study; and in a drama of 2,500 lines, the absence of two feet was unlikely to be noticed by the audience, much less to send them storming out of the theater in protest.

Dramatists may design incomplete lines in the interest of forceful or comic effect, as can be seen with Don Ferolo Whiskerandos's dying words in the interpolated play in Richard Brinsley Sheridan's *The Critic*:

> WHISKERANDOS
> O cursëd parry!—that last thrust in tierce
> Was fatal—Captain, thou hast fencëd well!
> And Whiskerandos quits this bustling scene
> For all eter—
>
> BEEFEATER
> —nity—he would have added, but stern death
> Cut short his being and the noun at once!

Divided lines also appear sometimes in nondramatic verse. Their purpose is usually to mark transitions in narrative or argument. For example, in "Tintern Abbey" Wordsworth divides a line (111) to mark the completion of his meditation on Nature and the beginning of his direct address to his sister Dorothy. Nature is

> The guide, the guardian of my heart, and soul
>
>   x /   x   / x /x
> Of all my moral being.
>
>   /   x   /
>   Nor perchance,
> If I were not thus taught, should I the more
> Suffer my genial spirits to decay:
> For thou art with me here upon the banks
> Of this fair river; thou my dearest Friend.

Nondramatic poems in blank verse may also feature short lines now and again. For example, the tenth and twenty-seventh lines of Emerson's twenty-eight-line "Snow-Storm" are tetrameters rather than pentameters. (The twenty-seventh line—the "Built in an age . . . " line below—has a feminine ending.)

Come see the north-wind's masonry
Come see | the north- | wind's ma | sonry

Built in an age, the mad wind's night-work
Built in | an age, | the mad | wind's night-work

This practice is sometimes said to derive from the precedent of the incomplete lines in Shakespeare's plays. Occasionally, short lines may result because the poet loses track of the foot count.

English contains a few disyllabic words of indeterminate accent that can be fore-stressed or rear-stressed, depending on metrical context. Possibly the most significant of these words, on account of its frequency in speech, is "into." As *The Random House Dictionary of the English Language* notes, one pronunciation of the word is "*unstressed* in′ tŏo." That is, though the word is treated in the abstract as being accented on the first syllable, we do not always stress "in-" in speech. And in verse the word can go either way, as suits the poet's convenience, as is apparent in this couplet (*Gotham*, 2.127–28) by Charles Churchill, who first rear-stresses and then fore-stresses the word in describing how virtue, presented in fine poetry, steals a march on the hearts of even the most obdurate readers:

$$\text{x} \quad /$$
They see not, till they fall | into | the snares,

$$\text{x} \quad / \quad \text{x} \quad /$$
Delud | ed in | to vir | tue unawares.

Other verbal switch-hitters (in poetry at any rate) include "whereby," "thereby," "thereto," "thereon," "without," and "within." These differ, however, from "into," in that dictionaries treat them today as unequivocally rear-stressed.

A double condition also appears in disyllabic adjectives whose first element is the negative prefix "un-." Words like "unknown" and "untried" are rear-stressed, but can comfortably occupy an accented-unaccented sequence in an iambic line, when followed by a heavy monosyllable or by a fore-stressed word of two or more syllables. Consider, for example, that passage (5.1.362–65) in Philip Massinger's *New Way to Pay Old Debts* in which the greedy Giles Overreach tries to draw his sword on his enemies but feels paralyzed by the ghosts of the helpless people whom he cheated of legacies:

Some undone widow sits upon my arm
And takes away the use of 't, and my sword

> Glued to my scabbard with wrong'd orphans' tears
> Will not be drawn. . . .

Most of us will read the first line iambically, with no sense of strain or un-usual rhythm, even though normally we stress "undone" on the second syl-lable, as in this couplet (31–32) from John Denham's "Cooper Hill," in which Denham describes Londoners hurrying to and fro on business:

> Where, with like haste, through several ways, they run,
> Some to undo and some to be undone.

Some metrists have argued that, during earlier stages in our poetry, a similarly ambiguous condition affected other disyllabic adjectives. Such metrists include Bridges, who calls the phenomenon "recession of accent" and suggests that words like "complete" and "supreme" were fore-stressed when followed by a heavy monosyllabic noun or a longer noun whose first syllable was heavily stressed. (I have added accent marks in the examples below to indicate clearly the alleged shift in pronunciation.)

> Than all the cómplete armour that thou wear'st
>
> (Shakespeare, *Richard III*, 4.4.190)

> Our súpreme foe in time may much remit
>
> (Milton, *Paradise Lost*, 2.210)

I wonder, however, if people altered pronunciation in such cases. Pronounc-ing the adjectives normally would result in the comparatively unusual com-bination of a light iamb followed by a heavy one. Yet this combination has been, as we have observed, admissible since Chaucer's time.

Would that we had tapes of Richard Burbage, John Heminges, and Henry Condell reading scenes from Shakespeare's plays, and recordings of Milton dictating *Paradise Lost*. Then we could resolve the recession-of-accent ques-tion. Unfortunately, the Poet's Audio Library did not exist in the sixteenth and seventeenth centuries.

Occasionally, we will encounter a foot that admits of two metrical inter-pretations. This can happen when, for instance, a line begins with a new clause or phrase, and the first foot consists of two light monosyllabic words. Consider the first of these lines (11–12) from Hardy's "At Lulworth Cove A Century Back," lines in which Hardy imagines Keats's looking up at the star that inspired his last sonnet:

> And as the evening light scants less and less
> He looks up at a star, as many do

The initial foot can be delivered iambically or trochaically. If one pauses slightly between "And" and "as," "And" probably takes precedence. If one does not pause, "as" probably does. But it does not matter, in terms of metrical convention, which reading one gives. Since inverted first feet are historically admissible in iambic verse, both readings are conventional. The ambiguity need not concern us unless we are interested in it.

A more specific ambiguity occurs in the opening line of Hamlet's celebrated soliloquy:

To be, | or not | to be: | that is | the question

Probably most actors and readers will treat the fourth foot as inverted: *that is the question*. Such a reading stresses the crux of Hamlet's situation: should he live and suffer the corruption he sees about him or should he oppose it to the hilt and thereby almost surely bring on his death? Yet it is also possible to speak the fourth foot as a conventional iamb: that *is* the question. This construction emphasizes the immediacy of Hamlet's predicament and the urgent necessity of resolving it.

As in Hardy's line about Keats, however, either reading is metrically conventional. After a mid-line pause, an inverted foot is as admissible as a regular iamb.

In closing this chapter I should like to emphasize the point made in the previous one. The main source of variety in English iambic verse is the internal rhythmical modulation of the line. I fear that this point may have been obscured in our survey of metrical substitutions and variants. However, if the point has drifted out of view, it will shortly come back into sharp focus.

3

Additional Sources of Rhythmical Modulation, Including Enjambment, Caesural Pause, and Word Length

In chapter 62 of part 2 of Miguel de Cervantes' *Don Quixote*, the hero falls into conversation with a bookseller and remarks of translation:

> [I]t appears to me that translating from one language to another, unless it be from one of those two queenly tongues, Greek and Latin, is like gazing at a Flemish tapestry with the wrong side out: even though the figures are visible, they are full of threads that obscure the view and are not bright and smooth as when seen from the other side.

We call a literary work a "text," and Cervantes' simile about translations may remind us that "text" comes from the Latin *texere*, meaning "to weave." Lovers of verse will find this etymology appropriate, because excellent poetry has a texture as palpable as that of beautifully woven cloth. Poets do not literally interlace lines warp-and-woof fashion, but they do draw them together into a single verbal fabric. And this process contributes, no less than does the modulation of individual lines, to the distinctive rhythms of a poem.

In this chapter, we will explore how poets weave, from the strands of individual lines, the fabric of their verse. We can begin by examining a poem of some length, Robert Browning's "My Last Duchess." The poem is a "dramatic monologue." This term indicates that the voice speaking the poem is not the poet's, but that of a fictional or historical character the poet creates or recreates and gives words to, in the same manner that a dramatist creates and gives words to characters in a play. In Browning's case, the speaker is a sixteenth-century duke, Alfonso II d'Este of Ferrara. The "last duchess" of the title is Lucrezia de' Medici, who at age fourteen married the duke and died several years later under suspicious circumstances. Rumor was that she had been poisoned by her husband. Shortly after her death, the duke initiated negotiations with the Count of Tyrol for the hand of his niece. (In the poem, the duke alludes to the count's "daughter"; Browning may have made the relationship closer to make it more immediate.) When the poem opens, the duke has just concluded a round of deliberations with an emissary the count has sent to Ferrara to discuss the marriage, and the duke has now drawn aside a curtain covering a portrait of his late wife, about whom he proceeds to reminisce. In the course of his recollections, a second portrait emerges—a portrait, in the subject's own words, of a tyrannical and jealous man who squelched the spirit and perhaps the life of a warmhearted young woman who had the misfortune to marry him. Fra Pandolf, the painter mentioned in the second line of the poem, and Claus of Innsbruck, the sculptor referred to in the final line, are fictitious.

> That's my last Duchess painted on the wall,
> Looking as if she were alive. I call
> That piece a wonder, now: Frà Pandolf's hands
> Worked busily a day, and there she stands.
> Will 't please you sit and look at her? I said   5
> "Frà Pandolf" by design, for never read
> Strangers like you that pictured countenance,
> The depth and passion of its earnest glance,
> But to myself they turned (since none puts by
> The curtain I have drawn for you, but I)   10
> And seemed as they would ask me, if they durst,
> How such a glance came there; so, not the first
> Are you to turn and ask thus. Sir, 't was not
> Her husband's presence only, called that spot
> Of joy into the Duchess' cheek: perhaps   15
> Frà Pandolf chanced to say, "Her mantle laps
> Over my lady's wrist too much," or "Paint
> Must never hope to reproduce the faint
> Half-flush that dies along her throat": such stuff
> Was courtesy, she thought, and cause enough   20
> For calling up that spot of joy. She had
> A heart—how shall I say?—too soon made glad,
> Too easily impressed; she liked whate'er
> She looked on, and her looks went everywhere.

Sir, 'twas all one! My favor at her breast,   25
The dropping of the daylight in the West,
The bough of cherries some officious fool
Broke in the orchard for her, the white mule
She rode with round the terrace—all and each
Would draw from her alike the approving speech,   30
Or blush, at least. She thanked men—good! but thanked
Somehow—I know not how—as if she ranked
My gift of a nine-hundred-years-old name
With anybody's gift. Who'd stoop to blame
This sort of trifling? Even had you skill   35
In speech—which I have not—to make your will
Quite clear to such an one, and say, "Just this
Or that in you disgusts me; here you miss,
Or there exceed the mark"—and if she let
Herself be lessoned so, nor plainly set   40
Her wits to yours, forsooth, and made excuse,
—E'en then would be some stooping; and I choose
Never to stoop. Oh sir, she smiled no doubt,
Whene'er I passed her; but who passed without
Much the same smile? This grew; I gave commands;   45
Then all smiles stopped together. There she stands
As if alive. Will 't please you rise? We'll meet
The company below, then. I repeat,
The Count your master's known munificence
Is ample warrant that no just pretense   50
Of mine for dowry will be disallowed;
Though his fair daughter's self, as I avowed
At starting, is my object. Nay, we'll go
Together down, sir. Notice Neptune, though,
Taming a sea-horse, thought a rarity,   55
Which Claus of Innsbruck cast in bronze for me!

Browning has written this poem in iambic pentameter, and all of the fifty-six lines reflect the metrical norm in conventional ways. Eight lines (1, 2, 7, 17, 28, 43, 45, and 55) begin with an inverted foot, and one or two others (e.g., 9) may as well. Yet as we have observed, the trochee-for-iamb switch in the first foot appears so frequently in English verse that it is scarcely a divergence. The only other possible variation occurs in line 30, whose fourth foot may be read as an anapest ("the approv-") or as an iamb with an elision ("th' approv-"), elision being a topic we will discuss in the next chapter. To put the matter another way, "My Last Duchess" consists of 280 feet, of which approximately 270 (over 95 percent) are iambs and of which the 10 or so variants are so common as to be readily absorbed into the meter. In strictly metrical terms, the poem is a model of regularity.

For all its metrical regularity, however, the poem has an extraordinarily complex rhythmical texture. Though most lines of "My Last Duchess" maintain the iambic fluctuation, no two sound exactly alike. Their differences partly reflect the sorts of modulations that we examined in chapter 1. Some lines alternate emphatically between offbeats and beats and thus bring the speech rhythm and the metrical norm into close proximity:

> She **rode** with **round** the **terrace**—**all** and **each**
> Which **Claus** of **Innsbruck cast** in **bronze** for **me**

But other lines have fewer than five prominent stresses,

> The **depth** and **passion** of its **earnest glance**
> The **dropping** of the **daylight** in the **West**

while others have more than five:

> **Quite clear** to such an **one**, and say, "**Just this**
> Then **all smiles stopped** together. **There** she **stands**

We also find lines in which two successive feet have four degrees of rising stress:

>   1   2   3   4
> Broke in the orchard for | her, the | white mule

We find as well lines that have a light foot at one point and a heavy foot at another (in this case, the feet in question not being adjacent), with the result that—to return to our mountain-range trope—one of the line's peaks is a little lower than one of its valleys. One of the metrical beats, that is, receives less speech stress than one of the metrical off-beats:

> She looked on, and her looks went everywhere.

Three additional factors contribute to the rhythmical texture of "My Last Duchess" and give the fabric of the verse its special character.

The first involves grammatical pauses within lines. These are customarily called "caesuras," from *caesura,* the Latin word for "cutting." As has been noted, "caesura" refers, in ancient prosody and in modern French prosody, to a more or less obligatory division with a verse line. The ancient hexameter generally has a break between words within the third foot, and the traditional alexandrine pauses after the sixth syllable. In contrast, in English pentametric verse it is essential for the maintenance of rhythmical interest that the caesura be allowed to float to different positions in the line. Even when poets like Gascoigne and Pope have suggested that the caesura should fall near the middle of the pentameter, their good ears have nullified this counsel and have led them to introduce sense breaks at other positions. Indeed, because English lines are not governed by a fixed pause, some prosodists have urged that "caesuras" are not relevant to our verse and that we should not use the word in connection with it. As long as we remember, however, that we are not designating regularized division of line, I believe that we may safely and helpfully use the term.

As regards the caesural pauses in "My Last Duchess," we will note that Browning breaks his pentameters at different points and often breaks them not just in one place, but in two or even three or four. We will also note that the caesuras rarely occur at the same spot in successive verses. Consider, for example, the passage consisting of the short exclamation, "Sir, 'twas all one!" and the long sentence that follows it. The passage runs for six and a half verses, the iambic tread of which is interrupted only by the trochaic "Broke in" foot that opens the fourth line of the group and by the possibly anapestic "the approv- " foot in the sixth line. The proper way to scan the lines is to mark, with the exemptions just mentioned, a succession of iambic feet across the lines. Yet throughout the passage Browning shifts the sense breaks every which way:

> Sir # 'twas all one # My favor at her breast
> The dropping # of the daylight # in the West
> The bough of cherries # some officious fool
> Broke # in the orchard for her # the white mule
> She rode with # round the terrace # all and each
> Would draw from her alike # the approving speech
> Or blush # at least #

The first of these pentameters pauses after syllables 1 and 4, the second after syllables 3 and 7, the third after syllable 5, and so on. Indeed, during these six and a half lines, Browning pauses at every possible position, save after the eighth and ninth syllables—and he breaks at these positions elsewhere in the poem, as in this couplet:

At starting # is my object # Nay # we'll go
Together down # sir # Notice Neptune # though

In brief, though the form of the iambic pentameter is constant, Browning arranges, in an ever changing manner, the grammatical components that fill out the form. These syntactical shifts and angularities help to create, from line to line, rhythmical vivacity.

The running-on of one verse into another is a second factor that contributes to the distinctive texture of "My Last Duchess." This technique is called "enjambment," a term that derives from French prosody and from the French verb, *enjamber,* meaning "to stride over, to span." To illustrate Browning's use of enjambment, we can once more refer to that passage beginning, "Sir, 'twas all one!" Three of the passage's six full lines (the first, second, and sixth) are "end-stopped," a term meaning the opposite of "run-on" or "enjambed" and indicating that the conclusion of a line corresponds with the completion of a grammatical unit. In each of these three lines, this correspondence is visually evident: a mark of punctuation appears at the end of the verse. Yet the three other lines in the passage are to varying degrees enjambed. They conclude with constructions that are grammatically incomplete and that require us to read on through the line ending. This mixture of end-stopped and run-on lines contributes, no less than do the variations of the caesuras, to the rhythmical fluidity of Browning's versification.

Browning's enjambments also suit the contexts in which they occur. Contrary to what we might think when we first read "My Last Duchess," Browning is not enjambing his verses willy-nilly. In most instances, he uses the run-ons to suggest rhythmically the thing he is describing. For example, when he writes

The bough of cherries some officious fool
Broke in the orchard for her . . .

the enjambment—the breaking of the pentameter over into the next verse —serves as a rhythmical analogue to the activity of the branch-snapper.

Similarly expressive enjambments appear after the lines involving "the white mule" and "all and each." By means of the line-turn

. . . the white mule
She rode with round the terrace . . .

Browning suggests the circumambulations of the animal. And when he writes

>   . . . all and each
>   Would draw from her alike . . .

and when he refers to the calling of

>   . . . that spot
>   Of joy into the Duchess' cheek . . .

the enjambments convey the Duchess's warm responsiveness to—and her spontaneous and candid delight in—the world around her. Reading these lines and reading through their turns, we may remember getting off a plane or a bus and catching sight of someone we loved whose eyes lit up and whose face blushed happily to see us.

Browning also expressively employs enjambment when the Duke imagines Frà Pandolf's banter with the Duchess while she sat for her portrait:

>   . . . perhaps
>   Frà Pandolf chanced to say, "Her mantle laps
>   Over my lady's wrist too much," or, "Paint
>   Must never hope to reproduce the faint
>   Half-flush that dies along her throat" . . .

The turn involving the lapping mantle suggests, rhythmically, a fold of drapery. And just as "the faint / Half-flush . . . dies along" the Duchess's throat, so the words describing that phenomenon subside from one line into another.

Because enjambment can prove disruptive, setting as it does metrical units and grammatical units at odds, it is most effective when used, as Browning uses it, in coordination with sense. A poet who runs lines on frequently, without contextual justification, may lose hold of grammatical structure, and the reader may lose all sense of the shape and meaning of the poem. Using enjambment, poets should try, like fine slalom skiers, to execute turns with sinuous grace.

The poet's working vocabulary, particularly as regards the lengths of the words that comprise it, is a third factor that crucially contributes to the rhythmical texture of a poem. Verse composed chiefly of monosyllables and disyllables will sound different from verse that more frequently mixes with shorter words trisyllables and polysyllables. A succession of monosyllabic words tends to slow down lines or passages, whereas trisyllables and polysyllables tend to speed them up. Monosyllables, when brought into close proximity with each other, require that we articulate them carefully to maintain their distinction. In contrast, no matter how long a polysyllabic word is, only one syllable will carry the chief stress, and we will usually skate over the other syllables without minute discrimination. Even "antidisestab-lishmentarianism" has just a single primary accent falling on the eighth syl-lable, the other eleven syllables having varying amounts of lesser stress. In consequence, the word takes much less time to say than "Tom filched Steve's new watch, then pinched Brad's notes on George Sand," an utterance which also has twelve syllables, but which demands greater enunciation of and separation between syllables.

Given this circumstance, poets with good working vocabularies can alter the pace of their verse by varying the kinds of the words that they lay across the meter. To return to "My Last Duchess," a line like "How such a glance came there: so, not the first"—a line comprised of monosyllables—moves more heavily than "The Count your master's known munificence," which is swifter on account of its disyllable and polysyllable. So, too, "Too easily im-pressed; she liked whate'er," flows more quickly than, "Or blush, at least. She thanked men—good! but thanked," though in this latter line the greater number of pauses also contributes to slowing it down.

These three factors, then—caesural pause, enjambment, vocabulary as it relates to word length—all contribute to verse texture. All help to create, over the course of a poem, qualities that subtly affect our experience of it.

These factors may be further explored, and the points that we have made about them can be clarified and extended, by examining other works of other poets. As regards pauses within lines, Andrew Marvell's "The Nymph Complaining for the Death of Her Fawn," a poem in iambic tetrameter, il-luminates ways in which caesural breaks may contribute not only to rhyth-mical variety, but also to expressive signification. Consider, for instance, the following passage (63–68), in which the woman who speaks the poem de-scribes how her deer loved to chase and play with her:

> It is a wondrous thing, how fleet
> 'Twas on those little silver feet.
> With what a pretty skipping grace,
> It oft would challenge me the race:
> And when 't had left me far away,
> 'Twould stay, and run again, and stay.

Until the last line of this passage, the grammatical units flow smoothly across the tetrameters. The final line, however, consists of three short phrases, with pauses in between. And this rhythm suggests, almost as much as the words do, the way that the animal sprints off, then stops to encourage its human companion to follow it, and then dashes further on. (Also, the en-

jambment from the first line to the second—"how fleet / 'Twas on . . . "—
nicely indicates the deer's quickness.)

Janet Lewis's "Days" demonstrates that even in a line as short as the iambic
dimeter, a poet may manage caesural pauses to achieve impressive effects.
Written when Lewis was suffering from tuberculosis in the 1920s and was
immobilized in a sanitarium in Santa Fe, the poem compares the swift passage of human life to the action of a loom. (In view of the weaving motif of
this chapter, this poem may be especially appropriate.) The poem's first line
is "clipped," to use a term discussed in the previous chapter. That is, the line
lacks its initial unaccented syllable.

> Swift and subtle
> The flying shuttle
> Crosses the web
> And fills the loom,
> Leaving for range
> Of choice or change
> No room, no room.

One of the virtues of this small masterpiece is the introduction of a caesura
in the last line. The grammatical division, coming after the rapid transver-
sals of the previous lines, alters and sharpens the rhythm, and the repetition
of "no room" piercingly communicates the constraint the speaker feels.

Lewis's poem brings to mind another purpose to which poets may put
caesural pauses. Poets can signal the close of a poem or passage by introducing a line in which they handle the caesura in a manner different from
that in which they have handled it in previous lines. Dryden is particularly
adept at this technique, as is evident when in *Absalom and Achitophel* he
depicts (543–50) the notorious George Villiers in the guise of the Old Testament figure of Zimri. Here Dryden spins out a number of long, impres-
sively balanced clauses and phrases. When, however, he closes down the key
section of his portrait, he varies his syntactical patterns and pauses:

> Some of their chiefs were princes of the land:
> In the first rank of these did Zimri stand;
> A man so various, that he seem'd to be
> Not one, but all mankind's epitome:
> Stiff in opinions, always in the wrong;
> Was everything by starts, and nothing long:
> But, in the course of one revolving moon,
> Was chemist, fiddler, statesman, and buffoon.

The enumeration, in the final line, of Villiers's pursuits not only summarizes the volatility of his character; it also provides, by means of the staccato pauses and the rapid succession of one-word subject complements, an energetic conclusion to this part of the poem.

We see the reverse of this procedure in Vikram Seth's "Prandial Plaint":

> My love, I love your breasts. I love your nose.
> I love your accent and I love your toes.
> I am your slave. One word, and I obey.
> But please don't slurp your coffee in that way.

At various points in his first three lines, Seth pauses. Even in the second verse, in which no mark of punctuation appears, most readers will hear a caesura between the fifth and sixth syllable, where one ordinate clause ends and another is introduced by the conjunction "and." In the fourth line, however, there is no definite pause. After listing in short clauses the qualities he loves in the person addressed, as well as stating the depth of his devotion, he sets down in a single long clause the one trait he does not appreciate. In addition to indicating a departure from the previously encomiastic vein, this shift nicely shapes the poem to closure.

A poet's treatment of caesural pauses may also reflect stylistic ideals or preferences. We see this situation in Ben Jonson, who was interested in the classical plain style and in the poetic genres—such as epigram, satire, elegy, and verse epistle—that had been associated with it in antiquity. Interestingly, the Latin word for the plain style, *subtilis,* means "refined, discriminating, finely woven," and is a cognate form of *subtexere,* "to weave together beneath, to connect, to join." Because the plain style aims at exactness of statement, it forgoes elaborations of the two other styles associated with it in ancient rhetorical theory, the middle or pleasant *(temperatus)* style and the high or grave *(gravis)* style. The plain stylist will especially avoid, as Cicero observes *(Orator* 84), "clauses of equal length . . . or identical cadences." And since Jonson seeks an acuity whose force might be undermined by mellifluousness, he steers clear of balanced lines and syntactical correspondences.

To appreciate Jonson's style, as it relates to his handling of caesuras, we can examine his three superb middle-length heroic-couplet poems, "To draw no envy, Shakespeare, on thy name," "Inviting a Friend to Supper," and "To Penshurst." A passage (45–66) from the last-named of these exemplifies his practice. Penshurst was the country house of the Sidney family, and Jonson admired it not only for the modest utility of its design and the fruitfulness of its gardens and grounds, but also for the hospitality of its inhabitants, who kept their doors open to all people regardless of social class and who maintained the house so that it served rather than burdened the community around it. (In the passage, "clown" means "a rustic"; the final couplet refers to dining at a banquet at which one gets such meager fare that one has to go out and supplement one's meal elsewhere afterwards.)

> And though thy walls be of the country stone
>> They're rear'd with no man's ruin, no man's groan,
> There's none, that dwell about them, wish them down;
>> But all come in, the farmer, and the clown:
> And no one empty-handed, to salute
>> Thy lord, and lady, though they have no suit.
> Some bring a capon, some a rural cake,
>> Some nuts, some apples; some that think they make
> The better cheeses, bring 'hem; or else send
>> By their ripe daughters, whom they would commend
> This way to husbands; and whose baskets bear
>> An emblem of themselves, in plum, or pear.
> But what can this (more than express their love)
>> Add to thy free provisions, far above
> The need of such? whose liberal board doth flow,
>> With all, that hospitality doth know!
> Where comes no guest, but is allow'd to eat,
>> Without his fear, and of thy lord's own meat:
> Where the same beer, and bread, and self-same wine,
>> That is his Lordship's, shall be also mine.
> And I not fain to sit (as some, this day,
>> At great men's tables) and yet dine away.

An appealing feature of such verse, and of the plain style when well managed, is its intellectual scrupulosity. It engages its subject sincerely, but without flourishes. And its exactness of statement here is achieved in part by the careful and varied placement of pauses within the line. The reader feels that each detail is given due attention and, if need be, due qualification.

Jonson indents the second lines of his couplets, and it may be worth a moment to explain his reason for doing this. Apparently, Jonson regards the heroic couplet as the English equivalent of the common ancient couplet form, the elegiac couplet. This consisted of a dactylic hexameter, plus a dactylic pentameter. In medieval manuscripts and in early printed versions of the elegiacs of such Latin poets as Ovid and Martial, the pentameters are generally indented inward from the hexameters. This practice apparently originated in antiquity. Not long ago, archeologists discovered a papyrus book, dating from the first century B.C., containing elegiacs by Cornelius Gallus, and in it the pentameters are regularly set in from the hexameters. Even though the English couplet involves metrically identical lines, when Jonson uses it for epigrams and elegies—genres which in antiquity were written in elegiacs—he usually indents the second in emulation of the ancient form.

This explanation gains plausibility if we consider those times in Jonson's work when he does not indent the second line of his heroic couplets. Though his practice is by no means uniform, when he employs heroic couplets for verse epistles—a genre which in antiquity was customarily written in continuous hexameters—he is less likely to indent the second line. Nor does Jonson indent the second lines of his heroic couplets when he employs them translating Horace's hexametric epistle to the Pisos, *The Art of Poetry*.

Later practitioners of the heroic couplet, however, usually align everything flush left, regardless of genre or subject. Very occasionally, Jonson also writes in rhyming couplets whose first lines are pentameters and whose second lines are indented tetrameters. This scheme might seem a closer analogue to the hexameter-plus-pentameter arrangement of ancient elegiacs than the heroic couplet is. However, when Jonson employs the pentameter-tetrameter couplet, he is evidently imitating not the elegiac couplet, but rather the ancient iambic strophe, a unit consisting of an iambic trimeter (in antiquity, a twelve-syllable line) plus an iambic dimeter (in antiquity, an eight-syllable line). "The Praises of a Country Life," Jonson's translation of the iambic strophes of the second of Horace's *Epodes*, illustrates this other couplet type.

Turning to enjambment, we can further explore its expressive capacities by scrutinizing a sonnet by Frederick Goddard Tuckerman. The sonnet has an unorthodox rhyme pattern, which resembles, yet does not exactly follow, the Petrarchan scheme. Instead of rhyming the octave, in Petrarchan fashion, *abbaabba*, the poet develops an *abbaabaa* sequence; and whereas the sestet of the Petrarchan sonnet rarely ends with a couplet, Tuckerman rhymes his last six last lines, *cddcee*. But this is by the by. The sonnet draws an analogy between the course of a life and a river's course, an analogy that Tuckerman redeems from banality by means of memorable description and by the haunting sense of a baffled search for meaning. As does "My Last

Duchess," this poem has a foot that can be read either as an anapestic substitution or as an iamb by elision. Here the foot in question is the fourth of
the second line: "the assum-" or "th' assum-."

> As when, down some broad river dropping, we,
> Day after day, behold the assuming shores
> Sink and grow dim, as the great water-course
> Pushes his banks apart and seeks the sea—
> Benches of pine, high shelf and balcony,
> To flats of willow and low sycamores
> Subsiding—till where'er the wave we see
> Himself is his horizon utterly:
> So fades the portion of our early world.
> Still on the ambit hangs the purple air;
> Yet, while we lean to read the secret there,
> The stream that by green shore-sides plashed and purled
> Expands, the mountains melt to vapors rare,
> And life alone circles out flat and bare.

Tuckerman's very line turns suggest a river's windings and the way that
riverine landscapes change from upstream cliffs and palisades to sparsely
wooded flats and flood plains as the stream broadens and approaches its es-
tuarial passage into the sea. When Tuckerman says

> . . . the assuming shores
> Sink and grow dim, as the great water-course
> Pushes his banks apart . . .

and

> Benches of pine, high shelf and balcony,
> To flats of willow and low sycamore
> Subsiding . . .

the enjambments fortify the images of the river's enlarging breadth and of
the shore's growing more level and, from the perspective of someone trav-
eling on the water, more distant. So, too, when the river issues into the ocean
and the poet observes

> The stream that by green shore-sides plashed and purled
> Expands . . .

it is as if the pentameter also increases its bounds.

Another excellent poem that employs expressive enjambment is Christina Rossetti's "A Pause of Thought." The poem concerns a persistent but unrealistic hope, and though Rossetti does not specify the object of this hope, she renders strikingly the psychic paralysis that it causes. The poem consists of five stanzas, each having four lines. The first three lines of each stanza are pentameters; the fourth is a trimeter. Particularly effective is the extension of a subordinate clause from the second to the third line of this, the second stanza. The turn rhythmically manifests the elusiveness of what the poet desires, as well as the ineffectuality of the desire itself:

> I watched and waited with a steadfast will:
>   And though the object seemed to flee away
>   That I so longed for, ever day by day
>   I watched and waited still.

Likewise, in the poem's final stanza, the enjambment from the next-to-last to the last line quietly conveys the speaker's inability to forswear her futile pursuit:

> Alas, thou foolish one! alike unfit
>   For healthy joy and salutary pain:
>   Thou knowest the chase useless, and again
>   Turnest to follow it.

No discussion of enjambment would be complete if it failed to mention Milton, who is the patron saint of this device. Indeed, Milton's *Paradise Lost* is an epic not only about the fall of man, but also about the expressive effects of enjambment. Milton continually turns the line, and the energy of his poem derives in no small part from the way his long sentences ride across pentameter after pentameter. We feel this quality particularly in the poet's descriptions of how the angels who rebel against God are thrown from heaven to hell. To emphasize their downward mobility, Milton sends them on their way with forceful enjambments. For instance, of the fate that Satan suffers, Milton writes (1.44–47):

> . . . Him the Almighty Power
> Hurl'd headlong flaming from th' ethereal sky
> With hideous ruin and combustion down
> To bottomless perdition . . .

The first line here ends with a subject in need of its verb, so we have to read through the line ending. Milton in essence hurls the line down into its successor, just as God hurls Satan down into the abyss. And just as Satan keeps falling, after his initial hellward propulsion, so the pentameters keep tumbling through their line endings.

Related effects appear in Raphael's more detailed account (6.871–77) of the rebel angels' translation from heaven to hell:

> Nine days they fell; confounded Chaos roar'd
> And felt tenfold confusion in their fall
> Through his wild anarchy, so huge a rout
> Encumber'd him with ruin: hell at last
> Yawning receiv'd them whole, and on them closed,
> Hell their fit habitation fraught with fire
> Unquenchable, the house of woe and pain.

Note that when the angels "fall / Through his [Chaos's] wild anarchy," the verse falls with them, and that when "hell at last / Yawning received them whole," the second of the two pentameters involved in this process yawns, in a sense, to receive the first. Further, just as hell is "fraught with fire / Unquenchable," so the pentameter that refers to the fire is unquenched at its close and runs on into the next line.

In the first stanza of "Sunday Morning," Stevens put enjambment to quieter but no less arresting ends, when he describes (6–7) how his protagonist, relaxing in her peignoir and enjoying her morning coffee, is reminded of mortality and of Jesus's crucifixion:

> She dreams a little, and she feels the dark
> Encroachment of that old catastrophe

We must read through the first line, since it ends with an adjective in need of its noun, and the resulting line turn communicates rhythmically the encroachment, on the woman, of the serious concerns with which she and the poem will soon grapple. (Because Stevens has established that it is morning, neither the woman nor the reader is thinking of "dark" in the nominative sense; and to my knowledge no reader has mistaken, at least not for long, the adjective for a noun.).

Even when poets do not wholly enjamb a line, they can use its ending in interesting ways. To take an example from Shakespeare, Antony's lines on seeing the dead Caesar (*Julius Caesar*, 3.1.149–50),

> Are all thy conquests, glories, triumphs, spoils,
> Shrunk to this little measure? Fare thee well.

derive expressive force from the carrying-on of the question through the line end, even though it concludes with a grammatical pause. It is as if Caesar's greatness—his "conquests, glories, triumphs, spoils"—cannot be contained or expressed in one line alone. By the same token, the abrupt pause in the following line in the middle of the fourth foot communicates something of the brusque curtailment of Ceasar's power and of the poverty of death, which reduces one and all to the same "little measure."

A similar effect occurs in the opening lines of *Antony and Cleopatra,* when Philo says (1.1.1–2) of Antony's infatuation with the Egyptian queen,

> Nay, but this dotage of our general's
> O'erflows the measure . . .

Just as Antony's affection is excessive, so the line that expresses this fact spills over its metrical bound.

By means of semi-enjambment, poets can make line endings do double duty. A poet can conclude a verse in a way such that its sense sounds complete, but can then supply additional material that alters or enhances meaning. This happens in the following lines (9–10) from the seventh poem of Tennyson's tetrametric *In Memoriam,* in which the poet stands at dawn in Wimpole Street in London, before the home of his deceased friend, Arthur Henry Hallam:

> He is not here; but far away
> The noise of life begins again . . .

Initially, we might read the first of these lines as alluding simply to Hallam: he is not in the house, but far away in death. Yet reading on, we see that the poet is also saying that, distant from the residential district in which he is situated, the metropolis is rousing itself. The surprise provided by the line turn is small, but brings collateral elements before us. Having first thought of Hallam's terrestrial home versus the remote and unknown house of death, we are presented with a further and geographical contrast between the spot where Tennyson grieves for his friend and the city center—a place where human commerce continues regardless of the loss of this or that individual. We also are presented with a juxtaposition between the silent absentness of death and "the noise of life."

A similar extension of meaning occurs in "My Last Duchess" when the duke describes his suppression of his wife's vivacity and friendliness:

> . . . Oh sir, she smiled no doubt,
> Whene'er I passed her; but who passed without
> Much the same smile? This grew; I gave commands;
> Then all smiles stopped together. There she stands
> As if alive. . . .

"There she stands" is grammatically complete. The sentence could stop at the line end. However, Browning has only, we discover, suspended sense. He adds, "As if alive." But the duchess is not alive, and the tacked-on phrase reminds us of the fact. She is dead, maybe because the man discussing her murdered her. As in Tennyson's poem, the touch is small. At the same time, it adds a *frisson* to Browning's oblique but powerful portrait of the duke.

As regards word length and verse texture, poets can, if they wish, create interesting counterpoints by juxtaposing lines of short words with lines of longer ones. When, for instance, in Shakespeare's *Taming of the Shrew* (2.1.170–76), Petruchio announces that he will not let Kate's ill temper discourage him from wooing her, he hypothesizes, in verses comprised of monosyllables, ways in which she may insult him and then imagines, in verses featuring di-, tri-, and polysyllabic words, complimentary replies to deflect her rudeness:

> Say that she rail, why then I'll tell her plain
> She sings as sweetly as a nightingale.
> Say that she frown, I'll say she looks as clear
> As morning roses newly washed with dew.
> Say she be mute and will not speak a word,
> Then I'll commend her volubility
> And say she uttereth piercing eloquence.

Another notable juxtaposition of this type appears toward the close of *Hamlet*. Mortally wounded, the prince is concerned for the reputation that he will leave behind him. He realizes that unless he has an advocate to tell the world his side of his family's sad story, he may be blamed for the catastrophes that have befallen the Danish court. So he begs his distraught friend Horatio, who himself wishes to commit suicide, to live at least a little longer and give a fair accounting of all that has happened. As Hamlet puts it to Horatio (5.2.349–50):

> Absent thee from felicity awhile,
> And in this harsh world draw thy breath in pain

Though it is the thought that touches us in these lines, the thought is memorable precisely on account of the contrast between the first line's graceful paraphrase (for "Don't die yet") and the second's clotted density. Both lines are conventional pentameters, but the first, with its disyllables and polysyllable and its alliteration, seems rhythmically to carry a sense of the happy (to Hamlet's way of thinking) realm of death, whereas the congested rhythm of the second suggests the acerbic domain of earthly experience.

At times a single trisyllable or polysyllable can alter the movement of a whole passage or poem, giving it rhythmical interest that it might otherwise lack. An example of this appears in an epigram, in iambic tetrameter, that John Hoskyns wrote to his son. A great jurist who had intimate knowledge of the courts of Elizabeth I and James I, Hoskyns saw many people rise high, only to end up in the Tower or at the executioner's block. Sometimes these reversals resulted from mere verbal indiscretions, and Hoskyns cautioned his son,

> Sweet Benedict, whilst thou art young
> And knowst not yet the use of tongue,
> Keep it in thrall whilst thou art free:
> Imprison it or it will thee.

Coming after two lines that consist of monosyllables, the word "imprison" ripples the final line, giving it a dark and silky quality appropriate to the context.

In revising a poem, a poet may alter words and types of words, sensing that initial choices have ill suited a line or passage. For instance, Edward Fitzgerald evidently felt that clunkiness afflicted the first line of his first version of one of the most famous quatrains in *The Rubáiyát of Omar Khayyám*. In the first edition of the poem, the quatrain began:

> Here with a Loaf of Bread beneath the Bough,
> A Flask of Wine, a book of Verse—and Thou

In later editions, Fitzgerald changed these to,

> A Book of Verses underneath the Bough,
> A Jug of Wine, a Loaf of Bread—and Thou

This second version probably sounds more pleasing to most ears. Because of its mid-line disyllable and trisyllable, it flows more lithely than the original line. The internal falling rhythm of the word "Verses," and the accented-unaccented-accented contour of "underneath," give a trochaic movement to the line. This quality nicely contrasts with the character of the following line, which has a purely rising rhythm—produced by an alternation of monosyllabic particles and monosyllabic nouns or pronouns—and which, far from moving uninterruptedly, as the first line does—is divided by two heavy caesural pauses.

The factors that contribute to the texture of a poem are often interrelated and cooperative. Frequently we will notice effects produced not simply by variations in caesural pauses or from the use of enjambment or from the blending of words of different lengths, but rather by a combination of two or even all three of these elements. Consider, for example, Louise Bogan's "Last Hill in a Vista," a poem which contrasts a life that is safe but dull with one that is chancy but exciting. Bogan writes the poem in iambic tetrameter couplets, with feminine endings in the first, second, and fourth couplets; and, like Lewis's "Days," Bogan's poem has a "clipped" line (the fourth)—a line lacking its initial unaccented syllable.

> Come, let us tell the weeds in ditches
> How we are poor, who once had riches,
> And lie out in the sparse and sodden
> Pastures that the cows have trodden,
> The while an autumn night seals down
> The comforts of the wooden town.
>
> Come, let us counsel some cold stranger
> How we sought safety, but loved danger.
> So, with stiff walls about us, we
> Chose this more fragile boundary:
> Hills, where light poplars, the firm oak,
> Loosen into a little smoke.

Particularly notable in terms of verse texture is the poem's ninth line— "So, with stiff walls about us, we." Unlike the previous lines, it pauses in the middle of both the first and the last foot. Also unlike the previous lines (save the third), this one is enjambed, and the resulting movement is especially apt, since at this point the poet is moving from the domain of the "wooden town" and its "stiff walls" to the natural world. It is not just the caesural pauses that secure this transition, nor is it just the enjambment. The two factors work together.

Caesural pause and enjambment also cooperate in Milton's *Samson Agonistes,* in that passage (1648–51) in which the messenger relates the hero's destruction of the temple at Gaza:

> ... those two massy pillars
> With horrible convulsion to and fro,
> He tugg'd, he shook, till down they came and drew
> The whole roof after them ...

The short "he tugg'd, he shook," clauses break up the flow of the passage and indicate the strain-and-jerk quality of Samson's action, while the line turn, " ... and drew / The whole ... ," suggests how readily the no-longer-supported roof answered the call of gravity.

The following lines show how word length and caesural pause can cooperate:

> Where both deliberate, the love is slight:
> Who ever loved, that loved not at first sight?
>
> (Marlowe, *Hero and Leander*, 1.175–76)

Would we say that the pleasing texture of the couplet results from the combination of the smooth first line, with its polysyllabic "deliberate," and the slower second line, with its nine monosyllables and one disyllable? Or would we argue that the texture results from the neat shifting of the caesura, so that the first line divides into phrases of six and four syllables and the second into phrases of four and six? I suspect that most of us would urge that the effect is produced by both factors, working together.

A poem that employs the devices we have discussed is not necessarily better than a poem that does not use them. Many intangibles go into the making of good verse. Complexity of technique is not invariably an advantage. Consider, for example, these lines (2.2.85–106) from the balcony scene of Shakespeare's *Romeo and Juliet*. Juliet has just learned that Romeo, hidden in the garden below, has heard her confession of love for him. Though embarrassed, she does not retract what she has said, but instead pleads with him to tell her his feelings, since she has revealed, however unwittingly, hers. The fourth and fifth lines of the passage mean, "I'd rather that we could meet and talk coolly and formally. I'd rather that you didn't know how I feel. But this isn't possible now. So good-bye to niceties of social exchange: let's discuss matters openly."

> Thou knowest the mask of night is on my face,
> Else would a maiden blush bepaint my cheek
> For that which thou hast heard me speak tonight.
> Fain* would I dwell on form—fain, fain deny   *Gladly
> What I have spoke; but farewell compliment!

Dost thou love me? I know thou wilt say, "Ay";
And I will take thy word. Yet, if thou swear'st,
Thou mayst prove false. At lovers' perjuries,
They say Jove laughs. O gentle Romeo,
If thou dost love, pronounce it faithfully.
Or if thou thinkest I am too easily won,
I'll frown and be perverse and say thee nay,
So thou wilt woo; but else, not for the world.
In truth, fair Montague, I am too fond,
And therefore thou mayst think my havior light;
But trust me, gentleman, I'll prove more true
Than those that have more cunning to be strange.* *distant, unfriendly
I should have been more strange, I must confess,
But that thou overheard'st, ere I was ware,
My truelove passion. Therefore pardon me,
And not impute this yielding to light love,
Which the dark night hath so discoverëd.

There is virtually no enjambment here. All the lines, with the exception of the fourth, conclude with a pause in sense. Neither are the caesural pauses unusually placed. Indeed, they almost invariably fall in the middle of the line, after the fourth, fifth, or sixth syllable. As for the diction, it is relatively simple. Of the 183 words in the passage, 155 are monosyllabic; only the last is polysyllabic, and this depends on the sounding of the -ed that forms the past participle of "discover." (Here and elsewhere, Shakespeare appears to treat the different forms of the now obsolete -est inflection for verbs as equally asyllabic; it would also appear that we are to read "easily" as a disyllable by elision.) Shakespeare's handling of the meter is straightforward, too. Save for a first-foot inversion in the last line, and for possible first-foot inversions in the fourth and fifth lines, the verse regularly follows the iambic pattern.

Despite being technically unremarkable, however, the speech has extraordinary vibrancy. It freshly and alertly captures the psychological reality of the speaker. Juliet is alive here in all her humor, intelligence, and candor, a candor so direct and rich that it can admit being capable of deceit. Reading this passage may remind us that a poet does not need to use lots of big words, tricky caesuras, and run-ons to write great verse.

In closing this chapter, I will take a cue from Juliet and candidly admit an anxiety. I worry that I may have appeared, in discussing the expressive potentials of form, to have recommended the view that form is or should be a reflection of content. This view is far from my sense of poetry. Form is distinguishable from content. If this were not so, it would be impossible to study rhetoric and literary style, much less the particular discipline of versification, and we should have to define anew the simplest figure of speech or prosodic phenomenon whenever it occurred.

Nevertheless, form and content can be correlated, and the factors that we have been examining are important to versification. In giving their works distinctive texture, poets can and do vitally connect sense with rhythm. It is well, then, to note these factors, even at the risk of exaggerating their operation. As Bridges says on this subject:

> The relation of the form of the verse to the sense is not intended to be taken exactly; it is a matter of feeling between the two, and is misrepresented by any definition. Poetry would be absurd in which there was perpetual verbal mimicry of the sense; but this is not to deny that matter and form should be in live harmonious relation.

4

The Story of Elision, Including the Famous Rise, Troublesome Reign, and Tragical Fall of the Metrical Apostrophe

1. The Practice and Conventions of Elision

UNDER CERTAIN CIRCUMSTANCES, poets may, for the sake of metrical convenience, contract or slur two adjacent syllables into one. The practice is called "elision." The word derives from the Latin *elidere*, "to strike out," and indicates the omission or blurring of a speech sound. The equivalent term in Greek is *synaloepha*, "a blending or coalescence of two syllables into one."

These terms are often associated with a specific kind of contraction. In ancient Greek verse, words that ended with a short vowel would lose it when the following word began with a vowel or diphthong. The word-ending vowel was deleted, from both text and pronunciation, and was replaced by an apostrophe. (Also, words ending with the diphthong *ai* or *oi* sometimes lost the diphthong if the following word began with a vowel.) The apostrophe itself was originally an instrument of elision. "Apostrophe" is short for *apostrophos prosôidia*, "a turning away mark," though we today use the mark not only for contractions, but also for possessives (e.g., "Mary's car and Peter's bike") and some plurals (e.g., "The scandal involved several V.I.P.'s").

The eighteenth line of Sophocles' *Women of Trachis* illustrates elision. The line is an iambic trimeter, the customary meter for dialogue in Greek drama. Deianeira is speaking of having been unhappily engaged to Achelous, a river god with the head and face of a bull. Shortly before the intended nuptials, she was rescued by Heracles, who outwrestled her unprepossessing fiancé and then married her himself. (As has been mentioned, the Greeks treated two iambic units as a single *metron:* hence their "trimeter" has twelve rather six syllables. Here and elsewhere in this book, the circumflexes indicate not accents but long vowels—in this case, omega rather than omikron and eta rather than epsilon.)

> chronôi d' en husterôi men, asmenêi de moi
> (but in time there came, to my glad relief)

Here the conjunction *de* (but, and) loses its epsilon, on account of being followed by *en* (in, after) whose first letter is an epsilon. And instead of having an extra short syllable in the first *metra*, we have by contraction a single short syllable (*d' en*) that fits seamlessly into the measure:

> chronôi d' en hūs | terôi men, ās | menêi de moi

Similarly, in Latin verse a vowel or diphthong at the end of a word is elided if followed by a word that starts with a vowel or diphthong. Though "elision" is a Latin term, Latin practice does not involve literally striking out the elided vowel, as happens in Greek. Elision is merely understood. For instance, in Catullus's dactylic hexameter (85.1) about his confused feelings during an unhappy love affair,

> Odi et amo. Quare id faciam, fortasse requiris.
> (I hate and love. How can I do this? you may ask.)

there are two elisions. But they are not marked. If we scan the line, we must note them ourselves by, for example, parenthesizing the elided element:

> Ōd(i) et ā | mō. Quā | r(e) īd faci | ām, for | tasse re | quiris.

(A poet writing dactylic hexameters may contract, as Catullus does here in the second and fourth feet, two short syllables into one long. The last foot of the hexameter is always disyllabic and treated as a spondee, regardless of whether the final syllable is long or short.)

Additional terms describe other kinds of metrical contractions in ancient and modern verse, and some English prosodists prefer to restrict "elision" to losses or slurrings of a word-ending vowel:

>   > / x / x / x / x /
> T' explore a passage hid from human tract
>
> > > > (Thomas Campion, "Elegy on Prince Henry," 55)

> x / x / x / > / x /
> To rise from earth and sweep th' expanse on high
>
> > > > (Phillis Wheatley, "On Imagination," 42)

While I sympathize with the desire for precision, the different types of metrical contraction in English verse are, as we shall see, related. An elaborate technical vocabulary might obscure this fact. Hence, I shall only mention in passing the additional terms and shall use "elision," as have Bridges and others, in a catch-all fashion.

However finicky the topic may appear, we must understand elision. English is notoriously susceptible to compression and slurring, especially so far as weakly stressed syllables are concerned. Syllabic ambiguities are a natural part of our language, and they have been artfully manipulated by poets from Chaucer to the present. And though elision occurs in but a small percentage of feet in English verse—even in Milton, our elider as well as our enjamber par excellence, the figure is perhaps 6 or 7 percent—we need to recognize elisions when they occur. Otherwise, the rhythms of lines in which they appear will confuse us. This issue is crucial today, when editions of earlier poets often modernize spelling in ways which obscure shortened word forms and which remove apostrophes that marked contractions in the original texts.

Before launching into the main material of this chapter, I should stress that English poets have never practiced elision in as consistent and as regulated a manner as, for instance, French or Latin poets have. Though we can and will set forth general phonetic conditions under which poets elide, particular practices vary from age to age and from poet to poet. It would be misguided to imagine that we can reduce elision to rules that are universally applicable.

English verse features basically two types of elision.

The first concerns contractible adjacent vowels. Such vowels can occur within a word or—as in the examples already cited from Campion and Wheatley—the first vowel may end one word and the second vowel begin the following word. For contractions within a word, some metrists use the term "synaeresis." (When scanning adjacent-vowel elisions in English verse, I shall mark the contractions with an arrowhead. This device is not ideal: it does not distinguish between cases, like the ones below, where adjacent vowels glide together and cases, like the ones from Campion and Wheatley, where one of the vowels is, at least in theory, contracted away. But, as I hope will become clear, the arrowhead is a helpful visual aid for locating elisions.)

```
    x    /  x  / >  / x / x   /
Some frail memorial still erected nigh
```

(Thomas Gray, "Elegy Written in a Country Churchyard," 78)

```
x  /  x  /  x  /  >     /  x  /
```
Of all the horrid, hideous notes of woe

(Byron, Don Juan, 14.393)

```
x  /  x  /  >  / x      /    x  /
```
I saw, in gradual vision through my tears

(Elizabeth Barrett Browning, Sonnets from the Portuguese, 1.6)

As these examples suggest, the vowels involved in such elisions mostly consist or are part of lightly stressed syllables. Slurred together, they form a metrically unaccented syllable. Occasionally, however, the contraction entails a heavy and a light vowel that merge into a metrically accented syllable:

```
x  /    x   / x  /   x > x     /
```
Far-off, most secret, and inviolate Rose

(Yeats, "The Secret Rose," 1)

Adjacent-vowel elisions across a gap between words have an interesting orthographic history. In earlier times, words involved in such contractions were simply run together. For instance, in manuscripts of Chaucer's works, we find "thestaat" and "tharray" for "the estate" and "the array" (*The Canterbury Tales,* A 716 ["The General Prologue"]), "thenchauntementz" for "the enchantments" (*The Canterbury Tales,* A 1944 ["The Knight's Tale"]), and "tendite" for "to endite" (*Troilus and Criseyde,* 1.6). And in manuscripts of Lydgate's poems, we discover "Tamade" and "Talefft" for "To a [have] made" and "To a [have] left" ("A Defence of Holy Church," 12; 23). However, this practice of word fusion dies out in the sixteenth and early seventeenth centuries, when poets more and more often signify transverbal contractions by replacing the elided vowel or diphthong with an apostrophe. In the following transverbal elisions, "thou art" becomes "th' art," "She extorts" contracts to "Sh' extorts," and "the untasted" reduces to "th' untasted":

```
/  x     >    /  x    / x  /x /
```
Fortune, th' art vanquished: sacred deity

(Thomas Dekker, Old Fortunatus, 5.2.321)

```
>   /  x  / x     /  x   / x /
```
Sh' extorts a promise, that next day I dine

(Anne Finch, "Ardelia's Answer to Ephelia," 30)

```
x  / x  /    >   / x  /   x /
```
The cattle from th' untasted fields return

(James Thomson, The Seasons, "Winter," 123)

Like adjacent-vowel elisions within words, most transverbal elisions entail two light syllables which, contracted, make one metrically unaccented syllable. Yet, as with certain interverbal elisions of contiguous vowels, some transverbal elisions merge a light and a heavy syllable into a metrically accented syllable. Such contractions appear often in George Herbert's verse:

```
x  /   x   / x  /   x   / x  >
A new small-rented lease, and cancel th' old
```

                                                        ("Redemption," 4)

```
x    >   x   / x   /    x  / x   /
And th' other black and grave, wherewith each one
```

                                                        ("The Church-Floor," 4)

```
x  / x / x   /   x  >  x  /
Is deeply carvëd there. But th' other week
```

                                                        ("Jesu," 2)

Why Herbert uses this construction as much as he does, I do not know. Every poet has small, distinguishing stylistic features. This is one of Herbert's.

The apostrophizing of transverbal elisions declines after the middle of the eighteenth century, for reasons that will be discussed shortly. When, in the nineteenth and twentieth centuries, poets elide vowels across word-gaps, the elisions are usually unmarked. If we wish in scanning to register them, we must register them with parentheses, as we did with the elisions in Catullus's line:

```
 >   / x   / x   / x   / x  /
Th(e) old order changeth, yielding place to new
```

                (Tennyson, *Idylls of the King* [*The Passing of Arthur*], 408)

```
x  / x /    >   / x   /
The better for th(e) embittered hour
```

                (Housman, *A Shropshire Lad* 62 ["'Terence, this is stupid stuff'"], 54)

One might wonder if these are elisions. Might not the extra syllables instead result in an anapestic substitution in the first foot of Tennyson's pentameter and in the third foot of Housman's tetrameter? Lacking direct testimony from the poets, we cannot answer this question conclusively. And if we feel strongly about the matter, we can scan each line as having an extra unaccented syllable that produces an anapest:

```
x x  /  x  /  x  /  x  /  x  /
```
The old or | der chang | eth, yield | ing place | to new

```
x  /  x  /  x x  /  x        /
```
The bet | ter for | the embit | tered hour

However, Tennyson and Housman likely intended contractions. Though they in other works experiment with trisyllabic substitutions, in *Idylls of the King* and "Terence" they rarely introduce extra syllables. Given the prosodic context, if we can by elision resolve the extra syllable, we probably should do so.

The second basic type of elision concerns pairs of lightly stressed vowels that appear in the same trisyllabic or polysyllabic word and are separated by one of the liquid consonants (*l* or *r*) or by one of the nasal consonants. (*N* is the nasal consonant most frequently involved in elisions, though *m* fairly often figures in them, too.) In such cases, the first light vowel may—again, if it suits the poet's metrical convenience—be contracted away. "Syncope" is the technical term for such elisions, which entail the dropping of a vowel or syllable from the middle of a word. Especially in the seventeenth and the first half of the eighteenth century, poets indicated contractions of this sort by replacing, as they did in transverbal elisions, the elided vowel with an apostrophe:

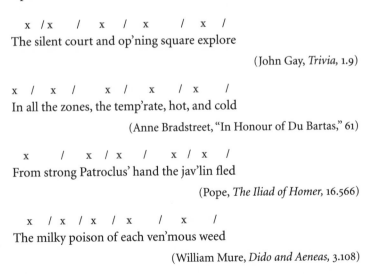

```
x  / x   /  x  /  x    /  x  /
```
The silent court and op'ning square explore

(John Gay, *Trivia*, 1.9)

```
x  /  x  /   x  /  x  /  x     /
```
In all the zones, the temp'rate, hot, and cold

(Anne Bradstreet, "In Honour of Du Bartas," 61)

```
x    /  x  / x   /  x  / x   /
```
From strong Patroclus' hand the jav'lin fled

(Pope, *The Iliad of Homer*, 16.566)

```
x  / x / x  / x    /  x    /
```
The milky poison of each ven'mous weed

(William Mure, *Dido and Aeneas*, 3.108)

Earlier poets may also produce such syncopations by shortened word forms, such as "harkning" for "harkening" or "dextrous" for "dexterous":

```
x  /  x  /  x    /  x  /  x  /
```
Where all sat harkning how her youthful age

(Donne, "Of the Progress of the Soul: The Second Anniversary," 68)

```
/   x x  /   x  /  x  /  x   /
```
Now at his head the dextrous task commence

(Pope, *The Dunciad*, 2.199)

It is an open question whether or not such cases should be called elisions, since many of these shortened word forms once coexisted equally with the longer ones. The *OED* indicates, for example, that only in the nineteenth century did "dexterous" decisively gain the upper hand over "dextrous."

As with transverbal elisions, the orthographic recording of metrical syncopations decreases after the middle of the eighteenth century. Usually, in nineteenth- and twentieth-century verse, such contractions are to be understood without shortened forms or apostrophes. If we wish them noted in scansion, we must indicate them ourselves:

```
x    /    x   /    x / x   / x  /
```
Too veh(e)ment light dilated my ideal

(Elizabeth Barrett Browning, *Sonnets from the Portuguese*, 30.12)

```
/    x   x  / x   /    x   /   x  /
```
Mark where the pressing wind shoots jav(e)lin-like

(George Meredith, *Modern Love*, 43.1)

```
x     /    x   / x / x  /    x  /
```
Some scriv(e)ning to the end against their fate

(Robinson, "Ben Jonson Entertains a Man from Stratford," 145)

```
x    /   x   /   x  / x /  x   /
```
But what would int(e)rest you about the brook

(Frost, "The Mountain," 48)

We may wonder, as we did with the unapostrophized transverbal elisions, whether the poets actually intended these internal syncopations. In Frost's case, we can consult the Library of Congress recording of the poet reading his poem, and can hear that he pronounces "interest" with two rather than three syllables. However, if we feel strongly, apropos of the other lines, that a trisyllabic substitution rather than an elision is occurring , we can scan in, as we did in the alternative scansions of Tennyson's and Housman's lines, an additional unaccented syllable that produces an anapest. Still, the poems from which the lines above are cited follow the decasyllabic norm of the pentameter closely, making it likely that the poets intended contractions.

Having discussed the two main types of elision, we may examine several subvarieties. For instance, metrists speak of "*y*-glides" and "*w*-glides." These contractions involve the two principal semivowels in English. *Y*-glides involve *i, e,* or vocalic *y,* all of which can become a consonantal *y* when followed by vowel. When this occurs, the consonantalized vowel merges into the vowel after it.

Y-glides occur in the line cited earlier from Gray's "Elegy" and in the line from Byron's *Don Juan.* In the first, "memorial" (pronounced "mem • or • e • al" when carefully enunciated) reduces to "mem • or • yal." In the second, "hideous" (conventionally pronounced "hid • e • us") reduces to "hid • yus." Additional lines with *y*-glides include

> x   /   x / >   / x   /   x /
> When his Meridian Glories were begun
>
> (Blake, "To Mrs. Anna Flaxman," 4)

> x   / x   / >   /   x   / x   /
> There are interiors none may map or chart
>
> (Henri Coulette, "Postscript," 10)

Two y-glides appear in this pentameter:

> x   /   x / >   /   x   / >   /
> Where green valerian tufts, luxuriant spread
>
> (Anna Seward, "An Old Cat's Dying Soliloquy," 25)

Three appear in this:

> x   /   >   /   >   / x   / >   /
> The Scythian, Indian, or Arabian war
>
> (Dryden, *The Aeneid of Virgil,* 7.837)

And Lewis Carroll evidently wishes us to hear a *y*-glide in the adjective he invented for the eighth line, an iambic trimeter, of "Jabberwocky":

> x   /   >   / x   /
> The frumious Bandersnatch

Though all of the *y*-glides just cited appear within words, such glides occur transverbally, too. A special case involves the phrase "many a," which from the fourteenth to the twentieth century often counts as two syllables, "man • ya." Two instances of this elision appear in each of these pentameters from Chaucer:

```
x  /   x   /  > / x   /  >   /
```
He hath maad many a lay and many a thing
    He has written many poems and many other things

(The Legend of Good Women, 430)

```
x     /  >   /   x    / >  / x  / (x)
```
And many a breem and many a luce in stuwë
    And many a carp and many a pike in fishpond

(The Canterbury Tales, A 350 ["The General Prologue"])

So familiar is this elision that it hardly needs illustration. Here, however, are two additional examples:

```
x /   x /  x  /  >   /  x  /
```
I sigh the lack of many a thing I sought

(Shakespeare, Sonnet 30, 3)

```
x   /  >  / x / x   /    x   /
```
Yet many a man is making friends with death

(Edna St. Vincent Millay, Fatal Interview, 30.7 ["Love is not all"])

In Donne's and Jonson's poems, we find transverbal *y*-glides marked by apostrophes—apostrophes that look odd to us because they do not replace a letter but simply indicate a glide. This procedure is illustrated by the following lines from Donne and Jonson. The Donne line is especially notable, since it comes from the one poem of his for which a manuscript copy survives in his own hand. In addition to apostrophizing the *y*-glide—"By' Occasion"—Donne notes, by replacing the *e* of "waked" with an apostrophe, that this verb is monosyllabic rather than disyllabic. However, I have added the dieresis in "Circumstantial." This word must be pronounced as having five syllables, or the line will be short a beat. Further, the poem is in rhyming tercets, and the word needs the fifth syllable to match the other tercet's two other rhymes, "several" and "all."

```
>   / x   /   x    / x  / x/
```
By' Occasion wak'd, and Circumstantiäl

(Donne, "A Letter to the Lady Cary and Mrs. Essex Rich, from Amiens," 35)

```
x     /  x   /   x   /   >    /  x  /
```
And we will have no Pooly' or Parrot by

(Jonson, "Inviting a Friend to Supper," 36)

Jonson and Donne occasionally apostrophize related transverbal contractions without deleting any letter involved in the process:

```
x      /     >   /  x    /   x  /    x   /
```
And which no' affection praise enough can give

(Jonson, *Epigrams,* 23.6 ["Donne, the delight of Phoebus"])

```
x  /   x   /  x  /   >   /    x   /
```
Above one sigh a day, I' allowed him not

(Donne, "Love's Diet," 7)

Because C. H. Herford and Percy and Evelyn Simpson have, in their careful
edition of Jonson, familiarized us with this apostrophe-without-the-loss-
of-vowel contraction, it has been called "Jonsonian elision"; but it appears
in other Renaissance poets.

Bridges, in his *Milton's Prosody,* cites transverbal *y*-glides from *Paradise
Lost* and *Paradise Regained.* Milton, however, does not apostrophize these
glides, apparently assuming that readers will recognize the contractions
without orthographic aid. Here are a couple of examples of such glides additional to those that Bridges adduces. The second is one of the great lines
in *Paradise Lost:*

```
x  /  x   /   x   /   >     /  x  /
```
The other none: in Mercy and Justice both

(*Paradise Lost,* 3.132)

```
/    x   x  /   x   /    x   /  >  /
```
Love hath abounded more than Glory abounds

(*Paradise Lost,* 3.312)

Certain words now clearly or marginally disyllabic, such as "riot," "diet,"
"crying," and "flying," have formerly been treated as *y*-glided monosyllables:

```
x  >  x   /   x  /    x   /  >    /
```
Of riot ascends above their loftiest tow'rs

(Milton, *Paradise Lost,* 1.499)

The Story of Elision | 125

```
x   >   x  /   x  /  x  /  x   /
```
Half flying; behooves him now both oar and sail

(Milton, Paradise Lost, 2.942)

I used to regard such elisions as obsolete, imagining that everybody today treats such words as unequivocally disyllabic. Then one evening, as I was driving home from work with the radio on, I heard Patty Loveless, the fine country music artist, perform a song ("You Can Feel Bad If It Makes You Feel Better," written by Matraca Berg and Tim Krekel) with the lines:

> Yeah, take another look at these tears I'm cryin'
> They're not fallin' on your shoulders, they're fallin' on mine.

In Ms. Loveless's vocal, the rhyme is exact and expressive. Miltonic elision is alive and well in Nashville.

"W-glides" concern such words as "shadowy," in which the middle vowel ("shad • o • ee") fuses with or glides into the "w" sound ("shad • wee"), though here, as in other elisions, the contracted syllable may still be faintly heard.

```
x   /   >   /   x   /  x /   x   /
```
The shadowy forms of cattle on the furze

(Edgar Bowers, "The Stoic," 15)

W-glides can also involve an *o* or *u* that, appearing before another vowel, is transformed into the semi-vocalic "w" sound. We saw an instance of this in one of Elizabeth Barrett Browning's lines. "Grad • u • al" (pronounced "graj • oo • al" when carefully enunciated) reduces "graj • wal." Again, most of us will probably hear at least the hint of the contracted syllable. Another *w*-glide appears in this line, which treats "echoing" (conventionally pronounced "ek • o • ing") as something closer to "ek • wing":

```
x    /   x   /  x  /   >    /    x    /
```
That most consists in echoing words and terms

(Ben Jonson, The Poetaster, 5.1.130)

Further, poets of the past have occasionally treated as *w*-glided monosyllables such words as "ruin" and "doing."

In English, as in Latin, silent or semi-silent *h* has been considered as being no barrier to elision. At earlier stages of our verse, when poets elide through *h* they may, as they do with transverbal adjacent-vowel elision, just run words together. For example, in poems in the Egerton manuscript in the poet's own hand, Wyatt contracts—rather bizarrely to our eyes—"the Hebrew moder [mother]" into "thebrew moder" ("In doubtful breast," 3) and "the howrs [hours]" into "thowrs" ("In Spain," 15). However, from the latter stages of the sixteenth century to the later eighteenth century, elisions through *h* generally feature apostrophes.

> x / x / >   / x /x   /
> I'd be content t' have writ the *British Prince*
>
> (Rochester, "An Epistolary Essay," 11)

> x /   >   /x / x/x /
> Who give th' hysteric or poetic fit
>
> (Pope, *The Rape of the Lock*, 4.60)

Later elisions through *h* are understood rather than marked:

> x   / x   / x /   > / x   /
> 'Twixt night and morn, upon th(e) horizon's verge
>
> (Byron, *Don Juan*, 15.786)

Many words now treated as disyllables once admitted of both monosyllabic or disyllabic pronunciation. These include *heaven, even, fallen, given,* and a number of other words concluding with weakly stressed, semi-syllabic *n* sound. With most such words the vowel in the second syllable was considered susceptible to syncopation or was regarded as merely a phantom vowel that owed its tenuous existence to orthographic convention. (Writers from Gabriel Harvey in the sixteenth century to Thomas Gray in the eighteenth indicate that the normal colloquial pronunciation of "heaven" was monosyllabic.) In some texts, when the monosyllabic version of the word is intended, it is indicated by an apostrophe—*heav'n, ev'n, fall'n, ris'n, driv'n.* *Even* was additionally rendered *e'en,* and we sometimes find the syncopated form of *ta'en* for *taken.* *Ne'er, e'er,* and *o'er* often appear in earlier poetry for *never, ever,* and *over,* and *evil* and *devil* are sometimes treated as monosyllables. A related case is "spirit," which formerly featured several reduced forms, including "spirt," "sprit," "sprite," and "spright," and could apparently be said either disyllabically, as we say it today, or monosyllabically, as homophonic with one of its variants.

In earlier verse, we also may find initial light vowels or light syllables dropped from words. Such elision is called "aphaeresis." Examples include *'gainst* for *against, 'fore* for *before, 'scape* for *escape,* and *'pointed* for *appointed:*

His youth 'gainst time and age hath ever spurned

> (George Peele, "A Farewell to Arms," 3)

Of these fair edifices 'fore my wars

> (Shakespeare, *Coriolanus*, 4.4.3)

And 'scape the martyrdom of jakes and fire

> (Pope, *The Dunciad Variorum*, 1.124)

As many springs their 'pointed space have run

> (Mary Leapor, "An Epistle to a Lady," 7)

In addition, people once subjected "it" to elision in ways that we no longer do. In previous chapters, we saw Massinger contract "of it" to "of 't" and Robert Browning compress "Will it" to "Will 't." And in other poems, we find "is't" and "was't" for "is it" and "was it," and additional contractions like the following:

> They do, we're sorry for't; it is our fate
>
> > (Cyril Tourneur, *The Revenger's Tragedy*, 1.2.17)

> My Lord, I know't; she is my prisoner
>
> > (Beaumont and Fletcher, *A King and No King*, 2.1.4)

Such constructions even figure in rhymes, as in Herrick's two-line epigram, "To God":

> If anything delight me for to print
> My book, 'tis this: that Thou, my God, are in't.

A similar construction is involved in a rhyme in Swift's "Progress of Marriage" (97–98), a satire in iambic tetrameter:

> She'll say, and she may truly say't,
> She can't abide to stay out late.

In Renaissance and seventeenth-century verse, one finds as well a form of elision by which the preposition and definite article in prepositional phrases are compressed into one syllable. *In the,* for example, becomes *i'th'* (in our second chapter we encountered this contraction in Herrick's "Upon His Departure Hence"), *of the* becomes *o'th'*, and *to the* becomes *to th'*. This procedure of dropping the final letter or syllable from the end of a word, though no vowel follows it, is called "apocope":

<pre>
x /   >   / x / > / x   /
</pre>
The love o'th' people, yea i'th' selfsame state

(Fletcher and Shakespeare, The Two Noble Kinsmen, 5.4.2)

<pre>
x   /   >   / x / x /   x   /
</pre>
For whilst, to th' shame of slow-endeav(o)ring art

(Milton, "On Shakespeare," 9)

Elisions like these, in which an apostrophe comes after rather than between the two fused syllables, can be confusing. When first encountering Milton's line about Shakespeare, I thought *th'* went with *shame* and attempted to pronounce the phantom collocation, *thsh*.

Though it is unusual for more than one elision to occur in a line, we have already seen cases where this happens. The line that follows is another such case. It features a *y*-glide that fuses the light third and fourth syllables of "Illyrian" and a *w*-glide that runs together the light second and third syllables of "Paduan":

<pre>
x / >   / x / >   / x /
</pre>
Illyrian lark or Paduan nightingale

(Alice Meynell, "The Poet to the Birds," 10)

This line has two syncopations before *r*:

A taste for hist'ry with a gen'rous aim

(Christopher Smart, "Epitaph on Henrietta,
Late Duchess of Cleveland," 13)

This line, like the earlier-cited verse from Dryden's translation of *The Aeneid*, has three elisions—the first and third of the elisions here being *y*-glides and the second being a *w*-glide:

<pre>
x / >   / > / x / >   /
</pre>
Irradiance, virtual or immediate touch

(Milton's, Paradise Lost, 8.617)

Or to scan the line phonetically:

<pre>
x / x   /   x / x / x   /
</pre>
Irra | dyance, vir | chwal or | imme | dyate touch

Rarely, a single word will be implicated in two elisions. In this line "adulterous" dings the *e* of a preceding "the," only to have its own *e* syncopated away:

The Story of Elision | 129

```
x    /    x   / x   /    >   /   x      /
```
Shall Troy, shall Priam, and th' adult'rous spouse

(Pope, The Iliad of Homer, 2.195)

And here a contracted form of "enemy" plunders the definite article of its vowel:

```
>      x x   /    x / x / x   /
```
Th' enmy of life, decayer of all kind

(Wyatt, "The en[e]my of life," 1)

Poets sometimes elide in successive lines to create aural counterpoints. For example, in the following couplet ("The Damp," 11–12), Donne introduces matching third-syllable contractions—this parallelism being complemented by the parallel phrasal breaks, which fall in both lines after the seventh syllable:

> First kill th' enormous Giant, your Disdain,
> And let th' enchantress Honor, next be slain

Contractible syllables may prove handy, moreover, to poets who impose special metrical constraints on their verse. Milton, for instance, mostly denies his blank-verse in *Paradise Lost* feminine endings. Partly because he is writing in the high epic genre, and partly because he is not pointing his line-endings with rhyme, he wishes to keep the meter as clear as possible and not to exceed its ten-syllable limit. Elision helps him meet this objective. In the line below (4.515), for instance, "forbidden," functions with its full trisyllabic value early in the line, but, at the close of the line, is trimmed of its final syllable so that it produces a masculine ending.

```
x   /  x    /  x /     /  x    x  /
```
Forbidden them to taste: knowledge forbidd'n

Pope, too, steers clear, in his serious verse, of feminine endings, and not infrequently uses metrical apostrophes to avoid suggestions of hypermetrical syllables at the ends of his lines. This policy is in force throughout his translation of Homer's *Iliad*, and can be seen, for instance, in Nestor's reproach (9.129–30; 143–44) to Agamemnon for abusing his power and mistreating Achilles:

> The laws and scepters to thy hand are giv'n,
> And millions own the care of thee and heav'n. . . .

But bold of soul, when headlong fury fir'd,
You wrong'd the man by men and Gods admir'd.

Elision is, I repeat and emphasize, *optional.* Depending on metrical context, a poet may on one occasion contract two syllables susceptible to elision and on another occasion fully articulate each. Shakespeare, for instance, avails himself of this freedom throughout *Romeo and Juliet,* in connection with the hero's and heroine's names. These vary between two and three syllables, according to the requirements of the pentameter. This alternation is noteworthy at the play's close (5.302–305, 310–311), when it is resolved that effigies should be made in memory of the lovers:

> x / x /x / x / x /
> There shall no figure at such rate be set

> x / x / x / x /x/
> As that of true and faithful Juliet.

> x / x / > / x /x /
> As rich shall Romeo's by his lady's lie—

> x / x/x / x / x/
> Poor sacrifices of our enmity! . . .

> x / x / x /x / x /
> For never was a story of more woe

> x / x /> / x / x/
> Than this of Juliet and her Romeo.

What is more, poets sometimes manipulate syllabic ambiguities to demonstrate metrical virtuosity. A sleight-of-hand popular in the Renaissance involves constructing a line in which the same word is featured both in its elided and unelided versions, as happens below with "ivory" and "being":

> x / x / x / x / x /
> If ivory, her forehand iv(o)ry ween

(Spenser, *Amoretti*, "Ye Tradeful Merchants," 10)

> > / x / x / x /x /
> Being red she loves him best; and being white,
> Her best is better'd by a more delight.

(Shakespeare, *Venus and Adonis*, 77–78)

An even trickier manipulation appears in this line (*Epigrams,* 96.3 ["Who shall doubt, Donne"]) by Ben Jonson, who first treats "so alone" as three syllables and then transverbally *w*-glides the phrase to two syllables:

<pre>
x   / x /   x   /   > /   x   /
</pre>
That so alone canst judge, so' alone dost make

Poets continue to play with syllabic ambiguities up to and through the second half of the eighteenth century, even as elision begins to be damned as overly arty. For instance, when Goldsmith opens (1–4) his "Deserted Village,"

> Sweet Auburn, loveliest village of the plain,
> Where health and plenty cheard the labouring swain,
> Where smiling spring its earliest visit paid,
> And parting summer's lingering blooms delayed. . . .

each line has a contractible trisyllabic word—"loveliest," "labouring," "earliest," "lingering"; and Goldsmith appears to intend not only this pattern, but also the alternation between adjacent-vowel glides (love • lyest . . . ear • lyest) and syncopations (lab'ring . . . ling'ring).

Though more recent poets have been less inclined to such ingenuities, they too have exploited ambiguities of elidable speech sounds. For example, Gerard Manley Hopkins treats "hour" as both monosyllabic and disyllabic in line 2 of "I wake and feel the fell of dark, not day," using a dieresis to indicate the word's disyllabic occurrence:

<pre>
x   /   x   /   x   / x   / x   /
</pre>
What hours, O what black hoürs we have spent!

If poets sometimes contract syllables, they also occasionally lengthen them. This procedure, however, is less significant to our verse than elision and principally concerns Renaissance poetry. We have seen a metrical lengthening already, in that line in which Donne treats "Circumstantial" as having five syllables—"Circumstantiäl." Metrical lengthenings fall chiefly into one of two categories. The first concerns suffixes or stem-additions like *-ion*, *-ious*, *-eous*, and *-ial*. Though currently monosyllabic, these once admitted, at least in theory, of disyllabic expansion. The second category involves the *-ed* inflection we use to form the past participles of many verbs. Though today this inflection is unsounded more often than not, formerly it could be pronounced if it suited the poet's metrical convenience.

Both types of lengthening appear in *1 Henry IV,* in that passage (1.3.145–50) in which Northumberland reports that Mortimer had been pronounced next in line for the throne by Richard II before the latter was killed. I shall scan only those lines in the passage that feature expansions.

```
    x  / x  /   x  / x / x /
He was, I heard the proclamati̇on:
And then it was when the unhappy king
(Whose wrongs in us God pardon!) did set forth
x  /  x / x  /  x  / x /
Upon his Irish expediti̇on;
From whence he intercepted did return
x  /  x  /   x    / x  /  x  /
To be deposed, and shortly murderëd.
```

Though diereses here mark the lengthenings, some texts use a grave accent to indicate when *-ed* endings are sounded (e.g., "murderèd"). Another procedure, which reflects a practice of poets and publishers from the sixteenth to the eighteenth century, is to ask the reader to sound all "-ed" endings printed thus and to recognize unsounded "-ed" endings by such spellings as "lov'd," "remov'd," and "track'd."

Also, a number of Middle English words have alternative forms, and Chaucer uses these to meet metrical exigencies. For example, our noun "year" existed in Middle English as monosyllabic "ye(e)r," and as disyllabic "ye(e)rë." And Chaucer employs both forms of the word in the following pentameter (*The Canterbury Tales,* B 1688 ["The Prioress's Prologue and Tale"]), which requires a monosyllable for the eighth position and a disyllable in the tenth and eleventh positions (to rhyme with "werë" and "therë"):

```
    x  / x  /   x   / x  /  x   /(x)
That lernëd in that scolë yeer by yerë
```

The most common manipulation of this type in *The Canterbury Tales* concerns the individual who guides the pilgrims and who referees their tale-telling. Depending upon metrical context, he is the "Hoost" or the "Hoostë."

Another kind of metrical lengthening involves such liquid and nasal consonants as *r, n,* and *l.* Very occasionally, these are given full syllabic value. Bridges cites examples from Shakespeare, including the eighth line of Sonnet 66:

```
   x      /   x /  x   / x / x /
And strength by limping sway disab-l-ed
```

If we do not say "dis • ab • l • ed" the line is short a syllable and a beat. Further, the word does not, in its unlengthened form, rhyme securely with "strumpeted," which concludes line 6 and with which, according to the pattern of the Elizabethan sonnet, line 8 must chime. Here is another example of semivocalic lengthening, this one from a poem in iambic tetrameter couplets:

> We would not with one fault dispense
>
> x / x / x / x /
> To weaken the resemb-l-ance.
>
> (Jane Austen, "To My Brother Frank, on the Birth of His Son," 13–14)

Just as poets play with ambiguities involving metrical contractions, so they play with those involving metrical lengthenings. A manipulation of this type appears in Shakespeare's *Romeo and Juliet,* just after Romeo has been banished from Verona for killing Tybalt. Because this punishment will separate him from Juliet, Romeo feels that it is a fate worse than death; and he expresses the feeling (3.3.19) in such a way that, in a single verse, the past participle of "banish" appears in both expanded and normal form:

> Hence banishèd is banished from the world.

Seldom will a word involve both a metrical contraction and a metrical lengthening, but this does happen, as is demonstrated by "amazed" in this line:

> x / > / x /   x / x /
> So that th' amazèd world shall henceforth find
>
> (Richard Lovelace, "To My Worthy Friend Mr. Peter Lely," 31)

2. Elision and Changing Views about Syllable Count

Elision is most significant in our poetry from Chaucer's time to about 1800. For most of this period, poets writing accentual-syllabics aspire to stick conscientiously to the syllable count of their meter, and elision provides them with small and welcome flexibilities in treating the syllabic component of their verse. And to put elision into historical perspective, we would do well to explore why for so long a time so many different poets with so many different outlooks and inclinations all wished to be exact with regard to syllable count. An obvious explanation is that they wanted to be true to the rules of their art, but there is another reason, too.

Earlier English poets are so concerned with syllable count partly as a result of viewing their metric less in a native context than in a pan-European one. They view English metric as part of the larger group of vernacular prosodies related to and yet different from classical prosody. They see English metric as one of all those vernacular versification systems that, like classical Greek and Latin, are concerned with regulating syllables, but that, unlike Greek and Latin, regulate *syllabic number* rather than *syllabic quantity.*

In ancient prosody, it will be remembered, one long syllable equals two shorts: a long syllable is considered to have a time value of 2, a short syllable a time value of 1. Hence, in some ancient verse forms, lines that are metrically equivalent may have different numbers of syllables, provided that the sum of longs and shorts adds up to the same figure. For example, the norm of the dactylic hexameter is seventeen syllables—five dactyls and a spondee. Yet the two short syllables in the first four dactyls may be contracted into a single long. (Contraction in the fifth foot is rare.) Though it is unusual, in any given hexameter, to find contractions in more than two of the first five feet, the line may theoretically have as few as thirteen syllables. Yet this thirteen-syllable line (spondee, spondee, spondee, spondee, dactyl, spondee: 11 longs [11 x 2 = 22] + 2 shorts [2 x 1 = 2] = 24) is prosodically equal to a hexameter that has the conventional seventeen syllables (five dactyls, one spondee: 7 longs [7 x 2 = 14] + 10 shorts [10 x 1 = 10] = 24).

No such proportional arrangements are possible in modern prosodies. The linguistic conditions on which ancient metric was based—the perception of syllabic length—had by the fourth or fifth century A.D. largely disappeared from European speech and been replaced by the dynamic rhythms that inform our modern languages. Admiring and seeking the strength and elegance of ancient verse, vernacular poets could follow the ancients in regulating syllables, but could only count them, not proportion them. Vernacular prosodies, English among the rest, became associated with this syllable-counting practice, as well as with the practice of end-rhyme, which was felt to add rigor to a metric sadly lacking the more complex, tightly knit correspondences of ancient versification. And their appreciation of the complex elegance of quantitative metric made it all the more important to modern poets that they regulate the syllabic component of their lines.

Here we might make an interesting side point. Though in recent times many poets have criticized rhymed accentual-syllabic verse as being confining and repressive, the chief complaint historically against modern-language measures has been not that they are too strict, but rather that they are insufficiently intricate or rigorous. Typical of this view is Ascham, who in his *Schoolmaster* (published 1570) characterizes poets of his day as "rash ignorant heads, which now can easely recken vp fourten sillabes [the iambic heptameter—"the fourteener"—was a common measure in Ascham's time], and easelie stumble on euery Ryme"; and Ascham wishes that modern poets could and would exercise "diligence in searchyng out not onelie iust measure in euerie meter, as euerie ignorant person may easely do, but also trew quantitie in euery foote and sillable, as onelie the learned shalbe able to do, and as the *Grekes* and *Romanes* were wont to do."

Middle English and Early Modern English poets adopted a pan-European prosodic outlook for other reasons, too. As has been noted, from the Norman Conquest to the fifteenth century England was virtually bilingual. As accentual-syllabic versification developed in Chaucer and Gower in the fourteenth century—and as it was reclarified and elaborated by poets from Wyatt and Surrey to Sidney and Spenser—French and Italian verse were the chief influences on native practice. The Old English accentual-alliterative tradition, in contrast, was little known or esteemed. (It is telling that when, in the second half of the sixteenth century, English poets and scholars discuss the possibilities of a prosody other than accentual-syllabic, they do not try to update the accentual-alliterative mode, but experiment with naturalizing the quantitative measures of classical antiquity.) And in view of how closely earlier English poets studied, translated, and imitated French and Italian poetry, it is not surprising that they would think of English metric in connection with other vernacular prosodies and, more specifically, with the isosyllabic traditions of French and Italian verse.

Reading such early treatises on English verse as Sidney's *Defence of Poesy* (composed circa 1583, published 1595), we see how the pan-European outlook, along with a grasp of the difference between modern and ancient prosodies, led to a highly syllabic interpretation of English meter. Discussing prosody, Sidney writes:

> Now, of versifying there are two sorts, the one ancient, the other modern: the ancient marked the quantity of each syllable, and according to that, framed his verse; the modern observing only number (with some regard of the accent), the chief life of it standeth in that like sounding of the words, which we call "rime."

To us, it seems odd that Sidney would suggest that English versification is concerned mainly with "number," with only "some regard of the accent." Isn't accent, we might ask, as important as (or even more critical than) number? The oddity of Sidney's analysis vanishes, however, when we read on and when Sidney makes clear that in referring to "modern" versifying, he is not speaking just of English poetry, but also of "Italian," "French," "Dutch," and "Spanish." And, actually, in view of the differences between Germanic languages like English and Dutch and Romance languages like French, Italian, and Spanish, Sidney's overarching description is pretty good. The problem is that there is more than one "sort" of modern versification. With relatively little qualification, we can fit, under the same umbrella, Greek metric and Latin metric. But we cannot quite do this for vernacular metric—for English, Dutch, French, Italian, and Spanish prosody. As a result, Sidney's characterization of modern metric more truly describes Romanic prosody than the Germanic-Romanic prosody of English verse.

In his *Arte of English Poesie* (1589), George Puttenham also juxtaposes the ancient regulation of syllabic quantity with the modern concern with syllabic number.

> Meter and measure is all one, for what the Greeks called *metron,* the Latins call *Mensura,* and is but quantity of a verse, either long or short. This quantity with them consisteth in the number of their feet [i.e., the key thing in, for instance, the dactylic hexameter is to have six feet, each of which has a quantity—a time value—of 4]: and with us in the number of syllables, which are comprehended in every verse, not regarding his [the ancient poet's] feet, otherwise than that we allow in scanning our verse, two syllables to make up one portion (suppose it a foot) in every verse.

Unlike Sidney, Puttenham does not explicitly connect English meter with other modern-language prosodies; but in his comparision between ancient versification—with its regard for "long or short"—and modern English versification—with its interest in "number of syllables"—he encourages a syllabic interpretation of the native metric no less than Sidney does. Also significant is the way that Puttenham even downplays the concept of the English foot. "[S]uppose it a foot," he says, meaning that English feet barely merit the name, since they do not have the precise arithmetic proportions of ancient feet. By downplaying the foot, he downplays syllabic accent, or at least the differentiation between syllabic accents that English feet involve.

Even when earlier metrists focus on the accentual element of English accentual-syllabic verse, they still regard our metric as part of a larger system of vernacular prosodies and consequently incline to a concern with syllable count. This tendency can be seen in Dryden's dialogue, *Essay of Dramatic Poesy* (1668), when Neander comments of verse that in Greek and Latin [it] consisted in quantity of words, and a determinate number of feet. But when, by the inundation of the Goths and Vandals into Italy, new languages were brought in, and barbarously mingled with the Latin, (of which the Italian, Spanish, French, and ours, made out of them and the Teutonic, are dialects), a new way of poesy was practiced. . . . This new way consisted in measure, or number of feet, and rhyme; the sweetness of rhyme, and observation of accent, supplying the place of quantity in words, which could neither exactly be observed by those bar-barians, who knew not the rules of it, neither was it suitable to their tongues, as it had been to the Greek and Latin. No man is tied in modern poesy to observe any farther rule in the feet of his verse, but that they be disyllables.

Here we have a distortion the opposite of that we find in Sidney. Instead of an overly syllabic characterization of English verse, we find an overly accen-tual and foot-based description of Romance-language verse. Italian, Spanish, and French poetry do not observe accent as regularly as ours does; neither do they centrally involve disyllabic feet. Again, though, the thing for us to note is that Dryden sees English versification in relation to versification in other modern languages. And while Dryden notices, more accurately than Sidney and Puttenham do, the role of accent in English poetry, syllable count is still essential. The poet must have a certain "number of feet," and those feet must be disyllabic.

The same pan-European context informs the most extremely syllabic in-terpretation of English meter, Edward Bysshe's *Art of English Poetry*, pub-lished in 1702. As A. Dwight Culler has observed, Bysshe adapted many of his ideas from a French manual of prosody, Claude Lancelot's *Four Treatises on Poetries, Latin, French, Italian, and Spanish* (1663). And Bysshe opens his remarks and establishes his central principles by taking from Lancelot a contrast between modern vernacular metric and ancient metric. Bysshe in fact alters Lancelot only to the extent of making a parenthetical insertion demanded by English poetry's having both rhymeless and rhymed modes, as opposed to French poetry's being traditionally all rhymed. Here is Lancelot:

> La structure ne consiste qu'en un certain nombre de syllabes, & non pas en pieds composez de syllabes longues & breves, comme les vers des Grecs et des Romains.

And here is Bysshe's appropriation:

The structure of our verses, whether blank or in rhyme, consists in a certain number of syllables; not in feet composed in long and short syllables, as the verses of the Greeks and Romans.

Contrary to what is sometimes said of Bysshe, he is aware of the role of accent in our verse. As he later remarks, "[T]he wrong placing of the accent is as great a fault in our versification, as false quantity was in that of the ancients." But seeing English poetry in the context of modern verse, he does not think twice about using an analysis of French prosody to examine English versification, nor does he hesitate to assert that in English poetry, as in other vernacular poetries, the key thing is to write lines with "a certain number of syllables," as opposed to the ancient practice of writing lines with proportional arrangements of "long and short syllables."

Only in the Romantic period does the study and practice of English metric take the nativist turn that leads to a greater attention to accent and a more relaxed treatment of syllable count. The nationalistic spirit of the Romantic movement, and the demand for greater freedom of expression, contribute to this development. England itself, as Paul Fussell has noted, shifts cultural allegiance, during and after the Napoleonic Wars, from France to Germany; and in the wake of this shift, writers see English more and more in terms of its roots in Old Germanic, instead of in light of its connections with Romanic languages. The Romantic movement also sees a growing interest in "primitive"—in the positive sense of "unaffected, original"—verse forms, such as folk ballads, which tend to be less strict as regards syllable count. This interest is subsequently reinforced by such developments as Frederick J. Furnivall's founding in 1864 of The Early English Text Society, which published, in some cases for the first time, a variety of non-accentual-syllabic Old English and pre-Chaucerian Middle English poems. For that matter, most of the Old English verse we read today remained unpublished until the nineteenth century. *Beowulf,* for example, does not appear until 1815, when Grímur Jónsson Thorkelin, a scholar from Iceland, brings out in Copenhagen the *editio princeps* under the title *Poema Danicum Dialecto Anglosaxonica (A Danish Poem in the Anglosaxon Dialect);* and only with John M. Kemble's edition of 1833 does the poem acquire its now-familiar title.

The prosodist who most clearly reflects the changing metrical climate is Edwin Guest. In his *History of English Rhythms* (1836–38), Guest basically argues that English metric took a wrong turn after the Norman Conquest, and he appears to view accentual-syllabic versification, and Modern English itself, as products of foreign corruption:

> [I]t was not till the rage for translation came upon us, during the latter half of the fourteenth century, that foreign words overspread the language. It is painful to think how many men of genius have forwarded the mischief. Perhaps we might point to the "ballades" and "envoys" of Chaucer and his school, as offering the worst French specimen of our language; and to Johnson as the writer, who has most laboured to swamp it in the Latin.

Guest further criticizes Chaucer, Shakespeare, Milton, Dryden, and Pope for not regulating their lines according to the sorts of medial caesuras that we find in Old English verse. Finally, he advocates that poets return to a version of the old accentual-alliterative system, on the principle that it will provide a metric more "*clear* and *definite* . . . [and] *well-defined*" (the italics are Guest's) than accentual-syllabic metric: "Of all the metres known to our poetry, that which has best succeeded in reconciling the poet's freedom with the demands of science, is the alliterative system of our Anglo-Saxon ancestors."

As late as 1816 it is reasonable (if not quite accurate) for Coleridge to announce that his "Christabel" is "founded on a new principle: namely, that of counting in each line the accents, not the syllables." For centuries, there had been little significant verse in English that did not regulate syllable-count. To be sure, poets of the nineteenth and twentieth centuries will continue to develop and enrich the standard accentual-syllabic measures. However, they are increasingly likely to adopt, at least once in a while, the looser iambic mode that we discussed in chapter 2. By the same token, they may now and again attempt, as Coleridge does in "Christabel," purely accentual verse. Tennyson's "Break, break, break" is another experiment of this kind. And in Hopkins, we find a poet cultivating a wholly accentual prosody.

Such changes affect the practice of elision. The orthographic marking of metrical contractions comes to be regarded as fussy or affected. In the nineteenth and early twentieth centuries, poets themselves, as we have seen, register elisions less and less—or perhaps one should say "apparent elisions," since one cannot always be sure that an unmarked elision is an elision. We also find poets starting to admit into the conventional iambic pentameter extra syllables:

   x / x   x   / x / x / x /
The sooner the better, to begin afresh

(Robert Browning, "Bishop Blougram's Apology," 253)

```
 x   /  x   /  x  /   x  /  x  x /
```
That runs out thro' the hawse, the clank of the winch

> (Bridges, "Elegy, The Summer-House on the Mound," 45)

```
 x  x  /   x   /  x   /  x / x  /
```
With a pride that may have been forgetfulness

> (Robinson, "Isaac and Archibald," 214)

(Here again, it not always clear whether the extra syllables are intended as such or are to be phonologically resolved according to earlier conventions.)

If recent poets are less likely to elide or to mark elisions in their poems, recent anthologists and editors often cease to record contractions that such poets as Ben Jonson, Milton, and Pope originally indicated. William Gifford anticipates this development in his 1816 edition of Ben Jonson. Gifford actually boasts of removing "[t]he barbarous contractions . . . the syncopes and apocopes which deformed the old folios," though these contractions mostly reflected speech habits in Jonson's day and were almost certainly supplied by the poet himself to indicate metrical structure.

This inclination to reject, condemn, or ignore elision has been even more widespread in our time. To the extent that editors and anthologists aim to make texts attractive and unintimidating to the contemporary reader, one sympathizes with them; but so far as they cease to register the metrical apostrophes in older verse, they risk misleading people about the versification of the poets of the past. Alexander Pope, for instance, becomes Alexander Anapest when his elisions are not recorded, as we can see by examining several current texts. The Oxford Poetry Library edition of Pope's verse prints 2.237 of *The Dunciad* thus:

> 'Twas chattering, grinning, mouthing, jabbering all

The current (fourth) edition of *The Norton Anthology of English Poetry* reads at 3.174 of *The Rape of the Lock,*

> And strike to dust the imperial towers of Troy

and *British and American Poets: Chaucer to the Present,* renders line 338 of Pope's "Epistle to Dr. Arbuthnot,"

> That flattery, even to kings, he held a shame

Unless schooled in elision, we might read the first line as having twelve syllables, with anapestic second and fifth feet:

```
  x    /  x x   /   x    /    x  /   x x   /
```
'Twas chat | tering, grin | ning, mouth | ing, jab | bering all

We might read the second line as having thirteen syllables and as consisting of two iambs, followed by three anapests:

```
x     /   x  /    x x  / xx  /  x x   /
And strike | to dust | the imper | ial tow | ers of Troy
```

And we might read the third line as having twelve syllables, with anapests in the second and third feet:

```
    x  /  x x /  x x /     x  /  x  /
That flat | tery, ev | en to kings, | he held | a shame
```

or as being an alexandrine with an inverted foot after the grammatical pause between the fourth and fifth syllables:

```
    x  /  x / / x   x  /    x  /  x   /
That flat | tery, | even | to kings, | he held | a shame
```

(One probably would not read the first two lines above as alexandrines: were we to construe them as having six feet, several would be awkwardly inverted, and the lines would not, in any case, sound like alexandrines.)

Only by being aware that Pope is probably treating "even" and "towers" as monosyllables, "flattery," "chattering," and "jabbering" as disyllables, "imperial" as a trisyllable, and "the imperial" as subject to transverbal elision, will we recognize that the lines are conventional iambic pentameters. That this is the case can be confirmed by consulting John Butt's Twickenham edition of Pope, which retains the poet's original spelling and which gives these readings,

> 'Twas chatt'ring, grinning, mouthing, jabb'ring all
> And strike to Dust th' Imperial Tow'rs of *Troy*
> That Flatt'ry, ev'n to Kings, he held a shame

In the great scheme of the universe, confusions regarding Pope's elisions are small beer. Still, the essence of Pope is his incredible diligence. He wrote exact iambics, taking pains to file every line to just the right alert correctness. If we miss his elisions, we miss his poetry.

Similar problems crop up with other poets. For instance, *The New Oxford Book of English Verse* prints the opening line of Shakespeare's Sonnet 129,

> The expense of spirit in a waste of shame

though the first foot almost certainly involves an elision, as was noted when the sonnet first appeared in the Quarto of 1609:

Th' expense of spirit in a waste of shame

The same anthology prints the last two lines of Donne's "Apparition":

I had rather thou shouldst painfully repent
Than by my threatenings rest still innocent

This reading suggests an anapest in the penultimate line's first foot and the final line's third foot:

x x   /
I had rath | er thou | shouldst pain | fully | repent

    x x /
Than by | my threat | enings rest | still in | nocent.

Yet the original 1633 edition of Donne's poems has a contraction in the first case and, in the second, prints "threatnings," an accepted spelling at the time.

I' had rather thou shouldst painfully repent
Than by my threatnings rest still innocent.

These readings maintain the meter.

 Though I think we should retain, on editorial principle, the orthographic elisions of earlier texts, this matter is perplexed. It would be absurd today to issue, for general consumption, texts that scrupulously reproduced original punctuation and orthography of Shakespeare, Dryden, or Milton. The question is not, To modernize or not to modernize? but rather, How far does one go, and is it legitimate to go a good ways in some areas and yet back off in others?

 Also, it may be unfair to censure contemporary editors for treating elisions erratically, since the original poets, scribes, and printers were scarcely models of consistency in this regard. Milton, for example, in the space of seven lines (*Paradise Lost*, 11.892, 11.898) writes:

And makes a Convenant never to destroy . . .
And call to mind his Conv'nant: Day and Night

Milton appears to wish "Convenant" to be disyllabic both times, but he marks the contraction only in the second case. Milton was blind when he wrote his epic, and so had diminished control over his text; but it is agreed that his printers and amanuenses did a good job of incorporating his aims, metrical and otherwise. It is not clear why no one caught this inconsistency, assuming it is unintentional.

Further, early poets and printers now and again introduce by mistake elisions that muddle rather than support the meter. In his *Chapters on English Metre,* Joseph B. Mayor cites a number of glitches from the First Folio of Shakespeare's plays. For instance, at 2.3.110 of *Macbeth* we read:

Th' expedition of my violent love

If one says "violent" with three syllables, the line has ten syllables, but the rhythm is off. In all likelihood, Shakespeare designed a more straightforward pentameter involving a disyllabic pronunciation of "violent":

x / x / x / x > x /
The expedition of my violent love

Shakespeare elsewhere uses both the uncontracted and contracted forms of "violent":

x /x / x / x > x /
These violent delights have violent ends

(*Romeo and Juliet,* 2.6.9)

And he probably intended the disyllabic form in the line from *Macbeth.* (Recently, in a bookstore, I consulted six contemporary paperback editions of the play. Four follow the apparently mistaken reading of the First Folio; two make the correction Mayor suggests.)

Whatever the future holds for English versification, we must be sensitive to the past when we deal with its poems. And whatever our feelings about elision, our appreciation of the verse of such poets as Shakespeare, Milton, and Pope will be stronger if we are aware of the ways that they have used the device.

3. How Real Is Elision? And What Are We, Finally, to Think of It?

Elision in English is a peculiar mix of genuine speech habits and highly artificial literary convention. This conclusion forces itself on anyone who examines the subject. Even so strong a proponent of elision as Bridges concedes that many of Milton's elisions are "historical" and "prosodic": they result from practices established in Homer or Virgil or Dante and do not represent full contractions in the poet's native language. Likewise, even so strong an opponent of elision as Saintsbury admits that many elisions registered by poets involve glides and compressions that occur all the time in speech.

One other conclusion forces itself on anyone who examines elision. At earlier stages of our language, people clipped or slurred more than we do now. Alexander Gill, Milton's schoolmaster at St. Paul's, testifies in his *Logonomia Anglica* that contractions like "for't" were "common forms of speech" *(communi loquendi formula)*. The same looks to be true of apocopations like "i'th'," since they appear in Renaissance prose texts, where there is no metrical need for them, as well as in poems. And to turn to the type of contraction that many of us most associate with elision—transverbal contractions of contiguous vowels—they, too, appear regularly in Renaissance prose texts. For example, in Golding's 1565 prose dedication for his translation of the first four books of Ovid's *Metamorphoses,* we find such contractions as "Thauthor" and "Thassured." And discussing elision in connection with "Fortune, Nature, Love," a song he wrote for *The Old Arcadia,* Sidney not only runs "the advantage" together into "thadvantage," but explicitly states that transverbal contractions such as "th' art" (for "thou art") are common in speech as well as writing:

> Elisiones, when one vowell metes with another, used indifferently [i.e., optionally] as thadvantaige of the verse best serves: for so in our ordinarie speache we do (for as well we saye 'thow art' as 'th' art'), and like scope dothe Petrarche take to hym self sometymes to use apostrophe sometymes not.

In the same vein, Puttenham writes of elision: "Your swallowing or eating up one letter by another is when two vowels meet, whereof th' one's sound goeth into other, as to say for *to attain t' attain.*" And though one might think that Puttenham's contracting "the one's" to the "th' one's" is a joke, whereby he is mimicking the very phenomenon he describes, in fact he frequently contracts transverbally elsewhere in his treatise.

Campion's *Observations in the Art of English Poesy* also seems to testify to tendencies to transverbal elision in colloquial English. If I am reading the sentence below correctly, Campion says that to avoid hiatus—the clashing of open vowels—in poetry, English poets should avail themselves of contractions current in speech ("in our toong"). Campion also recommends, for metrical convenience, additional elisions.

> The *Synalaephas* or *Elisions* in our toong are either necessary to avoid the hollownes and gaping in our verse, as *to* and *the, t'inchaunt, th'inchaunter,*

or may be usd at pleasure, as for *let us* to say *let's;* for *we will, wee'l;* for *every, ev'ry;* for *they are, th'ar;* for *he is, hee's;* for *admired, admir'd;* and such like.

Likewise, Dryden, in his "Dedication of Examen Poeticum," appears to suggest that gliding together contiguous vowels is as natural as or more natural than keeping them separate. Warning poets against hiatus and criticizing the hiatus in Chapman's tetrameter, "The army's plague, the strife of kings," Dryden writes:

> In these words, *the army's, the* ending with a vowel, and *army's* beginning with another vowel, without cutting off the first, which by it had been *th' army's,* there remains a most horrible ill-sounding gap betwixt those words.

A related point concerns Pope's couplet about bad critics who judge poetry merely by correct syllable disposition and count, regardless of how the syllables aurally cooperate or do not cooperate. (In the first line of the couplet, "These" is nominative and refers not to "Equal Syllables," but to the bad critics.)

> These Equal Syllables alone require,
> Tho' oft the Ear the open vowels tire.
>
> *(Essay on Criticism,* 344–45)

Many now doubt that anybody's ear was ever fatigued by open vowels; there is a suspicion that early metrists were not responding to native phonetic conditions, but were merely following ancient rhetoricians and grammarians who had argued against hiatus and for elision. But it is possible that even down to Pope's time, there was a tendency in English to run contiguous vowels together, whereas it seemed a little forced to keep perfectly distinct the vowels and syllables in phrases like "Tho' oft," "the ear," and "the open."

These conditions change partly because of the factors discussed in the previous section of this chapter; but the change is also due, I suspect, to the lexicographic labors and innovations of the eighteenth century. During this time, there is a widely felt need to clarify English speech. Swift anticipates this development in his 1712 "Proposal for Correcting the English Tongue," in which he, though a frequent elider, damns elisions used by the poets of the previous age, especially contractions that reduced disyllabic words to monosyllables:

There is another Set of Men, who have contributed very much to the spoiling of the *English* Tongue; I mean the Poets, from the Time of the Restoration. These Gentlemen, although they could not be insensible how much our Language was already overstocked with Monosyllables, yet to save Time and Pains, introduced that barbarous Custom of abbreviating Words, to fit them to the Measure of their Verses.

And the second half of the eighteenth century witnesses a great push to establish rules of orthoepy (proper pronunciation). This development appears in John Walker's *Critical Pronouncing Dictionary of the English Language* (1791), as well as in the dictionaries of Samuel Johnson (1755) and Thomas Sheridan (1780) and in Sheridan's *A Course of Lectures in Elocution* (1763). The same concern is reflected in *The Rivals,* the comedy that Sheridan's son Richard wrote in 1775 and that humorously engages the subject of accurate elocution: Mrs. Malaprop pronounces difficult words purely and exactly, but completely mistakes their meanings. Another expression of the concern with proper elocution is Hugh Blair's immensely popular *Lectures on Rhetoric and Belles-Lettres* (1783), which emphasizes that "every Public Speaker . . . must give every sound which he utters its due proportion, and make every syllable, and even every letter in the word which he pronounces, be heard distinctly; without slurring, whispering, or suppressing any of the proper sounds." Blair also urges that clear speech is not only a sign of an enlightened individual, but also of a morally virtuous one. This Blairian view, incidentally, was still strong among my own childhood teachers. They not only corrected me and my classmates for slovenly contractions like "s'posed" and "gonna," but also left us with the impression that if we remained elision-dependent, we would eventually slide down the slippery slope to shoplifting and auto theft.

English is less confusingly variable today than it was three or four hundred years ago; but our language still has its share of syllabic ambiguities. Though there are fewer today than there were in 1600, dictionaries still list contracted and uncontracted pronunciations for many words. To take a few cases involving the liquid *r, memory, interest, general, several,* and *opera* all allow, according to *The Random House Dictionary of the English Language,* disyllabic as well as trisyllabic pronunciations. Then again, there are words which dictionaries tell us are pronounced differently from one another, but which are nearly homophonic. *The Random House Dictionary,* for instance, indicates that *flour* is one syllable and that *flower* is two, but many of us find it hard to hear a distinction between the words, and it is only context that saves us when we told, "Put the flower in the vase, and add the flour to the batter."

What is more, while we no longer in our verse employ transverbal elisions like "th'expense" and "th'arch," there are still synalephic tendencies in our speech. I well recall how carefully, in elementary-school phonics classes, my friends and I were instructed to lengthen the quality of the *e* of *the*, when it was followed by a word beginning with a vowel. And the reason for this is that if we do not lengthen the *e* in constructions like "the expense" or "the arch," it almost disappears. By the same token, we add an *n* to our indefinite article when it precedes most words that begin with a vowel (e.g., an overture, an exit) or a silent *h* (e.g., an heir, an honor). Without the barrier and link of the *n,* we will either slur or find ourselves with the awkward gaping between words that Campion, Dryden, and Pope mention.

For these reasons, I believe that anti-elisionists are misguided when they insist that iambic feet involving elisions are anapests in disguise—anapests squished into shoes a size too small merely to meet the cruel demands of an arbitrary disyllabic measure. Saintsbury in particular seems wide of the mark when he asks, discussing elision and spellings like "tharray" in early Chaucer manuscripts: "Now is this also a matter of theory—a sprout of the idea that the three syllables *ought to be two?*" So far as I can judge from reading the poets of the past, and from talking with poets of the present, no one urges that three syllables ought to be two. The point is that in some cases three syllables are two, or are somewhere between two and three.

Similarly misguided seems Saintsbury's damnation of Bridges's discussion of Milton's elisions:

> Heaven forbid that I should say, "Off with Mr. Bridges' head!" but I must admit that his position is to me quite incomprehensible. Pronounce these syllables and you have trisyllabic feet at once—all the trisyllabic feet that I want, and all that I contend for. But, it seems, you must, under some strange theory of divorce of scansion and pronunciation, say that they are not trisyllabic feet.

I share Saintsbury's uneasiness with procedures that divorce scansion from pronunciation. And it would be much simpler to discuss prosody—one would not have to write a chapter about elision—if one could follow Saintsbury's suggestion and toss all metrical contractions, Miltonic and otherwise, into a general trisyllabic-foot category. Yet the haunting effect of Milton's *Paradise Lost* is that his elisions are not full trisyllabic feet. They embellish his verse with prosodic grace notes. A strange and wonderful ambiguity arises and builds through the poem, as a result of Milton's maintaining with such theoretical strictness his decasyllabic norm while continually producing hints and echoes of extrametrical elements.

In defense of Saintsbury, we should say that clipping and slurring are not, regardless of prestigious prosodic precedents we could cite on their behalf, habits of speech we would wish to cultivate. And even if we may still use in poetry normal-speech syncopations such as those involving *r* and *n* ("mem[o]ry," "glist[e]ning," etc.), it is unlikely any contemporary poet would wish to revive the metrical apostrophe, much less the whole panoply of glides and contractions that Donne, Jonson, and Milton employ. Further, though Puttenham refers to "[y]our swallowing or eating up one letter by another . . . when two vowels meet," I do not believe that we today must feel obliged, in encountering an elision, to gulp away the contracted syllable.

Also, though elision can produce interesting musical effects, manipulations of contractible syllables or shortened word forms can sometimes seem lazy or incongruous. Readers may be forgiven for smiling when, for instance, Wordsworth says in his effusion on the beauty of a London morning ("Composed upon Westminster Bridge, September 3, 1802," 11),

> Ne'er saw I, never felt, a calm so deep!

The poet may be enchanted by the tranquillity he beholds. Nonetheless, even in this beatific state, he circumspectly deploys both the mono- and the disyllabic forms of "never" to maintain his meter.

English verse derives both from the Old Germanic tradition, which is more isoaccentual than isosyllabic, and from the ancient Classical and Romance-language traditions, which carefully regulate syllables. Our meter is accentual-syllabic, and a view honoring both parts of the compound is best. Excessive accentualism encourages metrical crudity. Exaggerated syllabism —a refusal ever to allow extraneous syllables into the line or an insistence that they should be explained away whenever they appear—condemns our poetry to fussiness. And we can give the last word on this subject to Auden who, in the thirteenth of his *Academic Graffiti*, satirizes Bysshe and Guest, the representatives of extreme syllabic and extreme accentual positions, respectively. (Auden's poem is a "clerihew," which consists of four lines—with couplet rhymes and irregular rhythms—and which presents a thumbnail sketch of a historical figure. The form is named for its inventor, Edmund

Clerihew Bentley [1876–1956], best known for his detective story, *Trent's Last Case.*)

> Among the prosodists, Bysshe
> Was the syllable-counting old sissy,
> Guest
> The accentual pest.

5

Boundless Wealth from a Finite Store:
Meter and Grammar

REFLECTING IN 1947 on his experiences as a teacher of poetry, W. H. Auden remarks: "It's amazing how little students know about prosody. When you teach a college class, you find they read [verse] either as straight prose, or as deadly monotonous beat as in *Gorboduc.*" Auden's observation raises a crucial point. Poetry consists neither exclusively of grammatical prose-sense nor exclusively of meter, but is rather a fusion of the two. On the one hand, poets make themselves intelligible by the same means that prose writers do—by agreeably and coherently arranging words and phrases into clauses and sentences. On the other hand, poets compose according to a regular beat and recurring rhythmical pattern, a procedure not characteristic of prose writing.

This chapter will explore the relationship between meter and grammar and will discuss ways in which poets coordinate the two. We have already touched on this subject at various points, but I should like to focus more closely on it now. Though our discussion will in some respects take us beyond traditional metrical analysis, it is not my aim to challenge scansion and foot division. As I stated in the introduction—and as I hope the previous chapters have demonstrated—these usefully clarify verse structure when properly applied. Working poets, however, do not simply divide language into two- or three-syllable units and then fasten them together, one at a time, foot by foot, to form lines. Rather, they also fashion their lines out of larger segments of speech. In learning their craft, they acquire a special feeling for the shapes and rhythms of words and phrases that enables them to write, simultaneously, metrically and grammatically. They learn to hear when words and phrases fit a meter, or a section of it, and to make the necessary adjustments or alterations when they do not.

The elements of grammar most relevant to versification are syntax (the study of the forms of phrases and sentences) and morphology (the study of the structures and shapes of words). We can begin our discussion by examining the syntax of a common type of iambic pentameter represented by the following lines:

My mountain belly and my rocky face

(Ben Jonson, "My Picture Left in Scotland," 17)

A painted meadow or a purling stream

(Joseph Addison, "A Letter from Italy," 166)

The smoothest numbers for the harshest prose

(Crabbe, "The Newspaper," 32)

The wretched refuse of your teeming shore

(Emma Lazarus, "The New Colossus," 12)

Reading these verses aloud, we can hear their rhythmical similarity, and looking at their grammatical components, we can discover the reason for this likeness. Each line is composed of two noun phrases connected by a monosyllabic conjunction or preposition. The first of the phrases involves a fore-stressed disyllabic adjective and a fore-stressed disyllabic noun. The second involves a fore-stressed disyllabic adjective and a monosyllabic noun. And both phrases are introduced by an article or attributive pronoun.

Overall, the lines are plainly iambic, though the rhythm is unemphatic in the middle. Neither the fifth, sixth, nor seventh syllables have much speech stress, though the sixth is a little weightier than the fifth or seventh. Putting the matter another way, we may say that the verses are pentameters with light third feet. If in scanning the lines we wish to draw attention to the light foot, we can supplement the conventional descriptive notation with the four-level stress register discussed in the first chapter. That is, in addition to marking the syllables as metrically unaccented or accented, we can speak of them in terms of weak (1), semiweak (2), semistrong (3), or strong (4). To take the example from Jonson, we can render the line thus:

```
1   4     1   4   1 2     1   4   1   4
x   /     x   /   x /     x   /   x   /
My moun | tain bel | ly and | my roc | ky face
```

Note what happens if we reverse the order of the noun phrases:

My rocky face and my mountain belly

Even though the line has the same words and the same number of syllables, its rhythmical character has changed. In particular, "my mountain belly" no longer fits into iambic measure. Whereas the shape of the phrase suits the first five positions of the pentameter, it is not well adapted to the second five. In its altered situation, it puts strong stresses on the seventh and ninth syllables, while leaving the eighth and tenth weak. Further, "and," which in the original line could attract a little speech stress and a metrical accent, on account of being between two very light syllables, is now more weakly situated (it comes right after the strong monosyllable "face") and cannot function as a beat. Overall, the new line has a more tripping, semi-anapestic rhythm. Such a line might work in a poem in loose four-beat measure with feminine endings:

> x /   x x / x   /   x x   / (x)
> Behold the results of candy and jelly:
> x / x /   x   x   /   x   / (x)
> My rocky face and my mountain belly

But it is not in sync with the pentametric pattern.

Turning more particularly to morphology and word shape, we can examine another species of pentameter, which we encounter fairly often and which is exemplified by the following lines:

> When I am made unhappy by my skill
>
> (Drayton, *Idea,* 43.12)

> To write what may securely stand the test
>
> (Rochester, "An Allusion to Horace," 98)

> And afterwards remember, do not grieve
>
> (Christina Rossetti, "Remember," 10)

> And see the great Achilles, whom we knew
>
> (Tennyson, "Ulysses," 64)

> I may have looked attentive for a while
>
> (Wendy Cope, "So Much Depends," 6)

Though these lines are syntactically diverse (Drayton's, for instance, is a dependent clause, Tennyson's is a portion of a compound predicate, Cope's is complete sentence), their rhythmical similarity is no less hearable than was the rhythmical similarity among the earlier group of lines. In this case, the likeness seems chiefly to result from each line's having a middle-stressed trisyllabic word that runs from the fifth to seventh positions. The words themselves represent different parts of speech. We have a proper noun (Achilles), adjectives (unhappy, attentive), an adverb (securely), and a verb (remember). But their shape is the same. This, and perhaps the pause that generally follows the word, produce the corresponding movement.

As with the pentameters comprised of noun phrases, we can alter these lines in sundry ways without damaging their grammar and can in particular move the trisyllabic words to different positions. We could write, for instance,

> And remember afterwards, do not grieve
> For a while, I may have looked attentive

But metrically speaking, or at least pentametrically speaking, such changes make the verses jump the tracks. The altered lines fall into that swingy, four-beat measure that we observed a moment ago. Though in these instances the rhythmical dislocation may confuse scansion—different readers may construe the lines somewhat differently—most of us probably hear something like,

> x   x /   x / x x   / x   /
> And remember afterwards, do not grieve
> x x   / x / x   /   x / x
> For a while, I may have looked attentive

The strong syllables of the trisyllabic words run awkwardly counter to iambic expectation; and syllables (e.g., "-wards" and "For") that in the original lines attracted a small but significant degree of speech stress, and that assumed metrical accents, are now positioned ambiguously at best. To read the revised lines as pentameters, one would have to mispronounce some of the words and give peculiar articulation to some of the phrases:

> And remem**ber** afterwards, **do** not **grieve**
> For **a** while, **I** may **have** looked **attentive**

Meter and grammar are no longer in harmony, but are contradicting each other.

Beginning poets may have trouble harmonizing meter and grammar, especially when they write in iambic pentameter. This difficulty results from the line's asymmetry and flexibility. As we noted in the introduction, even when a pentameter falls into two five-syllable sections, the first half has only two metrical beats, whereas the second has three. And, as we also noted, though the pentameter is long, it has no obligatory caesura. It is not conventionally partitioned into more manageable subdivisions, as are long lines in some other poetries. Hence when poets first attempt the measure, they tend to fall back, often under the influence of popular song-lyric, on a four-beat line; they produce verses that have ten syllables but that are really in the loose, swingy, semi-anapestic, four-beat rhythm that characterizes the awkward alterations above of Jonson's, Rossetti's, and Cope's lines. Poets who wish to write pentameter must learn to distinguish between lines of this tripping four-beat sort and lines that may have fewer than five strong speech stresses but maintain the iambic fluctuation and merely feature a light iamb or iambs at some point:

```
1    4 1   2 1    4    1  4 1     4
x   / x / x      /    x / x     /
```
Bespotted as with shields of red and black

(Spenser, The Fairie Queene, 1.11.11.5)

```
 1    4    1    4 1    4 1 2   1   4
 x   /    x   / x    / x/   x  /
```
The clouds were low and hairy in the skies

(Frost, "Once by the Pacific," 5)

One can make related observations about shorter measures, though it is easier to acquire a competence in these. (This is not to say that it is easier to use them in a vital way.) If we wish to write iambic tetrameter, for instance, we must learn to distinguish between octosyllabic lines in which the rhythm wobbles,

```
 x  /  x  /  x  x   / x
```
I need to fix my complexion

```
  x  /  x  x  /  x   x  /
```
The sorrowful eyes of the toad

and octosyllabic lines which may have a light (or heavy) iamb or iambs, but which nonetheless conform to the lighter-to-heavier iambic movement:

```
 3    4   1 2   1   4 1    4
 x   /    x /  x   / x    /
```
Most strangely our complexion clears

(Marvell, "Upon Appleton House," 112)

```
1   4   1   4 1 2 1 4
x   /   x   / x / x /
```
The speechless sorrow of its eyes

(Elinor Wylie, "Cold-Blooded Creatures," 8)

Would that poets had a prosodic device, analogous to a voltage tester or a circuit analyzer, to enable them to assess the current in a doubtful line. But though an optimistic novice might fancy that determinations could be made merely by checking where stresses fall—and that trouble is signaled when a beat lands on an odd-numbered position or an offbeat lands on an even-numbered position—matters are not so simple. Since trochaic feet can conventionally appear in the first foot of iambic lines or after a mid-line pause, a pentameter may have strong stresses at syllables 1 and 7 (and weak stresses at 2 and 8) or strong stresses at 1 and 5 (and weak stresses at 2 and 6):

```
/   x                   /   x
```
Beauty provoketh thieves sooner than gold

(Shakespeare, As You Like It, 1.3.109)

```
/   x               /x
```
Older than age, drier than any drouth

(Mark Van Doren, A Winter Diary, 321)

Abstractly described, such verses may sound wayward, but when we hear them, they turn out to be perfectly fine.

What is more, a light iamb may appear anywhere in the line:

```
1   2
```
And at | the banquet all the Muses sang

(Arnold, "Empedocles on Etna," 451)

```
    1   2
```
Refin | ing, as | with great Apollo's fire

(Corrothers, "Paul Laurence Dunbar," 3)

```
        1   2
```
Of thy defaute, | and to | supporten it

(James Stewart [James I of Scotland], "The Kingis Quair," 1355)

```
            1 2
```
If ever wife was hap | py in | a man

(Anne Bradstreet, "To My Dear and Loving Husband," 3)

1   2
It seemed I was your only cus | tomer

> (Alan Shapiro, "Simon, the Barber," 1)

And a heavy iamb may appear at any point as well:

 3   4
Take heed | betimes, repent, and learn of me

> (John Oldham, "A Satyr: The Person of Spenser is Brought in,
> Dissuading the Author from the Study of Poetry," 33)

         3   4
The last | set out | the soonest did arrive

> (Dryden, "To the Memory of Mr. Oldham," 8)

                      3   4
They want the young | men's whis | pering and sighing

> (John Crowe Ransom, "Piazza Piece," 4)

                          3   4
So sweet the night, so long- | drawn-out | and late

> (Edna St. Vincent Millay, *Sonnets from an Ungrafted Tree*, 10.10)

                                 3   4
These tiny two, unseen from space, | know all

> (Rosalie Colie, "Earth's Sonnet," 13)

Yet even as we acknowledge the impossibility of formulating rules to enable us to spot faulty lines, we can offer suggestions that will hold for most cases. If, in writing iambic pentameter, we find that stresses land on the fifth or seventh syllables when no grammatical pause precedes them—and hence when they are not part of a trochee after a mid-line break—it is possible that the rhythm is out of kilter. This possibility is increased if the sixth and eighth syllables are weak. Were they weighty, the significantly stressed fifth or seventh syllable might merely be part of a heavy but nonetheless conventional iamb, as in the lines above from Ransom and Millay. Likewise, if a stress falls on the third syllable, we may have gone astray, and this likelihood grows if there is no other strongly stressed syllable in the first, second, or fourth positions. (In thus numbering and speaking of the syllable-positions, I am assuming that the lines neither are clipped nor have anapestic substitutions. In cases where such variations appear, the numbering and analysis would need adjustment.)

Sometimes more than one arrangement of words or phrases will prove metrically workable. In pentameters that divide into groups of four and six syllables, for instance, the phrases may be transposable, assuming no logical relationship or pattern of rhyme is violated. When Friar Lawrence advises the banished Romeo to console himself with "Adversity's sweet milk, philosophy" (Shakespeare, *Romeo and Juliet*, 3.3.55), he could just as well say, for metrical purposes, "Philosophy, adversity's sweet milk." Similarly, words in a line may sometimes be transposed with one another, especially if they are coordinate adjectives, nouns, or verbs, and have the same number of syllables and the same rhythmical contour. Thomas Hood, for instance, artfully flip-flops transposable words in his observation about "The Irish Schoolmaster" (12.7–8):

> He never spoils the child and spares the rod
> But spoils the rod and never spares the child.

If, for the poet, versification involves recognizing when words and phrases do or don't effectively fit a meter, it also entails recognizing when, among several correct alternatives, there is no significant difference. We may agree with Coleridge that poetry equals "the *best* words in the best order," but poetry is never entirely a succession of dazzling verbal moments. Often, poets are just trying to move from point A to point B, and it behooves them to recognize that there may be a number of equally good ways to negotiate the interval. As friends and spouses of poets can attest, it is difficult to bear cheerfully with someone who suffers paroxysms of indecision over whether to say "the clear, chill day" or "the chill, clear day."

Though certain grammatical patterns appear relatively frequently in our verse, metrical composition is by no means limited to these. The pentameter line in particular seems capable of accommodating almost any syntactical arrangement, and the serious poet will avoid relying on the more common ones. There are clichés of rhythm as well as speech, and the ear may be put off by familiar modulations no less than by stereotypical diction.

These remarks are pertinent to the line type featuring the two noun phrases. It has a kind of facile sweetness. What is more, it tends to feel padded, mainly because of the two disyllabic adjectives and their symmetrical positioning—one in the first phrase, one in the second. A historical factor is involved as well. Eighteenth-century poets were fond of this line type and milked it to exhaustion. Perhaps because they sought to make their pentameters as smooth as possible, and because they consequently and desperately needed sources of rhythmical modulation, the line type had a dual appeal for them. On the one hand, its paired noun phrases made for balance. On the other hand, its light third foot made for metrical variety. Unfortunately, when one hears the line several times in close proximity—as one does, for instance, toward the close (346, 354, 361) of Goldsmith's "Deserted Village"—

> The various terrors of that horrid shore
> The rattling terrors of the vengeful snake
> The breezy covert of the warbling grove

it sets one's teeth on edge.

If the line has become a rhythmical cliché, its familiarity has on occasion been put to good effect by modern poets. For instance, in their memorial tributes to Arthur Henniker and John Muir, respectively, Thomas Hardy and Yvor Winters use the line to indicate something of the simple, old-fashioned goodness of their subjects:

> His modest spirit in his candid look
>
> > (Hardy, "A. H., 1855–1912," 4)

> A gentle figure from a simpler age
>
> > (Winters, "On Rereading a Passage from John Muir," 18)

Also, if a heavy iamb appears at any point before or after the light third foot, the rhythm tilts in such a way that it loses its cloying quality and acquires (at least to our ears at this point in metrical history) a more interesting effect:

> 3   4
> A cleaving daylight, and a last great calm
>
> > (Robinson, "Ben Jonson Entertains a Man from Stratford," 380)

> 3   4
> The bare man Nothing in the Beggar's Bush
>
> > (Auden, "The Hero," 4)

It will be noted that, to produce this alteration, the poet must dispense with one of the disyllabic adjectives. Doubtless this morphological shift affects the change of rhythm.

So, too, a line of the paired-noun-phrases type may acquire rhythmical interest if it appears in the midst of enjambments. For example, when

Milton writes (*Paradise Lost*, 2.278–80), during Mammon's speech arguing against a second assault on God,

> . . . All things invite
> To peaceful counsels, and the settled state
> Of order . . .

even the most fastidious reader will not find the movement trite. Admittedly, "To peaceful counsels, and the settled state" might appear in isolation just another variation on a familiar rhythmical theme, in this instance the first of the noun phrases beginning with a preposition rather than an article or attributive adjective. Yet we do not hear the noun phrases as neatly balanced. The enjambments sever the close syntactical relationship between them. Grammatically, the first noun phrase goes with material from the line above and the second with material from the line below.

Many other syntactical arrangements can produce lines with a sense break after the fifth syllable, in the middle of a light third foot. Though the arrangement involving the two noun phrases is most common, we can cite different examples to give us some sense of the innumerable ways that this simple form of the pentameter may be realized:

> It frets the halter, and it chokes the child
>
> (Ralegh, "Sir Walter Ralegh to His Son," 12)

> The pipe, the tabor, and the trembling crowd
>
> (Spenser, "Epithalamion," 131)

> My sweet companion and my gentle peer
>
> (Abraham Cowley, "On the Death of Mr. William Hervey," 9)

> Resolved to ruin or to rule the state
>
> (Dryden, *Absalom and Achitophel*, 174)

> Of life reviving with reviving day
>
> (Scott, *The Lady of the Lake*, 2.1.4)

> There is a mountain in the distant West
>
> (Henry Wadsworth Longfellow, "The Cross of Snow," 9)

Ralegh fills out the line with two independent clauses joined by a coordinating conjunction. Spenser uses a series of three nouns, the last modified by an adjective. Cowley deploys two noun phrases—the first of which, however, differs from the more common pattern, by involving a monosyllabic adjective and a trisyllabic noun accented in the middle. Dryden offers a past participle followed by coordinate infinitives. In Scott's line, we see two prepositional phrases. In the Longfellow line, we have an anticipatory ("dummy") subject, followed by a verb, subject, and prepositional phrase.

A light middle foot may consist as well of a conjunction and an article:

> Of heightened wit | and of | the critic's art
>
> > (Anne Finch, "A Poem Occasioned by the Sight
> > of the Fourth Epistle, Lib. Epist: 1 of Horace," 60)

Or it may entail a syllable with weak stress, followed by a syllable with some degree of intermediate stress, in a polysyllabic or fore-stressed trisyllabic word:

> In sad simil | itude | of griefs to mine
>
> > (Pope, *Eloisa to Abelard*, 360)

> You know the moun | tainous | coiffures of Bath
>
> > (Stevens, "Le Monocle de Mon Oncle" 29)

The comparative frequency of iambic pentameters having a light third foot, and a grammatical pause at or near the middle of the line, has led some to suggest that the meter is an updated version of the old Germanic four-beat, medially divided line. According to this view, the pentameter represents a form of the rhythm that we find in the accentual-alliterative tradition:

> /   /   /   /
> Lîxte se lêoma   lêoht inne stôd
> ⠀⠀The light shined   gleaming from inside
>
> > (*Beowulf*, 1570)

> ⠀⠀/   /   /   /
> At the day of domë,   we dede as he hightë
> ⠀⠀At the day of doom,   we did as he commanded
>
> > (Langland, *Piers Plowman*, 7.200)

The only difference is that the syllable count has become, in the iambic pentameter, regularized at ten-per-line.

While this suggestion is beguiling, it is not borne out by the evidence of English verse. The possibilities for modulation in iambic pentameter are infinite. More specifically, light iambs can appear, as we have noted, anywhere in the pentameter. They turn up most commonly as a third foot. Yet they occur almost as often in the second or fourth foot; and though light first and fifth feet are relatively infrequent, they are by no means rare.

What is more, far from distributing stresses equally between the first and second halves of the line, as is the case with the accentual-alliterative line, pentameters may occur with a majority of syllables with heavy speech stress toward the front:

> Leave, leave, fair Bride, your solitary bed
>
> (Donne, "Epithalamion Made at Lincoln's Inn," 2)

or lines with a majority of heavily stressed syllables grouped toward the middle:

> From ev'ry Tongue flows Harmony divine
>
> (Samuel Johnson, "London," 128)

or lines with a majority of heavily stressed syllables clustered near the end:

> As yet ungolden in the dense, hot night
>
> (Thom Gunn, "The Allegory of the Wolf Boy," 13)

For that matter, sometimes lines may be weighted at their very beginnings and very ends, with light syllables and feet in the middle:

> 3   4 1 2   1   2   1   4   3   4
> False fugitive, and to thy speed add wings
>
> (Milton, *Paradise Lost*, 2.700)

Let us return to word shape and to middle-stressed trisyllables. Though in pentametric verse they seem to have a special rhythmical distinctness when they run from the fifth to seventh positions, such words commonly appear in all of the other possible locations in the line. We frequently find them, that is, running from the first to the third position, from the third to the fifth, from the seventh to the ninth, and from the ninth to the eleventh —in this last case the final unaccented syllable of the word comprising a feminine ending:

> *Divinely* imitate the realms above
>
> (Sarah Fyge Egerton, "The Emulation," 35)

> The late *appearance* of the northern lights
>
> (R. S. Gwynn, "Horatio's Philosophy," 12)

In marble quarried from *Carrara's* hills

(W. H. Davies, "A Strange City," 16)

Go, get you up; I will not be *entreated*

(Beaumont, *The Knight of the Burning Pestle,* 4.3.3)

Moreover, two different middle-stressed trisyllables may occur at different positions in the line:

In a *forbidden* or *forbidding* tree

(Donne, "The Blossom," 12)

Adulthood's high *romantic* citadel

(Kingsley Amis, "Romance," 8)

Or three may appear, as in this line, where the third middle-stressed trisyllabic word (actually, it is the same word all three times) produces a feminine ending:

Tomorrow, and tomorrow, and tomorrow

(Shakespeare, *Macbeth,* 5.5.19)

To shift morphologies, one can find as well, in the same line, a pair of trisyllables with chief stress on the first syllable and some degree of intermediate stress on the third:

Boys seek for *images* and *melody*

(Robert Browning, "Transcendentalism," 17)

The *singular* idea of *loneliness*

(Robinson, "Isaac and Archibald," 63)

For that matter, one can find both kinds of trisyllables mixed together in a single line, as was the case in Amis's verse cited a moment ago (in which "citadel" appears, as well as "Adulthood's" and "romantic"), and as is the case in the lines below. The first line has a trisyllable primarily stressed on the first syllable and intermediately stressed on the third, followed by a middle-stressed trisyllable. The second line has two middle-stressed trisyllables on either side of a trisyllable primarily stressed on the first syllable and intermediately stressed on the third. The third line has a middle-stressed trisyllable between two trisyllables whose stress-contour is heavy-light-intermediate:

No *shimmering deceptions* of the sun

> (N. Scott Momaday, "Before an Old Painting of the Crucifixion," 26)

Whatever hypocrites austerely talk

> (Milton, *Paradise Lost*, 4.744)

A *liquefied Palazzo Barbaro*

> (Hecht, "In Memory of David Kalstone," 20)

Indeed, because most English words of more than one syllable feature alternating stress, whether rising or falling, it is easy for poets, once they get the hang of it, to fit them at any point into the line. Here, for instance, are verses that integrate, into the pentametric pattern, words of four and five syllables with rising stress:

into *mythologies* of memory

> (Mary Jo Salter, "Letter from America," 3)

Procrastination is the thief of time

> (Young, *Night Thoughts*, 1.393)

And here are verses that integrate words of five and six syllables with falling stress.

and *tantalizingly* within his reach

> (Marilyn Nelson, "Balance," 11)

Of all this *unintelligible* world

> (Wordsworth, "Tintern Abbey," 40)

Likewise, it is possible to integrate two four-syllable words with different stress contours into the same pentameter:

A *desolation,* a *simplicity*

> (Wordsworth, *The Prelude*, 4.402)

Or two five-syllable words with different stress contours:

Involuntary immortality

> (Seth, "The North Temple Tower," 10)

Other combinations may be noted. One of these involves pentameters whose ten positions are filled out by a monosyllabic, a disyllabic, a trisyllabic, and a tetrasyllabic word. Sometimes the words will be disposed like tenpins at an American bowling alley. Just as the pins are set up in a sequence of one, two, three, and four, the pentameters in question will consist of a sequence of a one-syllable word, then a two-syllable word, then a three-syllable, and lastly a four-syllable word. To fit the iambic pattern, the monosyllable will be relatively light, the disyllable will be fore-stressed, the trisyllable will have a heavy-light-heavy rhythm, and the tetrasyllable will have stress on its second and fourth syllables.

> With senseless, amorous idolatry
>
> > (Thomas Shadwell, *The Virtuoso*, "Epilogue," 13)

Poets can produce different sequences involving four words whose syllables number from one to four. For example, Milton gives us in the following verse (*Paradise Lost*, 3.492) the four words in descending succession. The bowling pins are set up in reverse. To fit the iambic pattern, the first and second words, which have four and three syllables respectively, feature rising rhythm; the third word is a disyllable with falling rhythm, the fourth a relatively heavy monosyllable:

> Indulgences, Dispenses, Pardons, Bulls

Mono-, di-, tri-, and tetrasyllabic words can be mixed together in many ways in the pentameter line. It indicates the richness of the pentametric verse that even such an exotic pattern as this should have so many possible permutations. (Such permutations spiral off into the stratosphere once you go beyond the regularly iambic—i.e., substitutionless—model and try to count versions that have an inverted foot or feet.) Here are additional examples:

> Provocative, with blenkis* amorous   4,1,2,3   * glances
>
> > (Robert Henryson, *The Testament of Cresseid*, 226)

> Created only to calumniate   3,2,1,4
>
> > (Shakespeare, *Troilus and Cressida*, 5.2.121)

> Yet Coquettilla's artifice prevails   1,4,3,2
>
> > (Mary Wortley Montagu, *Court Eclogues*,
> > "Roxanna, or The Drawing Room," 39)

> Remote, unfriended, melancholy, slow   2,3,4,1
>
> > (Goldsmith, "The Traveller," 1)

Philosophers deduce you chastity   4,2,1,3

          (Robert Browning, "Bishop Blougram's Apology," 825)

Archaic and divine indifference   3,1,2,4

          (Bowers, "An Elegy: December, 1970," 8)

All renaissance grotesques electrified   1,3,2,4

          (Kenneth Fields, "Altamont," 6)

Impromptu demonstrations of support   3,4,1,2

          (Dana Gioia, "News from Nineteen Eighty-Four," 17)

I should reiterate here the point, made in the introduction, that poets do not generally pre-plan verbal effects. Once poets have learned their medium, they practice it intuitively. I had no idea that bowling-pins lines existed until I bit the apple of literary criticism. Subsequently, I have discovered in my own early poems pentameters that feature a monosyllabic, disyllabic, trisyllabic, and tetrasyllabic word. Writing the poems, I was unaware of this circumstance.

While the abstract norm of the pentameter has five accents, one common version of the line has only three strong speech stresses. In this type of line, which readers will recognize immediately once examples of it are given, the second and fourth feet are light, and strong beats fall on syllables 2, 6, and 10. Grammatically, this line most frequently involves two major fore-stressed disyllables (e.g., nouns or verbs), introduced or connected by particles (e.g., articles or monosyllabic conjunctions and prepositions). And the line customarily concludes with another major word, usually a monosyllable, though a fore-stressed disyllable is a possibility as well, in this latter case the light second syllable comprising a feminine ending.

This line-type appears frequently in Chaucer:

In Omer, or in Darës, or in Ditë

          (*Troilus and Criseyde*, 1.146)

In Southwerk at the Tabard as I lay

          (*The Canterbury Tales*, A 20 ["The General Prologue"])

The barbour, and the bocher, and the smyth

          (*The Canterbury Tales*, A 2025 ["The Knight's Tale"])

Later instances include:

A kingdom, or a cottage, or a grave

> (Edward De Vere, "A Choice," 6)

Or ravished with the whistling of a name

> (Pope, *Essay on Man*, 4. 283)

And listen to the flapping of the flame

> (Wordsworth, "Personal Talk," 1.13)

Their doubles and the shadow of my boat

> (Edward Thomas, "July," 2)

As with other species of pentameter, this one can be realized in many ways. The poet can introduce, so to speak, a trisyllable for one of the disyllables and delete one of the particles:

Nor wonder at *complainings* in your streets

> (Mary Barber, "On Seeing an Officer's Widow," 30)

Or one of the disyllables may be replaced by a monosyllable and a trisyllable may make up the difference by replacing a disyllable:

As *sweet* and as *delicious* as the first

> (John Ford, *'Tis Pity She's a Whore*, 5.3.9)

Or a rear-stressed disyllable can close the line, the initial unaccented syllable of this word standing, in a sense, in place of one of the particles:

The Paythan an' the Zulu an' *Burmese*

> (Rudyard Kipling, "Fuzzy Wuzzy," 3)

Or the pattern may be accomplished by two rear-stressed disyllables flanking a polysyllable whose primarily stressed syllable occupies the sixth position in the line:

Detained for *contemplation* or *repose*

> (Wordsworth, *The Excursion*, 1.42)

Or it may involve two middle-stressed trisyllables and a rear-stressed disyllable:

Distinguished, and *familiar,* and *aloof*

> (Cunningham, "And what is love?" 4)

Or a middle-stressed and a fore-stressed trisyllable and a rear-stressed disyllable:

> *Wherever* on the *virginal frontier*
>
> (Wilbur, "John Chapman," 2)

Once readers or poets acquire a sense of rhythmico-grammatical groups, they may be able to specify other common types of this or that meter. They also may develop an ear for less common correspondences. Below, for instance, are the opening iambic tetrameters of two well-known poems, which are centuries apart, but which have the same unusual rhythm. This involves a trochaic first foot and a fore-stressed disyllabic word laid across the fourth and fifth positions of the line; the unaccented syllable of this word in turn constitutes the first syllable of a light iamb, which is followed by a heavy iamb, with the result that four degrees of stress rise over the course of two successive feet:

```
             1   2    3   4
  /   x  x / x  /   x   /
Drink to me only with thine eyes
```

(Ben Jonson, "Song," 1)

```
           1   2   3    4
  / x   x / x  /   x   /
Just as my fingers on these keys
```

(Stevens, "Peter Quince at the Clavier," 1)

Here are two iambic pentameters that feature similarly contoured and coordinated parallel phrases:

> False Friend, false Son, false Father, and false King
>
> (Churchill, *Gotham*, 2.385)

> Sans Wine, sans Song, sans Singer, and—sans End!
>
> (Fitzgerald, *The Rubáiyát of Omar Khayyám*, 5th ed., 24.4)

And here are two lines whose similar syntax produces a heavy second foot and a light third one—a combination which in turn contributes to the sense of uncertainty or impairment that the authors are endeavoring to communicate:

> The hare limp'd trembling through the frozen grass
>
> (Keats, "The Eve of St. Agnes," 3)

> Her mind kept fading in the growing mist

(Nabokov, Pale Fire, 202)

It also should be said, by way of encouragement to younger writers, that even great poets make metrical mistakes, and that one should not be frightened of errors or feel that one is a tin-eared klutz if one on occasion fumbles a line. For instance, Philip Sidney, as surefooted a metrician as ever wrote, perhaps loses his balance at that point (9–11) in "With How Sad Steps" where he wonders if in heaven, as well as on earth, constant love is met with contempt:

> Then ev'n of fellowship, O Moon, tell me
> Is constant love deem'd there but want of wit?
> Are beauties there as proud as here they be?

One can make iambic sense of the first four feet of the first line, but in the final foot, the meter appears to strain against natural speech stress:

> x /   x / x   / x /   ?   ?
> Then ev'n of fellowship, O Moon, tell me

Normally, we would say the two-syllable imperative clause with the accent on the verb: tell me. Yet this gives us a trochaic substitution. Such a substitution in the last foot of a line is almost always awkward, and in this case it would spoil the rhyme with "be." Evidently, then, Sidney wishes us to render the foot "tell me." But such a reading seems odd, unless the moon has recently imparted the desired information to some other nocturnal wanderer and the poet feels slighted in consequence.

At times meter and syntax may seem to be at loggerheads, but will, upon closer examination, prove to be in interesting and lively concurrence. At times, that is, meter may seem to require an unusual reading which will turn out to be significant and appropriate for the context. A good illustration of this situation occurs toward the close of John Greenleaf Whittier's "Abraham Davenport." In this poem, an eclipse has spread darkness over the countryside, and in the Connecticut State House, most of the legislators are terrified that the Day of Judgment has arrived. Amidst a clamor for adjournment, Representative Davenport calmly rises and suggests that people cannot know the ways of divinity and that the lawmakers should therefore remain at their earthly tasks—in this case, amending an act to regulate state fisheries—until heaven explicitly orders them to do otherwise. And he concludes by saying:

Let God do his work, we will see to ours.

Were we to encounter the first clause in isolation, we would probably read it with stresses on the two nouns. Let *God* do his *work*. However, such a reading does not fit the iambic pentameter pattern, which instead suggests that the stress should fall on "his." Though normally we do not stress an attributive adjective at the expense of its noun, rendering the line in this evidently unconventional fashion not only recovers the rhythm, but also clarifies the poem's meaning. We see that Whittier intends that the pronominal forms be emphasized right down the line and that the line itself encapsulates the poem's key juxtapositions—God/man and God's work/ man's work:

Let *God* do *his* work, *we* will see to *ours*

Generally speaking, grammatical variety is as pleasing in verse as it is in prose. In terms of morphology and word shape, it is frequently the case that verse that naturally and unostentatiously mixes different types of words will appeal to the ear more than verse whose vocabulary is notably constrained or limited. As we observed in the third chapter, Shakespeare in his dramas time and again captivates us with the dexterous diversity of his language, often creating interesting verbal and rhythmical counterpoints simply by juxtaposing lines of short words with lines of longer ones. And even the briefest of poems may also benefit from syntactical variety, a point well illustrated by J. V. Cunningham's version of Catullus's two-liner *Odi et Amo:*

I hate and love her. If you ask me why
I don't know. But I feel it and am torn.

We have here, in two iambic pentameters, three short sentences. The first is a simple declarative sentence, with subject, (compound) verb, and object. The second sentence is complex, the dependent clause coming first, the main clause, "I don't know," following. The third sentence has yet a different structure, being introduced by a coordinating conjunction and having a compound predicate.

It is doubtful that Cunningham was solemnly deliberating about syntax when he did this translation. Like most excellent poets, once he had acquired the skills of his trade, he applied them with a natural grace and devoted most of his conscious energy to thematics or, in the case of translation, to philological and interpretive questions. (Because Latin is much more highly inflected than English, and because its grammar differs from ours, the cast of Cunningham's sentences is necessarily his own as well as Catullus's.) But the quiet variety of syntax is a key aspect of the translation and significantly contributes to its success.

It bears repeating that one need not use fancy words and intricate grammar to write great verse. Cunningham's translation is, despite its syntactical fluidity, composed entirely of monosyllables. And many of the most memorable passages and lines in our poetry are written in simple words, with straightforward sentence structure:

> Why should a dog, a horse, a rat, have life,
> And thou no breath at all? Thou'lt come no more.
>
> (Shakespeare, King Lear, 5.3.308–9)

> I must stop short of thee the whole day long
>
> (Alice Meynell, "Renunciation," 8)

> We love the things we love for what they are
>
> (Frost, "Hyla Brook," 15)

For that matter, there are fine poems written entirely in monosyllabic words. One of these is the "Elegy" that Chidiock Tichbourne wrote on the eve of his execution for participating in the Babington plot to assassinate Queen Elizabeth. (Tichbourne was only twenty-seven or twenty-eight when he was beheaded: hence the poem's emphasis on youth and life's brevity. Like "heaven" and "even," "fallen" could in the Renaissance be pronounced monosyllabically.)

> My prime of youth is but a frost of cares.
> My feast of joy is but a dish of pain.
> My crop of corn is but a field of tares,
> And all my good is but vain hope of gain.
> The day is past, and yet I saw no sun,
> And now I live, and now my life is done.
>
> My tale was heard and yet it was not told.
> My fruit is fallen and yet my leaves are green.
> My youth is spent and yet I am not old.
> I saw the world and yet I was not seen.
> My thread is cut and yet it is not spun,
> And now I live, and now my life is done.
>
> I sought my death and found it in my womb.
> I looked for life and saw it was a shade.
> I trod the earth and knew it was my tomb.

And now I die, and now I was but made.
My glass is full, and now my glass is run,
And now I live, and now my life is done.

In closing this chapter and this section of the book, I should like to say a few words about the benefits of considering meter in connection with grammar. The masterpieces of our poetry are an enduring resource. Yet if they are to exercise their regenerative function, they must be understood and experienced in the spirit in which they were written. We must be able to internalize their rhythms of thought and sensibility. We must read them not merely with the eye, but also with the ear and mind and heart. We must experience them as the integrated works they are. We must hear both their grammatical and their metrical structures, both their sense and their music. To return to Auden's comment, it is possible to read verse as pure grammar, rendering it as though it were prose, or as pure meter, simply singsonging or intoning it forth. But the magical paradox of verse is that it joins fixed measure with fluid idiomatic speech. The better we appreciate this union, the more deeply and comprehensively we can grasp and share in the art.

Finally, the relationship between meter and grammar is well worth attention, in that the two perhaps illustrate, in similar and concurrent ways, something of the very nature of our being. In his stimulating study, *Grammatical Man*, Jeremy Campbell writes:

> Biologists as well as philosophers have suggested that the universe, and the living forms it contains, are based on chance, but not on accident. To put it another way, forces of chance and of antichance coexist in a complementary relationship. . . . The proper metaphor for the life process may not be a pair of rolling dice or a spinning roulette wheel, but the sentences of a language, conveying information that is partly predictable and partly unpredictable. These sentences are generated by rules which make much out of little, producing a boundless wealth of meaning from a finite store of words; they enable language to be familiar yet surprising, constrained yet unpredictable within its constraints.

No less than grammar does, meter fuses and enacts those principles of constancy and of change that seem essential to life and to the world about us. Like grammar, meter involves simple structures that can nevertheless be manifested in varied and complex ways. It organizes the rhythms of speech while at the same time allowing for all sorts of modulations, shadings, and surprises. And when Campbell adds that "grammatical man inhabits a grammatical universe," poets and readers of verse might speculate that we also inhabit a metrical one.

TWO

Other Matters,
Other Meters

6

Rhyme

1. The Background and History of Rhyme

MUCH OF OUR VERSE RHYMES. In many English-language poems, that is, the terminal sounds of different lines correspond. This correspondence concerns the vowels of the final metrically accented syllables of the lines and any sounds (e.g., consonants or hypermetrical syllables) that may follow them. However, the correspondence does not customarily extend to identicalness, and the sounds that open the syllables generally differ. In this respect, rhyme is like other elements of poetic art. It involves the interplay of similarity and dissimilarity.

Coleridge's "On a Volunteer Singer" illustrates the nature and function of rhyme:

> Swans sing before they die: 'twere no bad thing
> Did certain persons die before they sing.

Here "thing" and "sing" are the last stressed syllables of the iambic pentameters in which they appear. Even as the opening *th* and *s* sounds distinguish the words from one another, they chime on account of having the same vowel, a short *i*, and the same syllable-closing *ng*. This agreement helps to establish the integrity of each line. We hear the lines, as lines, more clearly than we might otherwise. In addition, the rhymes link the lines harmoniously together, hone the wit of the poem, and provide an aid to memory. We could revise Coleridge's poem so that it consisted of a pair of rhymeless pentameters:

> Swans sing before they die: 'twere no bad thing
> Did some folks die before they vocalized.

But such a revision would diminish our pleasure in and appreciation of the poem's organization.

Some authorities call correspondences between terminations of different lines "end rhyme," so as to differentiate it from a type of rhyme that entails chiming a syllable in the middle of a line with one at the end of it. This latter device is "internal rhyme." We find it occasionally in ancient verse as a rhetorical ornament, as in this hexameter by Ovid (*Art of Love*, 1.59):

> Quot caelum *stellas*, tot habet tua Roma *puellas*
>> (Many the stars that heaven blesses, many the maids that Rome possesses)

Internal rhyme often serves as a regular, structure-shaping feature in medieval Latin poems, where it is called "leonine rhyme," a term of uncertain origin. Examples of internal rhyme in English verse are furnished by lines 1, 3, 5, and 7 of Walter Scott's "County Guy." Here is the first stanza, with italics added to the internal rhymes:

> Ah! County *Guy*, the hour is *nigh*,
>> The sun has left the lea,
> The orange *flower* perfumes the *bower*,
>> The breeze is on the sea.
> The lark, his *lay* who thrill'd all *day*,
>> Sits hush'd his partner nigh;
> Breeze, bird, and *flower*, confess the *hour*,
>> But where is County Guy?

Internal rhyme may also entail chiming the end of one line with the middle of the following line. This procedure appears in Edgar Allan Poe's "The Raven." Poe composes the poem in six-line stanzas, and in addition to rhyming the ends of the lines, and the middles and ends of lines 1 and 3, he chimes the end of the third line with the middle of the fourth. Here is the poem's opening stanza. (The first five lines of each stanza are trochaic octameters and the sixth is a trochaic tetrameter; in addition, the second, fourth, fifth, and sixth lines are "catalectic," meaning that they lack their final unaccented syllable.)

> Once upon a midnight *dreary*, while I pondered, weak and *weary*,
> Over many a quaint and curious volume of forgotten lore—
> While I nodded, nearly *napping*, suddenly there came a *tapping*,

As of someone gently *rapping*, rapping at my chamber door—
"'Tis some visitor," I muttered, "tapping at my chamber door—
Only this and nothing more."

In this first stanza, Poe also matches "rapping" at the beginning of the second half of line 4 with "tapping" at the beginning of the second half of line 5; however, unlike the other arrangments involving internal rhyme, this one is not repeated regularly throughout the poem.

Poets may sometimes rhyme the middle of one line with the end of the line that follows it. Thom Gunn does this in "Pierce Street," a poem in iambic pentameters organized into five-line stanzas. Line 1 of each stanza rhymes with line 3; line 2 rhymes with line 4; and the fifth line rhymes with the middle of the fourth line. To make clear the internal rhymes, Gunn divides the fourth line after the second foot, the point at which appears the syllable that will chime with the end of the fifth line. Here are the poem's first two stanzas:

Nobody home. Long threads of sunlight slant
Past curtains, blind, and slat, through the warm room.
The beams are dazzling, but, random and scant,
Pierce where they end
             small areas of the gloom
On curve of chair leg or a green stalk's bend.

I start exploring. Beds and canvases
Are shapes in each room off the corridor
Their colors muted, square thick presences
Rising between
             the ceiling and the floor,
A furniture inferred much more than seen.

In addition, prosodists employ the term "internal rhyme" to denote those occasional sound-pairings that now and again turn up in lines, but not necessarily at their middles and ends. Such rhymes may occur by accident, as is evidently the case in the seventh line of the second of Arthur Hugh Clough's "Commemoration Sonnets":

Teaching, up*on* the light Slav*onic* toe

Or the poet may introduce such correspondences for expressive effect, as Shakespeare does when, in *Love's Labor's Lost* (4.3.178–82), he has Berowne boast that he will never succumb to the follies of romance:

When shall you see me write a thing in rhyme?
Or *groan* for *Joan*? Or spend a minute's time
In pruning me?* When shall you hear that I   *In prettying myself up
Will praise a hand, a foot, a face, an eye,
A *gait*, a *state*, a brow, a breast, a waist . . .

Even as he denies that he will become a lover and rhymer, Berowne is head-over-heels in love with Rosaline and rhyming up a storm. Nor, as Shakespeare indicates, is mere end rhyme sufficient to express Berowne's elevated spirits: the young man must also press internal rhyme into service of his ebullience.

Internal rhyme can be sonically interesting. It can as well be sonically exciting when employed by such musically gifted poets as William Dunbar, Milton, and Hopkins. But it is not an important element of our versification. In fact, the most familiar form of internal rhyme—the chiming of middles and ends of lines that we illustrated with the stanzas from Scott and Poe—tends to sound jingly. And in this chapter when I speak of rhyme, I shall be referring to end rhyme unless I specify otherwise.

If meter embodies our love of rhythm, rhyme reflects our delight in verbal concordances and harmonies. Anyone who has heard children improvising rhymes while skipping rope, or rap singers linking verse after verse with a single rhyme, must suspect that our species has an instinctive curiosity about aural patterns and a happiness in them. Further, the very nature of human speech encourages these feelings. The number of phonemes (i.e., basic speech sounds) in any language is small, usually between twenty-five and forty-five, and consequently the syllables and words constructed from this limited phonemic supply will correspond with some frequency.

The extent to which poets use these correspondences to shape their verse, however, depends on their language's grammatical and verbal structure. Languages that best accommodate rhyme are those that have a fair number of monosyllabic words and/or a fair number of di-, tri-, or poly-syllabic words whose final syllable bears notable length, pitch, or stress. Rhyming works less well in languages that rely on light flexional suffixes to indicate the grammatical functions of words or that otherwise involve considerable compounding.

For these reasons, end rhyme is an element of Chinese poetry from its beginnings, but is not common in the ancient Indo-European languages of Sanskrit, Greek, and Latin. Chinese is essentially monosyllabic, each character equaling a syllable, and from the outset, Chinese poets must have found it relatively natural to use rhyme to point metrical units. (Rhyme appears in the earliest preserved collection of Chinese poems, the *Shih Ching—The Classic of Songs* or *Book of Odes*—an anthology assembled in the sixth or fifth century B.C., some of the poems of which go back to the late second millennium B.C.) In contrast, Sanskrit, Greek, and Latin are highly inflected, and their oblique cases, and their complex conjugations and declensions, discourage rhyming. To achieve full rhymes in these languages, the poet would have to chime both stem and flexional elements of words. This process would not only be taxing, but would also produce rhymes which, regularly extending to two or more syllables, would sound distractingly bouncy.

End rhyme does not become a major feature of European verse until the Middle Ages, a period that sees the rise of the vernacular languages, which are less compressed and more analytic than the classical languages. (Also during this time, the nature and metric of Greek and Latin alter.) If we think of the three major millennia of European poetry—the first millennium B.C., the first millennium A.D., and the second millennium A.D.—it is only the last that is a real Age of Rhyme. In this third millennium appear the European tradition's finest rhyming poets, including Dante, Petrarch, Chaucer, Ariosto, the Shakespeare of the sonnets, Racine, Molière, Pope, Goethe, Leopardi, Baudelaire, Valéry, Frost, and Rilke, to name just a few.

Ancient poets and prose writers use and discuss (e.g., Aristotle, *Rhetoric* 1410a23ff. and Demetrius, *On Style,* 26) a form of quasi rhyme called *homoeoteleuton.* This involves terminating, with the same case-ending or same word, two or more nearby phrases, clauses, or lines. To illustrate case-ending correspondences, Demetrius quotes a sentence from Isocrates' *Panegyricus*: "I have often marvelled at the men who convened the assemblies (*sunagagontôn*) and instituted the athletic games (*katastêsantôn*)." And as an instance of *homoeoteleuton* involving the repetition of a word, Demetrius cites the following sentence from an unknown author: "When he was living you spoke of him only evil (*kakôs*), now that he is dead you write of him only evil (*kakôs*)." Though such "rhymes" can point line or clause endings, they are faint and lack the sprightliness that true rhyme has when skillfully managed. Neither do ancient writers deploy *homoeoteleuton* for consistent structure-marking purposes; rather they treat it as an occasional stylistic adornment.

Rhyme may develop in a literature not only as a result of internal linguistic conditions, but also in conjunction with external influences. After establishing itself in a geocultural center, rhyme may spread to other places and peoples in the course of trade, travel, and intellectual exchange. For instance, Arabic poets communicated conventions of rhyme to Persian poetry; and though the development of English rhyme may have been influenced indigenously by the rhyming practices of early Celtic poetry, the pivotal factor was the Norman Conquest, which brought into Britain the influence of the Romance languages in general and of the rhyming poetry of Old French in particular.

Having become prominent in English poetry in the Middle Ages, rhyme continues to be a notable feature in our verse thereafter. Such has been its prominence that J. V. Cunningham once went so far as to observe that "the dominant principle in English poetry since the Norman Conquest has been rhyme. In the first edition of *The Oxford Book of English* Verse (1900), there are 883 selections; 16 are unrhymed, or minimally rhymed." That is, over 98 percent of the selections are rhymed.

Cunningham's remarks require two qualifications. First, though there are many wonderful long rhymed poems in English, beginning with Chaucer's *Troilus and Criseyde*, unrhymed iambic pentameter (i.e., "blank verse") has been widely used for extended works in verse. Such works include the plays of Marlowe, Shakespeare, and Jonson, as well as Milton's *Paradise Lost* and Wordsworth's *The Prelude*. While rhyme confers obvious pleasures and advantages on short poems, in long ones it can cloy. Verse dramatists especially must weigh this matter, since dialogue must sound as lifelike as possible. (This is not to suggest that rhymed drama cannot work on the English stage; Richard Wilbur's remarkable versions of Molière demonstrate that it can. Nor do I mean to imply that blank verse is suitable only for extended works. Unrhymed pentameter is the medium for many fine short poems in English, including Campion's "The Writer to His Book," Emerson's "The Snow-Storm" and "Days," Tennyson's "Tears, Idle Tears," and Frost's "An Old Man's Winter Night.")

The second qualification concerns opinions about rhyme. Despite its prevalence in English and other modern-language verse, the device is, from the Renaissance on, repeatedly challenged. Critics of rhyme attack it on three grounds. First, they point out that it was not used by the ancient Greek and Latin poets, who represent for many the highest level of poetic achievement. Second, critics disparage rhyme because it was introduced into European poetry during the Middle Ages, which has often been regarded as a period of barbarism. Third, it has been argued that rhyme forces poets to wrest words from their normal order and thereby distort syntax and meaning.

The most pointed Renaissance attack on rhyme is Campion's *Observations in the Art of English Poesie*. Drawing on ideas earlier developed by such writers as Ascham, Campion contends that English verse should be regulated by syllable duration, as ancient verse was; and, as a corollary, Campion urges that English should dispense with "the vulgar and unarteficiall custome of riming." Campion's arguments are answered by Samuel Daniel's *Defence of Rhyme*, in which Daniel urges that English poetry should develop native resources rather than pursuing conventions of a different language and prosody. Daniel notes that English verse "doth not strictly observe long and short syllables, yet it most religiously respects the accent" and argues that "Rhyme (which is an excellency added to this work of measure, and a harmony far happier than any proportion antiquity could ever show us) doth add more grace, and hath more of delight than ever bare numbers, howsoever they can be forced to run in our slow language, can possibly yield." Daniel is generally felt to have gotten the better of the argument, but Campion's objections to rhyme reappear (though usually without the accompanying advocacy of quantitative metric) in later writers.

Another notable Renaissance protest against rhyme, this one humorous and ironical, is Ben Jonson's "A Fit of Rime against Rime." Jonson's poem cleverly rhymes its way through the standard criticisms of the device. Writing in trochaics, Jonson concludes by apostrophizing rhyme and by cursing whoever invented it. In wishing ill to the inventor's "feet," Jonson refers not only to the anatomical extremities that enable us to walk, but also to metrical units:

He that first invented thee,
May his joints tormented be,
    Cramped forever,
Still may syllabes jar with time,
Still may reason war with rime,
    Resting never.
May his sense when it would meet,
The cold tumor in his feet
    Grow unsounder.
And his title long be fool,
That in rearing such a school,
    Was the founder.

By far the best known challenge to rhyme comes from John Milton, who explains in a preface to the second printing of *Paradise Lost:*

The Measure [of the epic] is English Heroic Verse [i.e., iambic pentameter] without Rime, as that of Homer in Greek and of Virgil in Latin,— Rime being no necessary Adjunct or true Ornament of Poem or good Verse, in longer Works especially, but the Invention of a barbarous Age, to set off wretched matter and lame meter; graced indeed since by the use of some famous modern Poets, carried away by Custom, but much to their own vexation, hindrance, and constraint to express many things otherwise, and for the most part worse, than else they would have expressed them.

(In calling rhyme "the Invention of a barbarous Age," Milton is referring to the fact that Greek and Latin poets do not use the device, which becomes common in European poetry only during the "barbarous Age" of the medieval period.)

Milton's argument—and by extension similar arguments against rhyme —is rebutted by Samuel Johnson, who in his *Life* of Milton discusses *Paradise Lost* at length. Johnson is generous in his praise of the poem, which he seems to prefer to all other epics, even Homer's. Johnson says of Milton and *Paradise Lost*, "[H]is work is not the greatest of heroic poems, only because it is not the first." But when Johnson examines Milton's versification, he contends that the poet, "finding blank verse easier than rhyme, was desirous of persuading himself that it is better." And Johnson continues:

"Rhyme," he [Milton] says, and says truly, "is no necessary adjunct of true poetry." But perhaps of poetry as a mental operation meter or music is no necessary adjunct: it is however by the music of metre that poetry has been discriminated in all languages, and in languages melodiously constructed with a due proportion of long and short syllables [e.g., classical Greek and Latin], meter is sufficient. But one language cannot communicate its rules to another; where meter is scanty and imperfect some help is necessary. The music of the English heroic line [i.e., the iambic pentameter] strikes the ear so faintly that it is easily lost, unless all the syllables of every line cooperate together; this cooperation can be only obtained by the preservation of every verse unmingled with another as a distinct system of sounds, and this distinctness is obtained and preserved by the artifice of rhyme. The variety of pauses, so much boasted by the lovers of blank verse, changes the measures of an English poet to the periods of a declaimer; and there are only a few skillful and happy readers of Milton who enable their audience to perceive where the lines end or begin. "Blank verse," said an ingenious critic, "seems to be verse only to the eye." [In his biography of Johnson, James Boswell identifies the ingenious critic as the art connoisseur William Locke, who apparently made the remark in conversation with Johnson.]

Johnson raises here several interesting points. For one thing, as far as we can tell, it was easier to hear ancient Greek and Latin poetry, unaccompanied by rhyme, than it is to hear rhymeless verse in Modern English. All the available testimony (e.g., Cicero, *De Oratore*, 3.195–96) indicates that even unschooled audiences, with no text before them and with no previous knowledge of what they were listening to, grasped metrical patterns and objected to violations or slips in their use. And as Paul Maas has commented in comparing the verse of ancient Greece to that of modern Europe, "[W]ithout the aid of rhyme one cannot achieve that impression of closely knit discourse which Greek poetry, even in the loosest metres and in the least elevated style, never fails to give."

Another interesting point is that English blank verse has been, as Johnson suggests, more prone to rhetorical excess than rhymed verse. Though we might at first think that poetry with rhyme would be likelier to lapse into exaggeration than poetry without it, this is not the case. On the contrary, when one writes unrhymed iambic pentameter, the line tends to go flat if one does not run it over from time to time. And, as was noted in the second chapter, a poet who enjambs lines frequently may lose control of them. Moreover, running lines on encourages syntactical complexity, and this practice, if unrelieved, may produce bombast. Finally, a poet may be tempted, when writing blank verse, to turn up the level of rhetorical intensity to compensate for the absence of rhyme. It is revealing that many English poems we most associate with colloquial energy, from Chaucer's *Canterbury Tales* down to Frost's lyrics, have been in rhyme, whereas many poems that strike us as unusually ornate in diction, such as *Paradise Lost* and Tennyson's *Idylls of the King*, are rhymeless.

Milton's attack on rhyme contains as well, as Johnson notes, a destructive illogicality, though it is not immediately evident and is doubtless unintentional on Milton's part. Poetry is an expression of the human spirit, and its essence will always be elusive and magical. Rhyme is in this respect extraneous to poetry. But so, in spiritual terms, is every other tool of versification, including meter. So for that matter is grammar. So are words—and there are twentieth-century poems (e.g., by John Cage) that dispense with words and consist of blank pages. Yet many readers and listeners have, for millennia, known poetry by its various metrical, grammatical, and rhetorical devices. A case can be made that English lines are, with meter, sufficiently determined so as not to need rhyme. But it is foolish to criticize artifice for being artificial; that is its function. Artifice fails if it is clumsy, and the artifice of rhyme can be used badly. But it also can be used graciously and unaffectedly, as Milton himself knew. One of his favorite poems was Dante's *Divine Comedy.* If rhyme can be made, as Dryden puts it in his *Essay of Dramatic Poesy,* "so properly a part of the verse that it should never mislead the sense, but itself be led and governed by it," then it seems wise to admit rhyme as one of the possible instruments of our poetry. Poets are not required to use it, but they can if they wish.

In the final analysis, English is fortunate to have vital traditions of both rhyming and rhymeless verse. Poets involved in the rhyme controversy have themselves, for all practical purposes, subscribed to this idea, regardless of their theoretical stances. Even those who have on occasion attacked rhyme, such as Campion and Milton, have at other times embraced and used it brilliantly. And those who have defended rhyme, and have doubted blank verse, have praised the latter. No sooner does Johnson make the argument cited above than he adds with respect to *Paradise Lost:* "But, whatever be the advantage of rhyme I cannot prevail on myself to wish that Milton had been a rhymer, for I cannot wish his work to be other than it is."

Over the centuries, "rhyme" has been spelled in different ways, and it may be worthwhile to explain the variants. *The Oxford English Dictionary* has illuminating discussions of the two most common spellings, "Rhyme" and "Rime." The dictionary's entry for the latter observes:

> In med[ieval] L[atin] the terms *rithmi* and *rithmici versus* were used to denote accentual in contrast to quantitative verse *(metra).* As similarity of the terminal sounds was a common feature of accentual verse, *rithmus* naturally came to have the sense of "rime."

In other words, "rhyme" or "rime" was, from early on, identified or associated with accentual "rhythm." And the *OED,* after observing that "rime" came into English from the Old French *rime,* goes on to say that the currently preferred form *(rhyme)* resulted from two somewhat conflicting desires. First, people in the sixteenth century wished to make the word's spelling reflect its derivation from the Latin *rhythmus.* Second, people a little later wanted to distinguish the word from "rhythm":

> Down to c. 1560 the original spelling *rime (ryme)* continued to prevail in English. About that date the tendency to alter orthography on classical models led to the new spellings *rithme, rythme, rhythm(e),* which continued to be current till about the close of the 17th cent. . . . Soon after 1600,

probably from a desire to distinguish between 'rime' and 'rhythm', the intermediate forms *rhime, rhyme* came into use, and the latter finally established itself as the standard form. . . . The original *rime,* however, has never been quite discontinued, and from about 1870 its use has been considerably revived, esp. by writers upon the history of the English language or literature. To some extent this revival was due to the belief that the word was of native origin, and represented O[ld] E[nglish] *rím* ['number,' 'computation'].

2. The Two Common Types of Rhyme in English—Full and Partial—and Some of Their Varieties

English verse features two basic types of rhyme. The most common is "full" or "exact" rhyme. In full rhymes, the syllable pairs begin differently, but there is a match between the vowels and all sounds that may follow. Full rhyme most frequently involves syllables in which a vowel is flanked by consonants, as in **thing/sing** in Coleridge's epigram and as in **turn/burn** in these lines:

> He watches me for Mother, and will turn
> The bier and baby-carriage where I burn.
>
> (Robert Lowell, "Between the Porch and the Altar," 4.27–28)

However, one of the syllables may begin with a vowel, while its mate begins with a consonant, as in **old/told**:

> Sure, 'twas not ever thus, nor are we told
> Fables of women that excelled of old.
>
> (Anne Finch, "The Introduction," 21–22)

Or both syllables may end with vowels, but be preceded by different consonants, as in **me**/proper**ty**:

> Unreal, you realize yourself in me.
> I thought your coldness was my property.
>
> (Helen Pinkerton, "The Romantic Eros," 7–8)

Or one of the syllables may consist of a vowel by itself, with the other syllable's vowel being preceded an initial consonant, as in **I**/there**by**:

> That fish that is not catched thereby,
> Alas, is wiser far than I.
>
> (Donne, "The Bait," 27–28)

Full rhyme may be subdivided into "masculine rhyme," "feminine rhyme," and "triple rhyme." When we speak of masculine rhyme, we are speaking of one-syllable rhymes, with the syllables themselves being accented, as with **talk/walk**, ca**boose/loose**, and **dress**/opal**esce**. Feminine rhymes, on the other hand, extend over two syllables, with the primary stress on the first syllable, as in **thinning/winning**, de**votion/ocean**, and **fated**/liber**ated**. Triple rhymes involve three syllables with the strong accent on the antepenultimate syllable, as in **deference/reference** and **busily/fizzily**. Some prosodists call these latter rhymes *sdrucciola,* an onomatopoeic Italian word meaning "slippery" that the Italians use to denote trisyllabic rhymes.

Triple-rhyme words may lead a dual existence. Consider, for example, the word "posterity" as it appears in the ninth stanza of the "Dedication" of Byron's *Don Juan.* Because "posterity" takes primary stress on its second syllable, it can serve as a triple-rhyme match with "spare it he" and "rarity":

```
  /   x x /    x  / x   / x /(x)(x)
He that reserves his laurels for posterity
```

    (Who does not often claim the bright reversion?)

```
  x   / x / x  /   x    / x  / (x) (x)
Has generally no great crop to spare it, he
```

    Being only injured by his own assertion;

```
  x   /  x   /  x   /  x   / >   /(x)(x)
And although here and there some glorious rarity
```

    Arise, like Titan from the sea's immersion,

The major part of such appellants go

To—God knows where—for no one else can know.

Yet because the final syllable of "posterity" has a little stress—it would probably be a "2" in our four-level register—and is weightier than the syllable that precedes it, it can also take a metrical accent and can serve as one of a pair of masculine rhymes, as in the third quatrain of the sixth of Shakespeare's sonnets:

Ten times thyself were happier than thou art,

If ten of thine ten times refigured thee:

Then what could death do if thou shouldst depart,

```
  /  x    x  / x /   x  / x /
Leaving thee living in posterity.
```

Note that the stanza from *Don Juan* features all three types of full rhyme: triple rhyme (postérity/spáre it he/rárity), feminine rhyme (revérsion/ immérsion/assértion), and masculine rhyme (go/know). The stanza itself is called "ottava rima" and consists of eight lines—in hendecasyllabic meter in Italian, where the stanza originated, and in iambic pentameter in English— rhyming *ababababcc*. And anyone interested in wildly inventive, over-the-top rhymes will enjoy *Don Juan* and Byron's two other long poems in ottava rima, *Beppo* and *The Vision of Judgment*.

Very rarely, rhymes extend over four syllables. Ambíguously/ contíguously, párdonable/hárdenable, and mátrimony/pátrimony are examples. Ogden Nash's work features a number of such rhymes. Usually, they result from his intentionally fracturing words. For instance, in his amusingly doggerelish "Hymn to the Sun and Myself," he chimes an unconventional comparative form of "natural" with a farcical version of the noun meaning "an unmarried man." This wayward match occurs (31–32) when the poet thanks himself

> For not having tried to impress my girl but being naturaler with her
> and naturaler;
> So that now instead of having to marry and all that I can continue to
> be a careless baturaler

Of the three familiar types of full rhyme—masculine, feminine, and triple—the one-syllable variety is the most common in English verse. It is also, functionally speaking, the most neutral. Employed extensively, feminine and triple rhymes incline verse toward comicality or intrusive virtuosity.

That said, feminine rhymes can be wonderfully expressive. In the second chapter, we saw this quality in the feminine rhymes with which Mary Wortley Montagu skewered Lord Lyttleton's *Advice to a Lady*. Another expressive use of feminine rhyme appears in Shakespeare's twentieth sonnet ("A woman's face, with Nature's own hand painted"). Here Shakespeare praises a young man for being graceful and attractive in a manner customarily credited only to women, and the poet emphasizes the feminine appeal of his subject by writing exclusively in feminine rhymes.

We see this same procedure in a less celebrated sonnet related to Shakespeare, John Weever's "Ad Gulielmum Shakespeare." Published in 1599, when the poet was in mid-career, this poem provides an arresting tribute to Shakespeare's *Venus and Adonis* and *The Rape of Lucrece* and his earlier dramas, such as *Romeo and Juliet*. Weever regards, as a feminine or "nymphish" excellence, the lyrical eloquence of these works and their protagonists; and suiting his technique to his occasion, Weever employs feminine rhymes entirely:

> Honey-tongued Shakespeare, when I saw thine issue
> I swore Apollo got them and none other;
> Their rosy-tainted features, clothed in tissue,
> Some heav'n-born goddess said to be their mother:
> Rose-cheek'd Adonis with his amber tresses,
> Fair, fire-hot Venus, charming him to love her,
> Chaste Lucretía virgin-like her dresses,
> Proud, lust-stung Tarquin seeking still to prove her,
> Romeo, Richard, more whose names I know not,
> Their sugar'd tongues and pure attractive beauty
> Say they are saints, although that saints they show not,
> For thousands vow to them subjective duty.
> > They burn in love thy children. Shakespeare, let them:
> > Go, woo thy muse, more nymphish brood beget them.

As was observed in the second chapter, "masculine" and "feminine" derive from French prosody and reflect the fact that in French the mute *e* is a common feminine suffix. In the late sixteenth and early seventeenth centuries, French poets develop specific rules to govern rhyme. One of these, designed to assure variety of rhyme, stipulates that masculine and feminine rhymes should alternate. Below are three extracts of four lines each that exemplify this rule. Accompanying the original texts are translations which reproduce in English the alternation of rhyme types. (To mark the rhymes that are feminine, I have added, to the French texts, diereses over the relevant syllables.) The first extract is from a poem in couplets:

> C'est en vain qu'au Parnasse un téméraire auteur
> Pense de l'art des vers atteindre la hauteur.
> S'il ne sent point du Ciel l'influence secrëtë
> Si son astre en naissant ne l'a formé poëtë.

(Nicolas Boileau, "L'Art Poétique," 1–4)

> An author may attempt, by his own lights,
> To scale the sheer sides of Parnassus' heights.
> But he must feel a heavenly spark and show it,
> His birth-star must have formed him for a poet.

The second is from a poem in cross-rhyming quatrains:

> Rubens, fleuve d'oubli, jardin de la paressë
> Oreiller de chair fraîche où l'on ne peut aimer,
> Mais où la vie afflue et s'agite sans cessë
> Comme l'air dans le ciel et la mer dans la mer.
>
> (Charles Baudelaire, "Les Phares," 1–4)

> Rubens, oblivion's stream, languorous garden,
> Pillow of cool flesh where love cannot be,
> But where life ceaselessly shuns rest or pardon
> Like air in sky or water in the sea.

In the third extract, the rhymes are enveloped: the first and fourth lines rhymingly embrace an interior second- and third-line couplet rhyme. Unlike the previous examples, this one is not in alexandrines, but in ten-syllable lines, though of course the lines that end femininely have an extra syllable.

> Si je n'ay plus la faveur de la Musë,
> Et si mes vers se trouvent imparfaits,
> Le lieu, le temps, l'aage ou je les ay faits,
> Et mes ennuis leur serviront d'excusë.
>
> (Joachim Du Bellay, "À Monsieur D'Avanson," 1–4)

> If now I lack the favor of the Muses,
> If my verse fails to strike the proper note,
> The place, the time, the age in which I wrote,
> And my ennui must serve as my excuses.

English poets have never governed rhyme as regularly as French poets have, but on occasion our poets will, for musical effect or for variety, alternate masculine and feminine rhymes. We can observe this principle in Herrick's "To the Virgins, to Make Much of Time," which is written in quatrains whose first and third lines rhyme masculinely and whose second and fourth lines rhyme femininely. We find a similar pattern in the enveloped quatrains of Hardy's haunting poem in iambic trimeter, "I Say I'll Seek Her." The speaker of this poem has made an assignation he does not keep, and he imagines his lover's response to his nonappearance. The first and fourth lines of each stanza feature masculine rhymes and the second and third lines feature feminine rhymes:

I say, 'I'll seek her side
  Ere hindrance interposes;'
  But eve in midnight closes
And here I still abide.

When darkness wears I see
  Her sad eyes in a vision;
  They ask, 'What indecision
Detains you, Love, from me?—

'The creaking hinge is oiled,
  I have unbarred the backway,
  But you tread not the trackway;
And shall the thing be spoiled?

'Far cockcrows echo shrill,
  The shadows are abating,
  And I am waiting, waiting;
But O, you tarry still!'

As the foregoing examples indicate, the key issue in rhyme is similarity of sound rather than of orthography. Words rhyme if they are pronounced alike, even if they are not spelled alike. Conversely, words that are spelled alike but pronounced differently (e.g., **bough/trough**) are customarily not considered rhymes, or are categorized among the second basic type of rhyme.

This second type comprises several species of partial rhyme. One of these variant species is, to recur to the example given immediately above, "eye rhyme," a kind of rhyme based on visual rather than audial identity. In some cases (e.g., **love/prove**) what are currently eye rhymes formerly rhymed for the ear as well. As a kind of license, these rhymes have been conventionally allowed in English versification long after they have ceased to rhyme for the ear. (Other words that were at earlier stages of our language pronounced differently than they are today include "join" and "tea": in the Augustan Age these rhymed with "line" and "day," respectively.)

In earlier stages of our language, when pronunciation was less settled than it is today, poets and readers evidently would, to maintain rhyme, adopt now one and now the other way of saying a syllable that had two possible pronunciations. Isaac Watts in his "Art of Reading and Writing English" analogizes between words that are syllabically ambiguous and subject to elision (e.g., "glittering" versus "glitt'ring") and words that are ambiguous with regard to rhyme. Watts urges that just as readers, when faced with a syllabically equivocal word, should choose the version that supports the meter, so they should lean, when encountering a word whose pronunciation is ambiguous, to the choice that secures the rhyme:

> [F]avour the rhime, . . . pronounce the last word of the line so as to make it chime with the line foregoing, where the word admits of two pronunciations; as,
>
>> 'Were I but once from bondage free,
>> 'I'd never sell my liberty.'
>
> Here I must pronounce the word *liberty,* as if it were written with a double *e, libertee,* to rhime to the word *free.*
> But if the verse ran thus:
>
>> 'My soul ascends above the sky,
>> 'And triumphs in her liberty.'
>
> The word *liberty* must be sounded as ending in *i,* that *sky* may have a juster rhime to it.

Today we pronounce the *y* in "liberty" as the *ee* sound in "free." Were we to pronounce "liberty," "perfectly," or "currency" so that they rhymed with "sky," those who heard us might think us affected. But poets still use such correspondences as eye rhymes. For instance, at the conclusion of "An Arundel Tomb," Larkin rhymes "prove" with "love."

Another species of unconventional rhyme is "rich rhyme." This phrase is a translation of the French *rime riche,* and indicates a kind of rhyme much more common in French verse and in Middle English verse than it is in Modern English verse. Rich rhyme involves words or syllables pronounced the same way without having the same meaning. Some authorities subdivide rich rhymes into "homographic" rhymes (i.e., rhymes that are written the same way, as with "state," meaning "government," and "state," meaning "to say") and "homophonic" rhymes (i.e., rhymes that sound alike, but are not written in the same way, as with "stare" and "stair").

Vikram Seth puts homographic rich rhymes to fine effect in his "Distressful Homonyms." In this poem, Seth matches "spare" (the verb) with "spare" (the adjective), "state" (the noun meaning "condition") with "state" (the verb), "rest" (meaning "remainder") with "rest" (meaning "repose"), and "even" (the adverb that suggests an unlikely instance) with "even" (meaning "smoothly" or "free from variation"):

> Since for me now you have no warmth to spare
> I sense I must adopt a sane and spare

Philosophy to ease a restless state
Fuelled by this uncaring. It will state

A very meagre truth: love, like the rest
Of our emotions, sometimes needs a rest.

Happiness, too, no doubt; and so, why even
Hope that "the course of true love" could run even?

Seth has mentioned in conversation that, following a convention of Tamil poetry, he also places similarly sounding syllables at the beginnings of the lines—"Since"/"sense," "Phil-"/"Fuel," "A ver-"/"Of our," and "Hap-"/"Hope."

There is as well a kind of approximate rhyme variously termed "slant" or "near" or "off" or "oblique." Such rhymes can be further subdivided into "consonantal" rhymes, involving a correspondence of final consonants but not final vowels (e.g., **fuss/face, moon/bone, balk/hulk**) and "assonantal" rhymes, involving a correspondence of final vowels but not final consonants (e.g., sur**prise/wide, grave/fate, note**/palin**drome**).

English poets interested in slant rhyme have experimented with consonance more than assonance. Two poets who often employ consonantal rhyme are Emily Dickinson and Wilfrid Owen. Characteristic of Dickinson's use of the device is the poem below, a poem written in quatrains of alternating tetrameters and trimeters, with the trimeters rhyming. The rhymes are **stir/door, match/stretch,** and **heal/hell**.

Remorse is memory awake,
Her parties all astir,
A presence of departed acts
At window and at door—

Its past set down before the soul
And lighted with a match,
Perusal to facilitate
And help belief to stretch.

Remorse is cureless, the disease
Not even God can heal;
For 'tis His institution and
The adequate of hell.

If remorse is the "adequate"—the equivalent—of hell, so would be any full account of all the subvarieties of rhyme. As well as those already examined, we could list double-consonant rhymes—rhymes with the same beginning and ending consonants but with different vowels in the middle (e.g., **damp/dump, bat/boat**). Another unusual species is apocopated rhyme, which in its most common form features a monosyllabic word paired with a disyllabic word whose first syllable chimes with the monosyllable (e.g., **tip/hip**po, **glad/rad**ish). "Mosaic rhyme" refers to feminine or triple rhymes in which at least one element is composed of more than one word. The second member of Byron's pos**terity/spare it, he/rarity** series thus produces or is a mosaic rhyme. **Back her/slacker** and **kidney stones/Sidney's tones** are other rhymes of this type. Oliver Wendell Holmes's "At the 'Atlantic' Dinner" has quite a few mosaic matches. Written in anapestics, the poem consists of sixty-eight lines of triple-rhymed couplets. **Catamount/that amount** and ma**hogany/jog any** are a couple of pairings that stick in the mind, as much as the mind would prefer that they didn't. People curious about rhyme at its most dizzyingly byzantine should read Holmes's poem, though they should rest for a few hours after doing so.

3. The Use of Rhyme

All other things being equal, those rhymes will most satisfy which have an element of surprise. For this reason, rhyme words that readily suggest one another (e.g., **breeze/trees, shame/blame, fly/high**) may sound trite to the reader. So, too, rhyme words may disappoint when they are synonymous or antonymous or nearly so (e.g., **light/bright, treasure/pleasure, breath/death, gladness/sadness**). Neither is it usually a good idea to rhyme a simple word with one of its compounds (e.g., **order**/dis**order**, **vision**/pre**vision**) or two compounds of the same class (e.g., con**duce**/intro**duce**). Such a procedure may give the reader the impression that the writer, when ending a line with one word, is not seeking thoughtfully for a mate for it, but is simply snatching the nearest, easiest rhyme available and slapping it down on the page.

It is also wise to make one's rhymes exact, unless one is deliberately working with a pattern of rich rhymes or slant rhymes. Once readers grow accustomed, in perusing a poem, to exact rhymes, an inexact rhyme may sound a false note. It is especially advisable to avoid inexact rhymes that involve pairing a singular noun with a plural of the same form (e.g., **back/cracks, hope/slopes**). Doubtful as well are rhymes in which one of the syllables is not accented (e.g., **pass/car**cass**, for**give**/dismis**sive**), though some critics and poets regard such pairings as daring and sophisticated. It is probably also prudent to be wary of the facile assonantal rhymes (e.g., **run/young** or **mist/kiss**) endemic in pop-song lyrics. Such rhymes are less of a problem in pop music, since they are supported and sometimes obliterated by the musical accompaniment. But in poetry composed for the individual voice and reader, such rhymes produce a sense of slippage.

Since rhymes please most when the words involved make unexpected yet persuasive connections between ideas, objects, and qualities, good rhymers often match different grammatical categories—nouns with verbs, verbs with adjectives, adverbs with nouns, and so forth. And if, when writing, a poet feels that the rhymes are flat, it may be beneficial to check to see whether the same parts of speech are being too regularly chimed. That may be the problem.

In addition, if one rhymes a common word with an unusual one, it may be well to have the unusual word come second. This point may be illustrated by a couplet from Frost's "Evening in a Sugar Orchard." Describing sparks which, rising from a sugarhouse chimney, catch in the bare maples above and form sublunary constellations, the poet says (15–16):

> They were content to figure in the trees
> As Leo, Orion, and the Pleiades.

Would anyone, hearing the initial "trees" termination, anticipate its being answered by "Pleiades"? Yet this word is perfect. It is visually apt. It is, moreover, intellectually striking, concluding as it does the arresting comparison between the small, transitory sparks in the trees and the vast, virtually immutable stellar groups in the heavens. And it is important that "Pleiades" clinches rather than sets up the rhyme. If we flip-flopped the lines, they would still make grammatical sense. But the rhyme would not startle us with the same pleasure.

These comments are pertinent as well to a type of intentionally strained rhyme that involves a fore-stressed trisyllabic word that has, in its final syllable, a "reduced vowel"—an indeterminate sound represented in most dictionaries by an upside-down *e*. This sort of rhyme, which is related to the kind of ambiguous rhyme that Watts discusses, is illustrated by the second and closing couplet of Hilaire Belloc's "Lord Finchley":

> Lord Finchley tried to mend the electric light
> Himself. It struck him dead: And serve him right!
> It is the business of the wealthy man
> To give employment to the artisan.

The tenuous **man**/arti**san** rhyme (and the stagger-and-stop enjambment from line 1 to line 2) well suit the dark humor of the poem. And as Belloc may have realized instinctively, the rhyme is all the more telling for the more complex word's coming second. This sequence encourages us to buck up the final syllable of "artisan" and to convert its reduced vowel back to its full value; and this conversion in turn has the effect of making the rhyme seem more important than poor Lord Finchley's demise. Were we to revise the couplet to read,

> To give employment to the artisan
> Should be the business of the wealthy man.

the rhyme would not be so goofily effective.

Having emphasized the advantages of inventive rhyme, I should add that commonplace rhymes are not inevitably bad. Critics often suggest that poets ought to shun at all costs the more familiar pairings, citing in support of this position Pope's phrase (*Essay on Criticism,* 349) about the "sure returns of still expected rhymes" and his related comment (350–53),

> Where-e'er you find *the cooling western breeze,*
> In the next line, it *whispers through the trees;*
> If *Crystal streams with pleasing murmurs creep,*
> The reader's threaten'd (not in vain) with *sleep,*

Yet a rhymer, especially one writing a longish poem, can hardly help introducing a commonplace match now and then. What causes, in poor verse, an impression of weak rhyming is not so much the banality of this or that rhyme, but rather, as Pope indicates, the presence of other insipidities, such as bromidic diction and clichéd figures of speech. Deployed sparingly, and placed in fresh phrases and sentences, "dull" rhymes can prove as effective as their snazzier brethren.

Demonstration of this point is supplied by Frost, who begins "Into my Own," the first poem in his first book, with the granddaddy of all trite rhymes:

> One of my wishes is that those dark trees,
> So old and firm they scarcely show the breeze . . .

When reading this couplet, however, we do not feel that the rhyme is amateurish. Instead, we are struck by the fine image of the rigid, ancient trees, stiff even when the breeze blows through them. And to mention only a few other instances of extraordinary poems with ordinary rhymes, Shakespeare's

Sonnet 129 ("Th' expense of spirit in a waste of shame") features (1, 3) **shame/blame**; George Herbert's "Antiphon I" introduces (3–4) **high/fly**; and Pope's "Elegy to the Memory of an Unfortunate Lady" (31–32) and Gray's "Elegy Written in a Country Churchyard" (42, 44) both feature **breath/death**.

These comments suggest an additional point. When poets rhyme, they connect not only words, but also phrases, sentences, feelings, and ideas. In "The Constant Symbol," Frost says he felt more confident and less self-conscious as a rhymer when he "came to see words as phrase-ends to countless phrases just as the syllables ly, ing, and ation are word-ends to countless words." If a poem's thoughts are poorly conceived and developed, no amount of ingenious rhyming will redeem it. By the same token, if the larger grammatical and conceptual units correspond gracefully and sincerely, the rhymes will do the same, regardless of how commonplace they may appear in the abstract.

For these reasons, rhyming dictionaries do not necessarily benefit poets. No less than other elements of a poem, rhyme is most effective when rooted in its subject. If stumped for a rhyme for, for instance, "car," poets should work their way mentally through sequences like **are**/Zanzi**bar**/**far**/bi**zarre**, testing words and sounds against the inner ear until something clicks. Simply lifting rhymes out of a book and tucking them into a poem is like buying seedlings from a nursery and thrusting them into the garden without considering whether the soil and sunlight conditions suit the plants.

When all is said and done, poems succeed by means of the acute presentation of subject matter. A poem with arrestingly apt imagery, movingly expressed emotion, or profound thought will, regardless of its rhymes, more impress a reader than a poem that has clever rhymes but little else.

The glossary at the back of this book defines such "fixed forms" as the villanelle, rondeau, ballade, triolet, sestina, and pantoum, but with the exception of the sonnet, these are not historically central to English verse, so I will offer only a few brief and general observations about them here. Fixed forms have a specified number of lines, a particular pattern of rhymes, and (often) refrains or repeated lines. Most fixed forms derive from Romance-language poetry and require that two or three rhymes be sustained over many lines, a requirement harder to meet in English than in the Romance languages. Contrary to what is sometimes said, English has a wonderful wealth and variety of rhymes. However, we do better with rhyme-pairs than with multiple rhymes—rhymes entailing sets of three or more corresponding words or syllables. One reason for this is that English words end in so many different ways, as opposed to, for example, Italian words. Another reason is that rich rhyme, though an interesting variant in Modern English poetry, is not as conventionally satisfying as it is in French or Middle English verse. Yet another reason is that we tend, in Modern English, to place the accent toward the front of words of two or more syllables, a circumstance that renders many words suitable for only feminine rhymes. (Chaucer's rhyming fluency with ballade and rhyme-royal stanzas results not only from his genius, but also from his having the option of giving rear-stressed, Romanic pronunciation to words that in Modern English have become unequivocally fore- or middle-stressed.)

A critical point about fixed forms concerns those with repeating or refrain lines. The poet should try to create a context in which these recurrences are not just repetitions, but take on, with each reappearance, additional meaning. In her fine villanelle, "Lonely Hearts," Wendy Cope exemplifies this procedure, venturing into and developing new areas of feeling even as she recurs to previous lines. Cope's poem deals with personal advertisements of people seeking prospective lovers or mates, and one of its recurring pentameters is:

Can someone make my simple wish come true?

Initially, the line seems straightforward, expressing the desire that we all have to find someone whom we love and who will love us in return. However, as the poem progresses, and as the line comes back again and again, it grows both funnier and sadder. Wishing for love is simple; finding it is not.

An observation might be made about the sonnet, which has proved for English-language poets the most useful of all the fixed forms. The most satisfying sonnets make economical use of each of the form's sub-divisions. To produce a fine sonnet, the poet should make each part contribute to the overall development. This is true whether the poet divides the sonnet, in the Italian fashion, into an octave and sestet, or arranges it, in the English manner, into three quatrains and a concluding couplet, or uses one of the more heterodox sequences sometimes favored by such poets as Tuckerman, Siegfried Sassoon, and Auden.

This consideration is especially pertinent to the English sonnet. Because it falls into three quatrains and a couplet, it is prone to mechanicality. Many fine English sonnets have been written, but others merely introduce a theme in the first quatrain, repeat it with variations in the next two, and, in the couplet, summarize the preceding material. Even Shakespeare can make the English sonnet seem aridly contrapuntal. Consider, for instance, his eighty-fifth sonnet:

> Hearing you praised, I say, "'Tis so, 'tis true,"
> And to the most of praise add something more;
> But that is in my thought, whose love to you,
> Though words come hindmost, holds his rank before.
> I think good thoughts whilst other* write good words,   *others
> And, like unlettered clerk, still cry "Amen"
> To every hymn that able spirit affords
> In polished form of well-refinëd pen.
> My tongue-tied Muse in manners holds her still
> While comments of your praise, richly compiled,
> Reserve their character with golden quill
> And precious phrase by all the Muses filed.
>   Then others for the breath of words respect,
>   Me for my dumb thoughts, speaking in effect.

For all its grace, this sonnet is structurally inert. Indeed, I have reversed the order of the three quatrains, so that the version above opens with lines 9 through 12, proceeds with lines 5 through 8, moves on to lines 1 through 4, then closes with the couplet. Not a word is changed. Despite this scrambling of the form, no transition is violated, no train of thought is derailed. It would be churlish to criticize Shakespeare, since he has bequeathed us such a rich and joyous legacy of verse. But a poem which can be thus re-arranged, with no damage to its argument, is not using its formal potentials as fully as it might.

Though the form of the Italian sonnet is more exigent than that of the English sonnet, the Italian structure perhaps has greater musical complexities and encourages more energetic development. The octave's *abbaabba* rhyme scheme can be treated as two envelope stanzas, with the "a" rhymes embracing the "b's." Yet the octave has as well three couplet rhymes (running from lines 2 to 7), and another envelope stanza (running from lines 3 to 6), though in this case it is the "b" rhymes that envelop the "a's." And this fluid interrelationship of the octave's rhymes, plus the historical preference for avoiding in the sestet a closing couplet (*cdecde* is the most common sestet rhyme sequence), may check the repetitive quality that afflicts many English sonnets.

As was suggested early in this chapter, rhyme is a natural outgrowth of our gift for and delight in speech. Rhyme seems to satisfy a basic human desire for symmetry and surprise, for resemblances and contrasts. Well-presented rhyme is, in all its varieties, pleasurable. And there is no better way to conclude this chapter than to cite Robert Burns's remarks, in one of his poems in the Scottish dialect ("Epistle to James Smith," 25–30), about his own love of rhyme:

> Some rhyme a neebor's name to lash;
> Some rhyme (vain thought!) for needfu' cash;
> Some rhyme to court the countra clash*   *gossip
>   An' raise a din;
> For me, an aim I never fash;*   *I never trouble about an aim
>   I rhyme for fun.

7

Stanzas

ADMIRERS OF BURNS will have recognized that the excerpt that closes the previous chapter is, in a formal sense, characteristic of the poet's work. Burns often arranges his poems in groups of six lines, the first, second, third, and fifth of which are iambic tetrameters that all rhyme together and the fourth and sixth of which are iambic dimeters that chime with each other. This arrangement appears not only in many of his verse epistles, such as the one to James Smith, but also in his two satirical masterpieces, "To a Louse" and "Holy Willie's Prayer." Here are the opening twelve lines of the latter, a monologue spoken by a smug religious hypocrite. The lines refer to and distort the doctrine that if we receive God's blessing, we do so as a result of His grace rather than of our works.

> O Thou that in the Heavens does dwell,
> Wha,* as it pleases best Thysel,   *Who
> Sends ane* to Heaven an' ten to Hell   *one
>   A'* for Thy glory,   *All
> And no for onie guid or ill*   *And not for any good or ill
>   They've done before Thee!
>
> I bless and praise Thy matchless might,
> When thousands Thou has left in night,
> That I am here before Thy sight,
>   For gifts an' grace,
> A burning and a shining light
>   To a' this place.

Indeed, so frequently and spiritedly does the poet use this six-line unit that, though he did not originate it, we identify it with him. We call it "Burns stanza."

This phrase reminds us that poets not only write in metrical lines, but also sometimes organize those lines into stanzas. A stanza may be defined as a group of lines arranged in a pattern that specifies the number of lines in the group, their meter, and the sequence of their rhymes. Customarily, this pattern is established at the beginning of a poem and repeats thereafter for as long as the poem continues. The stanzas are, in other words, structurally identical. They feature "responsion." As the poem proceeds, they answer one another.

The Oxford English Dictionary reports that "stanza" ultimately derives from the Latin verb *stare,* "to stand" and that our word descends from the Italian *stanza,* meaning "stopping place, room." Art lovers will recall that *stanze,* the plural of the Italian word, is applied to that suite of rooms in the Vatican for which Raphael painted his celebrated frescoes. The most stunning of these, *The School of Athens,* is in the Stanza della Segnatura, where the Papal tribunal met to discuss matters of canon law (hence the name "Room of the [Papal] Seal").

John Donne alludes to the etymology of "stanza" when in "The Canonization" he says (31–32) to his beloved:

> And if no piece of chronicle we prove,
> We'll build in sonnets pretty rooms.

Donne is telling his love that if their romance is not deemed appropriate for a lengthy history, then they will record it in short poems composed of elegant stanzas—"pretty rooms." (Until at least the middle of the eighteenth century, "sonnet" denoted not only the fourteen-line verse genre, but also lyrical poems in general. In addition, until the early eighteenth century, "pretty" meant, to cite the *OED* once more, "ingenious, artful, clever," salient qualities of Donne's often fiendishly intricate stanzas.)

Though a few texts use "stanza" to refer to any recurring group of two or more lines, most authorities suggest that stanzas have a minimum of four lines. "[A]n arrangement of a certain number of lines, usually four or more," is the way that *The Random House Dictionary of the English Language* puts it. Two-line units are commonly termed "couplets" and three-line units "tercets" or "triplets." These last two words in turn have differing connotations, which we will distinguish later in this chapter.

Stanzas usually involve rhyme, and the sequence of rhymes is customarily one of the defining characteristics of a stanzaic structure. Such sequences are called "rhyme schemes" and are commonly registered by a kind of prosodic algebra. For example, the rhyme scheme of Burns stanza is *aaabab*.

Historically speaking, nonrhyming stanzaic poems are rare in our verse, and when they appear they are for the most part written not in accordance with native measures but in imitation of stanzaic forms of classical lyric verse. These include the sapphic stanza (or "strophe" to use the ancient word most nearly equivalent to "stanza") and the alcaic stanza. Ancient Greek and Latin verse does not feature end rhyme, and English-language poets working in these ancient stanzas have usually followed the ancient practice of not rhyming them. In the ninth chapter, we will discuss classical stanzas and English adaptations of them.

In the past one hundred and fifty years, however, nonrhyming stanzaic poems do appear increasingly in English. An early example is Tennyson's "Tears, Idle Tears," which consists of four five-line stanzas in blank verse. (Even this poem alludes in form to a five-line strophe that Theocritus sometimes uses in his *Idylls*, though Tennyson does not try to write in or suggest Theocritus's meter.) Wallace Stevens is a twentieth-century poet who favors nonrhyming stanzas, usually of blank verse. His "Sunday Morning," for example, consists of eight fifteen-line stanzas of rhymeless iambic pentameter, and his "Monocle de Mon Oncle," also in blank verse, has twelve eleven-line stanzas.

Stanzas serve chiefly two functions. The first is indicated by the word's original meaning. Just as rooms can divide an apartment or building into subunits that enable people to organize different facets of domestic or professional life, so stanzas can partition a poem in such a way as to help poet and reader alike find their way through its components. To be sure, perspicuous organization is possible in nonstanzaic forms. Yet the poet can, in composing stanzaic verse, give aural-spatial shape to the parts of a narrative or an idea; and the reader can, in reading stanzaic verse, readily see the relationships between those parts.

We can appreciate the organizational capacity of stanzas by examining the eighteenth poem of Housman's *Shropshire Lad*:

> Oh, when I was in love with you,
>   Then I was clean and brave,

And miles around the wonder grew
   How well I did behave.

And now the fancy passes by,
   And nothing will remain,
And miles around they'll say that I
   Am quite myself again.

This poem juxtaposes life with love and life without it. When we fall in love, we feel ennobled. When love fails us—or when we fail it—we lapse back into our customary ignobility. And the juxtaposition is pointed by Housman's having divided the poem into two stanzas, each of which discusses one of the contrasting states. Though Housman could have written the poem in six or seven blank-verse lines or in several heroic couplets, its rueful humor would probably not have been as memorable. The stanzaic structure provides us with an immediate purchase on the thematic and emotional elements of the poem.

The second basic function of stanzas is musical. Stanzas permit the poet to experiment with patterns of rhymes, to mix together lines of different lengths, and to achieve thereby verbal melodies unattainable in nonstanzaic verse—verse which repeats the same metrical unit over and over (e.g., blank verse) or which merely rhymes adjacent lines of the same length (e.g., the heroic couplet).

Metrists have various names for stanzas. As was noted in the previous chapter, four-line stanzas are called "quatrains," though this term tells us only that the stanzas have four lines and says nothing about the lengths of those lines or the sequence of their rhymes. These more particular characteristics may be indicated by additional terms, three of which derive from hymnology and seem to have been popularized by the hymnist Isaac Watts in his preface to *The Psalms of David Imitated in the Language of the New Testament and Applied to the Christian State and Worship* (1719). Introducing the section of his preface titled "Of the Metre and Rhyme," Watts writes: "I have formed my verse in the three most useful metres to which our psalm-tunes are fitted: namely, the common metre; the metre of the old xxvth psalm, which I call short metre; and that of the old cth psalm, which I call long metre."

"Common meter"—so named because it is so prevalent in hymns and other species of short poems—is a quatrain rhyming *abab* and alternating between iambic tetrameter and iambic trimeter. It is the stanzaic form that

Housman employs in the poem cited above. A well-known hymn in common meter is Watts's "Our God, our help in ages past."

Scarcely less common than common meter, "long meter" is a quatrain of cross-rhyming iambic tetrameters. It may be illustrated by Elinor Wylie's "Cold-Blooded Creatures":

> Man, the egregious egoist
> (In mystery the twig is bent)
> Imagines, by some mental twist,
> That he alone is sentient
>
> Of the intolerable load
> That on all living creatures lies,
> Nor stoops to pity in the toad
> The speechless sorrow of his eyes.
>
> He asks no questions of the snake,
> Nor plumbs the phosphorescent gloom
> Where lidless fishes, broad awake,
> Swim staring at a night-mare doom.

Some writers also include under the heading of "long meter" quatrains of tetrameters rhyming *aabb*.

"Short meter" consists of quatrains whose first two lines are trimeters, whose third is a tetrameter, and whose fourth is another trimeter. The second and fourth of these lines rhyme. Lines 1 and 3, however, may be rhymed or unrhymed at the poet's discretion. An outstanding short-metered poem which rhymes its odd-numbered as well as its even-numbered lines is Hardy's "I Look into My Glass." A fine short-metered poem that leaves lines 1 and 3 unrhymed is Emily Dickinson's "I never saw a moor":

> I never saw a moor,
> I never saw the sea;
> Yet know I how the heather looks
> And what a billow be.
>
> I never spoke with God,
> Nor visited in heaven;
> Yet certain am I of the spot
> As if the checks were given.

A related term, not mentioned by Watts, is "half meter," which refers to quatrains, usually cross-rhyming, of iambic trimeter. A number of twentieth-century American poets have used this stanza to fine effect, including Louise Bogan ("Homunculus"), Yvor Winters ("An October Nocturne"), Theodore Roethke ("My Papa's Waltz"), Richard Wilbur ("To His Skeleton"), Anthony Hecht ("It Out-Herods Herod. Pray You, Avoid It"), and Helen Pinkerton ("Good Friday").

"Ballad meter"—or, as it is sometimes called, "ballad stanza"—consists of four lines that alternate between iambic tetrameter and iambic trimeter. As such, the form is like common meter. But whereas lines 1 and 3 as well as 2 and 4 rhyme in common meter, in ballad stanzas only 2 and 4 rhyme. An early nineteenth-century poem in ballad stanzas is Christian Milne's "Sent with a Flower-Pot Begging a Slip of Geranium":

> I've sent my empty pot again
> To beg another slip;
> The last you gave, I'm grieved to tell,
> December's frost did nip.
>
> I love fair Flora and her train
> But nurse her children ill;
> I tend too little, or too much;
> They die from want of skill.
>
> I blush to trouble you again,
> Who've served me oft before;
> But, should this die, I'll break the pot
> And trouble you no more.

Different people may use the same stanza name to mean different things. Ambiguities abound with regard to "ballad" and "ballad stanzas." Though these are widely understood to indicate quatrains of alternating tetrameters and trimeters, with only the trimeters rhyming, poets will on occasion rhyme all four lines of their quatrains and still call the result "a ballad," as John Clare does in his "Ballad" beginning, "We'll walk among the tedded hay." Likewise, a recent editor says of Cowper's "Epitaph on an Hare," a poem in quatrains of tetrameters and trimeters rhyming *abab,* that it is "is written in common ballad metre"—thus conflating "ballad meter" and "common meter." Further, we now and then find "ballads" whose stanzas have more than four lines. An example is Oscar Wilde's "Ballad of Reading Gaol," which —though alternating in conventional ballad-style between unrhymed tetrameters and rhymed trimeters—features stanzas of six rather than four lines. In Auden's "Ballad of Barnaby," we find quatrains that feature couplet rhymes rather than cross rhymes; what is more, the lines do not alternate between four and three stresses, but rather all have four beats. For that matter, the word "ballad" may be applied to any work of a romantic or sad character, as is the case with Carson McCullers's prose novella, *The Ballad of the Sad Café*. Lastly, if some writers use "ballad" broadly, others urge that the term should be restricted to the sorts of popular verses and folk songs collected in volumes like Thomas Percy's *Reliques of Ancient English Poetry* and F. J. Child's *English and Scottish Popular Ballads*. Though such ballads customarily follow an accentual pattern of four-three-four-three, they are often looser in meter than are the ballads of more consciously literary poets like, for example, Wordsworth.

We need not dwell upon such terminological tangles. Knowing that they exist, however, may prevent our being confused by them.

In the Renaissance, two stanzaic forms are lineated differently than they are today. Poems that sound to us as if they are in ballad meter are printed as rhyming iambic heptameter couplets. These are also called "fourteeners." Because the seven-foot lines usually break after the fourth foot, and because the couplets themselves tend to be grammatically and conceptually complete, they have the effect of stanzas of alternating tetrameters and trimeters, with the trimeters rhyming. For example, when we read these fourteeners (9–12) from Robert Southwell's "Burning Babe,"

> My faultless breast the furnace is, the fuel wounding thorns;
> Love is the fire, and sighs the smoke, the ashes shame and scorns.
> The fuel justice layeth on, and mercy blows the coals;
> The metal in this furnace wrought are men's defilëd souls.

we are likely to hear:

> My faultless breast the furnace is,
>   The fuel wounding thorns;
> Love is the fire, and sighs the smoke,
>   The ashes shame and scorns.
> The fuel justice layeth on,
>   And mercy blows the coals;
> The metal in this furnace wrought
>   Are men's defilëd souls.

In fact, when Arthur Quiller-Couch included "The Burning Babe" in his *Oxford Book of English Verse*, he printed the couplets in this fashion. Such a departure from the original lineation is an editorial no-no, but one can see Quiller-Couch's point. While his revision changes our visual sense of the poem, the rhythm is the same.

Some Renaissance poets who write fourteeners try to avoid the regular tetrameter-plus-trimeter effect of the measure. For instance, in his translation of Homer's *Iliad*, George Chapman is careful to enjamb the line now and then and to introduce grammatical pauses at different places within the line, though even in Chapman's hands, the line often breaks down into the shorter measures. (That Chapman himself may have grown dissatisfied with the fourteener is suggested by his having dropped it in favor of the heroic couplet when he later translated *The Odyssey*.) And despite its more recent association with or transformation into the ballad stanza, poets originally regarded the fourteener as, on account of its length, a possible equivalent of the ancient heroic hexameter. Indeed, perhaps the most interesting English verse in fourteeners is in Chapman's *Iliad* and Arthur Golding's translation of Ovid's *Metamorphoses*. Though these works are not widely read today, poets have always prized them; in a famous sonnet, Keats celebrates the former, and, in *ABC of Reading*, Pound generously and rightly praises the latter.

The term "ballad meter" seems not to have become common until the Romantic period, which witnessed, as was noted in our fourth chapter, a rise of interest in ballads and other forms of popular verse. This was long after the vogue of fourteeners, lineated as such, had passed. In 1755, in the "Grammar of the English Tongue" section of his *Dictionary*, Samuel Johnson, though not actually speaking of "ballad meter," indicates the conceptual change that the fourteener had undergone: "The verse of fourteen syllables is now broken into a soft lyric measure of verses consisting alternately of eight syllables and six."

However, here and there in Romantic and post-Romantic verse, the fourteener survives. Thomas Hood's "The Desert-Born," Wordsworth's "Star-Gazers" and Frances Cornford's "At the End" all feature heptameters lineated in the old manner. A famous American poem in fourteeners is Ernest Lawrence Thayer's "Casey at the Bat," the first quatrain of which appears below:

> The outlook wasn't brilliant for the Mudville nine that day;
> The score stood four to two with but one inning more to play.
> And then when Cooney died at first and Barrows did the same,
> A sickly silence fell upon the patrons of the game.

Just as ballad meter has a differently lineated Renaissance equivalent, so does short meter. Here the Renaissance analogue is "poulter's measure," which consists of rhyming couplets whose first line is an iambic hexameter and whose second is an iambic heptameter. This form is embodied in Surrey's "When summer took in hand," which opens:

> When summer took in hand the winter to assail
> With force of might and virtue great, his stormy blasts to quail,
> And when he clothëd fair the earth about with green,
> And every tree new garmented that pleasure was to seen,
> My heart 'gan new revive, and changëd blood did stir
> Me to withdraw my winter woe, that kept within my door.

Here the hexameters divide into two three-foot units, and the heptameters into four- and three-foot units. Consequently, we experience not just a succession of couplets, but also a sequence of short-metered quatrains:

> When summer took in hand
> The winter to assail
> With force of might and virtue great,
> His stormy blasts to quail . . .

(In his *Certain Notes Concerning the Making of Verse or Rhyme in English* of 1575, George Gascoigne explains that "poulter's measure" comes from a custom among poultry-men, who "giveth xii for one dozen and xiiii for another.")

Stanzaic verse often features indented lines. Poets indent principally for two reasons. First, indentations can mark length variations among the lines of a stanza. Indentations, that is, can enable the poet to distinguish visually on the page the longer from the shorter lines. Robert Herrick, for example, employs indentations for this purpose in "To the Yew and Cypress to Grace his Funeral." Herrick writes the poem in quatrains whose iambic lines follow a sequence of dimeter, trimeter, monometer, and tetrameter. And to cue readers to this arrangement, he justifies the longest line to the left-hand margin and indents the other three in proportion to their brevity—the trimeters slightly, the dimeters moderately, and the monometers severely:

> Both you two have
> Relation to the grave;
> And where
> The Fun'ral-Trump sounds, you are there.

I shall be made
Ere long a fleeting shade:
Pray come,
And do some honor to my tomb.

Do not deny
My last request; for I
Will be
Thankful to you, or friends, for me.

The second reason for indenting is to highlight rhyme pairs. If a poem's rhymes involve either a crossing or an embracing scheme—if any of the rhymes is suspended and a line or more intervenes before the rhyme is answered—the poet can, by indenting, enable the reader to perceive in a glance the suspension. Tennyson's *In Memoriam,* which features iambic tetrameter quatrains rhyming *abba,* illustrates this procedure. Though all the lines in the stanza are tetrameters, Tennyson sets the second and third in from the left-hand margin, so as to throw into relief their rhyme correspondence. This at the same time emphasizes the correspondence between the unindented first and fourth lines. It is as if the arrangement says to the reader, "Now the first line is not going to be rhymed immediately. But don't panic. After matching the indented second and third lines, we'll move back out to the left-hand margin, and we'll chime line four with line one." Below is the twenty-seventh section of *In Memoriam*:

I envy not in any moods
The captive void of noble rage,
The linnet born within the cage
That never knew the summer woods;

I envy not the beast that takes
His license in the field of time,
Unfetter'd by the sense of crime,
To whom a conscience never wakes;

Nor, what may count itself as blest,
The heart that never plighted troth
But stagnates in the weeds of sloth:
Nor any want-begotten rest.

I hold it true, whate'er befall;
I feel it, when I suffer most;

> 'Tis better to have loved and lost
> Than never to have loved at all.

Because *In Memoriam* is the best-known instance of this stanza, some hand-books call it "*In Memoriam* stanza." Tennyson, however, did not invent the form, which appears as early as Ben Jonson's "Elegy" ("Though beauty be the mark of praise").

Often, indentation serves simultaneously the two functions that we have been examining. Poets will indent to distinguish shorter lines from longer ones, while rhyming the long lines with other long lines and the short lines with other short lines. In Housman's "O, when I was in love with you," for instance, the indentations signify not only that the trimeters are shorter than the tetrameters, but also that the trimeters rhyme among themselves while the tetrameters likewise rhyme together. So, too, in Burns's six-line stanza, the indented fourth and sixth lines not only are dimeters as opposed to the tetrameters prevailing elsewhere in the stanza, they also rhyme with each other.

Because indentation can alert us to rhyme-pairings and to differences and correspondences between line lengths, the device is especially useful in signaling structural properties of complex stanzas. We can explore this point by considering George Herbert's "The Flower," the first two stanzas of which run:

> How fresh, O Lord, how sweet and clean
> Are thy returns! Ev'n as the flowers in spring,
> To which, besides their own demean,*   *demesne
> The late-past frosts tributes of pleasure bring.
> Grief melts away
> Like snow in May,
> As if there were no such cold thing.

> Who would have thought my shrivel'd heart
> Could have recover'd greenness? It was gone
> Quite underground, as flowers depart
> To see their mother-root when they have blown;
> Where they together
> All the hard weather,
> Dead to the world, keep house unknown.

The arrangement of lines on the page helps us to see that the moderately in-dented first, third, and seventh lines are iambic tetrameters, that the unindented second and fourth lines are iambic pentameters, and that the severely indented fifth and sixth lines are iambic dimeters. The arrangement also helps us to grasp the rhyme scheme, which runs *ababccb,* though the indentations do not entirely reflect this pattern. Whereas the first two tetrameters rhyme with each other, and while the pentameters and trimeters rhyme with their mates, the slightly indented final tetrameter rhymes not with the earlier tetrameters, but with the unindented pentameters.

While experienced readers will usually be able to discern the purpose of indentations that appear in this or that poem, the device has never been consistently practiced. A poet may on one occasion employ indentation for a certain stanzaic form and then on another occasion use the same stanza without indenting anything in it. Wordsworth, for example, employs common meter for four of his "Lucy" poems; in three of these, he indents the even-numbered lines, but in one ("Strange Fits of Passion Have I Known") he aligns everything with the left-hand margin. Likewise, Frost uses ballad stanzas for both "Stars" and "The Peaceful Shepherd," indenting lines 2 and 4 in the stanzas of the first poem, but setting to the left-hand margin all the lines of the second poem.

Further, though indentation frequently distinguishes shorter lines from longer ones, poets may indent long lines more than or instead of short ones. This occurs, for example, in the hymn section of Milton's "On the Morning of Christ's Nativity." Milton writes this portion of the poem in stanzas of eight iambic lines, whose sequence runs trimeter, trimeter, pentameter, trimeter, trimeter, pentameter, tetrameter, and hexameter. And as can be seen from this, the fourth stanza of the hymn, Milton aligns with the left-hand margin all of the trimeters (along with the hexameter), whereas he indents the two pentameters:

> No war or battle's sound
> Was heard the world around:
>> The idle spear and shield were high up hung;
> The hookèd chariot stood
> Unstained with hostile blood;
>> The trumpet spake not to the armèd throng,
> And kings sat still with awful eye,
> As if they surely knew their sovran Lord was by.

Indentational variants turn up as well in certain of the fixed forms, particularly Petrarchan sonnets. Some sonneteers align, as Robinson does in "The Clerks," all fourteen lines with the left-hand margin. Milton, on the other hand, takes an approach derived from standard editions of the sonnets of Dante and Petrarch, an approach involving what we today call "hanging indents." It places the first, fifth, ninth, and twelfth lines against the left-hand margin and indents the rest of the lines an equal distance to the right. We can see this procedure in the first of the two sonnets that Milton wrote for Cyriack Skinner, a student and friend of the poet, and the grandson of Edward Coke, the famous judge and legal scholar.

> Cyriack, whose grandsire on the royal bench
>> Of British Themis, with no mean applause
>> Pronounced, and in his volumes taught, our laws,
>> Which others at their bar so often wrench:
> Today deep thoughts resolve with me to drench
>> In mirth, that after no repenting draws;
>> Let Euclid rest, and Archimedes pause,
>> And what the Swede intend, and what the French.
> To measure life, learn thou betimes, and know
>> Toward solid good what leads the nearest way;
>> For other things mild Heav'n a time ordains,
> And disapproves that care, though wise in show
>> That with superfluous burden loads the day,
>> And, when God sends a cheerful hour, refrains.

Thus indented, the Petrarchan sonnet is seen not only as an octave and sestet, but also as two quatrains and two tercets—the poet registering this structure by leaving at the left margin the first line of each of the four divisions.

Other poets writing Petrarchan sonnets use indentation to mark rhyme arrangement. Keats does this in "On the Grasshopper and Cricket." In the octave, he indents the *b* rhymes to distinguish them from the *a* rhymes. In the sestet, he aligns the *c* rhymes with the left-hand margin, indents the *d* rhymes a little, and indents the *e* rhymes even further.

> The poetry of earth is never dead:
>> When all the birds are faint with the hot sun,
>> And hide in cooling trees, a voice will run
> From hedge to hedge about the new-mown mead;
> That is the Grasshopper's—he takes the lead
>> In summer luxury,—he has never done
>> With his delights; for when tired out with fun
> He rests at ease beneath some pleasant weed.
> The poetry of earth is ceasing never:

> On a lone winter evening, when the frost
> > Has wrought a silence, from the stove there shrills
> The Cricket's song, in warmth increasing ever,
> And seems to one in drowsiness half lost,
> > The Grasshopper's among some grassy hills.

English sonnets, on account of their simpler rhyme scheme, offer fewer options for indentive poets. Even here, however, enough mutations exist to frazzle a person trying to summarize them. Sometimes all lines are aligned with the left-hand margin. Sometimes this arrangement is varied by indenting the closing couplet. Sometimes a poet will indent the even-numbered lines, in order to mark the alternating rhyme pairs, and align the couplet with the left-hand margin. Keats follows this latter scheme in several of his English sonnets, including his amusing and trenchant sonnet on Fame ("Fame, like a wayward girl, will still be coy").

In long poems in blank verse (e.g., Milton's *Paradise Lost*) or heroic couplets (e.g., Pope's *The Rape of the Lock*), indentation may be used to mark transitions from one passage to another. In other words, poets may use indentation just as prose writers do—to signal the start of a new paragraph. Indeed, students of poetry sometimes speak of "paragraphs" in connection with substantial sections, of variable length, of long poems.

If contemporary editions often ignore elisions in early poetry, so they often ignore indentations that poets originally designed. It is not unusual to see, for instance, all the lines of Milton's and Keats's sonnets aligned with the left-hand margin, and in current anthologies, Gray's "Elegy Written in a Country Churchyard" is equally likely to appear with or without the second and fourth lines of its quatrains indented. (Gray intended those lines to be indented.) It is futile to weep and wail about the decline in appreciation of indentation, but neither is our editorial haphazardness a cause for celebration.

In addition to their other functions, stanzas can serve expressive purposes. In an earlier chapter, we noted how poets can dispose lines—end-stopping one here and enjambing one there—so as to sharpen and vivify aspects of their subject matter. In much the same manner, poets can manipulate stanzas—now closing them up, now running them on—with a view to rendering as precisely as possible a quality of movement, image, or idea.

Richard Wilbur's "Hamlen Brook" provides excellent examples of ways in which stanzaic management can be lively and significant. The lines in this poem are iambic (with some anapestic substitutions) and are arranged in quatrains that rhyme *abba* and that follow a trimeter-tetrameter-pentameter-trimeter sequence.

> At the alder-darkened brink
> Where the stream slows to a lucid jet
> I lean to the water, dinting its top with sweat,
> And see, before I can drink,
>
> A startled inchling trout
> Of spotted near-transparency,
> Trawling a shadow solider than he.
> He swerves now, darting out
>
> To where, in a flicked slew
> Of sparks and glittering silt, he weaves
> Through stream-bed rocks, disturbing foundered leaves,
> And butts then out of view
>
> Beneath a sliding glass
> Crazed by the skimming of a brace
> Of burnished dragon-flies across its face,
> In which deep cloudlets pass
>
> And a white precipice
> Of mirrored birch-trees plunges down
> Toward where the azures of the zenith drown.
> How shall I drink all this?
>
> Joy's trick is to supply
> Dry lips with what can cool and slake,
> Leaving them dumbstruck also with an ache
> Nothing can satisfy.

Wilbur communicates the rich complexities and movement of the natural world not only by the line-enjambments (e.g., " . . . he weaves / Through stream-bed rocks . . ." and " . . . a white precipice / Of mirrored birch-trees plunges down / Toward where . . ."), but also by letting the stanzas overflow from one to another during that long sentence that runs from the eighth to the nineteenth line. Just as, for instance, the minnow trout "darts out" from shallows along the bank, so the stanza describing this flight shoots away from and beyond its margins into the next stanza. And just as the minnow "butts out of view" at the end of the third stanza, so the stanza itself disappears into its successor. It would be wrong to say that the stanza replicates the fluid multiplicity of subject, since at every point the poet is sensitively guiding the verse; yet the stanzaic movement is vitally correlated with the subject, and we, as readers, feel the scene all the more strongly because of this correlation.

Wilbur's poem raises another important point. Just as varying its rhythmical modulations gives a metrical line fluidity and spirit, varying the kinds of sentences within a stanza may lend it life and energy. As do meters and rhymes, stanzas can enchant us by manifesting similarity in dissimilarity and dissimilarity in similarity. Their repeating structure makes stanzas identical, while the varying shapes and lengths of the sentences that poets lay into or across them makes them different. A pleasing element of "Hamlen Brook" is that, after giving us that extended sentence running from the end of the second stanza through the penultimate line of the fifth stanza, Wilbur concludes the fifth stanza with a short interrogative sentence: "How shall I drink all this?" This syntactical shift nicely modulates the stanza to its conclusion and signals the imminent summary statement and close of the poem.

Interesting correlations between meaning and stanzaic management also occur in Philip Larkin's "Whitsun Weddings." This poem features eight ten-line stanzas that rhyme *ababcdecde,* all the lines being iambic pentameters except for the second, which is an iambic dimeter. The poem describes a railway journey, from Hull in northeastern England down to London, that the poet takes on Whitsunday weekend. Whitsunday commemorates the descent, related in the second chapter of Acts, of the Holy Spirit on the Apostles on the day of Pentecost. The holiday falls on the seventh Sunday after Easter, hence in late May or early June and hence at a time of year popular for weddings. The first two stanzas of the poem tell of the train's departure from the station in Hull and of the countryside through which the train passes in the earlier stages of the journey. Each of these stanzas concludes with a period. During the third stanza, however, the poet notices that, at every station where the train pauses, just-married couples are climbing aboard to begin their honeymoons. And at this juncture, Larkin opens the stanza up, and the movement of the poem shifts:

> At first, I didn't notice what a noise
>   The weddings made
> Each station that we stopped at: sun destroys
> The interest of what's happening in the shade,
> And down the long cool platforms whoops and skirls

I took for porters larking with the mails,
And went on reading. Once we started, though,
We passed them, grinning and pomaded, girls
In parodies of fashion, heels and veils,
All posed irresolutely, watching us go,

As if out on the end of an event
    Waving goodbye
To something that survived it. Struck, I leant
More promptly out next time, more curiously,
And saw it all again in different terms:
The fathers with broad belts under their suits
And seamy foreheads; mothers loud and fat;
An uncle shouting smut; and then the perms,
The nylon gloves and jewellery-substitutes,
The lemons, mauves, and olive-ochres that

Marked off the girls unreally from the rest.
    Yes, from cafés
And banquet-halls up yards, and bunting-dressed
Coach-party annexes, the wedding-days
Were coming to an end. . . .

Notice the transition from the first to the second of these stanzas. Speaking of the girls who attended the wedding and who are now seeing their married friend off into her new life, Larkin says that they seem

All posed irresolutely, watching us go

As if out on the end of an event
    Waving goodbye
To something that survived it. . . .

This releasing of the stanza into its successor accomplishes two things. First, it conveys a sense of the train's departure. Just as the train leaves the station, so the stanza advances out of its enclosure into a new development of thought. Second, the stanza's run-on reinforces the feeling, on the part of the watching girls, that a person and a situation they long have known is going away from them and in some respects will never return. It may be extreme of the poet to suggest, if this is what he is suggesting, that when a friend marries, her earlier relationships do not "survive." But earlier ties are altered. And the way that the description of the girls is suspended at the end of the stanza contributes to our appreciation of their pathos. They are left on a physical and psychic platform or promontory, while the couple newly transformed by marriage is moving out with the train.

Much the same movement accompanies the transition from the stanza describing the apparel of the young women to the stanza mentioning that the wedding days are drawing to a close. In the running-on of the first of these stanzas, and in the isolation, at the top of the second, of the phrase about the girls' being "[m]arked off . . . unreally from the rest," we have an aural and visual intimation of the girls' distinctness. The stanza-break marks them off no less than does their colorful apparel, and the very line that mentions this quality stands by itself, neither grammatically a part of the stanza it introduces nor organically a part of the stanza in which it originates.

Long stanzas like the one Larkin uses in "The Whitsun Weddings" have special potentials. Stanzaic extension encourages complication of syntax and argument. Such complication is not necessarily beneficial. If uncontrolled, it can lead to elaboration for its own sake. Well managed, however, an extended stanza may give the poet more room than a shorter stanza might to move between image and idea, or between event and meditation on event.

More specifically, extended stanzas seem particularly to suit a kind of middle-length poem—a poem of, say, fifty to one hundred lines—well represented by such works as Keats's "Ode to a Nightingale" and "Ode on a Grecian Urn," Yeats's "Prayer for My Daughter," Winters's "California Oaks," and Larkin's "Whitsun Weddings" and "Church Going." Though these poems differ in many respects from one another, they all combine lyrical grace with a thematic and argumentative richness that we customarily encounter only in much longer poems or in such prose forms as the essay, short story, or novel. On the page, these poems sometimes look like the neoclassical odes of Milton and Dryden. Yet they escape the ceremonial effusiveness that makes those earlier poems easier to admire than to enjoy.

This is not to imply that "The Whitsun Weddings" is better than more simply arranged poems such as Dickinson's "I never saw a moor," which is, in its memorable compactness, as exemplary a poem as Larkin's. Nor do I wish to imply that relatively simple stanzas are incapable of sophistications of argument or narrative. The quatrains of Wilbur's "Hamlen Brook" perfectly capture and follow complicated perceptions of and reflections about our physical universe; and, to cite another poem, Edgar Bowers's "The Stoic" presents, in straightforward pentameter quatrains, a powerful and detailed meditation on the effects of war on the human spirit. The point is merely that one can do things in extended stanzas that one cannot do in simpler forms—and vice versa.

Poets interested in creating a complex stanza may do so by combining two or more simpler ones. For instance, the ten-line stanzas Keats uses in his odes about the Nightingale, Melancholy, the Grecian Urn, and Indolence consist of the opening quatrain of an English sonnet, followed by the sestet of an Italian sonnet. The first four lines of the stanzas are alternately rhymed pentameters; the remaining six pentameters have three additional rhymes. (This pattern is varied, however, in the Nightingale ode, in which the eighth lines of the stanzas are trimeters instead of pentameters. The Autumn ode, having an eleven-line stanza, is a variation on the English-quatrain-plus-Italian-sestet technique.) The stanza that Larkin employs for "The Whitsun Weddings" follows the same principle of fusing a cross-rhyming quatrain with a Petrarchan sestet, though Larkin makes the second line of each stanza a dimeter rather a pentameter.

One can also invent, as Herbert and Hardy often do, complex stanzas more or less out of thin air—stanzas, that is, like those of "The Flower" that do not readily or neatly resolve themselves into simpler and more familiar forms.

In addition to stanzas already mentioned, several stanzas of fixed length have been adopted by English-language poets. One of these is *ottava rima*, which we illustrated in our previous chapter. Another fixed stanza important in English poetry is "rhyme royal." This has seven lines of iambic pentameter, rhyming *ababbcc*. Chaucer employs the stanza in *Troilus and Criseyde*, as well in most of his short lyrics, including "Gentilesse," one of the great ethical poems of our language. Later poems in rhyme royal include John Davies's *Orchestra* and Shakespeare's *Rape of Lucrece*. An excellent recent poem that uses the stanza is Thom Gunn's "Merlin in the Cave: He Speculates without a Book."

Though not a stanza by the four-line-or-longer criterion, *terza rima* deserves mention here. It involves interlocking tercets, rhyming *aba bcb cdc* . . . , and was invented by Dante for his *Divine Comedy*. *Terza rima* has not been much used in our poetry, because of the difficulty of sustaining in English the three-part, interlocking rhymes. However, Wyatt uses the form for his verse epistles to John Poins and Francis Brian. Certain poets, moreover, have fused the form with the sonnet by following four interlocking tercets with a closing couplet that rhymes with the middle line of the fourth tercet. We see this procedure in Frost's "Acquainted with the Night," Larkin's

"Whatever Happened?" and Shelley's five-sonnet sequence "Ode to the West Wind." The final piece of the sequence appears below:

> Make me thy lyre, even as the forest is:
> What if my leaves are falling like its own!
> The tumult of thy mighty harmonies
>
> Will take from both a deep autumnal tone,
> Sweet though in sadness. Be thou, Spirit fierce,
> My spirit! Be thou me, impetuous one!
>
> Drive my dead thoughts over the universe
> Like withered leaves to quicken a new birth!
> And, by the incantation of this verse,
>
> Scatter, as from an unextinguished hearth
> Ashes and sparks, my words among mankind!
> Be through my lips to unawakened earth
>
> The trumpet of a prophecy! O, Wind,
> If Winter comes, can Spring be far behind?

Such exercises depart from Dante's original form, in that the *terza-rima* cantos of *The Divine Comedy* conclude with a single line rather than a couplet. For example, the Paolo and Francesca episode ends (*Inferno*, 5.139–142) with the poet's saying:

> Mentre che l'uno spirto questo disse,
>   l'altro piangëa; sì che di pietade
>   io venni men così com' io morisse.
> E caddi come corpo morto cade.
>
> During the time that the one spirit painted
>   their tragic tale, the other one was crying;
>   and, overcome with pity there, I fainted.
> And fell just like a body falls in dying.

As was mentioned earlier, some metrists distinguish between "tercets" and "triplets." Tercets are defined as three-line units that do not necessarily all rhyme together and triplets as three-line units that do. Walter Savage Landor's "Little Aglae" may serve to illustrate triplets in this sense and may serve as well to conclude this chapter. The poem is subtitled, "To Her Father, on Her Statue Being Called Like Her." As he does elsewhere, Landor wittily contrasts art with life and no less wittily affirms the precious vitality of the latter:

Father! the little girl we see
Is not, I fancy, so like me;
You never hold her on your knee.

When she came home the other day,
You kissed her; but I cannot say
She kissed you first and ran away.

8

Trochaic and Trisyllabic Meters

ONE OF THE MOST COLORFUL figures in the history of classical scholarship, Benjamin Jowett was Regius Professor of Greek at Oxford from 1855 until 1893, serving also for much of that time as Master of Balliol College. An opponent of emerging tendencies in the academic profession to stress research at the expense of teaching, he fostered in his students a sense of social as well as intellectual responsibility. His many distinguished pupils included Herbert Henry Asquith, who eventually became prime minister of Britain, the poets Gerard Manley Hopkins and Algernon Charles Swinburne, and the future archbishop of Canterbury, Cosmo Gordon Lang. Jowett was in addition a longtime correspondent of Florence Nightingale's, and he produced a translation of Plato, which achieved, despite its chilly reception from other classical scholars, immense popularity. Though capable of great bonhomie, Jowett could be tactless. Once, when his friend Tennyson visited Oxford and read a new poem to a gathering in the Master's Lodge at Balliol, Jowett commented, after the poet had finished his performance, "I wouldn't publish that, if I were you, Tennyson." (Notoriously sensitive to criticism, Tennyson responded, "Well if it comes to that, Master, the sherry you gave us at luncheon was beastly.") The arbitrary side of Jowett is captured by Henry Charles Beeching in an epigram in which the subject is the speaker:

> First come I. My name is Jowett.
> There's no knowledge but I know it.
> I am Master of this College:
> What I don't know isn't knowledge.

In addition to testifying memorably to Jowett, this poem reminds us that while iambic meters are particularly well suited to English, our poets have employed other rhythms. In Beeching's epigram, the movement involves, no less than iambic does, an alternation of lighter and heavier syllables. However, rather than rising from unaccented to accented syllables, it falls from accented to unaccented. Its basic unit is not an iamb but a trochee, repeated in this case four times per line:

```
 /   x   /  x   /   x  /  x
First come | I. My | name is | Jowett.

   /    x    /  x     /  x   /  x
There's no | knowledge | but I | know it.

/ x     / x  /  x   / x
I am | Master | of this | College:

  / x   /    x   / x   /  x
What I | don't know | isn't | knowledge.
```

This chapter will discuss accentual-syllabic meters in English other than iambic. These include meters involving trochaic and trisyllabic feet, and we can best proceed by further exploring trochaic verse.

Aside from the iamb, the trochee is the only disyllabic foot that serves as a basis for English meters. Even metrists who believe that English verse often features pyrrhics and spondees regard them merely as variants in other measures. Nobody speaks of poems composed wholly in "pyrrhic trimeter" or "spondaic pentameter."

The most familiar line length for English trochaics is the tetrameter. In fact, after the iambic pentameter and iambic tetrameter, the trochaic tetrameter is the most common line in our verse. The measure appears not only in Beeching's epigram on Jowett, but also in the best-known trochaic poem in English, Henry Wadsworth Longfellow's *Song of Hiawatha*. Below is a passage (3.64–78) that describes Hiawatha's grandmother's home on Lake Superior and relates how she raised the boy after his mother's death. I will place scansion marks over the lines, though in only the first four lines will I introduce foot divisions: if used throughout the passage, they might make fluent reading difficult.

```
  /   x    /   x    /  x    /  x
By the | shores of | Gitchee | Gumee

  /   x   / x   /   x    / x
By the | shining | Big-Sea | -Water,
```

```
 /    x   /  x    /  x   /  x
Stood the | wigwam | of No | komis,
  /   x   /  x   /    x   /  x
Daughter | of the | Moon, No | komis.
   /   x /  x /   x / x
Dark behind it rose the forest,
  /   x  /  x   /   x /    x
Rose the black and gloomy pine-trees,
  /   x /  x   /   x /   x
Rose the firs with cones upon them;
   /    x / x  /    x / x
Bright before it beat the water,
  /    x  /  x   /  x / x
Beat the clear and sunny water,
  /   x / x   /   x   / x
Beat the shining Big-Sea-Water.
    /   x   /  x  /   x / x
  There the wrinkled old Nokomis
 /      x / x /x  /  x
Nursed the little Hiawatha,
 /     x  / x  / x   / x
Rocked him in his linden cradle,
 / x   /  x   /  x   /  x
Bedded soft in moss and rushes,
  / x /    x  /  x   / x
Safely bound with reindeer sinews.
```

Because the last syllable in trochaic lines is an offbeat, final-syllable correspondences in trochaic verse do not produce full rhymes. Rather, they match unaccented syllables and result in comparatively weak pairings like serene**ly**/mum**my**, bur**bling**/hon**king**, and no**strum**/panjan**drum**. To achieve in trochaics conventional full rhyme, poets must rhyme the entire final foot. They must, in essence, employ feminine rhyme. (Some might object, in this context, to the term "feminine," because the rhyme does not entail, as feminine rhymes customarily do, syllables that extend beyond the meter. Correspondences like **Jowett/know it** and **college/knowledge** rest within the boundary of the trochaic lines in which they occur. Nevertheless, the rhymes are disyllabic, with falling rhythm, and have the effect of feminine rhymes.) As has been observed, feminine rhymes can, when mixed with masculine rhymes, provide engaging verbal melody. As has also been noted, however, rhymes involving hypermetrical syllables tend to jingle. In a poem like Beeching's, the brevity and humor may render this quality inconspicuous or even pleasingly appropriate. But in longer poems, a total reliance on such rhymes might weary the reader. For this reason, poets composing in trochaics have mostly either eschewed rhyme, as Longfellow does in *The Song of Hiawatha,* or have cut the last unaccented element from the line, so as to be able to rhyme firmly on a single syllable.

This latter procedure is called "catalexis," a Greek term that means, in the words of Liddell and Scott's *Greek-English Lexicon,* "ending, termination" or, more specifically, "the last foot [of a line of poetry] when it wants one or more syllables." A trochaic poem that features catalexis—that regularly drops final unaccented syllables, thereby facilitating monosyllabic rhymes —is Elizabeth Barrett Browning's "The Best." This is composed in tetrameters, the first five of which I shall scan, indicating with a caret the missing syllable at the end:

> /   x /   x /   x /   ^
> What's the best thing in the world?
> /   x   / x / x /   ^
> June-rose, by May-dew impearl'd;
> /   x   /   x /   x /   ^
> Sweet south-wind, that means no rain;
> /   x / x / x /   ^
> Truth, not cruel to a friend;
> / x   / x /   x /   ^
> Pleasure, not in haste to end;
> Beauty, not self-deck'd and curl'd
> Till its pride is over-plain;
> Light, that never makes you wink;
> Memory, that gives no pain;
> Love, when, *so,* you're loved again.
> What's the best thing in the world?
> —Something out of it, I think.

Barrett Browning could have cast her poem in complete (also called "acatalectic") trochaics. As regards the closing lines, she might have said something like

Beauty not as hard as granite,
Matched with pride that's even tougher;
Light that never leaves you winking;
Memory that needs no buffer;
Love that doesn't make you suffer.
What's the best thing in the planet?
—Something out of it, I'm thinking.

But by omitting the last unaccented syllable of her lines, she secures rhymes that are stabler and more in tune with her sad intelligence than are the alternate rhymes. These fill out the meter but sound flippant. Other outstanding poems written in catalectic trochaic tetrameters include Thomas Hardy's "The Reminder," Yvor Winters's "Before Disaster," and Thom Gunn's "Words for Some Ash." In addition, eight of the ten poems in Ben Jonson's sequence "A Celebration of Charis" are in catalectic trochaic tetrameter, though Jonson occasionally introduces complete trochaic lines.

Some observers call the line that Barrett Browning employs "clipped," "truncated," "headless," or "acephelous" iambic tetrameter. Rather than treating the line as being trochaic and lacking its final unstressed syllable, such observers explain the line as being iambic and lacking its first unstressed syllable. Thus construed, the line is not

/ x / x / x / ^
Pleasure, | not in | haste to | end;

but rather

^ / x / x / x /
Pleas | ure, not | in haste | to end;

Though I have no theoretical quarrel with this latter explanation, the rhythm does not seem iambic. In his "Metrical Feet," Coleridge writes,

Trochee trips from long to short

a line which is itself a catalectic trochaic tetrameter and which refers to the original Greek meaning of *trochaios*—"running, tripping." And that is how the line sounds. It has a forward-skipping movement, even if the final syllable is lacking and the line ends on a beat.

This species of tetrameter—whether one considers it as catalectic trochaic or as headless iambic—first appears as a variant in Middle English poems in iambic tetrameter. It is to this headless iambic or catalectic trochaic line that Chaucer refers when in *The House of Fame* he speaks (1098) of verses that "fayle in a sillable." Two instances of this line occur a little later in the poem when Chaucer introduces (1429–32) Josephus, author of the *Antiquitates Judaicae.* Chaucer calls Judaism the "sectë saturnyn" because he and his time regarded it as the oldest of all religions. Because *The House of Fame* is mainly iambic, I shall scan the short lines as clipped iambic rather than catalectic trochaic:

```
^   /  x /   x   / x /
    Alderfirst, loo, ther I sigh
    x / x /x   /   x   /
    Upon a piler stonde on high,
    x   / x / x   / x   /
    That was of led and yren fyn,
^   /   x / x / x  /
    Hym of sectë saturnyn
```

First of all, lo, there I saw, upon a high pillar made of fine lead and iron, him of the sect of Saturn.

Poets working in rhymed trochaics may mix, in some kind of regular sequence, acatalectic and catalectic lines. Samuel Johnson's "Short Song of Congratulation" illustrates this technique. The poem is in cross-rhyming trochaic tetrameter quatrains, lines 1 and 3 of which are complete and lines 2 and 4 of which are catalectic. Ironically addressing a feckless young aristocrat who has just attained his majority, the poem begins,

```
  /   x   / x  /   x    / x
Long-ex | pected | one and | twenty
  /   x   / x  / x  /   ^
Ling'ring | year at | last is | flown,
  /   x    /  x   /   x    /  x
Pomp and | pleasure, | pride and | plenty,
  /   x   /  x   /  x   /   ^
Great Sir | John, are | all your | own.
```

Loosen'd from the minor's tether,
Free to mortgage or to sell,
Wild as wind, and light as feather,
Bid the slaves of thrift farewell. . . .

Since the four-beat line is easy to hear, iambics and trochaics cooperate in tetrametric verse more readily than they do in the longer and more flexible pentameter. Nowhere are the tetrametrically cooperative capacities of the two rhythms more evident than in Milton's "L'Allegro" and "Il Penseroso." In these companion poems in rhyming tetrameter couplets, Milton shifts, irregularly but gracefully, between the various possible forms of the iambic and the trochaic tetrameter. For example, he sometimes matches acatalectic trochaic tetrameters with iambic tetrameters with feminine endings (e.g., "L'Allegro," 45–46):

```
   /   x  /   x    /  x  /  x
Then to come in spite of sorrow,

   x   /  x  /  x  /  x     / (x)
And at my window bid good morrow
```

More often, and at other points (e.g., "Il Penseroso," 31–38), he mixes regular iambic tetrameters and catalectic trochaic lines:

```
Come, pensive nun, devout and pure,

  / x   /   x   /   x  /   ^
Sober, steadfast, and demure,

All in a robe of darkest grain,

  / x   /   x / x   /   ^
Flowing with majestic train,

And sable stole of cypress lawn

Over thy decent shoulders drawn.

  /   x  /   x  /  x  /   ^
Come, but keep thy wonted state,

With even step and musing gait . . .
```

A poem that further demonstrates the cooperative potentials of iambic and trochaic (acatalectic and catalectic) tetrameters is Keats's little tour de force, "Give me women, wine, and snuff," which may be quoted in full:

```
   /   x / x   /   x    /  ^
Give me women, wine, and snuff                catalectic trochaic tet.

  x  / x  / x    /  x /
Until I cry out, "Hold, enough!"              iambic tet.

  /   x  / x /  x / x
You may do so sans objection                  acatalectic trochaic tet.
```

```
    /   x  /  x   /x   /  x
Till the day of resurrection;                          acatalectic trochaic tet.

    x   /   x   /    x   /   x   /
For, bless my beard, they aye shall be                        iambic tet.

    /  x  /  x    /  x /  ^
My belovëd Trinity.                                      catalectic trochaic tet.
```

Other iambo-trochaic-tetrametric mixtures could be cited, but adducing them might make readers of this book cry out, "Hold, enough!"

Because poets writing in trochaics often resort to catalexis, we might wonder if they also use the opposite device of adding an extra syllable to the measure. Is there a trochaic equivalent to the feminine ending in iambic verse? Do poets ever add a ninth syllable to the trochaic tetrameter?

Generally, they do not. An iambic line with a feminine ending keeps its identity because the beat count remains the same. In contrast, an extra syllable in a trochaic line would assume or require, to maintain the prevailing rhythm, some degree of stress. As a result, the syllable would produce an extra beat and change the measure.

An exception to this rule involves triple rhymes. In this case, because the main rhyme syllable establishes the end of the line, one can identify the ninth as well as the eighth syllable as hypermetrical. Had, for example, the second couplet of Beeching's poem on Jowett run,

> Students make me no defiances:
> Things I don't know are not sciences.

we could still hear the seventh syllable as the line's metrical termination:

```
    /  x     /    x  /  x /(x) (x)
Students make me no defiances:

    /  x  /    x   /   x    /(x)(x)
Things I don't know are not sciences.
```

Conversely, poets writing English iambic verse do not usually employ catalexis. Because the final syllable in iambic lines is metrically accented, to drop it is to omit one of the beats and thus to shorten the meter. If in *Two Gentlemen of Verona*, Silvia had at 5.1.8 said not,

```
    x  /  x  /    x  /   x   /  x   /
Amen, amen! Go on, good Eglamour
```

but had shortened her agent's name, the effect would have been of a tetrameter with a feminine ending rather than a pentameter minus a syllable:

```
x  /  x  /   x  /   x    / (x)
Amen, amen! Go on, good Egla
```

Poets occasionally use trochaic measures other than tetrameter. Campion, for instance, employs trochaic pentameter for twelve epigrams he incorporates into his *Observations in the Art of English Poesie*. Here is the third:

> Kate can fancy only beardless husbands,
> That's the cause she shakes off ev'ry suitor,
> That's the cause she lives so stale a virgin,
> For, before her heart can heat her answer,
> Her smooth youths she finds all hugely bearded.

(Though for the poems in his *Observations,* Campion tries to arrange his verse according to syllabic length—as it was then conceived—he also endeavors, as Derek Attridge has pointed out, to make syllabic length correspond with syllabic stress; and as a result, most of the poems in the *Observations* produce, as this one does, a regular English accentual pattern.)

In the nineteenth century, a number of poets tried their hands at the trochaic octameter. In the previous chapter, we encountered this line in Poe's "Raven." We encounter the line as well in Tennyson's "Locksley Hall" and Robert Browning's "A Toccata of Galuppi's," in both of which the lines are regularly catalectic. Here is the next to last triplet (40–42) of Browning's poem:

> As for Venice and her people, merely born to bloom and drop,
> Here on earth they bore their fruitage, mirth and folly were the crop:
> What of soul was left, I wonder, when the kissing had to stop?

Poets working in trochaic octameters tend to pause, as Browning does here, midway through the line (i.e., after the fourth foot), and the line consequently sounds like a pair of trochaic tetrameters. Because Browning's lines are catalectic, their overall effect is of a complete trochaic tetrameter followed by one that is missing its final unaccented syllable. In acatalectic trochaic octameters, such as those Poe writes in the first and third lines of the stanzas of "The Raven," the effect is of two complete trochaic tetrameters. And so far as Poe rhymes the middles of these lines with their ends, he increases the impression of a tetrametric couplet:

Presently my soul grew stronger; hesitating then no longer (19)

   / x / x /   x   /   x

[Presently my soul grew stronger;

   / x / x   /   x /   x

hesitating then no longer]

The two principal trisyllabic feet in English verse are the anapest and the dactyl. The anapest consists of two metrically unaccented syllables followed by a metrically accented one; the dactyl is composed of one metrically accented syllable followed by two that are metrically unaccented. Because our poets have used dactylics less frequently than anapestics—and because dactylics have not been afflicted with the descriptive problems from which, as we shall see, anapestics have at times suffered—we can discuss the dactyl first.

Though Renaissance poets interested in ancient prosody endeavored to imitate classical quantitative dactylics, it was not until the nineteenth century that English poets seriously experimented with native, accentualized dactylics. As late as 1755, in his essay on versification in his *Dictionary,* Samuel Johnson did not even include the dactyl as an English foot, limiting himself to the iamb, trochee, and anapest. The same classification appears in Jefferson's "Thoughts on English Prosody" of 1786. There are, Jefferson suggests, "three measures" in English verse: "Imparisyllabic . . . made up of Trochees," "Parisyllabic . . . composed of all iambuses," and "Trisyllabic . . . [which] consists altogether of anapests." Such discussions reflect no bias against the dactyl. It is just that when Johnson and Jefferson were writing, there was no indigenous dactylic tradition.

The poet most responsible for developing such a tradition is Robert Southey. In the mid-1790s, he began to explore dactylic rhythm, encouraged by his friend Coleridge and by William Taylor, who had recently translated dactylic verses by the eighteenth-century German poet, Friedrich Gottlieb Klopstock. Southey's efforts did not attract much attention until 1821, when he achieved a *succès de scandale* with the publication of *A Vision of Judgment.* In a preface to this work, Southey not only defended the dactylic hexameters in which he had written the poem, but also attacked Byron and the "Satanic School" of English verse. Never one to duck a fight, Byron responded with *The Vision of Judgment,* in which he ridiculed (721) Southey's "spavin'd dactyls" and depicted (817–24) him reading his hexameters at the gates of heaven and sending the angels and demons assembled there running for cover:

Those grand heroics acted as a spell:
    The angels stopp'd their ears and plied their pinions;
The devils ran howling, deafen'd, down to hell;
    The ghosts fled, gibbering, for their own dominions—
(For 'tis not yet decided where they dwell,
    And I leave every man to his opinions);
Michael took refuge in his trump—but lo!
His teeth were set on edge, he could not blow!

Though in their verbal duel Byron scored a greater number of palpable hits than Southey, the latter's poem initiated a vogue for English dactylic hexameters, and several poets later in the nineteenth century did interesting work in the meter. This group included Arthur Hugh Clough, who composed in dactylic hexameters two fine poems, *The Bothie of Tober-na-Vuolich* (1848) and *Amours de Voyage* (1858), and Longfellow, who used the hexameters for two of his popular narratives, *Evangeline* (1847) and *The Courtship of Miles Standish* (1858). This last poem sold fifteen thousand copies the day it was published.

Since we will shortly examine a specimen in tetrameters of Southey's dactylics, we might do well to cite a passage from *The Courtship of Miles Standish* to illustrate English dactylic hexameters. The passage (653–61) is spoken to John by Priscilla, at that point in the poem when she is at her wit's end at having been manipulated by the men in her community. She points out that while the men dither about her possible marriage, she is expected to stand meekly by and to consign her future to their fumbling keeping. And from her own plight, she draws trenchant generalities about the conditions under which women often are forced to live. The ancient dactylic hexameter allowed, as has been mentioned, for spondees to be substituted for dactyls at any point in the line except, customarily, the fifth foot; by prosodic analogy, Longfellow allows himself to replace dactyls with trochees in any foot except the fifth. In addition, because the ancient hexameter's sixth foot had only two syllables, regardless of whether the final syllable was long or short, Longfellow makes—again, analogously—the sixth feet of his lines invariably trochaic rather than dactylic. He furthermore imitates the classical practice of placing the line's caesura within the third foot. (Southey also uses these conventions in his hexameters.)

/ x x / x x / x x / x   /   x x / x
"No!" inter | rupted the | maiden, with | answer | prompt and de | cisive;

```
  /  x   x    /  x   /   x x    /  x   x   /  x x    /  x
"No; you were | angry | with me, for | speaking so | frankly and | freely.
  /   x     /   x x    /  x     x / x   x  /  x x   /  x
It was | wrong I ac | knowledge; for | it is the | fate of a | woman
   /   x  x   / x   x    / x   x   /  x  x    /   x x   /   x
Long to be | patient and | silent, to | wait like a | ghost that is | speechless,
   /  x      /  x x    /   x  /    x   /  x x   / x
Till some | questioning | voice dis | solves the | spell of its | silence.
   /   x   x  /  x  /  x  x   / x   /  x x     /  x
Hence is the | inner | life of so | many | suffering | women

  /   x x     / x  x    /   x   /  x  /  xx    / x
Sunless and | silent and | deep, like | subter | ranean | rivers
   /  x     x    /  x   x   /  x x    /    x   /   x   x
Running through | caverns of | darkness, un | heard, un | seen and un
   /   x
 | fruitful,
  / x    x     /  x  x    /    x  /  x  x      / x  x
Chafing their | channels of | stone, with | endless and | profitless |
   /   x
 murmurs."
```

English-language poets have employed other dactylic measures, chiefly dactylic tetrameter. Southey uses this measure for "The Soldier's Wife," which protests the lack of compensation and support for widows whose husbands had been killed in military service. In this poem, Southey writes exclusively in dactyls, without trochaic substitutions, and this uniformity reflects the prevailing practice among poets working in dactylic tetrameters. Though trochees appear in hexametric poems, in poems in short lines the preference is to stick to dactyls. Here are the first two of four tercets of "The Soldier's Wife." Some readers may be puzzled that unaccented marks appear over the weighty monosyllables at the ends of lines 1, 2, 3, and 5. One difficulty (to be discussed shortly) with English dactylics—and with English trochaic and trisyllabic meters generally—is that they do not harmonize as naturally with normal pronunciation and phraseology as iambics do. Reading, we must exaggerate beats and underplay offbeats if we wish to maintain a sense of the meter.

```
   /  x x    /  x x   /  x  x    /  x   x
Weary way-wanderer, languid and sick at heart,
```

```
/ x x    /   x x / x   x /  x   x
```
Travelling painfully over the rugged road,

```
/    x x      /   x x    /   x    x    /   x x
```
Wild-visaged Wanderer! God help thee, wretched one!

```
/   x  x  / x x     /    x   x   /    x  x
```
Sorely thy little one drags by thee bare-footed,

```
/   x   x / x   x   /   x   x /   x    x
```
Cold is the baby that hangs at thy bending back,

```
/    x x   / x  x      /   x   x   / x x
```
Meagre and livid and screaming for misery.

Longfellow's and Southey's dactylics are rhymeless, and poets have found rhyming in this rhythm as hard as rhyming in trochaics. If complete trochaic lines require the rhyming poet to rely on feminine rhymes, dactylics oblige a rhymer to stick to triple rhymes or, in the case of the catalectic hexameter, double rhymes. Hence, just as poets rhyming trochaics often drop the line's final unaccented syllable, so poets rhyming dactylics often end on the stressed syllable of the final foot and cut the remaining two syllables. To distinguish this operation from single-syllable catalexis, some metrists use the term "brachycatalexis." ("Brachy-" or "brachys" is a Greek combining form meaning "short"; "brachycatalexis" thus signifies major abridgment of the line's final foot.)

If poets rhyming in trochaics tend either to resort to catalectic lines or to alternate between catalectic and acatalectic lines, poets rhyming in dactylics often structure all their lines brachycatalectically or alternate between full lines and brachycatalectic ones. Byron follows the former procedure in his "Song of Saul before His Last Battle," a poem in dactylic tetrameters, the first stanza of which appears below. "Corse" is an archaic form of "corpse."

```
/ x    x     /    x     x  / x   x  /    ^  ^
```
Warriors and chiefs! should the shaft or the sword

```
/       x x / x    x  / x   x /    ^   ^
```
Pierce me in leading the host of the Lord,

```
/   x   x /    x    x /   x   x    /    ^  ^
```
Heed not the corse, though a king's, in your path:

```
/ x x     / x   x / x   x    /    ^   ^
```
Bury your steel in the bosoms of Gath!

Thomas Hood, on the other hand, alternates between full and brachy-catalectic lines in the opening stanzas of his "Bridge of Sighs," a poem mainly in dactylic dimeters. Like Southey's poem, this concerns the plight of impoverished women—here members of the London poor who drowned themselves in the vicinity of Waterloo Bridge, an appallingly regular venue for suicides in the mid-nineteenth century. In line one, "Unfortunate" is nominative, not adjectival.

```
/    x   x  / x x
One more Unfortunate,
  / x x   /    ^  ^
Weary of breath,
  /   x x   / x x
Rashly importunate,
  /   x  x   /   ^   ^
Gone to her death!
```

To illustrate anapestic measures, we can cite the first two stanzas of another poem of Byron's, "The Destruction of Sennacherib." Written in tetrameters, this may be the best-known short English poem in trisyllabic feet.

```
  x x  / x   x     /   x   x / x   x /
The Assyrian came down like the wolf on the fold,
x    x  / x    x    /  x   x  / x x    /
And his cohorts were gleaming in purple and gold;
x    x  / x   x   /   x x   / x   x /
And the sheen of their spears was like stars on the sea,
   x   x  /   x   x   /  x x   /   x x /
When the blue wave rolls nightly on deep Galilee.

  x    x /   x   x / x    x   /  x x    /
Like the leaves of the forest when Summer is green,
  x  /   x    x   / x x  / x   x    /
That host with their banners at sunset were seen:
  x    x /  x   x  / x    x  / x    x    /
Like the leaves of the forest when Autumn hath blown,
   x  /  x   x  / x   x  / x   x     /
That host on the morrow lay withered and strown.
```

The sixth and eighth lines of Byron's poem feature a variation common in anapestic verse. The first syllable of the line is dropped. In his *Dictionary*, Johnson comments on this practice, saying of anapestics,

In this measure a syllable is often retrenched from the first foot, as

> Diógenes súrly and próud
> I thínk not of Íris, nor Íris of mé

In some anapestic poems, a majority of the lines will lack the first unstressed syllable or—if you prefer a different description—will have a first-foot iambic substitution. Consider, for example, Cowper's "Verses Supposed to Be Written by Alexander Selkirk, During His Solitary Abode in the Island of Juan Fernandez." Though composed in anapestic trimeter, thirty-six of the fifty-six lines open with a disyllabic rather than a trisyllabic foot. Here is the poem's first stanza:

```
x x    /   x   x /  x x  /
I am mon | arch of all | I survey,
      x /    x  x /   x  x /
   My right | there is none | to dispute;
   x    x /   x x   /    x  x /
From the cen | tre all round | to the sea,
   x x   /  x   x /  x    x   /
   I am lord | of the fowl | and the brute.
   x  /  x x    /  x   x   /
Oh sol | itude! where | are the charms
      x  / x  x   /  x   x /
   That sag | es have seen | in thy face?
   x  x  /  x   x  /   x x /
Better dwell | in the midst | of alarms,
      x   /  x  x  /  x x  /
   Than reign | in this hor | rible place.
```

Again, in some spots we may have to demote or promote a syllable somewhat unnaturally to keep the meter going; for instance, we must downplay the normally strong first syllable of "Better" to maintain the three-beat measure.

Similarly, in Frost's "Blueberries," roughly three-quarters of the 105 anapestic tetrameters start with an iamb. The poem is a dialogue between two characters, and in the following passage (13–21) one of them expresses incredulity at the news that blueberry bushes have appeared in a pasture recently consumed by fire. However, the speaker revises this opinion upon recalling that blueberries love ashy soil and readily colonize burn-areas.

```
    x   x   /   x  x   /   x   x /   x  x   /
Why, there has | n't been time | for the bush | es to grow.
    x   /   x   x  /   x   x  /   x  x   /
That's al | ways the way | with the blue | berries, though:
    x   /   x   x   /   x   /   x x /
There may | not have been | the ghost | of a sign
  x   x  /  x   x   /   x   x  /   x   x   /
Of them an | ywhere un | der the shade | of the pine,
   x   /   x x   /   x   x  /   x   x   /
But get | the pine out | of the way, | you may burn
   x   /   x   x   /   x x /   x x  /
The pas | ture all ov | er until | not a fern
  x   /   x   x /   x  x   /   x   x  /
Or grass- | blade is left, | not to men | tion a stick,
  x   /   x   x   /   x  x /   x   x   /
And pres | to, they're up | all around | you as thick
  x   /   x x   /   x x  /   x  x   /
And hard | to explain | as a con | juror's trick.
```

The practice of introducing a first-foot iamb into anapestic verse may bespeak necessity more than anything else. Whether rising or falling, trisyllabic measures are hard to sustain. Poets composing in them will find it advantageous to be permitted a disyllabic foot here and there. Further, iambs seem to be only minimally disruptive at the head of anapestic lines, perhaps for the same reason that trochees are minimally disruptive at line beginnings in iambic verse: at the boundary of a line or unit of syntax, the ear assimilates variation easily. What is more, a two-syllable foot with rising rhythm may fit well into anapestic measure for the same reason that trochees fit into dactylic verse. Though the length of the foot is different, iambs and anapests are both rear-stressed, just as trochees and dactyls are both fore-stressed. In other words, just as the disyllabically falling trochee blends rhythmically with the trisyllabically descending dactyl, so the disyllabically rising iamb substitutes well for the trisyllabically rising anapest.

Readers may have noted that, in the third line of the passage from "Blueberries," Frost places an iamb in the third foot as well as the first foot of the line. While the first foot is by far the likeliest place for iambs to appear in anapestic verse, poets may introduce them elsewhere in the line.

Many metrists argue that our versification involves a third trisyllabic foot.

This is the amphibrach, whose syllabic sequence runs unaccented-accented-unaccented. Other metrists believe that this foot is, as far as English is concerned, a prosodic mirage and that what some poets and readers call amphibrachic rhythm is really a subspecies of anapestic rhythm. I believe in the amphibrach, but only lukewarmly; and I can best discuss the opposing views about the foot by explaining my own Laodicean attitude towards it.

If asked to illustrate amphibrachic rhythm, I would begin by citing George Colman the Younger's epitaph "On Sir Nathan Wraxall the Historian":

> Misplacing—mistaking—
> Misquoting—misdating—
> Men, manners, things, facts all,
> Here lies Nathan Wraxall.

However dangerous it is to let morphology or phraseology influence metrical interpretation, the word shapes and punctuation in the poem's first two lines appear to signal amphibrachic feet. Moreover, the poem does not cohere rhythmically unless we read all four lines as amphibrachic dimeters —as having an unaccented-accented-unaccented pattern, twice repeated.

<pre>
    x   / x   x / x
Misplacing |—mistaking—

    x   / x   x / x
Misquoting |—misdating—

    x   / x   x   / x
Men, manners, | things, facts all,

    x   / x   x   / x
Here lies Na | than Wraxall.
</pre>

And while these lines will admit of another metrical interpretation, which we shall examine shortly, the present scansion looks to be the most logical.

Similarly, Hardy's translation of Pietro Bembo's epitaph on Raphael is evidently conceived as amphibrachic tetrameters:

<pre>
    x   / x   x   / x   x   / x   x   /x
Here's one in | whom Nature | feared—faint at | such vying—

   x /   x   x /   x   x /   x   x /x
Eclipse while | he lived, and | decease at | his dying.
</pre>

Additional support for the amphibrach is supplied by eighteenth-century poems that systematically mix amphibrachic and anapestic lines. In the following air from *Polly*, for example, John Gay casts the first lines of his tetrametric couplets in amphibrachs and the second lines in anapests—the amphibrachic lines being catalectic.

<pre>
    x   /   x   x   /   x   x   / x   x   /   ^
The sportsmen | keep hawks, and | their quarry | they gain;
    x   x   /   x   x   /   x   x   /   x x   /
Thus the wood | cock, the part | ridge, the pheas | ant is slain.
    x   / x   x   /   x   x   /   x   x   /   ^
What care and | expense for | their hounds are | employed!
    x   x   /   x   x   /   x   x   /   x   x   /
Thus the fox | and the hare | and the stag | are destroyed.
    x   / x   x   / x   x   / x   x   /   ^
The spaniel | they cherish, | whose flatter | ing way
  x   x   /   x   x   /   x   x   /   x   x   /
Can as well | as their mas | ters cringe, fawn | and betray.
    x   /   x   x / x   x   /   x   x   /   ^
Thus staunch pol | iticians, | look all the | world round,
  x   x   /   x   x   /   x   x   /   x   x   /
Love the men | who can serve | as hawk, span | iel or hound.
</pre>

In the nineteenth century, Christina Rossetti uses this technique in satirizing David Garrick's jingoistic "Heart of Oak." Here Rossetti quotes one of Garrick's amphibrachic tetrameters, then answers it with her own anapestic tetrameter:

<pre>
    x   / x   x   /   x   x   / x   x   /   ^
"Come cheer up, | my lads, 'tis | to glory | we steer"—

  x   x   /   x   x   /   x   x   /   x   x   /
As the sol | dier remarked | whose post lay | in the rear.
</pre>

Those who deny the existence of amphibrachic verse argue that it is just anapestic verse that lacks the first unaccented syllable. Such observers would note that lines I have scanned as catalectic amphibrachic lines may be treated as clipped anapestic ones and that acatalectic amphibrachic lines may be construed as clipped anapestic lines with feminine endings:

<pre>
^   x   /   x   x   / (x)
Misplac | ing —mistaking—
^   x   /   x   x   /   x   x   /   x   x   /(x)
Here's one | in whom Na | ture feared—faint | at such vying—
</pre>

```
 ^   x   /    x  x   /    x   x   /   x  x   /
The sports | men keep hawks, | and their quar | ry they gain;
 ^   x     /   x   x /    x  x   /  x  x   /
"Come cheer | up, my lads, | 'tis to glor | y we steer"—
```

This interpretation has the virtue of simplifying our metrical vocabulary. If we adopt this view, we no longer need the amphibrach. But the interpretation is questionable, to the extent that we hear, in poems like Gay's, the presence of a rhythm in addition to anapestic. Even in such poems as Matthew Prior's "Jinny the Just," Mary Wortley Montagu's "The Lover," Robert Browning's "How They Brought the Good News from Ghent to Aix"—poems in which there are possibly amphibrachic lines, but no consistent disposition of them vis-à-vis the plainly anapestic lines—we may feel that the poet is working with two distinct, albeit cooperative, trisyllabic rhythms.

Would that we knew how the poets mentioned in the preceding paragraphs regarded their trisyllabic poems. Would that they had left clear indications as to whether they saw them as anapestic, or as amphibrachic as well as anapestic, or as just generally trisyllabic. Unfortunately, no such testimony exists as far as I know. Further, the testimony of their fellow poets and prosodists is conflicting on this point. Johnson, as has been noted, admits only anapests in the category of trisyllabic feet. Likewise, Goldsmith appears to consider the anapest as the sole trisyllabic foot. "What criticisms have we not heard of late," he remarks in his dedication to *The Traveller*, "in favour of blank verse, and Pindaric odes, chorusses, anapests and iambics, alliterative care, and happy negligence." And introducing, in his "State of Literature," a parody of Thomas Gray's "The Bard," Goldsmith characterizes his effort as "a blank Pindaric Ode . . . of my own making; consisting of Strophe, Antistrophe, Trochaics, Iambics, Sapphics, Pentameters, Exameters, and a Chorus." On the other hand, Gray describes Prior's light verse as an irregular mixture of amphibrachic and anapestic tetrameters, observing, as Johnson does, that anapestic lines frequently begin with an iamb. (It is possible that Gray may be saying that amphibrach tetrameter can be construed as anapestic tetrameter with an iambic first foot; but his sentence structure indicates that he is drawing a distinction between amphibrachs and anapests and that iambic substitutions are relevant only to the latter.)

We now and then in subjects of humour use a free verse of eleven or twelve syllables, which may consist of four Amphibrachees, or four Anapaests, or the first may be an Iambic, &c.; so Prior:

```
  x    /x  x    / x   x /    x  x  /
As Chloe came into the room t'other day

   x  x /    x   x  / x   x    / x x    /
'Tis enough that 'tis loaded with baubles and seals
```

Similarly, Coleridge mentions in his *Notebooks* "Amphibrach tetrameter catalectic" as a familiar English line; and he devotes a couplet (7–8) of his "Metrical Feet" to the amphibrach, with the couplet itself being two amphibrachic tetrameters catalectic. I have added scansion marks to the first line of the couplet and have changed to x's and /'s the breves and macrons which Coleridge places over the second line:

```
   x   / x  x /    x  x    / x  x    /   ^
One syllable long, with one short at each side,

   x    / x  x /    x  x / x   /   ^
Amphibrachys hastes with a stately stride.
```

Readers may observe that the second line is missing the unaccented syllable that should follow the third beat ("state-") or precede the final beat ("stride"). Coleridge may have been seeing "stately" as three syllables: "statëly." Though this is hard to believe, it is not inconceivable, especially since Coleridge had too sensitive an ear not to hear a slip; and had he heard an error, he could have restored the meter simply by substituting a three-syllable synonym like "elegant" or "dignified" for "stately."

If in our inquiry into the existence or nonexistence of the amphibrach has been inconclusive, it does not greatly matter how one construes the individual feet in poems in disputable trisyllabic measures. The key thing is just to see where the beats fall. If you can locate the beats, you can enjoy the poem and recite it cogently to others. Ultimately, foot-division is neither as illuminating or as clear a matter in trisyllabic verse as it is in iambic verse. You can treat the opening stanza of Hardy's "Ruined Maid" as catalectic amphibrachic tetrameters,

```
   x   /x   x  /   x   x  /  x   x   /   ^
"O 'Melia, | my dear, this | does every | thing crown!

   x  /    x   x  /  x   x    /  x   x  /    ^
Who could have | supposed I | should meet you | in Town?

   x    /    x   x  / x     x    / x x /   ^
And whence such | fair garments, | such prosper | i-ty?"

   x  / x   x   /  x   x   / x    x    /  ^
"O didn't | you know I'd | been ruined?" | said she.
```

or as anapestic tetrameters lacking their first unstressed syllables:

```
 ∧    x   /  x    x  /    x   x  /    x   x    /
 "O 'Mel | ia,  my dear, | this  does ev | ery thing crown!
 ∧     x  /    x   x  /    x  x     /    x  x   /
 Who could | have supposed | I should meet | you in Town?
 ∧   x     /     x   x  /   x    x     /   x x  /
 And whence | such fair gar | ments, such pros | peri-ty?"
 ∧   x  /   x  x    /  x   x  /  x     x     /
 "O did | n't you know | I'd been ru | ined?" said she.
```

What is important is to recognize that the poem is in trisyllabic rather than
iambic rhythm and to locate the stresses.

Trochaic and triple meters run against the natural rhythms of English,
and it is mainly for this reason that such meters have been employed less
often by our poets than iambic measures. The poet who adopts trochaics or
trisyllabics must pound out the beats to maintain the meter. Further, the
reader is almost inevitably asked to override at points natural rhetorical stress
for the meter's sake. Were we to encounter, outside of its metrical context,
the following verse from Byron's "The Destruction of Sennacherib,"

> And the blue wave rolls nightly on deep Galilee

we would pronounce "Galilee," as habit and the dictionary direct us, with
primary stress on the first syllable, and would probably subordinate, to that
syllable, the adjective ("deep") that precedes it. Yet because the line appears
in a poem in anapestic tetrameters, the measure asks us to lay heavy stress
on "deep" and "-lee" and to subordinate "Gal-":

> And the **sheen** of their **spears** was like **stars** on the **sea**
> When the **blue** wave rolls **night**ly on **deep** Galilee.

Likewise, were we to encounter anywhere but in *The Song of Hiawatha*
("Introduction," 34),

> The blue heron, the Shuh-shuh-gah

it is unlikely that we would emphasize the two definite articles at the expense of "blue" and the first syllable of "Shuh-shuh-gah." But that is what
Longfellow wishes us to do, since he is writing in trochaic tetrameter:

```
  /   x    / x     /   x     /  x
 The blue | heron, | the Shuh | -Shuh-gah
```

And if we were unaware of the meter Southey was using in "The Soldier's Wife," it might be difficult for us to hear

> Wild-visaged Wanderer! God help thee, wretched one!

as four dactyls,

> /   x x   /   x x   /   x   x   /   x x
> Wild-visaged Wanderer! God help thee, wretched one!

Even with the dactylic rhythm firmly in mind, we tend, in the last two feet of the line, to give "help" and "one" stresses the meter does not permit.

Two questions might be raised about my analysis. First, am I failing to grant a license to trochaic and trisyllabic measures that I have extended to iambic ones? Is it fair of me to point out that trochaics and trisyllabics often require the reader to accentuate lines oddly when I have urged that the metrical character of such a possibly puzzling iambic line as

> Affliction is enamored of thy parts

> (Shakespeare, *Romeo and Juliet*, 3.3.2)

can be resolved by reading it in context:

> x /   x   /   x /   x   /   x /
> Afflic | tion is | enam | ored of | thy parts

Why, that is, am I reluctant to let pass muster, in an anapestic poem, a line like "When the blue wave rolls nightly on deep Galilee"? If we simply refer the line to the poem's meter and scan it

> x   x   /   x   x   /   x x   /   x x /
> When the blue wave rolls nightly on deep Galilee.

what is wrong with that?

My answer is that though the line from *Romeo and Juliet* is relatively unusual in its modulation of the iambic pentameter paradigm—the stress peaks over syllables 4 and 8 are not high—the line still follows the paradigm's iambic fluctuation. Byron's line, in contrast, seems not to follow the anapestic pattern. We have to cheat, in pronouncing the words and phrases, to give them the requisite rhythmical shape.

The second question that might be raised about my analysis is related to the first. Have I not overlooked the possibility that just as iambic verse can in places accommodate trochees or anapests, so also can trochaics and trisyllabics accommodate various substitutions? Indeed, have not I already pointed out that dactylic verse accepts trochees and that anapestic verse is receptive to iambs? Further, to speak of trochaic verse specifically, is it not possible that iambic first feet may be as natural in trochaics as trochaic first feet are in iambics? In other words, if trochees may appear at the beginnings of iambic lines and after mid-line pauses, why can we not consider Longfellow's line about the heron as being trochaic with an iambic substitution in the first foot and an iambic substitution after a mid-line pause?

<pre>
     x   /   / x   x /   /   x
The blue | heron, | the Shuh | -shuh-gah
</pre>

To this question, I would respond that, unless we stress the first syllable of Longfellow's line, we lose the meter. It dissolves. Whereas our ears can re-cover the rhythm of an iambic line that begins with trochee or has a trochee after a mid-line pause, the opposite is not true.

We can clarify this issue by examining other lines (9.200, 14.104) that open, as does the one about the heron, with a light syllable followed by a heavier one. In the second of these, Longfellow evidently wishes us to syn-copate for the meter the middle syllable of "separate," though this point is irrelevant to the matter at hand.

> And three useless arrows only
> For each song a separate symbol

If we utter these lines naturally, with more stress on the second than the first syllable, we lose the metrical pattern. If, to refer to the linguists' four-level stress-register, we read the openings of the lines,

<pre>
1   3 4
And three useless arrows only

1 3   4
For each song a separate symbol
</pre>

the lines sound different from trochaic tetrameter; they sound more like loose iambic trimeters.

Because trochaics and trisyllabics are so emphatic, it has been suggested that readers of poems in these measures might do well to ignore the met-rical pattern and to approach the poems purely in terms of prose sense. Longfellow evidently felt this way with regard to *Evangeline*, as is revealed in his response to Nathaniel Hawthorne's congratulatory letter on the pub-lication of the poem. A mutual friend of the two writers, the Reverend H. L. Conolly, who knew the legend of Evangeline and Gabriel, had first offered it to Hawthorne as a subject for a work of prose fiction. Only after considerable time had elapsed without Hawthorne's using the legend did Longfellow ask if he might try his hand at it, whereupon the novelist relinquished rights to the story to the poet. And after thanking Hawthorne for his good opinion of the finished poem, Longfellow alludes to Hawthorne's bequest: "Still more do I thank you for resigning to me that legend of Acady. This success I owe entirely to you, for being willing to forego the pleasure of writing a prose tale which many people would have taken for poetry, that I might write a poem which many people take for prose."

Longfellow, that is, indicates that, faced with the choice of having his readers boom out the lines or having them read the poem in prosier manner, he was not averse to having them do the latter.

Since our speech falls into iambics so readily, it is hard for poets to avoid that rhythm when writing in the other measures that we have been examining. Such is especially the case with anapestics, probably because they have rising rhythm and thus may recall or verge on iambics more readily than dactylics or trochaics do. In any case, if poets writing anapestic measure are not vigilant, they may intermittently slip back into what sound like iambic lines and may thereby confuse readers. Consider the fifth line of the earlier cited stanza of Cowper's "Verses Supposed to Be Written by Alexander Selkirk":

> Oh solitude! where are the charms

In isolation this looks like a conventional iambic tetrameter, as does this line (21) later on in the poem:

> My sorrows I might then assuage.

Such lines would fit in iambic-tetrameter verses like the following made-up ones:

> Now condos are replacing farms.
> Oh solitude! where are the charms
> Of country living in this age?
> Could I but grow some beets and sage,
> My sorrows I might then assuage.

The foregoing comments are not intended to disparage trochaic or triple measures. Much less do I wish to criticize the efforts of such great writers as Prior, Montagu, Goldsmith, Cowper, Byron, and Longfellow, who have enriched our literature by exploring them. Trochaics and triple meters have a distinctive music. However, they have not the suppleness and capacity for fluid modulation that iambic measures have, nor do they tolerate the range of variations that the texture of iambic verse can absorb.

Yet rather than end this chapter on a negative note, I should like to close with a passage from a fine poem in anapestic-amphibrachic tetrameter or, if one prefers, in anapestic tetrameter with many iambic first feet. The poem is Goldsmith's "Retaliation," and the passage (29–40) is devoted to Edmund Burke. Despite his gentle humor, Goldsmith writes with a tragic accuracy about his friend's condition and career. Having previously mentioned that identifying the beats is the important thing in the recitation of poems in trisyllabic measures, I shall not divide the passage into feet, but shall merely mark the metrical accents:

> Here líes our good Édmund, whose génius was súch,
> We scárcely can práise it, or bláme it too múch;
> Who, bórn for the úniverse, nárrow'd his mínd,
> And to párty gave úp, what was méant for mankínd.
> Though fráught with all léarning, kept stráining his thróat
> To persuáde Tommy Tównsend to lénd him a vóte;
> Who, too déep for his héarers, still wént on refíning,
> And thóught of convíncing, while théy thought of díning;
> Though équal to áll things, for áll things unfít,
> Too níce for a státesman, too próud for a wít;
> For a pátriot too cóol, for a drúdge, disobédient,
> And too fónd of the *ríght* to pursúe the *expédient*.

9

Alternative Modes of
Versification in English

THOUGH ENGLISH-LANGUAGE POETS have written mostly in accentual-syllabic measure, they have explored four other types of verse: accentual verse, syllabic verse, free verse, and imitation-classical verse. While these additional modes are secondary to the main tradition, they all are interesting, and I should like briefly to describe each, in order to round out the picture of English versification drawn in the previous chapters.

1. Accentual Verse

In accentual verse, the number of accents in the poetic line is constant, but the number of syllables is variable. Old English verse is written principally in a single accentual meter, which in a modified form is employed as well by some Middle English poets. This meter apparently originated in Ancient Germanic, a language which developed in the centuries before Christ, but of which no written record survives. The meter was brought to Britain by the peoples from northwestern continental Europe who migrated to the island in the fifth century, after the departure of the Romans. Initially invited to England by the southern Celts—who, as Roman influence declined, were seeking allies against the northern Scots and Picts—the newcomers soon turned on their hosts and assumed dominance in their adopted country. They spoke several West Germanic dialects that provided the basis of what became English. That their meter is called not only "Old English," but also

"Old Germanic" or "Germanic" indicates it occurs throughout the poetries of the early Germanic languages—Old High German, Old Saxon, Old Norse, and Scandinavian as well as Old English. Another term applied to Old English language and meter is "Anglo-Saxon." It refers to the Angles and the Saxons, who, along with the Jutes, were the chief Germanic groups that settled in England. Though a synonym for "Old English," "Anglo-Saxon" has a different connotation. Scholars who use it tend to see the language as distinct from Middle and Modern English, whereas those who speak of "Old English" are more likely to regard the language as the first of three stages in a continuous developmental process.

The Old English meter consists of a line that has four accents and is divided by a medial caesura into a pair of half-lines or hemistichs. Each half-line has two of the four beats or "lifts" as they are sometimes called. Usually, the final word in each half-line contains the second of its beats; and, usually, each half-line is grammatically independent, comprising a complete phrase or clause. Interestingly, sentences conclude more often at mid-line breaks than at line endings. Though rhyme appears only occasionally and ornamentally, metrically accented syllables are pointed by alliteration. They begin, that is, with the same sound. The pivotal syllable in the line is the first metrically accented syllable in the second hemistich. This syllable determines the line's alliterative motif. At least one of the accented syllables in the first half-line alliterates with it, and, more often than not, both do. Only rarely, however, does the fourth of the line's accented syllables alliterate with the other three. Michael Alexander schematizes the meter as

BANG . . . BANG: BANG . . . CRASH

Old English meter is exemplified by *Beowulf,* a short passage of which will be cited in a moment. However, because Old English looks alien to anyone who has not studied it, we can best illustrate Old English meter initially with a section of C. S. Lewis's "The Planets," which realizes in Modern English the antique form. At this point (44–52) in his poem, Lewis is speaking of the sun and of the beneficial effects of its light. I shall place acute accents over the metrically stressed syllables and shall underscore the alliterating elements. Notice that each line falls into two grammatical sections, even when, as in the second and the last of the lines, the pause is unpunctuated.

Through <u>m</u>órtal <u>m</u>índ, <u>m</u>ísts are párted
And <u>m</u>íld as <u>m</u>órning the <u>m</u>éllow wísdom
<u>Br</u>éathes o'er the <u>br</u>éast, <u>br</u>óadening éastward

Cléar and cloudless. In a clós'd gárden
(Unbóund her búrden) his béams fóster
Sóul in sécret, where the sóil puts fórth
Páradisal pálm, and púre fóuntains
Túrn and re-témper, tóuching cóolly
The uncómely cómmon to córdial góld.

We can see why such verse is called accentual. The lines above have a fixed number (four) of accents, but the syllable count varies. Lines 1 and 4 have eight syllables; lines 3 and 5 have nine; lines 2 and 9 have ten. Further, the metrically accented syllables appear at different places in the lines. In line 1, syllables 2, 4, 5, and 7 carry beats; in line 4, syllables 1, 3, 7, and 8 do; in the last line, the beats fall on the third, fifth, eighth, and tenth syllables. It would seem arbitrary to divide such verse into feet. No consistent pattern of iambs, trochees, anapests, or dactyls would emerge. Rather, the rhythmical integrity of the verse is established by the regular number of accents, the two-and-two division of the lines, and the alliteration.

This summary of Old English meter requires qualification. While the syllable count of the line overall is variable, the half-lines from which the poet makes complete verses fall into five basic types, and these somewhat restrict the range of syllabic divergence. Over a century ago Eduard Sievers, whom we mentioned in our introduction, expounded these five basic hemistichs and their accentual patterns. And though subsequent scholars have debated various aspects of Old English versification, and though in his later years Sievers himself expressed dissatisfaction with his analysis, its descriptive usefulness and accuracy are acknowledged by most authorities today. Here are Sievers's five types; a grave accent (\) indicates a secondary stress:

Hemistich A:	/ x / x
Hemistich B:	x / x /
Hemistich C:	x / / x
Hemistich D:	/ / \ x or / / x \
Hemistich E:	/ \ x /

These five line types are susceptible to variation, as regards additional unaccented or secondarily stressed syllables. Some of these variations occur because Old English has true long and short vowel pairs, and its prosody has a significant durational component. Most metrical accents fall on long syllables, but not all do; and a long-and-accented syllable can be "resolved" (to use the word Sievers preferred) or "broken" (to use the term J. R. R.

Tolkien favored) into a metrically accented short syllable, plus a weak, un-accented syllable.

Old English poets do not combine the half-lines willy-nilly, but generally, while trying to avoid undue repetition, follow what we might today call a loosely trochaic or trochaic-dactylic rhythm. The trochaic-like "A" half-line is the most common in Old English verse—40 percent of *Beowulf*'s hemi-stichs are A's—and A is especially frequent in the first hemistich. As A. J. Bliss remarks: "The poet combines his pairs of verses in such a way as to achieve greater variety, both of rhythm and of phrasing, than chance would dictate; and at the same time to ensure that the falling rhythm of Type A, the norm of Old English metre, is maintained in as many lines as possible."

The following lines from *Beowulf* illustrate the procedure Bliss describes. The hemistich-types are registered in the margins, and the alliterating ele-ments are underscored. With regard to the third of the lines below, we will recall that word-opening vowels and diphthongs alliterate, even if the dif-ference in their spelling makes it appear to the eye that they do not. Thorns and eths—Old English letters that have not survived into Modern English, though they are still used in Icelandic—have been transliterated to "th"; and long vowels are marked with circumflexes. Also, I follow the practice, common in modern editions of *Beowulf*, of putting space between the hemistichs to make their divisions clearer. (In its single surviving manu-script codex—the Cotton manuscript of circa 1000—the poem is written out like prose. Because parchment, the writing material of that time, was relatively scarce and expensive, scribes could not always afford to leave empty areas around texts.)

```
       x    /   / x      /  x x   / x
  C  Oft Scyld Scêfing    sceathena thrêatum  A

     / x \    /   x      / x \ xx  /
  A  monegum mægthum    meodo-setla oftêah;  E

     / x x /  x    x    x  / x    /
  A  egsode eorlas   syththan ærest wearth  B

     /  x   /  x    x  x  / x x /
  A  fêasceaft funden;  hê thæs frôfre gebâd ... B
     Often Scyld Scefing    seized mead-benches
     from enemy troops,   from many a clan;
     he terrified warriors,    even though first he was found
     a waif, helpless.    For that came a remedy ...
```

(trans. Howell D. Chickering, Jr.)

In the wake of the Norman Conquest, accentual-alliterative verse declines. Eventually, the two principal meters of medieval French verse, the octosyllabic and decasyllabic lines, are adopted and naturalized, becoming our iambic tetrameter and iambic pentameter. This development may well have been affected by Italian verse, too. Chaucer traveled in Italy in the early 1370s, and his creation or elaboration of the pentameter may reflect not only Anglo-Norman influence, but also that of the Italian hendecasyllabic line. So far as the eleventh syllable of the hendecasyllabic line is light, its structure is not unlike that of the Chaucerian pentameter, which ends with a hypermetrical eleventh syllable much more frequently than pentameters in Modern English do.

Nevertheless, the influence of the Old Germanic tradition persists throughout the Middle English period. At times we have a blend of the accentual-alliterative mode with the emerging syllable-regulating and rhyming style. For instance, Layamon's *Brut* (early thirteenth century) is written in medially divided accentual lines, but Layamon uses alliteration only irregularly and rhymes his half-lines frequently. We find a later variation on this technique in *Gamelyn* (anon., mid-fourteenth century) in which the medially divided accentual lines are end-rhymed, couplet-style. And in *Pearl,* the anonymous mystical masterpiece of the fourteenth century, we have a poem that, in its rhyme and its complex stanzaic structure, seems very much of the Anglo-Norman school. Yet *Pearl* features alliteration—it is not structural, admittedly, but there is a lot of it—and the syllable count seems less important to the poet than the four metrical beats per line. There is not, that is, the degree of syllabic regulation that we find in the octosyllabics of Gower's *Confessio Amantis* or Chaucer's *Book of the Duchess* and *House of Fame.* Similarly, *Sir Gawain and the Green Knight,* authorship of which is traditionally ascribed to the *Pearl*-poet, features long stanzas of unrhymed accentual-alliterative lines which, however, conclude with five shorter "bob-and-wheel" lines rhyming *ababa,* the bob line having one beat, the four wheel lines having three beats each.

What is more, the second half of the fourteenth century witnessed a phenomenon that scholars call "The Alliterative Revival." Especially in the north and west of England, there appear a number of poems—*Sir Gawain and the Green Knight* is a leading example—that metrically revert to the more accentual mode of the Old English period. Some regard this movement as a conscious protest against the emerging accentual-syllabic tradition and as a nationalistic effort to turn English verse back to its Germanic origins. Others suspect that the Alliterative Revival was not a revival at all. They believe that the accentual-alliterative tradition survived in the centuries following the Norman conquest, but that works in the tradition were not adequately recorded and published; and there are gaps in the historical record, chiefly between the later eleventh and the early thirteenth century, a time from which virtually no English-language poetry of any kind survives. Still other people argue that the Alliterative Revival is a new but natural outgrowth from the mixed alliterative-rhyming modes of the thirteenth and fourteenth centuries. If in fact the same person wrote *Sir Gawain* and *Pearl*—both of which mix Romanic and Germanic elements, with *Sir Gawain* being more Germanic and *Pearl* more Romanic—this last view would seem to be closest to the truth. Another circumstance supporting this view is that the revived alliterative line is longer and looser than the Old English measure. If the new line descends from the older measure, it is refracted through intervening forms and practices.

The quintessential poem of the Alliterative Revival is *Piers Plowman*, authorship of which is attributed to William Langland. The opening lines appear below. The poem exists in three versions, called A, B, and C; our excerpt comes from the B text, which is thought to be the best of the three. As with the lines from *Beowulf*, I have slightly modernized the spelling. In the passage, the narrator relates that one summer he dressed up as a hermit—"unholy of workës" refers to a practice whereby people passed themselves off as religious mendicants to dodge honest labor—and went forth wayfaring. One morning on Malvern Hills something remarkable happened to him. He fell asleep on a bank near a sweetly purling stream and (subsequent to our passage) had a dream-vision to which the main part of the poem is devoted.

> In a sómer séson   whan sóft was the sónnë
> I shópe me in shróudës   as I a shépe wérë,
> In hábite as an héremite   unhóly of wórkës,
> Went wýde in this wórld   wóndres to hérë.
> Ac on a Máy mórnynge   on Málverne húllës
> Me byfél a férly,   of fáiry, me thóughtë;
> I was wéry forwándred   and wént me to réstë
> Únder a bróde bánkë   bi a bórnës sídë
> And as I láy and léned   and lóked in the wáteres,
> I slómbred in a slépyng,   it swéyued so mérye.

We can see how Langland's meter resembles and differs from the Old

English measure. As in Old English verse, Langland's lines have customarily four beats and are divided by a medial caesura, with two beats on either side. The stressed syllables are pointed by alliteration, and the key syllable is the first stressed syllable in the second half of the line. The syllable count is, however, more variable than it is in the older tradition. Line 3, for example, has fourteen syllables, line 4 has ten, and line 7 has thirteen. Also (and this is characteristic of accentual verse during the Alliterative Revival), we are more likely to find all four beats alliterating, as they do in line 1, though this variant is still relatively uncommon. Further, extended three-beat hemistichs, such as "Únder a bróde bánkë," occur more frequently than they do in Old English verse.

Despite its triumphs in the fourteenth century, accentual-alliterative versification did not survive the development of the more precisely and flexibly organized accentual-syllabic system. For all of its vigor, the accentual-alliterative line—with its requirements of structural alliteration and medial division—is restrictive and thumping. There are many areas of psychological, emotional, and intellectual experience with which the line cannot deal. It would be difficult to write, in the accentual-alliterative manner, something like the speech of Juliet cited in chapter 3, or like Marvell's "The Garden."

That said, modern poets have on occasion fruitfully revived the Old English meter. Richard Wilbur has written two excellent poems, "The Lilacs" and "Junk," in it. And W. H. Auden adopted it for his *Age of Anxiety,* a long semidramatic poem (the poet himself called it "a Baroque Eclogue"), set against the backdrop of the Second World War. Here (6–19) one of the characters silently interrogates himself before the mirror in a bar. By now I hope that the principles of the measure are sufficiently clear as to make it unnecessary to highlight graphically the alliterative patterns and the accented syllables in the lines. It should be mentioned, however, that in the eighth line below, Auden treats the *h*s as silent, so that "hiding" and "heart" alliterate with "angel."

> How glad and good when you go to bed,
> Do you feel, my friend? What flavor has
> That liquor you lift with your left hand;
> Is it cold by contrast, cool as this
> For a soiled soul; does your self like mine
> Taste of untruth? Tell me, what are you
> Hiding in your heart, some angel face,
> Some shadowy she who shares in my absence,
> Enjoys my jokes? I'm jealous, surely,

Nicer myself (though not as honest),
The marked man of romantic thrillers
Whose brow bears the brand of a winter
No priest can explain, the poet disguised,
Thinking over things in thieves' kitchens . . .

In addition, the alliterative tradition inspired one modern poet, Gerard
Manley Hopkins, to attempt an accentual prosody all his own. Hopkins
characterizes his technique as "sprung rhythm"; and in remarks written evidently in the early 1880s but not published until after his death, Hopkins
correlates his practice with that of Langland. Hopkins says that "[medieval?]
Greek and Latin lyric verse . . . and the old English verse seen in *Pierce
Ploughman* are in sprung rhythm." Though Hopkins's measures are highly
idiosyncratic, and though rhyme is crucial to his verse, we can readily perceive connections between his poems and those of the Germanic tradition.
For example, in his sonnet, "Spelt from Sibyl's Leaves,"—a sonnet described
by Hopkins as being in an eight-beat line, with four stresses on each side of
a medial caesura—we can see, as in earlier accentual poems, the concern
with rhythmical balance and energetic alliteration. Here is the sonnet's sestet, which imagines the Last Judgment, when Divinity will rigidly and ir-
revocably separate the saved from the damned. Hopkins describes Hell in
terms of a ghastly nightfall and connects it with that place in the Under-
world where, as the Cumaean Sibyl indicates (*Aeneid*, 6.540ff.) to Aeneas,
the road branches one way to Elysium and the other way to Tartarus. To
better enable readers to follow his rhythms, Hopkins himself supplies accent marks over certain syllables and superscripted vertical bars to divide
the half-lines from each other.

Only the beakleaved boughs dragonish | damask the tool-smooth
    bleak light; black,
Ever so black on it. Óur tale, O óur oracle! | Lét life, wáned, ah lét
    life wind
Off hér once skéined stained véined varíety | upon, áll on twó
    spools; párt, pen, páck
Now her áll in twó flocks, twó folds—black, white; | right, wrong;
    reckon but, reck but, mind
But thése two; wáre of a wórld where bút these | twó tell, each off
    the óther; of a rack
Where, selfwrung, selfstrung, sheathe- and shelterless, | thóughts
    agáinst thoughts ín groans grínd.

And here, in its entirety, is Hopkins's "Inversnaid," a lovely proto-ecology poem in a simple (by Hopkins's standards) four-beat line. The poem is set in Scotland—the title refers to a summer resort on the eastern side of Loch Lomond, and the poem depicts a stream and falls that empty there into the loch—and some of the words are from Scottish or North English dialect. "Burn" means "stream"; a "coop" is a "hollow"; "degged" means "sprinkled"; "braes" means "hillsides"; "heathpacks" refers to "heather," and "flitches" are "clumps" or "tufts." "Twindles" looks to be a portmanteau word that Hopkins invented from "twists" and "dwindles." As in "Spelt from Sybil's Leaves," the accent marks are Hopkins's.

> This darksome burn, horseback brown,
> His rollrock highroad roaring down,
> In coop and in comb the fleece of his foam
> Flutes and low to the lake falls home.
>
> A windpuff-bonnet of fáwn fróth
> Turns and twindles over the broth
> Of a pool so pitchblack, féll-fró́wning,
> It rounds and rounds Despair to drowning.
>
> Degged with dew, dappled with dew
> Are the groins of the braes that the brook treads through,
> Wiry heathpacks, flitches of fern,
> And the beadbonny ash that sits over the burn.
>
> What would the world be, once bereft
> Of wet and of wildness? Let them be left,
> O let them be left, wildness and wet;
> Long live the weeds and the wilderness yet.

At the risk of belaboring the obvious, we can note what makes this an accentual poem. There is constancy in the beat count—four per line—whereas there is variability in the number of syllables, which range from seven in line 9 to twelve in line 12. If it be objected that poems in iambics sometimes have trisyllabic substitutions and thus vary syllable count, we can reply that such variations are not as marked as those here and that the lines still admit of easy foot-divisions that can enable us, if we wish, to locate where and how the extra syllables function. "Inversnaid," in contrast, features lines, like the seventh, that are not readily construable by conventional foot-analysis.

Some metrists might consider such poems as Coleridge's "Christabel" and Shelley's "Sensitive Plant" to be additional examples of accentual verse. However, to hear these poems accurately we must bring to them our experience and habits of reading accentual-syllabic verse. Specifically, we have to recognize the sorts of promotions and demotions that we find in accentual-syllabics. For instance, when we encounter the lines below (8, 28, 448, 644) from Coleridge's four-beat "Christabel," we must, to get the requisite number of stresses, identify as metrically accented the relatively light syllables "from," "of," "in," "hos-" and "-ty." (I will mark these syllables with grave rather than acute accents.)

> Fròm her kénnel benéath the róck
> Òf her ówn betróthëd kníght
> And fóndly ìn his árms he tóok
> And áll his hòspitálitỳ

Likewise, when we read, in Shelley's "Sensitive Plant," such lines as

> Wrapped and filled by their mutual atmosphere. (68)

we must recognize that "wrapped" is demoted or we will lose hold of the four-beat measure. To keep the verse going, we must fight our tendency to give the word a beat:

> Like young lóvers whom yóuth and lóve make déar
> Wrapped and fílled by their mútual átmosphére.

This kind of verse is not truly and independentally accentual in the way *Piers Plowman* is or Hopkins's poems are. It is more a subspecies or variant of accentual-syllabic verse.

We do, however, find other instances of accentual verse in nursery or chanting rhymes. In *Jack and the Beanstalk*, for example, the giant speaks in four-beat accentual verse when he threatens to use the hero's skeleton as a wheat substitute:

> Fé fí fó fúm
> Í smell the blóod of an Énglishmán;
> Bé he alíve or bé he déad,
> I'll grínd his bónes to máke my bréad.

2. Syllabic Verse

If accentual verse regulates the number of accents in the line, but not the number of syllables, syllabic verse does the opposite. It is determined by a fixed syllable count, but the number and placement of the beats may vary.

Some have proposed that certain poems of the English Renaissance may be syllabic in conception. Apparent support for this hypothesis has been discerned in Sidney's comment about modern verse's "observing only number (with some regard of the accent)." But, as we noted in the fourth chapter, when Renaissance metrists like Sidney emphasize syllable count, they do so primarily to distinguish the procedure, in vernacular prosodies, of regulating syllabic number from the procedure, in ancient prosody, of regulating syllabic quantity. And however syllabic the metrical theory of the English Renaissance may at times seem, the metrical practice is as concerned with the arrangement of accents as it is with the counting of syllables.

Yet John Donne, in his five extended *Satires,* does write what might be called purely syllabic verse. Donne composes the satires in decasyllabic couplets, but does not consistently dispose his beats according to the iambic pentameter pattern or any other accentual scheme. Readers have long recognized the heterodox versification of these poems. It may well have been with them mind that Ben Jonson complained to William Drummond, "That Donne, for not keeping of accent, deserved hanging." Alexander Pope found the rhythms of the satires so harsh that he "versified" the second and fourth —rewriting them, that is, as smooth Augustan pentameters. In a less censorious mood, Thomas Gray in his "Observations on English Metre" remarked, "Dr. Donne (in his Satires) observes no regularity in the pause, or in the feet of his verse, only the number of syllables is equal throughout."

The following lines (5–16) from the fourth of Donne's *Satires* illustrate their versification. At this point in the poem, its speaker laments that he has received a reputation for corruption as a result of going to the royal court, though he did not go to curry favor, but merely to learn what the place was like. The speaker compares his plight to that of a person (here called "Glaze," a name suggesting someone prone to "stare" or "gawk") who in Germany during the Reformation went to Catholic mass for curiosity rather than out of religious conviction and who, caught there by the authorities, was fined for engaging in proscribed observances. Both the first line and fourth-to-last line may look to have an extra syllable. But Donne probably wishes us to read "neither" as monosyllabic, as is commonly done in the Renaissance verse; and he likely intends us to read "to all" as an elision (to' all). A few lines earlier, on the same principle, "To a" is reduced to "To' a."

> My mind, neither with pride's itch, nor yet hath been
> Poison'd with love to see, or to be seen,
> I had no suit there, nor new suit to show,
> Yet went to Court; but as Glaze, which did go
> To'a Mass in jest, catch'd, was fain to disburse
> The hundred marks, which is the Statute's curse,
> Before he 'scapt, so'it pleased my destiny
> (Guilty of my sin of going) to think me
> As prone to all ill, and of good as forget-
> ful, as proud, as lustful, and as much in debt,
> As vain, as witless, and as false as they
> Which dwell at Court, for once going that way.

Some of these lines can be scanned as iambic pentameters, but others (e. g., the two in the next-to-last couplet) cannot. The jaggedness of rhythm is augmented by the jerky pauses within the lines and by the violent enjambments (as in "forget-/ful"). Since Donne in other poems handles the pentameter with consummate skill, one must assume that the irregularities here are intentional.

Though the verse of his *Satires* is syllabic, Donne does not look to have composed them as metrical experiments. Instead, Donne's technique likely involves his attitude towards the genre in which he is working. In his day, people thought that "satire" derived from "satyr" and that satirists might well write in the riotous manner of that lascivious woodland creature of classical mythology. ("Satire" actually derives not from "satyr" but from the Latin word *satura,* meaning "medley.") In other words, Donne's syllabism probably issued from generic rather than metrical considerations.

In view of apparent rhythmical irregularities in Wyatt's poems in pentameter, some observers have speculated that he may have conceived some of his poems in that line as syllabic. His translations and adaptations of Italian poems certainly could have led him in this direction: accent is not so prominent a feature of Italian verse as it is in English verse. However, scholars disagree about Wyatt's versification. Some urge that if one allows Wyatt certain features of earlier English pronunciation—the sounding of silent "e's" and Romanic accentuation of words like "nature" and "balance"—he emerges as a more regular prosodist than he is often said to be. Others see him as consciously experimental. Still others see him simply as a transitional figure from the somewhat confused pentametric practice of such Early Tudor poets as Stephen Hawes to the surer practice of Surrey and, eventually, Spenser and Sidney. But whatever is going on in Wyatt's verse, it is not pure syllabism. If irregularities exist, they produce variations in syllable count no less than in accent pattern.

Renaissance conundrums aside, English syllabic verse appears during and is part of the prosodic restlessness of the twentieth century. Fine modern poets who have experimented with syllabics include Robert Bridges, Elizabeth Daryush, Marianne Moore, Auden, Dylan Thomas, and Thom Gunn.

Some twentieth-century syllabic poems suggest traditional accentual-syllabic arrangement. Daryush's "For ———" is an example. Written in a seven-syllable line, this is a study of a person who, while superficially sympathetic, is profoundly self-centered. That Daryush conceives of the poem as syllabic is plain from its not having line-beginning majuscules unless grammar calls for them. As Daryush indicates in an appendix to one of her collections, she conventionally opens lines with capitals in her accentual-syllabic verse, but does not do this in her work in syllabics. Despite the syllabic conception of the poem, many readers may hear most of its lines as iambic trimeters with anapestic substitutions.

> It is pleasant to hang out
> this sign at your open gate:
> "*Succour for the desolate*"—
> your neighbours praise you, no doubt;
>
> but woe to whoe'er in need
> at the inner door has knocked,
> found the snug room barred and locked
> where alone you fatly feed.

More often, however, syllabic verse has been characterized not by lyrical effects, such as one finds in Daryush's work, but by more conversational tones. This circumstance is not surprising. One principle of syllabic verse is that no pattern of accent should establish itself. To the extent that this principle is realized, rhythm will be de-emphasized, since rhythm requires some form of grammatical repetition or regularly recurring beat. Neither is it surprising that poets working in syllabics have usually found that lines with an odd number of syllables are best suited to their aims. Writing lines of five, seven, nine, or eleven syllables, poets are less apt to slip unconsciously into iambics than they would be if they were writing lines of four, six, eight, or ten syllables. And though poets in writing lines with an odd number of syllables may risk falling into trochaics, this danger is not so grave. As was noted in the last chapter, trochaic rhythms are emphatic; it requires effort and awareness to sustain them.

Gunn's "Considering the Snail" is a syllabic poem which well illustrates less lyrical and more conversational tones than Daryush's. Gunn composes in a seven-syllable line and in six-line stanzas slant-rhymed *abcabc*. The adjective in the last line is evidently to be heard in its syncopated form— "delib'rate."

> The snail pushes through a green
> night, for the grass is heavy
> with water and meets over
> the bright path he makes, where rain
> has darkened the earth's dark. He
> moves in a wood of desire,
>
> pale antlers barely stirring
> as he hunts. I cannot tell
> what power is at work, drenched there
> with purpose, knowing nothing.
> What is a snail's fury? All
> I think is that if later
>
> I parted the blades above
> the tunnel and saw the thin
> trail of broken white across
> litter, I would never have
> imagined the slow passion
> to that deliberate progress.

However understated his rhythms, Gunn nicely correlates the movement and subject of his verse. The enjambment from line 2 to line 3, for instance, gives a sense of the impending weight of the soaked grass, and the way it arches and meets over the snail is well suggested by the turn from line 3 to line 4. Likewise, the simultaneous division and running together of stanzas 2 and 3 indicate the duality of the human speaker's "part[ing]" something that was for the snail indivisible and ongoing.

Some syllabic poems, especially those by Marianne Moore and Dylan

Thomas, feature stanzas of Byzantine complexity. The seven stanzas of Thomas's "Poem in October," for example, are of ten lines each, with the syllabic structure running 9, 12, 9, 3, 5, 12, 12, 5, 3, 9. Similarly intricate is the strophic arrangement of Moore's "No Swan So Fine," whose seven-line stanza runs 7, 8, 6, 8, 8, 5, 9. Since this latter poem is only two stanzas long, it can be conveniently cited. The poem contrasts the impermanence of life, even at its grandest and most royal, with the permanence of art. In a note on the poem, Moore reports that she took its opening quotation from an article by Percy Phillip that appeared in the *New York Times Magazine* of May 10, 1931. Lines 2 and 5 in each stanza rhyme. Otherwise, the poem is un-rhymed, though there are hints of rhymes or slant rhymes elsewhere, as in the poem's final two lines ("sculptured/dead").

"No water so still as the
     dead fountains of Versailles." No swan,
with swart blind look askance
and gondoliering legs, so fine
     as the chintz china one with fawn-
brown eyes and toothed gold
collar on to show whose bird it was.

Lodged in the Louis Fifteenth
     candelabrum-tree of cockscomb-
tinted buttons, dahlias,
sea-urchins, and everlastings,
     it perches on the branching foam
of polished sculptured
flowers—at ease and tall. The king is dead.

3. Free Verse

Free verse is verse without traditional metrical arrangement. As such, it re-sists definition according to any consistent principle of measure. Nor are different exercises in free verse readily susceptible to typological classifica-tion. So many kinds of composition have, in the past one hundred years, come forth under the aegis of free verse, that no taxonomy can adequately comprehend them all. As early as 1921, Paul Valéry remarked of the explo-sion and proliferation of free verse: "Our epoch has seen the birth of almost as many prosodies as it has counted poets."

Nevertheless, we can specify several common varieties of free verse. One is long-lined and syntactically repetitive. It is often said to derive ultimately from the translations of the Psalms in the King James Bible, translations which are in prose, but which are rhythmical and which use, as the originals do, a great deal of parallelism. First developed and popularized by Martin Farquhar Tupper in his *Proverbial Philosophy* (the first of four installments of which was published in 1838), this variety of free verse became, in the hands of Walt Whitman, an instrument capable of great personal urgency and observation. However, neither Tupper nor Whitman nor their early readers characterized the medium as "free verse," which is a translation of *vers libre,* a French coinage of the 1880s.

Characteristic of the long scriptural line is Whitman's "Are You the New Person Drawn toward Me?"

> Are you the new person drawn toward me?
> To begin with take warning, I am surely far different from what
>   you suppose;
> Do you suppose you will find in me your ideal?
> Do you think it so easy to have me become your lover?
> Do you think the friendship of me would be unalloy'd satisfaction?
> Do you think I am trusty and faithful?
> Do you see no further than this façade, this smooth and
>   tolerant manner of me?
> Do you suppose yourself advancing on real ground toward
>   a real heroic man?
> Have you no thought O dreamer that it may be all maya, illusion?

Like the translators of the King James Psalms, Whitman employs parallelism to establish a sense of rhythm. He additionally uses anaphora, that related figure of speech that involves beginning successive clauses with the same grammatical construction. Here the anaphoric element consists of the interrogative "Do you" plus a verb. As often happens in Whitman, parallelism and anaphora not only set the verse going and keep it moving, they also give the poet a way to end the poem. To signal closure he simply departs from his scheme of repetition. In "Are You the New Person . . . " after his series of "Do you" questions, he opens a line with "Have you." If we are familiar with Whitman's technique, as soon as we hear this change in his formula, we know that he is rounding the poem (or, in a longer poem, a section or passage) to its conclusion.

Another common variety of free verse involves short lines that correspond to syntactical units. Each line comprises one element of the larger sentence structures operating in the poem. Such free verse is exemplified by the remarkable Imagist poems of H.D. (e.g., "Pear Tree" and "Oread"), Pound (e.g., "The Coming of War: Actaeon"), and Stevens (e.g., "Disillusionment of Ten O'Clock"); and the mode is anticipated by some of the poems in Stephen Crane's *The Black Riders and Other Lines* (1895), including the third:

> In the desert
> I saw a creature, naked, bestial,
> Who, squatting upon the ground,
> Held his heart in his hands,
> And ate of it.
> I said, "Is it good, friend?"
> "It is bitter—bitter," he answered;
> "But I like it
> "Because it is bitter,
> "And because it is my heart."

The first five lines are a single sentence. Line 1 consists of an introductory prepositional phrase. Line 2 gives us the main clause, which contains a subject, verb, and direct object, plus two adjectives ("naked, bestial") in apposition to the object ("creature"). Line 3 begins a relative clause and features the relative pronoun "who," modified by the participial phrase "squatting upon the ground." The predicate of the relative clause then follows in lines 4 and 5, with the parallel verbs ("Held . . . And ate") dividing, so to speak, the predicate material between them. Line six is a short question, introduced by "I said." Lines seven through ten consist of a compound-complex sentence, with two independent clauses ("It is bitter—bitter" . . . "I like it") and two dependent clauses ("Because it is bitter" . . . "because it is my heart"). Each of these four clauses is accorded a single line, with the first clause being closed with the tag, "he answered." If we do not have in the poem the organized rhythmical repetition that meter supplies, the grammar is compressed and urgent, and the line divisions reflect the syntactical current.

Yet another variety of free verse blends the short-lined approach we find in Crane with lots of enjambment. William Carlos Williams is the poet most identified with this mode, though it is not the only mode he employs, nor is it, in my opinion, the mode in which he most excels. (Williams is arguably strongest in such poems as "The Widow's Lament in Springtime," "Complaint," and "To Waken an Old Lady," where the enjambment is less frequent and more pointed; or in a poem such as "Danse Russe," which features Whitmanian syntactical repetition, but which does so in a line much tauter and livelier than Whitman's.) A good way to appreciate Williams's short, heavily enjambed line is to listen to recordings of him reading his work. He reads in an almost breathless rush his poems in this mode. Listening to him, we may be reminded that he once suggested that he wanted to do in free verse what Milton had done in blank verse—"to make the verse paragraph rather than the line his basic unit." To facilitate run-ons, Williams will end his lines in mid-phrase—with prepositions, conjunctions, articles, attributive words, or with adjectives whose nouns appear at the beginning of the line below. On occasion he concludes poems without a closing mark of punctuation. "The Yellow Chimney" illustrates these qualities:

> There is a plume
> of fleshpale
> smoke upon the blue
>
> sky. The silver
> rings that
> strap the yellow
>
> brick stack at
> wide intervals shine
> in this amber
>
> light—not
> of the sun not of
> the pale sun but
>
> his born brother
> the
> declining season

It testifies to the prevalence of iambic rhythms in our speech that even so fine a vers-libriste as Williams falls into them, apparently without being aware of it. For instance, the first stanza of "The Yellow Chimney" is regularly iambic:

> There is a plume of fleshpale smoke upon the blue

To be sure, the effect of this poem is partly intended to be visual. Its slender appearance on the page may be designed to intimate the fragility or sketchiness of the things described. Still, the iambic undercurrent is notable.

A final type—or possible type—of free verse is a betwixt-and-between variety that hovers intermittently around, in, and out of meter. T. S. Eliot is the best-known practitioner of the mode, which can be seen in such poems as "Gerontion" and in various passages in *Four Quartets*, including the following ("Burnt Norton," 31–46):

> So we moved, and they, in a formal pattern,   31
> Along the empty alley, into the box circle,
> To look down into the drained pool.
> Dry the pool, dry concrete, brown edged,
> And the pool was filled with water out of sunlight,   35
> And the lotos rose, quietly, quietly,
> The surface glittered out of heart of light,
> And they were behind us, reflected in the pool.
> Then a cloud passed, and the pool was empty.
> Go, said the bird, for the leaves were full of children,   40
> Hidden excitedly, containing laughter.
> Go, go, go, said the bird: human kind
> Cannot bear very much reality.
> Time past and time future
> What might have been and what has been   45
> Point to one end, which is always present.

Visually, this passage suggests blank verse. In fact three of the lines above (37, 41, 43) scan as regular pentameters. Other lines (e.g., 35, 38) could be scanned as iambic pentameters with anapestic substitutions. Another line (45) can be scanned as an iambic tetrameter, and others (e.g., 33 and 46) could be construed as tetrameters, though given the uncertain rhythmical context, we may feel not entirely confident in treating them thus. Still other lines (e.g., 44) do not lend themselves to any one obvious interpretation. Overall, the verse hovers around iambic rhythm, sliding between, mostly, tetrameter and pentameter. If it is free verse, it is not as directly free as Crane's poem nor as inventively free as, say, Stevens's "Disillusionment of Ten O'Clock." If it is metrical, it is only tenuously so and requires that its reader have a sure ear for meter to catch the ways that it alludes to and plays off of conventional measure.

4. Imitation-Classical Verse

Imitation-classical verse attempts either to realize or to suggest in English the quantitative measures of ancient Greek and Latin poets. Poets writing imitation-classical verse endeavor to produce poems according to arrangements of long and short syllables (rather than accented and unaccented ones) or try to dispose accented and unaccented syllables in patterns that correspond to the long and short positions in classical lines and stanzas.

The most notable attempt to realize in English a prosody of long and short syllables occurs in the sixteenth century. This effort is spurred by classical scholars such as Roger Ascham, whose *Schoolmaster* advocates, as was indicated in our fourth chapter, that English metric should base itself, as ancient metric had, on the classification and measurement of long and short syllables. Philip Sidney, who read and admired Ascham's work, wrote several poems in imitation-classical measures for his *Old Arcadia*, which he drafted evidently between 1578 and 1581. Other poets of Sidney's acquaintance, including Edmund Spenser and Edward Dyer, expressed interest in quantitative metric, and these writers have come to be known as the "Areopagus" group. The name comes from a lighthearted comment that Spenser, referring to the ancient Athenian council, makes in a letter to Gabriel Harvey. Sidney and Dyer had, Spenser tells Harvey, "proclaimed in their *areiôi pagôi* a generall surceasing and silence of balde Rymers ... [and] prescribed certaine Lawes and rules of Quantities of English sillables for English Verse."

Sidney, however, seems to have grown doubtful of his experiments. At points in drafts or transcriptions of *The Old Arcadia* prior to the final one, he introduced two items that dealt with quantitative metric. The first is a dialogue discussing the relative merits of quantitative verse and rhymed accentual-syllabic verse; the second is a group of notes setting forth rules for determining syllabic length in English—notes from which I quoted in chapter 4. Neither item makes it into the final transcription of *The Old Arcadia* or into the expanded *New Arcadia*, which Sidney left unfinished at his death. Robert Kimbrough speculates that "Sidney suppressed both of these passages ... for it seems clear that after his experimentations he realized that the natural thrust of English poetry could be maintained only within the rhythms and meter of accentual-syllabic verse." This speculation gains in plausibility when we recall that it was probably in 1582 that Sidney wrote *Astrophel and Stella*, his brilliant cycle of love poems in native meters. These poems marked a great leap forward in his own work and may have persuaded him, if persuasion was needed, that the potentials of the accentual-syllabic mode were greater than those of quantitative metric.

In any event, interest in quantitative metric fizzles after the 1580s. English poets continue to write quantitative verse into the seventeenth century, but the last vital argument that our prosody might be made quantitative is Thomas Campion's *Observations in the Art of English Poesie,* which, as has been noted, was published in 1602, but was probably written at least a decade earlier. Even William Johnson Stone's *On the Use of Classical Metres in English* (1898), the best-known relatively recent exploration of the possibility of a quantitative metric in English, has attracted little attention from poets other than Bridges.

The sixteenth-century concern with quantitative metric reflects the condition of our language and verse at that time. In the early decades of the century, Modern English was still in a process of formation, and its grammatical and phonological structures were not well understood. English had produced no indisputably great poet except Chaucer, whose prosody had become incomprehensible because of the changes English had undergone since his day. Further, though by midcentury poets had reclarified and adapted accentual-syllabic measures to Modern English, there existed as yet no impressive body of native verse. The work in, for example, *Tottel's Miscellany* of 1557 represents real and growing achievement. But neither in subject nor in technique could such work be said to rival the best poems of antiquity. Latin literature had matured in part by adapting itself to Greek metric; it was conceivable that English might profit from a similar accommodation.

Ultimately, however, the ancient quantitative meters proved unnecessary. Even during their classicizing experiments, Sidney and Spenser continued working with accentual-syllabic measures, demonstrating in the process the resources of the accentual-syllabic system. Because of their successes, and those of such younger writers as Marlowe, Shakespeare, Donne, and Jonson, the 1580s and 1590s witnessed a flowering of dramatic and lyric poetry in English that put to rest doubts about the efficacy of the native metric.

In addition, the nature of our language makes unfeasible the importation of a quantitative metric. A chief stumbling block is that Modern English does not have the true long and short vowel pairs that Greek and Latin and even Old English did. Though we speak of our vowels as being "long" and "short," we are referring mainly to vowel quality (tense vs. lax), not duration. Length in Modern English is phonetic rather than phonemic: the environment in which the vowel occurs is more critical to syllabic duration than the vowel itself. For instance, though "bit" and "beat" feature, respectively, short *i* and long *e* sounds, both syllables are short, on account of being stopped by the voiceless *t*. And though "beat" and "bead" both feature a long *e*, the first is short, whereas the second is long because of its voiced *d*. By the same token, while "beat" with its long *e* is short, "jazz" with its short *a* is long. Even after we ascertain that some syllables are short and others are long, when we encounter them in verse, as in these made-up ballad-stanza lines,

> They drew a bead on victory
> And beat the Utah Jazz

their differences or similarities of length are metrically irrelevant.

What we immediately hear and grasp is stress. We can recognize duration, particularly when it is pointed out to us, and the lengths of syllables contribute to the aural effects of our verse lines. But quantity is not central to our experience of our language. And as A. E. Housman remarks in his review of Stone's book, to ask English-speaking poets to elevate quantity over stress is like asking athletes to run on their hands and to catch and throw balls with their feet.

The sixteenth-century experiment with quantitative meters did, however, produce some fine verse. This is amply evident in the thirty or so poems that Campion wrote to illustrate the durational measures discussed in his *Observations in the Art of English Poesie*. The best-known of these poems is the elegantly flowing "Rose-cheekt Laura":

> Rose-cheekt Laura, come;
> Sing thou smoothly with thy beauty's
> Silent music, either other
> > Sweetly gracing.

> Lovely forms do flow
> From consent divinely framëd
> Heav'n is music, and thy beauty's
> > Birth is heavenly.

> These dull notes we sing
> Discords need for helps to grace them;
> Only beauty purely loving
> > Knows no discord;

But still moves delight,
Like clear springs renew'd by flowing,
Ever perfect, ever in them-
     selves eternal.

We may well be puzzled when Campion explains, for instance, that the first line of each stanza is a quantitative iambic dimeter, "two feet and one odd syllable. The first foot may be made either a Trochee or a Spondee or an Iambick . . . In the second place we must ever insert a Trochee or Tribrach [an ancient foot consisting of three short syllables] and so leave the last syllable (as in the end of the verse it is always held) common." If we are unfamiliar with the rules according to which Campion is measuring his quantities, his description is confusing; and we may grow more confused when we try to relate it to conventional classical prosody. Ancient iambic dimeters consist of two iambic *metra* and eight syllables, with the first syllable of each *metra* being "anceps"—either long or short—the second and fourth being long, and the third being short. Yet regardless of Campion's description of it, the poem is a beauty; and we can hear its stanzas as straightforward accentualized English trochaics, line 1 a catalectic trimeter, lines 2 and 3 tetrameters, and line 4 a dimeter, even if Campion himself did not conceive of the poem in quite these terms.

Instead of trying to write verse according to quantitative rules, most later English poets interested in ancient measures have tried to approximate, in stress-based rhythms, the patterns of classical lines. Southey's and Longfellow's experiments with the dactylic hexameter exemplify this accentualizing process. So does Frost's "For Once, Then, Something," which Englishes the "Phalaecean" hendecasyllabic line. (The adjective derives from the line's having been much used by the Greek poet Phalaecus.) In antiquity, this measure consists of a trochee, a dactyl, and three more trochees. Frost follows the ancient sequence of feet, but arranges the syllables within them not by length, but by accent. Here is his poem, with its first four lines scanned:

```
 /   x   /    x  x   / x     / x   /   x
Others | taunt me with | having | knelt at | well-curbs
 /  x    /   x  x  /    x   / x    / x
Always | wrong to the | light, so | never | seeing
  / x    /   x   x   /   x     /      x   / x
Deeper | down in the | well than | where the | water
 /     x   /  x x   / x     / x    / x
Gives me | back in a | shining | surface | picture
```

Me myself in the summer heaven, godlike,
Looking out of a wreath of fern and cloud puffs.
Once, when trying with chin against a well-curb,
I discerned, as I thought, beyond the picture,
Through the picture, a something white, uncertain,
Something more of the depths—and then I lost it.
Water came to rebuke the too clear water.
One drop fell from a fern, and lo, a ripple
Shook whatever it was lay there at bottom,
Blurred it, blotted it out. What was that whiteness?
Truth? A pebble of quartz? For once, then, something.

English-language poets have imitated not only ancient verse lines, but also ancient stanzaic forms. Tennyson employs for his "Milton," for example, an accentualized version of the alcaic stanza, named after the Greek lyric poet Alcaeus. In addition, poets have imitated the Sapphic stanza, which the Greek poet Sappho popularized and which consists of three hendeca-syllabic lines, with the pattern long-short-long-anceps-long-short-short-long-short-long-anceps, and a concluding five-syllable line, which runs long-short-short-long-anceps. Adapting this pattern to accentualized English results in the eleven-syllable lines having accents on the first, third, fifth, eighth, and tenth syllables, while the five-syllable lines are accented on the first and fourth syllables. Swinburne uses this pattern in his "Sapphics," which depicts Sappho herself and the final stanza of which envisions the ghosts of the poet's followers

Clothed about with flame and with tears, and singing
Songs that move the heart of the shaken heaven,
Songs that break the heart of the earth with pity,
        Hearing, to hear them.

An ancient modification of Sapphic stanza appears in Horace, who regularly makes long the fourth syllables of the hendecasyllabic lines and who generally sets word accents at the fourth and sixth syllables:

$$\bar{\text{mi}}\text{ttĕ } \bar{\text{ci}}\text{vi}\bar{\text{les}} \text{ sŭpĕr } \bar{\text{ur}}\text{bĕ } \bar{\text{cu}}\bar{\text{ras}}$$

        let go, moreover, your dutiful anxieties for the state

(Odes, 3.8.17)

Though this variation looks slight, if you incorporate it into English it alters the line's rhythm. If you stress syllables 4 and 6, and consequently de-emphasize syllables 3 and 5, you turn the line into a quasi-iambic pentameter, with a trochaic first foot and feminine ending. One possible advantage of the Horatian modification is that it produces rhythmical correspondence between all four lines of the stanza. The short Adonic line is, in its English version, basically an iambic dimeter with a trochaic first foot and feminine ending; thus the line answers, in miniature, lines that resemble pentameters with trochaic first feet and feminine endings.

A poem in English Sapphics on the Horatian model is Cowper's powerful "Lines Written During a Period of Insanity":

> Hatred and vengeance, my eternal portion,
> Scarce can endure delay of execution,
> Wait, with impatient readiness, to seize my
> Soul in a moment.
>
> Damn'd below Judas: more adhorr'd than he was,
> Who for a few pence sold his holy Master.
> Twice betrayed Jesus me, the last delinquent,
> Deems the profanest.
>
> Man disavows, and Deity disowns me:
> Hell might afford my miseries a shelter;
> Therefore hell keeps her ever-hungry mouths all
> Bolted against me.
>
> Hard lot! encompass'd with a thousand dangers;
> Weary, faint, trembling with a thousand terrors;
> I'm call'd, if vanquish'd, to receive a sentence
> Worse than Abiram's.
>
> *Him* the vindictive rod of angry justice
> Sent quick and howling to the centre headlong;
> *I,* fed with judgment, in a fleshly tomb, am
> Buried above ground.

The repeated inversions of the initial feet, and the heavy-light—or in some cases heavy-heavy—line-endings, give Cowper's verse distinctive rhythm; but it is different from that which we find Swinburne's Sapphics. (In "The Craftsman," a poem about Shakespeare, Kipling mixes Sapphic and Horatian hendecasyllabics and adds wrinkles of his devising.)

A final ancient form that we should note is the choral ode. In the late sixth and early fifth centuries B.C., it was practiced in its own right by Corinna, Pindar, and Bacchylides; and subsequently, Aeschylus, Sophocles, and Euripides featured it as a musical component of their tragedies. Choral odes were performed, as their name indicates, by choruses of singers and were often written in triadic groups that followed the sequence of strophe, antistrophe, and epode. The strophe and antistrophe were identically constructed; and though the epode differed in arrangement from them, it corresponded to the other epodes. Customarily, a choral ode would go through at least two of these complete three-part cycles. Metrists apply an alphabetic notation to the choral ode's triadic sequence (not unlike that which they apply to rhyme schemes), rendering the ode's form as AAB, AAB, and so on. The As stand for the strophes and antistrophes, the Bs for the epodes.

Because Pindar was the most famous writer of choral odes in antiquity, and because more of his work has survived than that of any other writer of choral odes, the form came to be associated with him. In the Renaissance, Ben Jonson on several occasions imitated the structures of the earlier poet's elaborate stanzas—explicitly appealing to "Pindar's Muse" at the beginning of his own "Ode to James, Earl of Desmond." And Jonson's "To the Immortal Memory and Friendship of That Noble Pair, Sir Lucius Cary and Sir Henry Morison" is considered by many to be the most successful English realization of the Pindaric manner. This poem offers Cary condolences on the early death of his friend Morison, and Jonson disposes the poem in the ancient tripartite fashion. The strophes and antistrophes are ten lines long and follow the same metrical and rhyme arrangement; the epodes, which exhibit a similar correspondence between themselves, have twelve lines. Each triad thus has thirty-two lines, and the poem runs four times through the sequence.

Would that I could illustrate, by citing from the poem, Jonson's technique; but to exhibit the correspondences of the strophes and antistrophes, the correspondences of the epodes, and the larger correspondences of the whole three-part schema, I would have to cite at least sixty-four lines. The best that can be done here is to encourage interested readers to lay hands on a copy of Jonson's verse and to examine the poem themselves. That Jonson labels his strophes and antistrophes "Turns" and "Counter-turns," and names his epodes "Stands," recalls conventions according to which the ancient odes were performed. The chorus would dance to one side of the stage while singing the strophes, would move back during the antistrophes, and would stand still to deliver the epodes.

Though Jonson understood the structure of the Pindaric ode, subsequent poets did not, and their misconceptions gave rise, in the middle and later seventeenth century, to an unusual poetic genre: the irregular Pindaric or pseudo-Pindaric ode. The key figure in this development was Abraham Cowley, who published in 1656 a volume of *Pindarique Odes*. Perhaps influenced by Horace's having commented (*Odes*, 4.2.5ff.) that Pindar's now lost dithyrambs sweep along in "verses released from rule" *(numeris lege solutis)*, Cowley emulated Pindar's elaborate style, but did not follow the principles of strophic responsion that governed the ancient poet's odes. In his "Discourse on the Pindarique Ode" in 1706, William Congreve protested. Like Jonson, Congreve recognized the order of the original form and observed: "The Character of these late Pindariques, is, a Bundle of rambling incoherent Thoughts, expressed in a like Parcel of irregular Stanzas, which also consist of such another Complication of disproportioned, uncertain and perplexed Verses and Rhimes." In the meantime, however, Cowley's odes had become popular and much emulated. Eventually, the pseudo-Pindaric vogue faded, as the work of translators and editors like Gilbert West and August Boeckh clarified the particular structures of the ancient poet's odes. But poets continued to write irregular odes down through the Romantic period. Among these later works are Wordsworth's immortality ode and Keats's "Ode to Psyche."

Congreve's complaints notwithstanding, the irregularities of the English Pindaric ode are limited. Cowley's lines are consistently iambic, though their lengths vary unpredictably from one to six feet and though the rhymes follow no repeating scheme. This passage (37–48) from Cowley's ode "To the New Year"—a passage in which the poet pleads with the new year not to vex him with disappointing romantic entanglements—typifies his technique:

> Nay, if thou lov'st me, gentle year,
> Let not so much as love be there,
> Vain, fruitless love I mean; for, gentle year,
>   Although I fear,
> There's of this caution little need,
>   Yet, gentle year, take heed
>   How thou dost make
>   Such a mistake;
> Such love I mean alone
> As by thy cruel predecessors has been shown;
> For, though I'have too much cause to doubt it,
> I fain would try, for once, if life can live without it.

It is difficult to imagine that such verse was once wildly popular.

All of the alternative modes that we have been examining—accentual, syllabic, free, and imitation-classical—have produced valuable poems and offer valuable opportunities to poets. At the same time, however, all lack something of the flexibility and order of the accentual-syllabic system.

Because any complete articulation in English has one and only one primary stress, accentual verse requires special devices to indicate which intermediate stresses count metrically and which do not. In accentual-syllabic verse, the foot pattern guides us. When we hear an iambic pentameter with only three strong speech stresses, as in

> Each **morn**ing they will **laun**der, for their **sin**

> (Gwen Harwood, "Home of Mercy," 12)

the metrical paradigm unobtrusively informs us (in reading naturally, we are not even aware of the process) that "they" and "for" also carry metrical accents:

> x / x / x / x / x /
> Each morning they will launder, for their sin

Conversely, if a pentameter is jammed with weighty syllables, as in

> This **soil breeds spin**sters! **Five miles round**, I **swear**

> (A. D. Hope, "Clover Honey," 2)

the measure instantly and quietly determines that "soil," "spin-," "five," "round," and "swear," are the metrically accented ones, whereas "breeds" and "miles" serve as offbeats:

> x / x / x / x / x /
> This soil breeds spinsters! Five miles round, I swear

Accentual verse provides no such natural and understated means of indicating which intermediately stressed syllables are metrically significant. To get around this problem, poets have three options: (1) they can highlight ambiguous syllables with accent marks, italics, and the like; (2) they can point beats with alliteration; or (3) they can confine themselves to simple rhythms that avoid (so far as is possible) intermediate stress and that rely on sharply contrasted weak and strong syllables. However, none of these options is especially appealing. Even in superb poems like Hopkins's, diacritical and related devices tend to be distracting and to leave an impression

Alternative Modes of Versification in English | 273

of typographic exaggeration. Nor, for all of the vigor of the Old English tradition, would poets today feel comfortable confining themselves to its regularly balanced and alliterating structures. As for the last option, it may be the least attractive, since it would deny poets so many notes from the scale of normal English speech.

If accentual verse risks overemphasis, syllabic verse risks tenuousness. Many readers have difficulty hearing syllabic lines as lines, and a number of prosodists have wondered if, in a language as accentual as ours is, any metric can profitably ignore stress.

In addition, it is sometimes hard, in reading syllabic verse, to resolve syllabic ambiguities. When we encounter, in an accentual-syllabic poem, a line with an extra syllable, we can hear where an elision or a substitution is occurring. We can precisely locate the variation, since we know the rhythmical pattern and can discern the individual feet. Consider the following pentameter:

> Which puts me in a worse-than-usual fix
>
> (Wendy Cope, "Another Unfortunate Choice," 2)

Here, if we enunciate carefully, we have eleven syllables and two possibilities for elision: we can slur *e* and *i* in "me in" or *u* and *a* in "usual." However, the foot pattern solves this dilemma. The first slur would gum up the meter (and would be odd in light of contemporary speech); the second would not. The poet, then, wishes us to hear,

> x   /   x / x   /   x /   >   /
> Which puts | me in | a worse- | than-us | ual fix

Or if somebody objects to elision and wishes to construe the line as having a full extra syllable, it results in an anapestic substitution in the fifth foot:

> x   /   x / x   /   x /   x x /
> Which puts | me in | a worse- | than-us | ual fix

Without any foot pattern, syllabic verse may leave us at a loss with respect to such quandaries. Illustrations of this situation appear throughout Bridges's philosophic epic in twelve-syllable lines, *The Testament of Beauty*. Consider, for instance, this verse (2.144):

> The unfathomable mystery of her awaken'd joy

If we say this line carefully, we have fifteen syllables. Apparently, then, we are to elide three of the syllables to get down to the twelve-syllable norm. Unfortunately, according to the conventions of elision Bridges analyzes in *Milton's Prosody,* four possibilities for contractions occur in the line—"Th' unfathomable," "unfath'mable," "myst'ry," and "mystery' of." My best guess is that Bridges intended the first three. However, Bridges urges in *Milton's Prosody* that Milton was reluctant to internally syncopate adjectives ending in -*able* and that we should scan, for example,

Of something not unseasonable to ask

(Paradise Lost, 8.201)

not as

x /   x   / x /   x / x /
Of something not unseas'nable to ask

but as

x /   x   / x / x / x >
Of something not unseasonable to ask

Did Bridges share the preference that he believed was evident in Milton's versification? If he did, and I syncopate "unfathomable" to "unfath'mable," I am probably misreading his line; and alternative elisive combinations I adopt may be wrong, too. Such uncertainties are small, but not inconsequential if we care about meter.

Free verse has some of the problematical elements that syllabics does. It is often hard to hear free verse as verse. The poet can obviate this difficulty by writing in short parsing lines like those that Crane employs in "In the desert." But such lines, with their regular phrasal clipping and end-stopping, may grow monotonous quickly, however brilliantly effective they may be for brief stretches.

Free verse may also require contextualization. So far as it avoids observable measure, its own rhythms can best be appreciated, as was suggested a moment ago in connection with Eliot, against the backdrop of the traditional meters that it eschews. Early free-versers could trust that their audience would know the forms of poetry and would hear the ways in which they were violating or improvising off of those forms. A century of experiment, however, has weakened the prosodic understanding of readers, and it is doubtful that many of them today have the internalized and intuitive metrical awareness to gauge the rhythms of *vers libre* against the modulatory capacities of the older and more definitely articulated verse measures.

Further, it takes a poet possessed of a rare ear to write free verse well. One advantage of meter is that it can lend its melodies to poets who lack a versatile musical sense, but who have a deep feeling for poetry and a vision to communicate. Few people would praise Gascoigne or Samuel Johnson as metrical virtuosi. Yet in poems like "Gascoigne's Woodmanship" or "The Vanity of Human Wishes," the meter combines with the poet's great heart, and the language soars and sings.

The difficulty with imitation-classical measures is simply that writing in them is a trifle factitious. A truly quantitative prosody is not feasible in Modern English, and today when we compose in classical lines and stanzas, we are really composing accentualized versions of them. Also, the ancient meters, even when accentualized, do not always suit the rhythms of Modern English; and if we write in them, we must guard against concentrating so narrowly on their unusual patterns that we forget what we are saying. Earlier, I mentioned Tennyson's "Milton," and this poem illustrates the problem:

> O mighty mouth'd inventor of harmonies,
> O skill'd to sing of Time or Eternity,
> > God-gifted organ-voice of England,
> > > Milton, a name to resound for ages;
> Whose Titan angels, Gabriel, Abdiel,
> Starr'd from Jehovah's gorgeous armories,
> > Tower, as the deep-domed empyrean
> > > Rings to the roar of an angel-onset!
> Me rather all that bowery loneliness,
> The brooks of Eden mazily murmuring,
> > And bloom profuse and cedar arches
> > > Charm, as a wanderer out in ocean,
> Where some refulgent sunset of India
> Streams o'er a rich ambrosial ocean isle,
> > And crimson-hued the stately palm-woods
> > > Whisper in odorous heights of even.

Tennyson subtitles the poem "Alcaics," and if we look up in a handbook the metrical pattern for the form, we will find that, by golly, the poet has presented rhythmically accurate modern equivalents of Alcaic stanzas. The poem's diction, however, may send us into sugar-shock. Even allowing that Tennyson is imitating Milton's high style, the word choice is baroque and the syntax convoluted. The poem's second sentence, which occupies the third and fourth stanzas, is particularly unusual, beginning as it does with a direct object ("Me") that hangs for three lines awaiting the verb ("Charm"). As a metrical exercise, the poem is highly accomplished, but it is simply an exercise. And if we write in imitation-classical measures, we should probably try our very best to make them native—in the sense of both "natural" and "of our own environment."

Whether this book has communicated insight into the nature of versification, only the reader can decide. Before closing, however, I should acknowledge the providence that enables the writing of books and that has allowed for poetry and the other arts. Somehow, on this little planet in the midst of this immense universe, life was born, and consciousness emerged and ramified. Not the least of the miracles that has occurred in this process is the appearance of language and the development of the elegant linguistic structures of verse that have helped us to explore, enjoy, understand, and preserve our experience.

We will never fully know why verse appeals to us in the mysterious ways that it does. Perhaps at a physiological level, it integrates our minds, encouraging us to experience language not only as a left-brain activity involving verbal content, but also as a right-brain response to tonal shades and rhythmical patterns. Perhaps in its numerical organization, verse connects us to the larger orders of our cosmos. Wherever the explanation lies, the very fact that we can compose and respond to poetry is a cause for hope that our species, despite its follies, may yet evolve to the full intelligence and sympathy of which it is capable.

Lastly, I should repeat that any poet who writes on technique, as I have done, is acutely cognizant that technique alone will never produce a good poem. Technique is crucial, but poems and poets need the assistance of their Muses. They need the gift of inspiration as well as the energies and intuitions that craft supplies. As Cunningham says in his "Predestined Space,"

> Simplicity assuages
> With grace the damaged heart,
> So would I in these pages
> If will were art.

But the best engineer
Of metre, rhyme, and thought
Can only tool each gear
To what he sought

If chance with craft combines
In the predestined space
To lend his damaged lines
Redeeming grace.

Notes

Glossary

Bibliography

Permissions and Copyrights

Index

Notes

Note to Introduction

For this book, I have used standard editions of the poets I cite. In the cases of Chaucer and Shakespeare, I have quoted from Larry D. Benson, general ed., *The Riverside Chaucer*, 3d ed., based on *The Works of Geoffrey Chaucer*, edited by F. N. Robinson (Boston: Houghton Mifflin, 1987) and from Sylvan Barnet, general ed., *The Complete Signet Classic Shakespeare* (New York: Harcourt Brace, 1972). In quoting from older poems, I have modernized spelling, except when doing so would have obscured the meter. I have less generally and less regularly modernized punctuation. Whereas today we punctuate chiefly to show grammatical organization, earlier writers are more likely to punctuate to indicate rhythm. Updating the punctuation of a Milton or a Pope may thus obscure modulations that the poets intended. Unless another translator is noted, I am responsible for the translations from foreign-language poems.

For the ancient works to which this book refers, I have consulted the following editions, all from the Loeb Classical Library, published by the Harvard University Press: *Apollodorus,* trans. James G. Frazer, 2 vols. (1921); Aristotle, *The "Art" of Rhetoric,* trans. John Henry Freese (1926); Aristotle, *The Poetics,* trans. W. Hamilton Fyfe (1932); Longinus, *On the Sublime,* trans. W. Hamilton Fyfe (1932); Demetrius, *On Style,* trans. W. Rhys Roberts (1932); Cicero, *Orator,* trans. H. M. Hubbell (1962); Cicero, *De Oratore,* trans. E. W. Sutton and H. Rackham, 2 vols. (1948); Horace, *Odes and Epodes,* trans. C. E. Bennett (1927); and Quintilian, *Institutio Oratoria,* trans. H. E. Butler, 4 vols. (1920).

Francis Jeffrey's epitaph on Peter Robinson appears in the following anthologies: Morris Bishop, ed., *A Treasury of British Humor* (New York: Coward-McCann, 1942), 93; David McCord, ed., *The Modern Treasury of Humorous Verse* (Garden City, N.Y.: Garden City Books, 1945), 359; Geoffrey Grigson, ed., *The Faber Book of Epigrams and Epitaphs* (London: Faber & Faber, 1977), 139; and Michael Roberts, ed., *The Faber Book of Comic Verse,* with a supplement chosen by Janet Adam Smith (London: Faber & Faber, 1974), 91. The epitaph exists in another version, written by John Gibson Lockhart. This appears in *The Journal of Sir Walter Scott, 1825–1832* (Edinburgh: David Douglas, 1910), 259 n. 2:

> Here lies that peerless paper peer Lord Peter,
> Who broke the laws of God and man and metre.

Lockhart, however, applies the poem to Lord Patrick ("Peter") Robertson (1794–1855), a distinguished writer and jurist, for whom there is an entry in the *Dictionary of National Biography.* There is no entry for any Peter Robinson. Since Jeffrey, Lockhart, and Robertson all lived and worked in Edinburgh at roughly the same time, it is possible that "Robinson" is a corruption for "Robertson."

For the different spellings of "meter" and "metre," see H. W. Fowler, *A Dictionary of Modern English Usage,* 2d ed., revised by Sir Ernest Gowers (Oxford: Oxford University Press, 1965), 363. A cogent statement of the difference between the organized rhythm of verse and the looser rhythm of prose is offered by Edwin Guest: "Verse may be defined as a succession of articulate sounds regulated by a rhythm so definite, that we can readily foresee the results which follow from its application. Rhythm is also met with in prose, but in the latter its range is so wide, that we never can anticipate its flow, while the pleasure we derive from verse is founded on this very anticipation" (Edwin Guest, *A History of English Rhythms,* 2 vols. [London: William Pickering, 1836–38], 1:1).

Many poets and readers, from the sixteenth century to our time, have observed that iambic rhythm is prevalent in or natural to English speech and poetry. In "Certain Notes of Instruction Concerning the Making of Verse or Rhyme in English" (1575), George Gascoigne writes: "[C]ommonly nowadays in English rhymes . . . we use none other but a foot of two syllables, whereof the first is depressed or made short, and the second is elevate or made long" (*George Gascoigne: The Green Knight, Selected Poetry and Prose,* ed. Roger Pooley [Manchester: Carcanet, 1982], 139). In his "Observations in the Art of English Poesie" (circa 1591, published 1602), Thomas Campion remarks that "Iambicks . . . fall out so naturally in our toong, that, if we examine our owne writers, we shall find they unawares hit oftentimes upon the true *Iambick* numbers"; and he comments more generally that "*Iambick* . . . is our most naturall and auncient English verse" (*The Works of Thomas Campion,* ed. Walter R. Davis [Garden City, N.Y.: Doubleday, 1967], 297, 301). Similarly, John Dryden, in his dedication (1664) to *The Rival Ladies,* speaks of unrhymed iambics as "that kind of writing which we call blank verse, but the French, more properly, *prose mesurée;* into which the English tongue so naturally slides that, in writing prose, 'tis hardly to be avoided" (John Dryden, *Of Dramatic Poesy and Other Critical Essays,* ed. George Watson, 2 vols. [London: Dent, 1962], 1:6). And the elder Samuel Wesley observes in his "Epistle to a Friend Concerning Poetry" (1700):

> If I our *English Numbers* taste aright
> We in the grave *Iambic* most delight. (507–8)

More recently, in "The Figure a Poem Makes" (1939), Robert Frost says: "All that can be done with words is soon told. So also with meters—particularly in our language where there are virtually but two, strict iambic and loose iambic" (*Robert Frost on Writing,* ed. Elaine Barry [New Brunswick, N.J.: Rutgers University Press, 1973], 125). John Thompson states, "The iambic metrical pattern has dominated English verse because it provides the best symbolic model of our language" (*The Founding of English Metre* [London: Routledge and Kegan Paul, 1961; reprint ed., with an introduction by John Hollander, New York: Columbia University Press, 1989], 12). And in a little article on the "Iamb," Raymond Chapman notes, "The iamb is the most frequently used foot in English verse . . . and is widely believed to fit the natural rhythm of the language" (Tom McArthur, ed., *The Oxford Companion to the English Language* [Oxford: Oxford University Press, 1992], 496).

Noam Chomsky and Morris Halle's discussion of the alternating-stress tendency of English words of more than one syllable appears in their *Sound Pattern of English* (New York: Harper & Row, 1968), 69ff. Eduard Sievers's essay on Old Germanic and Old English metrics appears in Jess B. Bessinger, Jr., and Stanley J. Kahrl, eds., *Essential Articles for the Study of Old English Poetry* (Hamden, Conn.: Archon, 1968), 267–88; Gawaina D. Luster is the translator of the essay. Old English scholars have noted that the rhythms of Germanic accentual verse shift from falling to rising with, as Ruth P. M. Lehmann puts it, "the loss of inflexions and regularization of the use of the article" ("Contrasting Rhythms of Old English and New English," in *Linguistic and Literary Studies in Honor of Archibald A. Hill*, ed. Mohammad Ali Jazayery, Edgar C. Polomé, and Werner Winter, 4:123 [The Hague: Mouton Publishers, 1978–79]). Originally part of his commentary on his translation of Alexander Pushkin's *Eugene Onegin*, Vladimir Nabokov's *Notes on Prosody* (New York: Pantheon, 1964) is also published in his *Notes on Prosody* and *Abram Gannibal* (Princeton: Princeton University Press, 1964). Otto Jespersen's criticism of foot scansion may be found in his essay, "Notes on Metre," which appears in Jespersen's volume of selected papers, *Linguistica* (Copenhagen: Levin & Munksgaard, 1933), 252; this essay is as well anthologized in Harvey Gross, ed., *The Structure of Verse*, revised ed. (New York: Ecco, 1979), 106–28. A compact and eloquent defense of standard scansion is provided in C. S. Lewis's "Metre," which appears in his *Selected Literary Essays*, ed. Walter Hopper (Cambridge: Cambridge University Press, 1969), 280–85. For a good overview of the history of the term "prosody," see W. Sidney Allen, *Accent and Rhythm: Prosodic Features of Latin and Greek: A Study in Theory and Reconstruction* (Cambridge: Cambridge University Press, 1973), 3–16.

Useful reference books on meter and versification include Alex Preminger and T. V. F. Brogan, eds., *The New Princeton Encyclopedia of Poetry and Poetics* (Princeton: Princeton University Press, 1993); Paul Kiparsky and Gilbert Youmans, eds., *Rhythm and Meter*, vol. 1 in the Phonetics and Phonology Series (San Diego: Academic Press [Harcourt Brace], 1989); and W. K. Wimsatt, ed., *Versification: Major Language Types* (New York: New York University Press, 1972). T. V. F. Brogan, *English Versification, 1570–1980* (Baltimore: Johns Hopkins University Press, 1981) is a descriptive bibliography of metrical studies of English poetry. Brogan's *Verseform: A Comparative Bibliography* (Baltimore: Johns Hopkins University Press, 1989) lists works devoted to different verse systems (e.g., French, Hebrew and Arabic, Chinese and Japanese) and to different structural topics (e.g., rhythm, stanza forms, visual prosody). George Saintsbury, *Historical Manual of English Prosody* (London: MacMillan, 1910), 233–62, and Derek Attridge, *The Rhythms of English Poetry* (London: Longman, 1982), 3–55, offer historical surveys of various approaches to metrical analysis that students of English verse have at one time or another pursued. General matters of phonetics and phonology are treated in McArthur, ed., *The Oxford Companion to the English Language* and David Crystal, *The Cambridge Encyclopedia of the English Language* (Cambridge: Cambridge University Press, 1995).

Any poet or student of poetry will benefit from having a good dictionary. The premier dictionary for etymology is *The Oxford English Dictionary,* commonly referred to as the *OED.* The citation from Carlyle's *History of the French Revolution* appears in the *OED*'s entry for "Prosody." The edition of *The Random House Dictionary of the English Language* to which I refer in this book is the Second Edition Unabridged (New York: Random House, 1987), whose editor in chief is Stuart Berg Flexner. For definitions of classical terms, I have consulted Henry George Liddell and Robert Scott, *A Greek-English Lexicon,* 8th ed. (Oxford: Oxford University Press, 1897) and D. P. Simpson, *Cassell's Latin Dictionary* (New York: Macmillan, 1977).

Note to Chapter One

Gerald Knowles is the author of the entry on "Stress" in *The Oxford Companion to the English Language.* A fine discussion of stress that parallels Knowles's, but that focuses more on verse, can be found in Alfred Corn, *The Poem's Heartbeat: A Manual of Prosody* (Brownsville, Oreg.: Story Line Press, 1997), 13–17. A recent linguistical-phonological study of stress, as it is manifested in different languages, is Bruce Hayes, *Metrical Stress Theory: Principles and Case Studies* (Chicago: University of Chicago Press, 1995).

In an interview in 1915 with William Stanley Braithwaite, Frost comments on the inextricability, in actual verse, of metrical norm and rhythmical modulation. When Frost mentions his interest in incorporating into his verse his own "sound of sense," Braithwaite asks: "[D]o you not come into conflict with metrical sounds to which the laws of poetry conform?" Frost replies: "No, . . . because you must understand this sound of which I speak has principally to do with tone. It is what Mr. Bridges, the Poet Laureate, characterized as speech-rhythm. Meter has to do with beat. . . . The two are one in creation but separate in analysis" (*Robert Frost on Writing,* 153). On this same subject, Attridge comments: "Though it remains true that the easiest way to talk about rhythmic tension is in terms of the relationship between an underlying metre and a verbal realisation, one should be fully aware that this does not imply two independent psychological levels, but a single complex experience" (*The Rhythms of English Poetry,* 172).

Jespersen's discussion and illustration of the four-level register may be found in his essay, "Notes on Metre," a full reference for which is given in the note to the introduction. More purely linguistic aspects of Jespersen's ideas are developed in George L. Trager and Henry Lee Smith, Jr., *An Outline of English Structure,* corrected ed. (Washington, D.C.: American Council of Learned Societies, 1957). Though adopting Jespersen's four-level stress register, Trager and Smith reverse its sequential significance. They use 1 to stand for strong (they use the term "primary") stress, 2 for secondary stress, 3 for tertiary stress, and 4 for weak stress, whereas Jespersen uses 4 for strong, 3 for "half-strong," 2 for "half-weak," and 1 for weak. I have followed Jespersen's terms and numberings because they are perhaps a little less clinical than Trager and Smith's

and because students have told me that, since 4 is greater than 1, they find it more natural to have 4 stand for strong and 1 for weak.

While associated with such twentieth-century linguists as Jespersen and Trager
and Smith, the principle of relative stress is anticipated by earlier writers. For instance,
Thomas Jefferson in his "Thoughts on English Prosody," distinguishes (*Writings,* ed.
Merrill D. Peterson [New York: Library of the Americas, 1984]) between four levels of
accent and scans according to these levels, giving the strongest metrically accented syllables four acute accents (⁗), the next-strongest three (‴), the next-strongest two
(″), and the weakest one (′). Jefferson's applies these levels only to metrically accented
syllables and leaves metrically unaccented syllables unscanned. (Occasionally, he
leaves light metrical beats unscanned as well.) Were the metrically unaccented syllables scanned, they would presumably require additional notation. According to this
procedure, Jefferson renders thus these lines from Shakespeare (*Julius Caesar,* 2.2.34
and *The Tempest,* 4.1.152):

> //　///　/　/　//
> Of all the wonders that I yet have heard
> 　///　//　///　//
> The cloud-capp'd towers, the gorgeous palaces

Jefferson notes that others may not hear the lines exactly as he does. His point is simply that there are different degrees of accent: "I am far from presuming to give this accentuation as perfect. . . . I have essayed these short passages to let the foreigner see
[Jefferson writes his essay to aid foreign readers of English verse] that the accent is not
equal; that they are not to be read monotonously" (611–12).

Ascham's remark about monosyllables and the unsuitability of dactylic rhythm to
English appears in G. Gregory Smith, ed., *Elizabethan Critical Essays,* 2 vols. (Oxford:
Oxford University Press, 1904), 1:30. Campion's comment on this subject occurs in
The Works of Thomas Campion, 296. Camden's remarks about monosyllables may be
found in William Camden, *Remains Concerning Britain,* ed. R. D. Dunn (Toronto: University of Toronto Press, 1985), 30. Gascoigne's recommendation of monosyllables appears in *George Gascoigne: The Green Knight, Selected Poetry and Prose,* 140. In his
*Short Treatise Containing Some Rules and Artifices to Be Observed and Eschewed in
Scottish Poesy* (1584), James VI also notes the metrical versatility of monosyllables,
though he treats them less favorably than Gascoigne: "Ye aucht likewise be war with
oft composing your haill lynis of monosyllabis onely (albeit our language haue sa
many as we can nocht weill eschewe it), because the maist pairt of thame are indiffer-
ent, and may be in short or lang place, as ye like" (Smith, *Elizabethan Critical Essays,*
1:215). Gascoigne's and James's observations have a twentieth-century parallel in
Frost's remark, about his own poems, to Sidney Cox: "I will find you the word 'come'
variously used in various passages as a whole, half, third, fourth, fifth, and sixth note"
(*Robert Frost on Writing,* 61). Though Frost gives no examples of his use of "come," attentive readers can point them out. For instance, in the opening lines of "Fireflies in
the Garden," "come" is metrically accented in the first line, but metrically unaccented
in the second:

```
x   /   x   /   x /   x /   x   /
```
Here come | real stars | to fill | the up | per skies,
```
x   /   x   /    x    /   x /  x    /
```
And here | on earth | come em | ulat | ing flies

Beth Bjorklund points out (*A Study in Comparative Prosody: English and German Jambic Pentameter* [Stuttgart: Heinz, 1978], esp. 225–308) that because German relies more on compounding and polysyllabic words than English does, German iambics are less fluid than English iambics, and trochaic rhythm is more important in German verse than it is in English poetry. See, too, Bjorkland's related and excellent analysis of German metric, "Iambic and Trochaic Verse—Major and Minor Keys?" in Kiparsky and Youmans, eds., *Meter and Rhythm,* 155–81. Jespersen's 1928 essay, "Monosyllabism in English" (*Linguistica,* 384–408) provides illuminating discussion of tendencies towards monosyllabism in our language; Jespersen does not, however, examine the matter in connection with its effect on our prosody. A good discussion of attitudes, among English writers in the Renaissance, toward monosyllables is Richard Foster Jones, *The Triumph of the English Language* (Stanford: Stanford University Press, 1953), 199–200; Dunn cites this study in his edition of Camden's *Remains.*

Valuable works on classical prosody include Paul Maas, *Greek Metre,* trans. Hugh Lloyd-Jones (Oxford: Oxford University Press, 1962); James W. Halporn, Martin Ostwald, and Thomas G. Rosenmeyer, *The Meters of Greek and Latin Poetry* (London: Methuen, 1963); Roger A. Hornsby, *Reading Latin Poetry* (Norman: University of Oklahoma Press, 1967); and M. L. West, *Greek Metre* (Oxford: Oxford University Press, 1982) and West's *Introduction to Greek Metre* (Oxford: Oxford University Press, 1987). Bridges's remarks about the rocks-caves-lakes-fens line in *Paradise Lost* appear in his *Milton's Prosody,* rev. final ed. (Oxford: Oxford University Press, 1921), 40.

The contrast between the comparative metrical flexibility of syllables in English verse, and the comparatively metrical inflexibility of syllables in ancient verse, is observed by Thomas Sheridan in his essay, "Of the Recitation of Poetic Numbers," in his *General Dictionary of the English Language* (1780): "[T]he quantity of our syllables is perpetually varying with the sense and is for the most part regulated by emphasis . . . this very circumstance has given us an amazing advantage over the ancients, in point of poetic numbers." Likewise, Yvor Winters comments: "In English verse, a syllable is accented or unaccented wholly in relation to the other syllables in the same foot, whereas in classical verse each syllable is arbitrarily classified by rule, and its length is in a very small measure dependent upon the context. This makes for a greater fluidity and sensitivity in English, I suspect, and with no loss of precision, perhaps with a gain in precision" (Yvor Winters, *In Defense of Reason* [Denver: Swallow, 1947], 108).

The scansions of the lines from Yeats's "Sailing to Byzantium" and from Pope's *Eloisa to Abelard* and *Epistle to Dr. Arbuthnot* appear in Paul Fussell, *Poetic Meter and Poetic Form,* rev. ed. (New York: Random House, 1979), 33, 36, 38. The scansions of line 369 of Pope's *Essay on Criticism* and of line 7 of Keats's "Eve of St. Agnes" appear in W. Jackson Bate and David Perkins, eds., *British and American Poets: Chaucer to the Present* (San Diego: Harcourt Brace, 1986), 995. Recent discussion of the question of whether or not spondees and pyrrhics are characteristic of English may be found in David Baker, ed., *Meter in English: A Critical Engagement* (Fayetteville: University of Arkansas Press, 1996). Brogan supplies even-handed summary of this question in general in his entry for "Spondee" in *The New Princeton Encyclopedia of Poetry and Poetics*. George T. Wright, in his *Shakespeare's Metrical Art* (Berkeley and Los Angeles: University of California Press, 1988), 9, implicitly advances a compromise position by using the terms "spondaic iamb" and "pyrrhic iamb."

Eliot's remarks on meter appear in his *To Criticize the Critic* (New York: Farrar Straus, 1965), 185–86. Additional observations on Eliot as a metrical theorist can be found in my *Missing Measures: Modern Poetry and the Revolt against Meter.* (Fayetteville: University of Arkansas Press, 1990), 63–64, 98. Frost's comment about placing meter and rhythm in "strained relation" appears in a letter to John Cournos printed in *Robert Frost: Collected Poems, Prose, and Plays*, ed. Richard Poirier and Mark Richardson (New York: Library of America, 1995), 680. And in a letter to John Freeman, Frost expresses, in a metaphor, the relationship of meter and speech rhythm: "All I ask is iambic. I undertake to furnish the variety in the relation of my tones to it. The crossed swords are always the same. The sword dancer varies his position between them" (*Robert Frost on Writing*, 81). See, too, Frost's "The Figure a Poem Makes," in which he notes: "The possibilities for tune from the dramatic tones of meaning struck across the rigidity of a limited meter are endless" (*Robert Frost on Writing*, 125).

Note to Chapter Two

Jakobson's remarks about inverted feet at linear and syntactical divisions appears in his essay, "Closing Statement: Linguistics and Poetics," in Thomas A. Sebeok, ed., *Style in Language* (Cambridge, Mass.: MIT Press, 1960), 364. Wright uses the term "false trochees" (*Shakespeare's Metrical Art*, 190–97) for verbal and other phrases in Shakespeare that initially look to have a falling rhythm but that are in fact iambic. Jespersen's comment that pauses may sometimes alleviate or smooth over metrical irregularities occurs in his *Linguistica*, 264–65. A detailed discussion of real and apparent conflicts, in iambic verse, between metrical pattern and phrasal shape may be found in Marina Tarlinskaja, "General and Particular Aspects of Meter," in Kiparsky and Youmans, eds., *Rhythm and Meter*, 121–54. It is in his "Figure a Poem Makes" that Frost speaks of "loose iambic": "All that can be done with words is soon told. So also with meters— particularly in our language where there are virtually but two, strict iambic and loose iambic" (*Robert Frost on Writing*, 125; also *Collected Poems, Prose, and Plays*, 776). This comment is also cited, in a different context, in the note to the introduction.

Many have complained that the application of ancient prosodic terms to modern verse has confused modern metrical studies; with "feminine caesura" modern vocabulary perhaps revenges itself on antiquity. Students of classical prosody have come to speak of feminine caesuras with reference to dactylic hexameters that pause after the first short syllable of the third foot (– ˘ <> ˘); by the same token, hexameters that pause after the long syllable of third foot are said to have masculine caesuras (– <> ˘ ˘, or, in cases in which the two short syllables are contracted into one long syllable, – <> –). West comments: "I do not know who introduced the sexual metaphor; the idea was probably that the - ˘ | ˘ division was *mollior* [tender, supple, soft]" (*Greek Metre,* 195); but what likely happened is that the modern term was applied at some juncture to a superficially similar but actually different situation in ancient prosody. In any event, the sorts of objections sometimes raised against ancient terms when they appear in modern contexts can be raised against the use of "feminine caesura" in ancient metrical analysis.

We can appreciate this point by examining the opening lines of *The Odyssey* and *The Iliad.* (Here and elsewhere in this book, circumflexes indicate the longer of paired vowels. For example, *Pêlêïadeô,* "son of Peleus," has as its second and fourth letter an eta rather than an epsilon, and its last letter is an omega rather than an omikron. In the first foot of *The Odyssey,* the diphthong in "moi" is shortened by "correption"—by being followed by a word beginning with a vowel.)

> Andra moi ennepe, Mousa, <> polutropon, hos mala polla
>> Tell me the tale, Muse, of the man of many turns, who [wandered] many ways
> Mênin aeide, Thea, <> Pêlêïadeô Achilêos
>> Sing, Goddess, of the wrath of Peleus' son, Achilles

The caesura in *The Odyssey* line is feminine, since it occurs after the second (and short) syllable for the Greek word for "Muse."

‾ ˘ ˘ | ‾ ˘ ˘ | ‾ ˘ ˘ | ‾ ˘ ˘ | ‾ ˘ ˘ | ‾ ‾
Andra moi | ennepe, | Mousa, po | lutropon, | hos mala | polla

In contrast, the caesura in *The Iliad* line is masculine because the pause occurs after the second and long syllable of the Greek word for "Goddess":

‾ ˘ ˘ | ‾ ˘ | ˘ ‾ | ‾ ˘˘ | ‾ ˘ ˘ | ‾ ‾
Mênin a | eide, The | a, Pê | lêïa | deô Achi | lêos

Yet as we can see, "feminine" and "masculine" do not suit caesuras in classical verse, at least not if we think of the terms as indicating the presence or absence of an extra syllable. The classical feminine caesura does not have a hypermetrical element, nor is the masculine caesura deficient in such an element. Regardless of whether the caesura is feminine or masculine, the third foot stays durationally the same. It has either a long syllable plus two shorts, or two long syllables.

Skeat's discussion of Chaucer's clipped pentameters appears in his edition of *The Complete Works of Geoffrey Chaucer,* 5 vols. (Oxford: Oxford University Press, 1900), 3:xliv–xlvii. Robert O. Evans discusses the opening line of the "General Prologue" to *The Canterbury Tales* in "Whan That Aprill(e)?" *Notes and Queries* 202 (June 1957): 234–37. Saintsbury's comments about clipped lines appear in his *History of English Prosody,* 3 vols. (New York: Russell & Russell, 1961), 1:170–71.

Most scholars believe that Chaucer composed iambic verse, but a few argue that the poet wrote a looser cadential verse related to the accentual-alliterative Anglo-Saxon tradition. This position has been most forcibly advocated by James G. Southworth in his *Verses of Cadence: An Introduction to the Prosody of Chaucer and His Followers* (Oxford: Basil Blackwell, 1954) and *The Prosody of Chaucer and His Followers* (Oxford: Basil Blackwell, 1962). And elements of Southworth's arguments, blended with the standard view, appear in Ian Robinson, *Chaucer's Prosody: A Study of the Middle English Verse Tradition* (Cambridge: Cambridge University Press, 1971).

We have no recordings of Chaucer reading his work, and pronouncing dictionaries and word-lists for English begin to appear only in the later sixteenth and earlier seventeenth centuries. (Robert Cawdrey's *Table Alphabetical* of 1604 is often cited as the first published English dictionary.) Hence any interpretation of Chaucer's metric involves probabilities, not certainties. And Southworth's and Robinson's books deserve serious consideration by anybody interested in Chaucer's versification.

However, Southworth's and Robinson's views seem to me as conjectural as and less probable than the views they attack. Southworth, for instance, contends that in Chaucer's day final *es* were no longer sounded and that Chaucer would not have sounded them in his verse; and Robinson speculates that Romanic or dual pronunciation is largely an invention of Chaucerian scholarship and that Chaucer's pronunciation was more or less regularly Teutonic, even in the case of French words recently adopted into English. Yet no one knows exactly when the final *e* ceased to be sounded. For that matter, elements of speech may persist in poetry for some time after they have dropped from colloquial usage. Even if the final *e* was becoming or had become largely mute in the spoken dialects of Chaucer's contemporaries, it is quite possible that it, in the words of one scholar, "would have remained available for the more conservative register of poetry" (Thomas G. Duncan, ed., *Medieval English Lyrics 1200–1400* [Harmondsworth: Penguin, 1995], 254). As for the question of Romanic pronunciations, it was precisely in Chaucer's lifetime—in the second half of the fourteenth century—that borrowing from French reached its peak. Chaucer's own vocabulary is saturated with French. As Crystal notes (*The Cambridge Encyclopedia of the English Language*, 47), nearly 500 different loan words from French appear in the 858-line "General Prologue" to *The Canterbury Tales*. It is hard to imagine that Chaucer or other fourteenth-century English speakers immediately and universally nativized all the French words coming into their language. It is also hard to imagine that Middle English pronunciation was not affected by three centuries of intimate connection with Norman French. Even today, we allow certain French-derived words both Romanic and Teutonic pronunciation and accentuation. "Buffet," meaning "refreshment-table," is an example. "Research" is another.

Chaucer's rhymes, moreover, indicate that he often sounded final *es* and at least sometimes pronounced Romanically words that we today pronounce Teutonically. To take a well-known case, Chaucer rhymes **Rome/to me** (*Canterbury Tales*, A 671–72 ["General Prologue"]). And the theory that Chaucer gave exclusively Teutonic pronunciation to many Romanic and other words leaves us with such rhymes as, to cite several readings that Robinson proposes (109, 124, 125, 129), **lícour/flóur,** cómmune/Fórtune, sócour/lánguor, pénaunce/governáunce, and mérvaille/éntraille. The theory requires, in other words, that Chaucer rhymed unaccented syllables with other unaccented ones, and rhymed unaccented syllables with accented ones. But the general practice of rhyme in Chaucer and in Chaucer's time—whether one is looking at English, French, Italian, or accentual Latin verse—involves pairing accented syllables with other accented syllables.

But there is a more serious objection to be raised against Southworth and Robinson. Neither distinguishes meter from rhythm—or rather they deny that the two can be harmonized in verse. For both Southworth and Robinson, an iambic pentameter that does not alternate heavily between offbeats and beats is not an iambic pentameter. Arguing that "English poetry is essentially in 3/8 rhythm" (*Verses of Cadence*, 8), and using a form of musical scansion, Southworth takes a straightforward line from Chaucer's description of the Prioress,

x / x / x / x / x / (x)
She leet no morsel from hir lippes fallë

(*The Canterbury Tales*, A 128 ["General Prologue"])

and scans it (*Verses of Cadence*, 64) as a non-iambic "rhythmical" verse:

♪│♪.│♪.│ ♩ ♩ ♪ ♪│♪. ♪.│♪
She leet no morsel / from hir lip pes falle

With such a method of scansion, one can prove not only that Chaucer never wrote iambic pentameter, but also that Shakespeare, Milton, Pope, and Frost never wrote it either.

We should make an additional observation about the musical elements of Southworth's prosodic description. They are arbitrary. It is difficult to see, for instance, how the unaccented second syllable of "morsel" is three times as long as "She." This is important, since Southworth uses his musical notation to deny the iambic character of lines even more regular than the one just cited. He scans another line from Chaucer's description of the Prioress,

And she was clepyd madame Eglantinë

(*The Canterbury Tales*, A 121 ["General Prologue"])

this way:

♪ │ ♩ ♪│♪ ♪,│ ♪ ♩ │♪. ♪.│♪
And she was cle pyd / ma dame Eg lan tine

While noting that this line alternates between offbeats and beats, Southworth contends that it is "not strictly iambic, because, as I have pointed out, in a regular iamb the unstressed element of the foot receives only half the time of the stressed element. And if we heed the virgule, the second element . . . is essentially trochaic" (*Verses of Cadence*, 65). In other words, Southworth can take a construction "was clépyd," which fits naturally into the iambic texture of the line, and simply by assigning each of the three syllables the durational value of an eighth note, can dismiss them from participation in iambic rhythm. Another problem is Southworth's implied principle relative to the virgule, a scribal mark which appears in some early manuscripts of Chaucer. The significance of the mark has never been determined—Southworth believes that its function is "rhetorical" (*Verses of Cadence*, 62)—but it occurs most often at a caesura in the line. And Southworth's suggestion that it is a determining factor of prosodic structure means in effect that lines that pause after an odd-numbered syllable position cannot really be iambic.

Again, with this method, one could demonstrate that no one has ever written authentic iambic pentameter.

Likewise, Robinson adduces (52) a "model," "ideal," or "diagram" pentameter that goes

> De dum de dum de dum de dum de dum (de)

and suggests that those who believe Chaucer wrote iambics must believe that all his lines cleave to this paradigmatic norm or can readily be accommodated to a "De dum de dum de dum" reading; and Robinson further urges that complexity of metrical practice invalidates or precludes simplicity of metrical description:

> [T]he diagram can be seen as a rule which we obey by speaking the lines as much like it as we can. (Another way of seeing it, as an abstraction of what all pentameters have in common, I immediately dismiss, because not all pentameters are at all like the model.) (53)

A similar confusion seems to underlie Robinson's refusal, when he ultimately concludes that Chaucer composed in "balanced pentameter," to define what he means by that term: "I offer no definition of iambic pentameter (to *define* Chaucer's pentameter I would reprint his works) " (151). Possibly I am missing something, but this statement seems to refute Robinson's idea of having discovered a pattern in Chaucer's verse. A pattern is not a pattern if it cannot be characterized. To "define" is in the Latin sense "to limit," and it is difficult to imagine how this process would be served simply by reprinting thousands of lines of verse.

Another point in favor of the view that Chaucer wrote iambic pentameter is that, even if we do not sound final *e*s or allow Romanic pronunciations, the majority of Chaucer's lines still run iambically, not in the "de dum de dum de dum" sense, to be sure, but in the flexibly modulated manner that also characterizes the versification of later poets like Shakespeare and Wordsworth. That the majority of Chaucer's lines are conventionally iambic does not necessarily mean that they all are; but it gives us grounds, when questionable lines can be brought into sync by sounding a final *e* or rear-stressing a word—especially a Romanic word like *nature, color, justice,* or *lion*—for suspecting that Chaucer intended them as iambic.

Finally, Chaucer's apologizing, in *The House of Fame* (1098), for introducing lines that are merely a single syllable short indicates that he counted syllables and was not working in an asyllabic cadential mode like that of Langland. And though Southworth argues for "the basic similarity in the rhythms of Chaucer and *Piers Plowman*" (*Verses of Cadence,* 49), Chaucer's Parson sharply distinguishes *(The Canterbury Tales,* I 43–44 ["The Parson's Prologue"]) between the accentual-alliterative tradition, in which poets "'rum, ram, ruf,' by lettre," and the newer tradition of "rym." This distinction suggests that for Chaucer and his readers the two modes sounded, as they sound to most of us today, quite different.

Discussions of Chaucer's versification that are in my opinion sounder than Southworth's and Robinson's appear in Paull F. Baum, *Chaucer's Verse* (Durham, N.C.: Duke University Press, 1961) and in Norman Davis's section on "Versification" in the introduction to *The Riverside Chaucer,* xlii–xlv.

Ben Jonson's reminiscence about Shakespeare and about the line in *Julius Caesar* may be found at 671–79 of Jonson's *Timber, or, Discoveries.* I have cited from *Ben Jonson,* ed. Ian Donaldson (Oxford: Oxford University Press, 1985), 539–40. Volume 11 (231–33) of the Herford and Simpson edition of Jonson surveys and analyzes possible explanations for the original and revised line. Some have doubted that Shakespeare ever wrote the line that Jonson attributes to him. Others, while believing that Jonson did quote accurately, have hypothesized that it is Heminges and Condell, the editors of the First Folio, and not Shakespeare, who are responsible for the revision. Yet all poets blunder from time to time and, when the blunders are brought to their attention, they make the sorts of adjustments that Shakespeare seems to have made. Another well-known case, though it did not produce a variant metrical line, involves Wordsworth's "The Thorn" from *Lyrical Ballads* (1798) and the lamely specific description (32–33) of the puddle-pond: "I've measured it from side to side: / 'Tis three feet long, and two feet wide." In the seventeenth chapter of the *Biographia Literaria* (1817), Coleridge objected to this and other lines as "sudden and unpleasant sinkings"; and in all editions of the poem thereafter, Wordsworth substituted a revised couplet, "Though but of compass small, and bare / To thirsty suns and parching air." (For discussion of this matter, see Jack Stillinger, ed., *Selected Poems and Prefaces by William Wordsworth* [Boston: Houghton Mifflin, 1965], 510–11.)

No one knows to what extent other incomplete lines in Shakespeare's plays result from textual corruptions. A fine overview of the matter is supplied by Paul Werstine, "Line Division in Shakespeare's Dramatic Verse: an Editorial Problem," *Analytical and Enumerative Bibliography* 8 (1984): 73–125. In particular, Werstine demonstrates how the individual compositors of the First Folio were liable to distinctive types of baselineation. Werstine concludes by cautioning against the recent trend, among certain Shakespeare scholars, to attribute irregularities in the early texts of the plays to the poet himself and to praise, as expressive felicities, metrical irregularities produced by compositors' errors:

> By ignoring the significant role of compositors in the line-arrangement of Shakespeare's earliest printed texts, editors have deprived themselves of a rationale for metrical emendation, and critics . . . have come to prefer compositorial mislining to the generally regular patterns of Shakespeare's verse. (111)

Bridges's speculations about, and case for, "recession of accent" appear in *Milton's Prosody,* 67–77.

Note to Chapter Three

The quotation that begins the chapter is taken from Miguel de Cervantes, *Don Quixote,* trans. Samuel Putnam (New York: Modern Library, 1949), 923. Studies devoted to the expressive potentials of verse are many. Those that I have found especially useful include Paul Valéry's "Concerning *Adonis*" and "Memoirs of a Poem," both of which appear in Paul Valéry, *The Art of Poetry,* trans. Denise Folliot, with an introduction by T. S. Eliot (Princeton: Princeton University Press, 1985), 8–34, 100–32, and Winters's "The Influence of Meter on Poetic Convention," in *In Defense of Reason,* 103–50. Equally valuable in a different way are such appreciative analyses of individual poems as that which Thom Gunn gives of Hardy's "Near Lanivet, 1872" (in "Hardy and the Ballads" in Thom Gunn, *The Occasions of Poetry,* ed. Clive Wilmer [London: Faber & Faber, 1982], 94–97), and that which Richard Wilbur gives of Frost's "Birches" (in "Poetry and Happiness" in Richard Wilbur, *Responses* [New York: Harcourt Brace, 1976], 109–14). Studies of individual poets or particular periods include Wright, *Shakespeare's Metrical Art;* Wesley Trimpi, *Ben Jonson's Poems* (Stanford: Stanford University Press, 1962); Bridges, *Milton's Prosody;* George Hemphill, "Dryden's Heroic Line," *PMLA* 72 (December 1957): 863–879; Susanne Woods, *Natural Emphasis: English Versification from Chaucer to Dryden* (San Marino, Calif.: Huntington Library, 1985); Paul Fussell, *Theory of Prosody in Eighteenth-Century England* (New London: Connecticut College, 1954); and Brennan O'Donnell, *The Passion of Meter: A Study of Wordsworth's Metrical Art* (Kent, Ohio: Kent State University Press, 1995). On the manuscript of Gallus's elegies, see L. D. Reynolds and N. G. Wilson, *Scribes and Scholars: A Guide to the Transmission of Greek and Latin Literature,* 3d ed. (Oxford: Oxford University Press, 1991), 247.

For cautionary remarks against overly sensitive readings of verse and against notions of "representative meter," see Samuel Johnson's discussion, in his *Life* of Pope, of that poet's suggestion (*Essay on Criticism,* 365) that "sound must seem an echo to the sense." Johnson remarks: "Beauties of this kind are commonly fancied; and when real are technical and nugatory, not to be rejected and not to be solicited" (*Samuel Johnson: Selected Poetry and Prose,* ed. Frank Brady and W. K. Wimsatt [Berkeley and Los Angeles: University of California Press, 1977], 549). And exaggerated correlations of meter and matter are parodied by Richard Brinsley Sheridan in that passage in *The Critic* where Puff, Sneer, and Dangle watch the rehearsal of Tilburina's mad scene:

> TILBURINA
> The wind whistles—the moon rises—see
> They have killed my squirrel in his cage!
> Is this a grasshopper!—Ha! no, it is my
> Whiskerandos—you shall not keep him—
> I know you have him in your pocket—
> An oyster may be crossed in love! Who says
> A whale's a bird?—Ha! did you call, my love?
> —He's here! He's there!—He's everywhere!
> Ah me! He's nowhere!   [Exit TILBURINA.]

PUFF: There, do you ever desire to see anybody madder than that?

SNEER: Never while I live!

PUFF: You observed how she mangled the metre?

DANGLE: Yes—egad, it was the first thing made me suspect she was out of her senses.

> (Richard Brinsley Sheridan, *The School for Scandal and Other Plays*,
> ed. Eric S. Rump [London: Penguin, 1988], 183.)

The quotation that closes the chapter comes from Bridges, *Milton's Prosody*, 63.

Note to Chapter Four

Bridges's *Milton's Prosody* is the most thorough study of elision in English poetry, though Bridges's analysis is anticipated by the third chapter ("Syllable") of Guest's *History of English Rhythms*, 1:22–75. Guest's historical discussion of elision (1:178–83) is interesting as well. Also illuminating are the examples of elision that Bysshe offers in his *Art of English Poetry*, 3d ed., 1708, ed. A. Dwight Culler (Los Angeles: Augustan Reprint Society, 1953), 11–17. (Culler discusses Bysshe's debt to Lancelot on page iv of this volume.) A. C. Partridge, *Orthography in Shakespeare and Elizabethan Drama: A Study of Colloquial Contractions, Elision, Prosody and Punctuation* (London: Edward Arnold, 1964) provides helpful discussion of the relationship, in the late Middle English period and the Renaissance, between poetic elision and actual speech. On elision in Shakespeare and the Renaissance, see also Wright, *Shakespeare's Metrical Art*, 149–59, and Paul Ramsey, *The Fickle Glass: A Study of Shakespeare's Sonnets* (New York: AMS, 1979). An excellent discussion of elision in eighteenth-century verse may be found in Fussell, *Theory of Prosody in Eighteenth-Century England*, 68–100. See also Fussell's entry on "Poetic Contractions" in the enlarged first edition of the *Princeton Encyclopedia of Poetry and Poetics* (Princeton: Princeton University Press, 1974), where Fussell observes, "There is evidence . . . that the contemporary reader of 18th-c[entury] poetry derived much of his aesthetic delight from his deliberate and conscious 'regularizing,' through contraction, of normally irregularly phonetic materials." Other fine analyses of elision include George A. Kellog, "Bridges' *Milton's Prosody* and Renaissance Metrical Theory," *PMLA* 68 (March 1953): 268–85, and Edward R. Weismiller's "Triple Threats to Duple Rhythm," in Kiparsky and Youmans, eds., *Rhythm and Meter*, 261–90. Additionally illuminating is Weismiller's entry on the "Metrical Treatment of Syllables" in *The New Princeton Encyclopedia of Poetry and Poetics*. For discussion of Milton's spelling, and its metrical significance or lack thereof, see John T. Shawcross, "Orthography and the Text of *Paradise Lost*," in *Language and Style in Milton*, ed. by Ronald David Emma and John T. Shawcross (New York: Ungar, 1967), 120–53.

A lighter-hearted study of elision is Beerbohm's *Savonarola Brown*, which lampoons the metrical contractions and related prosodic gimmickry of Shakespeare's plays. An illustrative passage is the following (1.1.27–37). The Sacristan has just greeted Savonarola, to which Savonarola has responded that he would thank the Sacristan for his greeting, except that thanks are owed to God alone. A Friar present at the exchange then comments:

FRIAR
'Tis a right answer he hath given thee.
Had Sav'narola spoken less than thus,
Methinks me, the less Sav'narola he.
As when the snow lies on yon Apennines,
White as the hem of Mary Mother's robe,
And insuspectible to the sun's rays,
Being harder to the touch than temper'd steel,
E'en so this great gaunt monk white-visagèd
Upstands to Heaven and to Heav'n devotes
The scarpèd thoughts that crown the upper slopes
Of his abrupt and *aus*tere nature.

SACRISTAN
Aye.

In addition to the syncopations of the hero's name and of "Even"—and in addition to the expansions ("white-visagèd," "scarpèd")—we see the trick of using, in a single line, "Heaven" as both a disyllable and a monosyllable. ("Being" is another metrically ambiguous word here used in its contracted form.) The passage pokes fun as well at two devices discussed in chapter 2. First, according to the alleged principle of recession of accent, Beerbohm fore-stresses "austere" to reconcile it to regularized iambic rhythm. Second, he has one character end a speech within a line that is then completed by another character's dutifully chipping in with the missing element.

Ascham's comments on rhymed and syllable-counting verse may be found in Smith, *Elizabethan Critical Essays*, 1:31; Sidney's remarks on the same subject appear in Philip Sidney, *Selected Prose and Poetry*, ed. Robert Kimbrough (New York: Holt, 1969), 155; the citation from Puttenham's *Arte* appears in George Puttenham, *The Arte of English Poesie*, ed. Edward Arber (London: Constable, 1906 [reprint, introduced by Baxter Hathaway, Kent, Ohio: Kent State University Press, 1970]), 81; the quotation from Dryden's "Essay" may be found in *Of Dramatic Poesy*, 1:83. Bysshe's comments on syllable count appear in his *Art of English Poetry*, 1, 6.

It is in his *Poetic Meter and Poetic Form*, 71–73 that Fussell discusses the shift, in the nineteenth century, of England's cultural allegiance from France to Germany. Guest's arguments against Romanic elements in English and for the superiority of the old Anglo-Saxon meter appear in his *History*, 2:110, 275–77. Gifford's comments about Jonson's elisions appear in *The Works of Ben Jonson*, ed. William Gifford, with introduction and appendices by Lieutenant-Colonel F. Cunningham, 9 vols. (London: Bickers and Son, 1875), 1:186. Mayor's discussion of apparently erroneous elisions in Shakespeare's texts occurs in Joseph B. Mayor, *Chapters on English Metre*, 2d ed. (Cambridge: Cambridge University Press, 1901), 178ff.

Gill's remarks about elisions in the common speech of his day are cited by Kellog, "Bridges' *Milton's Prosody* and Renaissance Metrical Theory," 283; Sidney's, Puttenham's, Campion's, Dryden's, and Swift's comments on elision may be found in Philip Sidney, *The Poems of Sir Philip Sidney*, ed. William A. Ringler, Jr. (Oxford: Oxford University Press, 1962), 391; Puttenham, *The Arte of English Poesie*, 174; *The Works of Thomas Campion*, 314; John Dryden, *Essays of John Dryden*, ed. W. P. Ker, 2 vols.

(London: Russell & Russell, 1961), 2:11; and *The Prose Works of Jonathan Swift,* ed. Herbert Davis with Louis Landa, 14 vols. (Oxford: Basil Blackwell, 1939–68), 4:11. Golding's dedication to the first four books of Ovid's *Metamorphoses* is cited in *Shakespeare's Ovid, Being Arthur Golding's Translation of The Metamorphoses,* ed. W. H. D. Rouse (Carbondale: Southern Illinois University Press, 1961), iii. Blair's remarks about the virtues of distinct articulation appear in Hugh Blair, *Lectures on Rhetoric and Belles Lettres,* ed. Harold F. Harding, foreword by David Potter, 2 vols. (Carbondale: Southern Illinois University Press, 1965), 2:207–8. Saintsbury's comments about Chaucerian elision and about Bridges's discussion of Milton appear in Saintsbury's *History,* 1:173, 2:263.

Though admiring Bridges and thinking that his account of elision in Milton is correct in its essentials, I disagree with Bridges's insistence that traditional English metric is fundamentally "syllabic," as opposed to "accentual," and disagree with his apparent belief that syllabism and accentualism are somehow prosodically irreconcilable. In his clear and unobjectionable definition of blank verse, Bridges implicitly acknowledges that our verse is accentual as well as syllabic: "English blank verse may conveniently be regarded as a decasyllabic line on a disyllabic basis and in rising rhythm (i.e., with accents or stresses on the alternate even syllables); and the disyllabic units may be called *feet*" (*Milton's Prosody,* 1). However, Bridges never sufficiently distinguishes between metrical accent and speech stress, and observing that not all pentameters have five strong stresses, he concludes that the accentual element of the English pentameter is less important than the syllabic element. Bridges seems at times to forget that *the pattern of metrical accents* is important, even if *the number of speech stresses* is variable.

This confusion is evident when Bridges distinguishes between what he calls syllabic verse (but what most of us call accentual-syllabic verse) and accentual verse:

> When reading Milton's or Chaucer's ten-syllable verse aloud, the occurrence of a line deficient in one of the ten syllables (and such lines occur in Chaucer) proves extremely awkward both for hearer and reader, especially if the reader is unprepared for it. It cannot escape observation: and if a line occurs in which there are more than ten syllables, the "trisyllabic foot" is readily perceived; so that of every line, as it is read, the hearer can say at once of how many syllables it was composed, whether of nine, ten, eleven or twelve. But he will not observe a variety in the number of stresses in the same way; whether the line have its full complement of five, or only four (as is very frequent), or only three, no awkwardness or interruption of rhythm will be perceived; nor will the hearer be able to say readily at the close of any line how many true stresses it contained. This is syllabic verse.
>
> Of stressed verse exactly the contrary is true. The omission of an initial unaccented syllable from the line produces no awkwardness: hearer and reader alike are indifferent as to the number of syllables which go to make the line; nor, as each line is read, can they say how many syllables have gone to make it. But if a stress be omitted, they perceive the rhythm to be unsatisfactory, and readily detect the awkwardness of the false metrical stresses which they passed over in the syllabic verse. This is stressed or accentual verse. (*Milton's Prosody,* 111–12)

Bridges is right to say that we do not, when we read, tally the speech stresses in each line or register the precise stress fluctuations in the line. Nor, Bridges might have added, do we necessarily register such conventional metrical variations as inverted feet at line beginnings or after mid-line pauses. But if the accentual pattern is awry— if the speech stresses and metrical beats come in the wrong places—we hear it and are jarred by it. There is a great difference between a well-made conventional pentameter with only three strong speech stresses that goes

> x / x / x / x / x /
> Who misinterpret silence as repose

(Suzanne J. Doyle, "Near Dark," 17)

and a would-be pentameter like this made-up one, which also has ten syllables and three strong speech stresses, but which goes

> Who mistákenly práttle of sílence

The practical liabilities of Bridges's position are apparent in his late (1929) philosophical epic, *The Testament of Beauty*. The *Testament* features a twelve-syllable line without any regular arrangement of feet or beats, and it is consequently impossible to resolve many of the syllabic ambiguities in the poem. Oftentimes, lines have thirteen or fourteen syllables and several possible elisions, and, with no accentual pattern to refer to, one cannot determine which syllables Bridges is contracting. (This matter is further discussed in the ninth chapter of this book.)

I once wrote to Richard Wilbur, asking how he would scan the second foot of the fourth line of his "A Finished Man":

> His memory of the fourth begins to fade.

Would he read the line as

> x /
> His mem | (o)ry of | the fourth | begins | to fade

or as

> x x /
> His mem | ory of | the fourth | begins | to fade

or as something in between? Accompanying the question were listed the three possible responses:

> ____The case you cite, it seems to me,
> Is clearly one of syncope.
>
> ____Th' interpretation I like best
> Involves a foot-two anapest.
>
> ____ Upon this point, I'm undecided:
> Half anapestic? Half-elided?

Mr. Wilbur checked the second response, explaining,

> Not being overfond of slur,
> Instead of "memry" I prefer
> A foot-two anapest, provided
> It's fast, and *almost* seems elided.

He added, "In short, I'd have it said trippingly on the tongue."

Dick Davis, in response to an inquiry as to whether he heard "literal" as two syllables or three his iambic trimeter ("Heresy," 7)

> Is literal blood and bone

wrote:

> [R]e the line "Is literal blood and bone". I guess if I had to choose between saying "It's an anapaest" or saying "It's elided" I'd say "It's elided". I think what happens in the actual reading of a line like this, though, is that one has a feeling of both possibilities being there—that is that the extra unstressed syllable is too pronounced to be regarded as [a] total elision, but too slight for a "real" anapaest. A number of words . . . have a kind of indeterminate/ambiguous number of syllables that seem to make them acceptable as parts of "anapaests"—or "weak anapaests" perhaps—in an otherwise very regular iambic poem. The word "being" is another word that comes to mind (one or two syllables?). I very rarely (if ever) use "full"—i.e. real—anapaests in iambic lines, but I quite often use these kind of half anapaests.

And Wendy Cope, answering a similar question about "usual" in the following line ("Another Unfortunate Choice," 2),

> Which puts me in a worse-than-usual fix

commented:

> When I read the poem aloud I say "usual" as a two-syllable word, more or less, but with a hint of the middle syllable—I think the Bridges elision theory would cover it.
>
> I certainly don't agree with Saintsbury that all marginal syllables have to be counted. I think it's important to use the rhythm of ordinary speech—I say words out loud and ask my ears how many syllables there are, in the same way that I say rhyming words out loud, to check that I'm not being misled by my eyes. If a person actually pronounces "usual" as a three-syllable word, then it would be appropriate for them to use it that way in a poem. And I might break my own rule for comic effect.

Each of these poets expresses what I suspect is the view of many other poets on this subject. If one adopts the elision explanation, there remains a hint that the elision is not total; and if one takes the anapest interpretation, there remains the sense that the anapest is "fast" or "weak."

I am grateful to Mr. Wilbur, Mr. Davis, and Ms. Cope for taking the trouble to discuss this question and for granting me permission to cite their comments.

Note to Chapter Five

Auden's remark about the reading of verse appears in *The Table Talk of W. H. Auden*, by Alan Ansen, ed. Nicholas Jenkins, with an introduction by Richard Howard (Princeton: Ontario Review Press, 1990), 62. Coleridge's definition of poetry occurs in his *Table Talk:* "I wish our clever young poets would remember my homely definitions of prose and poetry; that is, prose = words in their best order;—poetry = the *best* words in the best order" (Samuel Taylor Coleridge, *Selected Poetry and Prose*, 2d ed. enlarged, ed. Elisabeth Schneider [San Francisco: Rinehart, 1971], 506). A poet who notes the possibility of discussing meter in relation to grammatical organization is J. V. Cunningham. In his "How Shall the Poem Be Written?" (*The Collected Essays of J. V. Cunningham* [Chicago: Swallow, 1976], 266), Cunningham suggests, "The descriptive problems raised by different modes of recitation can be avoided by regarding a meter, not as a schematic diagram of scansions, but as a collection of syllabic-syntactic types." Several fine studies have been written about the relationship of syntax to meaning in poetry. See especially Winters, *In Defense of Reason*, 30–74, and Donald Davie, *Articulate Energy: An Inquiry into the Syntax of English Poetry*, 2d ed. (London: Routledge & Kegan Paul, 1976). A study of versification that analyzes word shape and word stress in relation to metrical pattern is Paul Kiparsky, "The Rhythmic Structure of English Verse," *Linguistic Inquiry* 8 (Spring 1977): 189–247. In his "Closing Statement: Linguistics and Poetics," Jakobson comments aptly on the crucial but little appreciated role of word shapes and grammatical patterns in poetry: "The poetic resources concealed in the morphological and syntactic structure of language, briefly the poetry of grammar, and its literary product, the grammar of poetry, have been seldom known to critics and mostly disregarded by linguists but skillfully mastered by creative writers" (Sebeok, ed., *Style in Language*, 375). It is to these "poetic resources," I believe, that Frost refers when he is exploring in 1913–15 his ideas about "the sound of sense" and about the interplay between it and meter:

> [I]f one is to be a poet he must learn to get cadences by skillfully breaking the sounds of sense with all their irregularity of accent across the regular beat of the metre. Verse in which there is nothing but the beat of the metre furnished by the accents of the polysyllabic words we call doggerel. Verse is not that. Neither is it the sound of sense alone. It is a resultant from those two.... The living part of a poem is the intonation entangled somehow in the syntax idiom and meaning of a sentence. (*Robert Frost on Writing*, 60, 61)

In a comment that Frost makes in 1915 to Walter Pritchard Eaton, we see this same interest in coordinating meter and interesting, lively sentences:

> I have tried to see what I could do with boasting tones and quizzical tones and shrugging tones (for there are such) and forty eleven other tones. All I care a cent for is to catch sentence tones that haven't been brought to book.... But summoning them is not all. They are only lovely when thrown and drawn and displayed across spaces of the footed line. (*Collected Poems, Prose, and Plays*, 690–91)

Jeremy Campbell's observations about grammar can be found in his *Grammatical Man: Information, Entropy, Language, and Life* (New York: Simon & Schuster, 1982), 11, 12.

Note to Chapter Six

Books that discuss rhyme and fixed forms include Lewis Turco, *The New Book of Forms: A Handbook of Poetics* (Hanover: University Press of New England, 1986), Miller Williams, *Patterns of Poetry: An Encyclopedia of Forms* (Baton Rouge: Louisiana State University Press, 1986), John Hollander, *Rhyme's Reason,* enlarged ed. (New Haven: Yale University Press, 1989), and John Drury, *The Poetry Dictionary* (Cincinnati: Story Press, 1995).

An interesting speculation about the origin of rhyme is provided by Arthur Melville Clark in his and Harold Whitehall's entry for "Rhyme" in the enlarged first edition of *The Princeton Encyclopedia of Poetry and Poetics:*

> R[hyme] is to be traced ... to the fact that the number of sounds available for any language is limited and its many words must be combinations and permutations of its few sounds. Every language, therefore, is bound to jingle now and then. It will depend on a variety of factors whether the jingles will come to be used deliberately as a device in poetry and how far that device will be carried. . . . Men must have been pleased by verbal jingles long before they realized that the jingles had a use in organizing or pointing their verses. R[hyme] is indeed only one instance of that animating principle of all the arts: the desire for similarity in dissimilarity and dissimilarity in similarity. Other results within the literary art are: alliteration, anaphora, antithesis and balance, assonance, meter and stanzas, parallelism, and refrains. Perhaps because man is a creature with paired limbs and organs, he takes pleasure in repetitions, not merely simple duplications, but approximations, complements, and counterpoints.

And Isak Dinesen tells a story that well illustrates the appeal of rhyme. The episode she relates occurred during the corn harvest on her farm in Kenya:

> The Natives, who have a strong sense of rhythm, know nothing of verse, or at least did not know anything before the times of the schools, where they were taught hymns. One evening out in the maize-field, where we had been harvesting maize, breaking off the cobs and throwing them on to the ox-carts, to amuse myself, I spoke to the field labourers, who were mostly quite young, in Swaheli verse. There was no sense in the verse, it was made for the sake of the rhyme:—"Ngumbe napenda chumbe, Malaya-mbaya. Wakamba na-kula mamba." The oxen like salt,—whores are bad,—The Wakamba do eat snakes. It caught the interest of the boys, they formed a ring round me. They were quick to understand that the meaning in poetry is of no consequence, and they did not question the thesis of the verse, but waited eagerly for the rhyme, and laughed at it when it came. I tried to make them themselves find the rhyme and finish the poem when I had begun it, but they could not, or would not, do that, and turned away their heads. As they had become used to the idea of poetry, they begged: "Speak again. Speak like rain." Why they should feel verse to be like rain I do not know. It must have been, however, an expression of applause, since in Africa rain is always longed for and welcomed. (*Out of Africa* [New York: Vintage, 1972], 276–77)

X. J. Kennedy and Dana Gioia cite this passage in their *Introduction to Poetry,* 8th ed. (New York: HarperCollins, 1994), 132.

Cunningham's comment about the prevalence of rhyme in English following the

Norman Conquest appears in his *Collected Essays,* 263. Campion's disparaging comment about rhyme appears in *The Works of Thomas Campion,* 291. Daniel's discussion of length and accent in English, and his praise of rhyme, may be found in Walter Jackson Bate, ed., *Criticism: The Major Texts* (San Diego: Harcourt Brace, 1970), 109, 108. Johnson's discussion of the versification of *Paradise Lost* appears in *Selected Poetry and Prose,* 443, 444. Paul Maas's remarks about rhyme in modern-language verse may be found in his *Greek Metre,* 21. Dryden's comment about rhyme and sense appears in *Of Dramatic Poesy,* 1:25. Watts's discussion of rhyme may be found in *The Works of Isaac Watts,* ed. George Burder, 6 vols. (London: Barfield, 1810; reprint New York: AMS, 1971), 4:706–7. Frost's comment about rhymes serving almost as inflectional endings to verse lines appears in *Robert Frost on Writing,* 133. The structural weaknesses of certain of Shakespeare's sonnets have been noted by earlier readers, especially John Crowe Ransom in his "Shakespeare at Sonnets," which appears in John Crowe Ransom, *The World's Body* (Baton Rouge: Louisiana State University Press, 1968), 270–303. Ransom writes of the sonnets:

> They use the common English metrical pattern, and the metrical work is always admirable, but the logical pattern more often than not fails to fit it. . . . Probably Shakespeare's usual structural difficulty consists about equally in having to pad out his quatrains, if three good co-ordinates do not offer themselves, and in having to squeeze the couplet too flat, or else extend its argument upward into the proper territory of the quatrains. But when both these things happen at once, the obvious remark is that the poet should have reverted to the Italian sonnet. (273, 278)

In his lecture notes on "Rhythm and the Other Structural Parts of Rhetoric—Verse," Hopkins comments on the value of rhyming words of different types and from different grammatical categories: "[T]here are two elements in the beauty rhyme has to the mind, the likeness or sameness of sound and the unlikeness or difference of meaning" (*The Journals and Papers of Gerard Manley Hopkins,* ed. Humphrey House, completed by Graham Story [London: Oxford University Press, 1959], 286). And in Hopkins's dialogue, "On the Origin of Beauty," one of the character urges that rhyme embodies "disagreement joined with agreement" (*Journals and Papers,* 101), and another character notes, "[R]hyme is the epitome of your principle [of beauty]. All beauty may by a metaphor be called rhyme" (102). Frost, too, suggests that rhyme is an acoustic equivalent of metaphor, or an extension of metaphor into sound:

> [A]ll there is to thought is feats of association . . . Now, wouldn't it be a pretty idea to look at that as the under part of every poem: a feat of association, putting two things together and making a metaphor . . . Carry that idea a little further, to think that perhaps the rhyming, the coupling of lines is an outward symbol of this thing that I call feats of association. (*Robert Frost: Poetry and Prose,* ed. Edward Connery Lathem and Lawrance Thompson [New York: Holt, 1972], 380)

Citing the final stanza of Hardy's "Darkling Thrush," Corn provides an excellent explanation of effectively inventive rhyme: "Notice that we find only one monosyllabic pair of rhymes, otherwise all rhymes pair words of differing numbers of syllables. And rhymes are also different parts of speech, often with differently spelled rhyming syllables" (*The Poem's Heartbeat,* 77).

Note to Chapter Seven

Because stanza and rhyme are so closely related in English verse practice, many of the works mentioned in the note to the previous chapter are relevant to this one. Watts's discussion of hymn stanzas and their terminology appears in his *Works*, 4:122. It is in *William Cowper: The Task and Selected Other Poems*, ed. James Sambrook (London: Longman, 1994), 292, that Sambrook uses the term "common ballad metre" to describe the form of Cowper's "Epitaph on an Hare." (No poet better illuminates the resources of common meter than Cowper, who skillfully deploys the form both in the solemn religious verse of his *Olney Hymns*, such as "Oh! for a closer walk with God," and in his lighter secular pieces, such as those about his pet hare Tiney and his spaniel Beau.) Gascoigne's explanation of the term "poulter's measure" appears in *George Gascoigne: The Green Knight, Selected Poetry and Prose*, 144. On the structures of Keats's odes, and of their formal relationship to his sonnets, see Ian Jack, *Keats and the Mirror of Art* (Oxford: Oxford University Press, 1967). In an interview with *The Paris Review*, Frost comments illuminatingly on the value of grammatical variety in stanzaic verse: "I'm always interested, you know, when I have three or four stanzas, in the way I *lay* the sentences in them. I'd hate to have the sentences all lie the same in the stanzas" (*Collected Poems, Prose, and Plays*, 890).

Note to Chapter Eight

Over the years, I have seen several accounts of the exchange between Jowett and Tennyson. If memory serves, the wording is never exactly the same, though the gist is. I have cited the exchange as it is given in Jan Morris, ed., *The Oxford Book of Oxford* (Oxford: Oxford University Press, 1978), 276. Beeching's epigram on Jowett appears in *The Balliol Rhymes*, "edited from the Rare Original Broadsheet with the Notes of J. W. Mackail, Lord Sumner and F. A. Madan together with a Manuscript from Christ Church Library, by W. G. Hiscock" (Oxford: Basil Blackwell, 1939). An iambic variant of the epigram exists:

> I am the first: my name is Jowett:
> Whatever's to be known, I know it.
> I am the Master of this College,
> And what I don't know is not knowledge.

Attridge's analysis of Campion's use of imitation-quantitative may be found in Derek Attridge, *Well-Weighed Syllables: Elizabethan Verse in Classical Metres* (London: Cambridge University Press, 1974), 219–27. Jefferson's discussion of the number and nature of English feet appear in his *Writings*, 601, 602, 603. Goldsmith's remarks about meter may be found in Oliver Goldsmith, *The Collected Works of Oliver Goldsmith*, ed. Arthur Friedman, 5 vols. (Oxford: Oxford University Press, 1966), 4:246; 3:190. Gray's comments about trisyllabic feet appear in *The Works of Thomas Gray*, ed. Edmund Gosse, 4 vols. (London: Macmillan, 1884; reprint New York: AMS, 1968), 1:359. Coleridge's remark about amphibrach tetrameter catalectic appears in Samuel Taylor Coleridge, *Notebooks,* ed. Kathleen Coburn, 4 vols. (New York: Pantheon Books, 1957–1990), 2. entry 2224.22.15(38). This comment is cited by David Perkins in his illuminating "Wordsworth, Hunt, and Romantic Understanding of Meter," *JEGP* 93 (January 1994): 1–17. Longfellow's letter to Hawthorne about *Evangeline* is quoted by H. E. Scudder in his headnote to the poem in *The Poetical Works of Longfellow,* introduced by George Monteiro, based on the Cambridge Edition of 1893, ed. H. E. Scudder (Boston: Houghton Mifflin, 1975), 70a–b.

Martin Halpern, "On the Two Chief Metrical Modes in English," *PMLA* 77 (June 1962): 177–86, persuasively argues that trochaic and trisyllabic meters, regardless of their theoretical condition, sound more like accentual verse than accentual-syllabic iambic verse. Other critics have likewise noted the comparatively wooden nature of trochaic and trisyllabic rhythm. For instance, at the end of his discussion of trochaics, Jakob Schipper says: "It is common to all these trochaic metres that their structure, especially that of the longer ones, is (except for the varying caesura) very regular, and that they have only very few rhythmical licences, chiefly slight slurring" (*A History of English Versification* [Oxford: Oxford University Press, 1910; reprint, New York: AMS, 1971], 248). For a different opinion of trochaics and trisyllabics, see Annie Finch's "Metrical Diversity: A Defense of the Non-Iambic Meters," in Baker, ed., *Meter in English,* 59–74. See also Finch's *Ghost of Meter: Culture and Prosody in American Free Verse* (Ann Arbor: University of Michigan Press, 1993), 62–66, for a discussion of nineteenth-century attitudes toward dactylic meters.

Note to Chapter Nine

Michael Alexander's bang-bang-bang-crash characterization of the Old English accentual-alliterative meter occurs in his *Earliest English Poems,* 2d ed. (Harmondsworth: Penguin, 1977), 16. Lewis's "The Planets" may be found in his article "The Alliterative Meter," in his *Selected Literary Essays,* 15–26. Sievers's essay, "Old Germanic Metrics and Old English Metrics" appears in *Essential Articles for the Study of Old English Poetry,* 267–88, already cited in the note for the introduction. Another helpful discussion of Old English metric is J. R. R. Tolkien's "Prefatory Remarks" to the J. R. Clark Hall translation of *Beowulf and the Finnesburg Fragment,* 3d ed. rev. by C. L. Wrenn (London: Allen and Unwin, 1950). Useful analysis may be found as well in Howell D. Chickering, Jr., ed. and trans., *Beowulf* (New York: Anchor-Doubleday, 1977), 29–38; it is from Chickering's edition that I cite *Beowulf,* 4–7. Bliss's remarks about Old English versification conclude his *Metre of Beowulf* (Oxford: Basil Blackwell, 1958), 138. Many summaries of Old English meter are inadequate, on account of their authors' failing to point out that certain prosodic factors in Old English (e.g., the nature and treatment of vowels) are different from those in Modern English. On this matter, see James Sledd, "Old English Prosody: A Demurrer," *College English* 31 (October 1969): 71–74.

Works that address Middle English accentual-alliterative verse include Marie

Borroff, *Sir Gawain and the Green Knight: A Stylistic and Metrical Study* (New Haven: Yale University Press, 1962) and Thomas Cable, *The English Alliterative Tradition* (Philadelphia: University of Pennsylvania Press, 1991). See as well the introduction to Walter Hoyt French and Charles Brockway Hale, eds., *Middle English Metrical Romances*, 2 vols. (New York: Russell & Russell, 1964). Hopkins's discussion of sprung meter and its historical antecedents appears in *The Poems of Gerard Manley Hopkins*, 4th ed., edited by W. H. Gardner and N. H. MacKenzie (London: Oxford University Press, 1967), 49. "Spelt from Sibyl's Leaves" exists in two manuscript versions; Bridges, Hopkins's friend and first editor, called them A and B. The accent marks differ somewhat from one to the other; and Gardner and MacKenzie indicate that the stress marks in their text of the poem "are a selection from A and B" (284). Readers interested in navigating through Hopkins's sometimes confusing explanations of sprung rhythm will find assistance in Winters's "The Poetry of Gerard Manley Hopkins" (*The Function of Criticism* [Denver: Swallow, 1957], 103–56) and Paull F. Baum's "Sprung Rhythm" (*PMLA* 74 [September 1959]: 418–25). Bridges anticipates me in suggesting that "Christabel" is, regardless of its other merits, not entirely accentual verse: "[I]t is plain that he [Coleridge] did not ever shake off the tradition of . . . conventional, metric stresses" (*Milton's Prosody*, 88).

Jonson's comment about Donne's not maintaining the accentual pattern of his verse occurs in *Conversations with Drummond*, 36; I quote from *Ben Jonson*, 596. Gray's remarks about Donne's satires may be found in Gray's *Works*, 1:340–41. An interesting discussion of Wyatt's pentametric verse appears in R. A. Rebholz, ed., *Sir Thomas Wyatt: The Complete Poems* (New Haven: Yale University Press, 1981), 44–55. On Wyatt's metrics, see also Thompson, *The Founding of English Metre*, 15–36. Elizabeth Daryush's comments on her use of majuscules appear in her *Selected Poems by Elizabeth Daryush* (Oxford: Carcanet, 1972):

> The poems without line-capitals are those written in syllabic metres (by which I mean metres governed only by the number of syllables to the line, and in which the number and position of the stresses may be varied at will) and are so printed as a reminder to the reader to follow strictly the natural speech-rhythm, and not to look for stresses where none are intended. (93)

Marianne Moore's note on the quoted first line and a half of "No Swan So Fine" occurs in Marianne Moore, *Collected Poems* (New York: Macmillan, 1951), 154.

For the background of free verse, readers may be interested in consulting *Missing Measures* and my entry on "Vers Libre" in Ian Hamilton, ed., *The Oxford Companion to Twentieth-Century Poetry in English* (Oxford: Oxford University Press, 1994). Brogan's *English Versification, 1570–1980*, lists a number of prosodic studies of free verse. One of the best is Paul Ramsey's thoughtful and sympathetic treatment, "Free Verse: Some Steps Towards Definition," *Studies in Philology* 65 (January, 1968): 98–108. More recent studies include Charles O. Hartman, *Free Verse: An Essay on Prosody* (Princeton: Princeton University Press, 1980); Stephen Cushman, *William Carlos Williams and the Meanings of Measure* (New Haven: Yale University Press, 1985); Finch, *The Ghost of Meter;* Amittai F. Aviram, *Telling Rhythm: Body and Meaning in Poetry* (Ann Arbor:

University of Michigan Press, 1994); Philip Hobsbaum, *Metre, Rhythm, and Verse Form* (London: Routledge, 1996), 89–120; H. T. Kirby-Smith, *The Origins of Free Verse* (Ann Arbor: University of Michigan Press, 1996). The best account of the beginnings of free verse is Édouard Dujardin's *Les Premiers Poètes du Vers Libre* (Paris: Mercure de France, 1922). This important work has never been translated into English. There is, however, a summary of it in Clive Scott, *Vers Libre: The Emergence of Free Verse in France, 1886–1914* (Oxford: Oxford University Press, 1990).

Valéry's remark that our age has produced nearly as many prosodies as poets occurs in Valéry, *The Art of Poetry*, 13. It appears that Francis Vielé-Griffin was the writer who popularized the term *vers libre*. He begins his prefatory manifesto to his *Joies* (1889) with the sentence, "Le vers est libre"; and Dujardin cites the publication of this book and its manifesto as marking "the definitive establishment of free verse" (*Les Premiers Poètes du Vers Libre*, 37). As I observe in *Missing Measures* (16–18), there is a term in neoclassical French poetics, *vers libres* ("free verses"), that describes a verse mode that mixes together different metrical lines and rhyme patterns. We find this mode in, for example, La Fontaine's fables. Though this other term is homophonic with *vers libre*, we should probably point out, even at the risk of seeming pedantic, that it is not the same term and indicates something very different from *vers libre*.

It is in his entry for "Free Verse" in the enlarged first edition of *The Princeton Encyclopedia of Poetry and Poetics* that Williams comments on Milton's having made the verse paragraph rather than the verse line his basic unit of composition. Cunningham's "How Shall the Poem Be Written," which appears in his *Collected Essays*, 256–71, has a trenchant analysis of the versification of Eliot's "Gerontion"; the term Cunningham coins for Eliot's practice is "parasitic meter . . . meter [that] presupposes a meter by law which it uses, alludes to, traduces, returns to" (268). Eliot's versification seems to have been influenced by his own early (1917) argument that "the most interesting verse which has yet been written in our language has been done either by taking a very simple form, like the iambic pentameter, and constantly withdrawing from it, or taking no form at all, and constantly approximating to a very simple one" (Eliot, *To Criticize the Critic*, 185); as was mentioned when this statement was cited in our first chapter, Eliot appears to have been not entirely clear on the difference between modulating meter and violating it.

On Renaissance experiments with classical measure, see Thompson, *The Founding of English Metre*, 128–38, and Attridge, *Well-Weighed Syllables*. Spenser's areopagus letter to Harvey may be found in Smith, *Elizabethan Critical Essays*, 1:89. It is in his edition of Sidney's *Selected Prose and Poetry*, 5, that Kimbrough discusses Sidney's suppression, in the final transcriptions of *The Old Arcadia*, of materials relating to quantitative metric. Campion's characterization of the quantitative "Iambick Dimeter, or English march" appears in *The Works of Thomas Campion*, 301. Housman's remarks on Stone's appear in a review of Stone's *On the Use of Classical Metres in English*; this review has been collected in *The Classical Papers of A. E. Housman*, ed. J. Diggle & F. R. D. Goodyear, 3 vols. (Cambridge: Cambridge University Press, 1972), 2:484–88. Congreve's observations about English Pindarics may be found in *The Complete*

Works of William Congreve, ed. Montague Summers, 4 vols. (New York: Russell and Russell, 1964), 4:82. Bridges's discussion of 8.201 of *Paradise Lost,* and of Milton's treatment of adjectives ending in *-able,* occurs in *Milton's Prosody,* 25, 30–32.

On accentual-syllabic meter and the alternative modes of versification, James McAuley writes:

> The past century has seen a great deal of prosodic restlessness, with attempts at reform, or revolutionary overthrow, of the standard metrical system. . . . None of the alternatives proposed has displaced the accentual-syllabic system; all have difficulties of their own, and all sacrifice something of the unique complexity or variability-within-strictness of the traditional norm. On the other hand, all offer the poet certain possibilities, and valuable work has been done in them. *(Versification: A Short Introduction* [East Lansing: Michigan State University Press, 1966], 69)

Glossary

Some of the terms below have signified different things at different times to different people; in such cases, I have tried to indicate the nature or range of variant meanings. A more comprehensive survey of literary terms—terms relevant not only to versification, but to other areas of poetry and to other genres of literature—is M. H. Abrams, *A Glossary of Literary Terms*, 6th ed. (San Diego: Harcourt Brace, 1993). For a dictionary devoted to figures of speech and figures of thought, see Richard A. Lanham, *A Handlist of Rhetorical Terms: A Guide for Students of English Literature* (Berkeley and Los Angeles: University of California Press, 1968). Though concerned with the visual arts, J. J. Pollitt, *The Ancient View of Greek Art: Criticism, History, and Terminology* (New Haven: Yale University Press, 1974) contains as well materials and analyses that illuminate the origin and evolution of words and concepts related to the theory and practice of poetry. *The New Princeton Encyclopedia of Poetry and Poetics,* edited by Alex Preminger and T. V. F. Brogan (Princeton: Princeton University Press, 1993) has entries and bibliographies for a wide range of topics concerning verse and versification.

Accent: a term with many denotations. For some people, it is synonymous with "stress" and indicates the relative prominence of a syllable when uttered. For others, it more specifically indicates "pitch"—the tonic height or acuity of a syllable. "Accent" also denotes a manner of speaking characteristic of a region or locality, as in "a Southern accent" or "a Boston accent." In connection with poetry, "accent" most often refers to one of the regularly recurring beats of a metrical line.

This book draws a distinction between "metrical accent" and "speech stress." Metrical accent involves the prosodic nature of a syllable as determined by comparing it specifically and exclusively to the other syllable or syllables of the foot in which it appears. A syllable in an iambic foot, for example, is metrically accented if it is weightier than the other syllable in that foot; it is metrically unaccented if it is lighter than the other syllable. Speech stress, on the other hand, refers to the relative weight of a syllable when spoken and viewed in the larger phrase or clause in which it figures. Though metrically accented syllables usually have significant speech stress, the two properties do not always coincide. A syllable with little speech stress may take a metrical accent if the other syllable in its foot is even lighter. By the same token, a syllable with notable speech stress may be metrically unaccented if the other syllable in its foot is even heavier. (See, too, "Metrical Accent.")

Accentual Verse: verse in which the lines have a fixed number of accents but a varying number of syllables. The most common type of accentual verse in our language is the four-beat line featured in such Old English poems as *Beowulf* and in such Middle English poems as William Langland's *Piers Plowman*. This line has a medial pause, with two accents on either side of the pause. Generally, three of the metrically accented syllables are pointed by alliteration, though sometimes only two alliterate and occasionally all four do. The third of the line's beats customarily dictates the alliterative pattern, retrospectively communicating, as it were, the alliterating sound to the first two beats. The measure may be illustrated by this line (7.2) from *Piers Plowman:*

> To ţáken his ţéme and ţúlyen the érthë

After the Middle Ages, accentual verse is eclipsed by the accentual-syllabic system. In the nineteenth century, however, such poems as Coleridge's "Christabel" and Hopkins's in "sprung rhythm" revive accentual verse. And in the twentieth century there are fruitful experiments with the old accentual-alliterative line by such poets as Auden and Wilbur. (See, too, "Alliteration," "Old English," and "Sprung Rhythm.")

Accentual-Syllabic Verse: verse in which the lines have a fixed number of syllables and a fixed number and pattern of accents. The iambic pentameter, for instance, has ten syllables and five metrical accents per line, the accents falling on the even-numbered syllables. Most of the major poetry in English from Chaucer to the present is accentual-syllabic, which is commonly considered the standard mode of versification in English.

Acephalous: a Greek word meaning "headless" and referring to a metrical line lacking its initial syllable. In English prosody, the word is most often applied to iambic lines missing their first unaccented syllable. (See, too, "Clipped.")

Alexandrine: in English verse, a line of six iambic feet; in French verse, a line of twelve syllables.

Alliteration: the device of beginning with the same sound two or more syllables in a phrase, clause, sentence, or verse line, as in Charles Churchill's comment (*The Prophecy of Famine*, 85–86) about having

> . . . prayed
> For apt alliteration's artful aid

We hear alliteration most clearly when it involves metrically accented syllables, but it may also extend to unaccented syllables. In Churchill's line, for instance, the metrically unaccented third syllable ("al-") participates in the alliteration. "For" and "-ful" faintly alliterate as well. And though we commonly associate alliteration with the repetition of consonant sounds, as in Gavin Douglas's rendering of Aeneas's address to Hector's ghost in book 2 of *The Aeneid:*

O thou, of Troy the lemand* lamp of lycht,	*gleaming
O Trojane hope, maist ferm* defens in fyght	*most firm

it may involve word-beginning vowels, as in the example from Churchill.

Orthography is not always a sure indication of alliteration, since most syllable-opening vowels will alliterate, regardless of how they are spelled:

The <u>ea</u>rnest <u>a</u>gitator <u>u</u>pped the <u>a</u>nte

Further, identical consonant sounds may be registered by different letters:

Is <u>K</u>aren's <u>c</u>addy <u>c</u>oming to the <u>k</u>ermis

This point notwithstanding, the etymology of "alliteration" associates it with the repetition of the same letter. The word derives from Latin *al* or *ad* ("to") + *littera* ("letter")—"to [begin with the same] letter."

Amphibrach: a trisyllabic foot whose sequence is unaccented-accented-unaccented.

Amphimacer (also called "Cretic"): a trisyllabic foot whose sequence is accented-unaccented-accented. Poems in English amphimacers are rare and are mostly novelty items in monometer. One such poem is Tennyson's "The Oak," which is mentioned by Robert J. Getty in his entry for "Cretic" in the enlarged first edition of *The Princeton Encyclopedia of Poetry and Poetics*. Another is Pope's "Lilliputian Ode," a tribute to Swift's *Gulliver's Travels*. The last line is evidently intended as a double foot, though one has to cheat a bit to keep the rhythm going.

In Amaze
Lost, I gaze!
Can our Eyes
Reach thy Size?
May my Lays
Swell with Praise
Worthy thee!
Worthy me!
Muse inspire
All thy Fire!
Bards of old
Of him told,
When they said
Atlas head
Propt the Skies:
See! and believe your Eyes!

(Quoted by Maynard Mack, *Alexander Pope: A Life* [New York: Norton, 1985], 443)

Without mentioning amphimacers specifically, Cunningham notes that Thomas Nashe's "Adieu, farewell, earth's bliss" and certain other Renaissance songs mix together iambic rhythm with amphimaceric rhythm: "The six-syllable line [of Nashe's poem] glides from a regular iambic pattern into a triple movement—accented, unaccented, accented—and back again as if both were its mode of being and neither had precedence over the other. . . . The poem in this respect belongs to a curious episode in the history of English meter; for this phenomenon appears only to my knowledge in the songs written within a fairly short period, of perhaps ten or twenty years, in the 1590s and early 1600s" (*The Collected Essays of J. V. Cunningham*, 177).

Anapest: a trisyllabic foot whose sequence is unaccented-unaccented-accented.

Anceps: a Latin term (related to the Greek *amphikephalos*) meaning "two-headed" and, by extension, "of two natures, undecided." In discussions of ancient Greek and Latin versification, the term has two denotations. First, an "anceps position" is a position in a meter that can be filled with either a short syllable or a long syllable at the poet's discretion. In the Greek iambic trimeter, for example, the first, fifth, and ninth positions are anceps. Second, an "anceps syllable" is a syllable that can function as either long or short, "either because the vowel itself for some reason admits of different scansions or because a consonant following the vowel can be allocated alternatively to the same or to the next syllable [e.g., the first syllable of *teknon*, 'child,' is open and short when the word is syllabified *te-knon* and closed and long when it is syllabified *tek-non*]" (West, *Introduction to Greek Metre*, 12–13).

The concept of anceps syllables is not usefully applicable to English versification. It is helpful to speak of a syllable as having a dual and varying nature only in a prosodic system like that of classical antiquity, in which the metrical character of most syllables is single and definite, according to phonemic and phonetic principles. English meters are based on syllabic stress, and this can change—especially where monosyllabic words are concerned—according to sense and verbal environment.

Aphaeresis: a Greek word meaning "a taking away." In poetry, it is a form of elision involving the suppression of the first vowel or syllable of a word, as with *'gainst* for *against* or *'longing* for *belonging*. (See, too, "Elision.")

Apocope (or "Apocopation"): a Greek word, meaning "a cutting off." For prosodists, it generally denotes a species of elision involving the dropping of the last letter or syllable in a word, regardless of whether or not that word is followed by a word beginning with a vowel. An apocopation common in Renaissance prose and verse is *i'the* (or, alternatively, *i'th'*) for *in the*. An apocopation frequent in Chaucer is the use of *bet* as a monosyllabic alternative for *better*, as in these iambic pentameters:

```
 x  /  x   /    x  /  x    /     x    /
```
The lessë prees, the bet; com forth with me
   The fewer people, the better; come forth with me

(Troilus and Criseyde, 2.1718)

```
 /   x  x  / x  / x   /   x  /(x)
```
Bet than a lazar or a beggesterë
   Better than a leper or a beggar-woman

(The Canterbury Tales, A 242 ["General Prologue"])

(See, too, "Elision.")

Assonance: repetition of vowel sounds within a phrase, clause, sentence, or verse line, as with the long *a* sounds of

Since fate is graver now, let's say we paid.

"Assonantal rhyme" is a form of partial rhyme that matches the vowels of the last metrically accented syllables of corresponding lines, but that does not match the consonants that follow. **Hope/boat** and **seed/deep** are assonantal rhymes. (See, too, "Consonance" and "Partial Rhyme.")

Ballad Stanza (also called "Ballad Meter"): a four-line stanza whose first and third lines are unrhyming iambic tetrameters and whose second and fourth lines are rhyming iambic trimeters, as in Emily Dickinson's "My Life Closed Twice":

My life closed twice before its close—
It yet remains to see
If Immortality unveil
A third event to me . . .

Ballad stanza resembles common meter, which has the same metrical structure, but which rhymes lines 1 and 3 as well 2 and 4. (See, too, "Common Meter.")

Ballade: a fixed-form poem consisting (usually) of three eight-line stanzas—all rhyming *ababbcbc*—and a concluding four-line "envoy" rhyming *bcbc*. The last line of each stanza and of the envoy are the same. A famous practitioner of this form is François Villon (1431–?), whose ballades include *Ballade des Dames du Temps Jadis* ("Ballade of Ladies of Former Times") with its refrain, *Mais où sont les neiges d'antan?* ("But where are the snows of yesteryear?").

Beat: in this book, a term indicating a metrically accented syllable. Because of its associations with music and with the marking of musical rhythm (which involves factors additional to accent, such as tempo), some metrists object to employing the term in connection with poetry. However, other metrists, particularly Derek Attridge, have favored the term and have used it cogently for prosodic analysis. (See, too, "Offbeat.")

Blank Verse: unrhymed metrical verse, especially unrhymed iambic pentameter. (Not to be confused with "Free Verse.") Possibly, the term reflects the historical classification of rhyme as one of the rhetorical embellishments or "colors" of style. Blank verse—and the related French phrase for rhymeless verse, *vers blancs* ("white verses")—thus betoken poetry that is "colorless," in the sense that a significant ornament is stripped away or omitted. It is in this sense that Samuel Johnson, in his *Dictionary,* says that the term indicates verse "[w]ithout rhime; where the rhime is *blanched.*" Prior to his execution by Henry VIII, Henry Howard translated books 2 and 4 of Virgil's *Aeneid* into blank verse; and he is generally credited with having introduced the medium into English.

Burns Stanza: a six-line stanza, rhyming *aaabab*, lines 1, 2, 3, and 5 being iambic tetrameters, lines 4 and 6 being iambic dimeters.

Catalexis: a Greek word, meaning "termination." In connection with verse lines, the word refers to "the last foot when it wants one or more syllables" (Liddell and Scott, *Greek-English Lexicon*). In English, catalexis usually refers the dropping of the final unaccented syllable from a trochaic line. Metrically complete trochaic lines are sometimes called "acatalectic." Of the opening four lines of Frost's "To the Thawing Wind," the first two are trochaic tetrameter acatalectic, the second two trochaic tetrameter catalectic:

$$/ \quad x \quad / \quad x \quad / \quad x \quad / \; x$$
Come with rain, O loud Southwester!
$$/ \quad x \; / \; x \quad / \quad x \; / \; x$$
Bring the singer, bring the nester;
$$/ \quad x \; / \; x \quad / \quad x \quad / \quad \wedge$$
Give the buried flower a dream;
$$/ \quad x \; / \; x \quad / \quad x \quad / \quad \wedge$$
Make the settled snowbank steam.

Some metrists use the term "brachycatalexis" to signify the dropping of the two final unaccented syllables of a dactylic line.

Caesura (or "Cesura"): a word derived ultimately from the Latin *caedere*, "to cut." Generally, a caesura is understood to be a sense break—a grammatical pause— within a line. Thus we say of the following iambic pentameter that it has a caesura after its second foot (or its fourth syllable):

Full season's come, yet filled trees keep the sky

(Louise Bogan, "Simple Autumnal," 13)

In discussions of ancient versification, "caesura" also indicates "the ending of a word before the end of the metrical foot with the result that there is an overlapping of metrical feet and words" (Hornsby, *Reading Latin Poetry*, 261). "Dieresis" is the term for the opposite situation—the coincidence of a word ending and foot ending. In discussions of ancient poetry and certain modern-language poetries, "caesura" may additionally refer to a more or less obligatory pause in a meter. Ancient dactylic hexameters, for example, usually have a caesura (in the sense of a word's ending within a foot) in the third foot or, less frequently, the fourth; and the French alexandrine traditionally has a caesura (in the sense of a grammatical pause) after the sixth of its twelve syllables. English meters have no such fixed caesuras. (See also "Dieresis.")

Clerihew: a form of light verse invented by Edmund Clerihew Bentley (1875–1956). Clerihews consist of two rhyming couplets, which feature irregular rhythm and which offer thumbnail biographical sketches of historical figures. One of Bentley's best-known clerihews is the following:

Sir Christopher Wren
Said, "I am going to dine with some men.
If anybody calls,
Say I am designing St. Paul's."

Clipped: a term that most commonly refers to iambic lines that lack their initial unstressed syllable. For instance, two of the following lines (33–40) from Eliot's "Sweeney Erect" are clipped—are missing the opening element of the iambic tetrameter measure in which the poem is written. (To clarify the meter, I have given the full spelling of "Missus"; Eliot himself uses the conventional abbreviation "Mrs.")

> The ladies of the corridor
> ∧ /   x / x /   x /
> Find themselves involved, disgraced,
> Call witness to their principles
> And deprecate the lack of taste

> Observing that hysteria
> Might easily be misunderstood;
> ∧   / x   / x / x /
> Missus Turner intimates
> It does the house no sort of good.

Many metrists call clipped lines "headless." I prefer "clipped" because it suggests a haircut, whereas "headless" makes it sound as if the lines offended an irascible monarch, who sent them to the block.

Common Meter: a quatrain rhyming *abab*, the first and third lines being iambic tetrameters, the second and fourth being iambic trimeters. Metrically, common meter is the same as "ballad stanza." However, the first and third lines of ballad stanzas do not rhyme. (See, too, "Ballad Stanza.")

Consonance: the repetition of consonant sounds at the ends of syllables or words, as in the *nd* sounds of

> Le**nd** a bu**nd**le with your sa**nd**wich.

"Consonantal rhyme" is a species of partial rhyme in which the final stressed syllables of lines correspond in their closing consonants but not in the vowels that precede them, as in **moon/none, limb/comb,** and **nut/lute.** (See, too, "Assonance" and "Partial Rhyme.")

Cretic: see "Amphimacer."

Dactyl: a trisyllabic foot whose sequence is accented-unaccented-unaccented.

Dieresis: a word derived from the Greek *diairesis,* meaning "division into parts" and, in grammar, "the separation of a diphthong into two syllables:—or of one word into two" (Liddell and Scott, *A Greek-English Lexicon*). "Dieresis" also denotes the diacritical symbol (¨) that indicates that adjacent vowels are pronounced separately, as in "Laocoön" (La • ok′ • o • on′). In classical metrics, "dieresis" also refers to cases where the end of a word and the end of a foot coincide. (See also "Caesura.")

Doggerel: a word of unknown origin, signifying inept verse, though the nature of the ineptitude has been variously defined. The *OED* gives as the word's earliest appearance a passage in *The Canterbury Tales* (B 2115, "Link between Sir Thopas and the Tale of Melibee"). Here the Host uses the phrase "rym dogerel" in objecting to and interrupting Chaucer's own "Sir Thopas." Metrically, "Sir Thopas" is not incompetent. But the tale is related mainly in the old "Romance-six stanza," which rhymes *aabaab* or *aabccb*—lines 1, 2, 4, and 5 being tetrameters, lines 3 and 6 being trimeter—and the stanza sounds jingly and crude, compared to the stabler, more flexible, and less obtrusive heroic couplets and rhyme royal stanzas that generally prevail elsewhere in *The Canterbury Tales*. As Thomas Gray notes in his "Observations on English Metre" (1760–61?), the problem with "Sir Thopas" is that it suffers from too much rather than too little order:

> [N]othing can be more regular than this sort of stanza, the pause always falling just in the middle of those verses which are of eight syllables, and at the end of those of six. I imagine that it was this very regularity which seemed so tedious to *mine host of the Tabbarde,* as to make him interrupt Chaucer in the middle of his story. (*The Works of Thomas Gray,* 1:336)

However, long before Gray's "Observations," George Puttenham had, in *Arte of English Poesie* (1589), interpreted doggerel to mean verse insufficiently attentive to the rules of poetic art. Using Chaucer's phrase, Puttenham writes: "A rymer that will be tyed to no rules at all, but range as he list, may easily utter what he will, but such maner of Poesie is called in our vulgar [i.e., our vernacular language], ryme dogrell" (*Arte,* 89). Puttenham's view that doggerel is unregulated has become the most common.

Yet some recent writers employ the word in its original sense. Robert Frost, for example, returns to the Chaucerian meaning when he characterizes doggerel as verse with no liveliness of speech-sense intonation: "Verse in which there is nothing but the beat of the metre furnished by the accents of the polysyllabic words we call doggerel" (*Robert Frost on Writing,* 60). Similarly, in a poem written for Charles Causley's sixty-fifth birthday, Philip Larkin calls doggerel the smooth but overly predictable iambic tetrameters with which he addresses his friend:

> Dear CHARLES, My Muse, asleep or dead,
> Offers this doggerel instead. (1–2)

For a good discussion of doggerel, see David J. Rothman, "Ars Doggerel," *Hellas* 1 (Fall 1990): 311–17.

Early Modern English: see "Modern English."

Echo Poem: a poem in which lines conclude with or are followed by a word or phrase that echoes the syllable, word, or phrase that precedes it. A striking contemporary echo poem is the second poem in Thom Gunn's "Misanthropos," a sequence concerning a man who seems to be the sole survivor of a nuclear holocaust. Here are the poem's first three couplets:

At last my shout is answered! Are you near,
Man whom I cannot see but can hear?
                                        Here.

The canyon hides you well, which well defended.
Sir, tell me, is the long war ended?
                                        Ended.

I passed no human on my trip, a slow one.
It is your luck, down there, to know one?
                                        No one.

Gunn integrates, it will be noted, the echo elements into his meter. "Here" is the tenth syllable of the second pentameter of the first couplet; and "Ended" and "No one" are the tenth and eleventh syllables in the second lines of their feminine-ended couplets. George Herbert's "Heaven" is an echo poem in which the echo words are not part of the meter, but stand on their own as responses to complete lines.

Elegiac Quatrain: see "Heroic Quatrain."

Elision: the contraction, for metrical purposes, of two syllables into one or the slur-ring away of a syllable. This process may involve two vowels sitting side by side within a word (e.g., "tumultuous," treated as "tu • mul • chwus" rather than "tu • mul • choo • us"); the process may involve two vowels facing each other across a gap between words (e.g., *Th'expense* for *The expense*); or the process may involve the omission of a vowel, consonant, or a syllable from a word (e.g., *consid'rate* for *considerate, ta'en* for *taken,* or *'longing* for *belonging*). To describe different types of elisions, metrists employ such terms as "synaloepha," "synaeresis," "apocope," "syncope," and "aphaeresis," entries for which appear in this glossary. We need not commit these terms to memory, but should be aware that syllabic ambigui-ties exist in our language and that poets make use of them in regulating syllable count.

End-Stopped: a term that refers to lines that are complete not only in meter, but also in sense. End-stopped lines, that is, involve the coincidence of metrical units with grammatical ones. Because of this condition, end-stopped lines often feature a mark of punctuation at their close:

I ask'd thee, "Give me immortality."
Then didst thou grant mine asking with a smile,
Like wealthy men who care not how they give.

(Tennyson, "Tithonus," 15–17)

(See, too, "Enjambment," the technique that is the opposite of end-stopping.)

Enjambment (also called "Running-on" or "Running-over"): a term that derives from French (*enjambement,* from *enjamber*—"to stride over, to span") and refers to the practice of setting metrical units and grammatical units at variance, with the result that the reader must read through the line ending in order to determine the sense of a phrase or clause. Enjambment occurs at the end of the second line of these lines (1–3) from Edgar Bowers's "Astronomers of Mont Blanc":

> Who are you there that, from your icy tower,
> Explore the colder distances, the far
> Escape of your whole universe to night . . .

If enjambment is to seem natural and expressive rather than arbitrary and awkward, it should serve meaning, as it does here. Bowers's run-on, that is, suggests the expanding—the "escap[ing]"—nature of the cosmos itself. (See, too, "End-stopped," which is the antonym of "Enjambed.")

Envoy: a short valedictory stanza that is part and appears at the end of certain fixed-form poems, such as the ballade. The word comes from the French *envoyer*, "to send off." (See, too, "Fixed Forms.")

Epigram: a short, witty poem. Though epigrams are frequently satirical and humorous, the "wit" of the form is best thought of as memorable compactness. Many ancient epigrams—including Simonides' two-line memorial for the Greek dead at Thermopylae and Callimachus's succinct elegy for his fellow poet Heraclitus—are deeply felt, even while remaining "witty." Fine epigrammatists in Modern English include Ben Jonson, Robert Herrick, and Walter Savage Landor. In the twentieth century outstanding epigrams—sometimes funny, sometimes serious, sometimes both—have been written by Rudyard Kipling, Hilaire Belloc, Dorothy Parker, Louise Bogan, Janet Lewis, Ogden Nash, Countee Cullen, J. V. Cunningham, John Frederick Nims, Richard Wilbur, Catherine Davis, Helen Pinkerton, X. J. Kennedy, Thom Gunn, Dick Davis, Wendy Cope, R. L. Barth, Brad Leithauser, and Vikram Seth.

Falling Rhythm: a term that some metrists use to describe rhythm, such as trochaic or dactylic, that moves from heavier to lighter syllables. (See, too, "Rising Rhythm.")

Feminine Ending: an extra, metrically unaccented syllable at the end of a line of verse, as with the eleventh syllable of this iambic pentameter:

> x / x / x / x / x / (x)
> He makes a common scorn of handsome women
> $\qquad\qquad\qquad\qquad$ (Fletcher, *The Wild-Goose Chase*, 3.1.17)

The advantage, in scanning, of placing in parentheses the mark over the extra syllable is that this makes clear that the syllable is—to use another term for the feminine ending—"hypermetrical," literally "beyond the meter." (See, too, "Feminine Rhyme.")

Feminine Rhyme: a rhyme of two syllables, with a metrical accent falling on the first, as in the **áges/páges** and **Gíbbon/ríbbon** rhymes of Landor's "Distribution of Honors for Literature":

> The grandest writer of late ages,
> Who wrapped up Rome in golden pages,

Whom scarcely Livius equal'd, Gibbon,
Died without star, or cross, or ribbon.

Some writers also use the term "feminine rhyme" to refer to trisyllabic rhymes accented on the antepenultimate syllable (e.g. **rápturous/cápture us** and **gríttily/ wíttily**). Other writers speak of such rhymes as "triple rhymes" or "sdrucciola rhymes." (See, too, "Masculine Rhyme," "Sdrucciolo/a," and "Triple Rhyme.")

Figurative Language: language used in an unconventional manner, for the purpose of expressive effect. From the ancients onward, figurative language has been divided into two categories. One contains "figures of thought" or "tropes" (from the Greek *tropos,* "turn"). Tropes are devices that employ language in nonliteral manner. One such device is irony (a statement whose literal meaning and real meaning are exactly opposite, as in "It's a shame that Mahler's symphonies aren't longer"). Another is simile (a statement explicitly comparing two apparently disparate entities or ideas, as in Stevens's comment, in "Sunday Morning," that "The day is like wide water"). Yet another is personification (the attribution of human traits to inanimate objects or concepts, as when Milton, in his sonnet on his blindness, imagines Patience as a counselor who tells him, "They also serve who only stand and wait").

The second category of figurative language contains "figures of speech" or "schemes" (from the Greek *schêma,* "form, shape"). These refer to conspicuously pointed syntactical arrangements. Under this heading come parallelism ("of the people, by the people, and for the people"), antithesis ("not that I loved Caesar less, but that I loved Rome more"), asyndeton ("I came, I saw, I conquered"), and the like.

Figures of Speech: see "Figurative Language."

Figures of Thought: see "Figurative Language."

Fixed Forms: poetic forms—such as the sonnet and villanelle—that have one or more of the three following characteristics: (1) a specific number of lines; (2) a particular sequence of rhymes; and (3) a certain number and pattern of repeating lines. Fixed forms include, but should not be identified exclusively with, "French Forms," which generally have all three characteristics. (See, too, "Ballade," "French Forms," "Rondeau," "Sonnet," "Sestina," "Triolet," and "Villanelle.")

Foot: the fundamental rhythmic unit in a poetic line. In English poetry, feet consist of two or three syllables, one and only one of which bears a metrical accent. Exceptions to this definition include the "Amphimacer," the "Spondee," the "Pyrrhic," and the "Ionic" foot, though the first is unusual in English, and the second, third, and fourth are arguably rare, unnecessary, or illusory. (See, too, "Amphibrach," "Amphimacer," "Anapest," "Dactyl," "Iamb," "Ionic," "Pyrrhic," "Spondee," and "Trochee.")

Fourteeners: rhyming iambic heptameter couplets. Common in the Renaissance, the form appears less frequently thereafter, though some metrists regard ballad-stanza poems as being in fourteeners, on the grounds that a quatrain arranged in a four-three-four-three pattern of iambic feet is simply a differently lineated version of the old form.

Free Verse: verse without traditional metrical arrangement. (Not to be confused with "Blank Verse.")

French Forms: poetic forms—such as the ballade, triolet, rondeau, and villanelle—that generally have a specific number of lines, a particular sequence of rhymes, and a certain number and pattern of repeating lines. These forms developed in the late Middle Ages and early Renaissance among such French poets as Guillaume de Machaut, Eustache Deschamps, Charles d'Orléans, and François Villon. Because several of the forms have subtypes, the student interested in them may wish to consult a handbook of French verse forms, such as Maurice Grammont, *Petit Traité de Versification Française* (Paris: Armond Colin, 1965). (See, too, "Ballade," "Fixed Forms," "Rondeau," "Triolet," and "Villanelle.")

Haiku: a form of Japanese verse consisting of seventeen syllables, arranged in a three-line sequence of 5–7–5. In the twentieth century, this form has been adapted to English verse, though the complex associations and delicacies of the original form have not always survived the process of adaptation.

Half Meter: quatrains of iambic trimeters, customarily rhyming *abab*.

Headless: see "Clipped."

Hemistich: a compound word from Greek (*hêmi*, "half," + *stichos*, "line of verse"), meaning "a half-line of verse." The term is most often employed with reference to meters that have an obligatory mid-line break. Metrists apply the term, for instance, to the two halves of the Old English four-beat line, which divides near the middle, with two metrical stresses on either side of the divide. (See, too, "Caesura" and "Stichos.")

Heroic: an adjective sometimes applied to iambic pentameter, originally on the grounds of its being the English measure most suitable for epic subjects. Though employed earlier, the term appears to have gained wide currency in the second half of the seventeenth century, when Milton used unrhymed pentameters for *Paradise Lost* and Dryden used rhymed pentameter couplets for his translation of Virgil's *Aeneid*. In his prefatory note about "The Verse" of his epic, Milton himself uses the adjective in reference to his line: "The Measure is English Heroic Verse without Rime."

Because English meters have never been connected with particular poetic genres to the degree that ancient meters were, it may be misleading to call the pentameter "heroic." Our poets have employed the meter not only for epics, but also for lyrics, satires, plays, epigrams, elegies, and epistles. But the term has been with us for a long time now and must be acknowledged by any conscientious compiler of glossaries.

Heroic Couplet: a rhyming pair of iambic pentameters. Today we tend to associate the heroic couplet with the carefully regulated and self-contained couplets of Dryden, Pope, Goldsmith, and Crabbe. This type of couplet is exemplified by Crabbe's lines ("The Library," 37–50) about the disinterested generosity that books extend to all who seek the consolations of literature:

> But what strange art, what magic can dispose
> The troubled mind to change its native woes?
> Or lead us willing from ourselves, to see
> Others more wretched, more undone than we?
> This, books can do—nor this alone: they give
> New views of life, and teach us how to live;
> They soothe the grieved, the stubborn they chastise;
> Fools they admonish, and confirm the wise.
> Their aid they yield to all: they never shun
> The man of sorrow, nor the wretch undone;
> Unlike the hard, the selfish, and the proud,
> They fly not sullen from the suppliant crowd;
> Nor tell to various people various things,
> But show to subjects, what they show to kings.

Differently handled heroic couplets—couplets featuring greater diversities of caesural pause or enjambment or both—may be found in such earlier poets as Chaucer, Donne, and Ben Jonson and such later ones as Robert Browning, Bridges, Winters, and Robert Lowell. (See, too, "Heroic.")

Heroic Quatrain: a stanza consisting of four iambic pentameters and rhyming *abab*. The form is also called an "Elegiac Quatrain," in reference to its use by Thomas Gray for his "Elegy Written in a Country Churchyard." (See, too, "Heroic.")

Hexameter: a line of six feet. Hexameters in antiquity were generally written in dactylic-spondaic rhythm. English hexameters are customarily iambic, though poems by Southey, Longfellow, and Clough approximate the ancient dactylic measure. (See also "Alexandrine.")

Hiatus: the full and distinct pronunciation of two adjacent vowels, despite the fact that their adjacency makes them candidates for elision. For instance, when Milton says in the last line of his sonnet to Mr. Lawrence,

> x / x / x / x / x /
> To interpose them oft, is not unwise

phonetic conditions would admit the elision, "T' interpose." However, for metrical purposes, Milton keeps the vowels and syllables distinct.

Hiatus is not a central concern in English speech and prosody. In English—at least, present-day English—hiatus is generally more natural than elision. If someone requests, "Would you be willing to interpose?" we do not respond, "My God, a hiatus!" Conversely, if someone asks, "Do you think it is time t' interpose?" we may well answer, "Come again?" In French, in contrast, elision is more the norm (*il n'est pas l'écrivain, qu'est-ce? c'est un stylo*, etc.), and hiatus more the exception.

Hypermetrical syllable: a syllable extending beyond the meter and not counted as part of it. "Hyper-" is a Greek prefix, meaning "over," "past," or "beyond." (See also "Feminine Ending.")

Iamb: a disyllabic foot with the sequence unaccented-accented.

Ictus: a term derived from Latin (where it means "stroke" or "beat") used by some metrists to describe one of the regularly recurring accents in a verse line.

Ionic: a four-syllable foot employed by such ancient poets as Anacreon and Horace. The foot has two forms—the greater ionic, whose sequence is long-long-short-short, and the lesser ionic, whose sequence is short-short-long-long. The foot has never been the basis for a meter in English. However, some metrists use "ionic" to describe the phenomenon of four syllables rising, across two iambic feet, through four levels of stress, as in

1   2 3   4   1 2 3   4

Made human by old symbols of man's worth

(J. V. Cunningham, "A Letter," 26)

The present study prefers to treat such configurations as involving two iambs—a light one followed by a heavy one. If one construes Cunningham's line as having two ionics and an iamb, one winds up with an iambic pentameter that is three feet long, with the majority of the feet being uniambic. (And if one scans the first foot as a spondee, one winds up with a three-foot iambic pentameter with no iambs at all.) Metrical description is confusing enough without investing it with such paradoxes.

Isosyllabic: characterized by an equality of syllables. ("Iso-" is a Greek combining form meaning "equal.") Metrists consider verse "isosyllabic" when it maintains syllabic correspondences between lines and/or stanzas. The term has been applied both to metrical systems in which syllable count is the chief basis for the meter (e.g., French) or to systems in which syllabic equality coexists with another principle or principles (e.g., Modern English, in which accent number and accent pattern are as important as syllable count).

Limerick: A form of light verse, consisting of five lines that rhyme *aabba*. Lines 1, 2, and 5 have three beats, and lines 3 and 4 have two. Usually, but not always, the rhythm is rollickingly anapestic.

In his *Complete Rhyming Dictionary* (New York: Halcyon House, 1936), Clement Wood differentiates three types of limerick, distinguishing them by the character of their final line. In the first type, the opening and closing lines are identical, as in this Mother Goose nursery rhyme.

Hickory, dickory, dock!
The mouse ran up the clock.
  The clock struck one—
  The mouse ran down,
Hickory, dickory, dock!

In the second type, the opening and closing lines differ but their rhyme word is the same. This type of limerick was popularized by Edward Lear (1812–1888), who frequently uses the name of a city or geographical location as the first- and fifth-line rhyme word. Here, for instance, he rhymes on the name of the pass where for several days in 480 B.C. Leonidas and his small Spartan contingent held off Xerxes' huge Persian army:

> There was an old man of Thermopylae,
> Who never did anything properly;
>> But they said, "If you choose
>> To boil eggs in your shoes,
> You shall never remain in Thermopylae."

In the third type of limerick, represented by the following Mother Goose rhyme, the opening and closing lines are entirely different:

> There was an old soldier of Bister
> Went walking one day with his sister,
>> When a cow at one poke
>> Tossed her into an oak
> Before the old gentleman missed her.

The etymology of "limerick" is uncertain. The *OED* cautiously notes: "Said to be from a custom at convivial parties, according to which each member sang an extemporized 'nonsense-verse', which was followed by a chorus containing the words 'Will you come up to Limerick?'"

Long Meter: a quatrain stanza, all four lines of which are iambic tetrameters, their rhyme scheme being *abab*.

Masculine Rhyme: one-syllable rhyme, the rhyme syllables themselves being metrically accented, as with **pearl/girl** or **pale/detail**. (See, too, "Feminine Rhyme," "Sdrucciolo/a," and "Triple Rhyme.")

Meter (British spelling, "Metre"): a term derived from the Greek *metron*, meaning "measure." Used in connection with poetry, the term denotes *organized rhythm* and refers to the principle or principles that determine the length and structural character of the verse line. (See, too, "Rhythm.")

Metrical Accent: in this book, a term that refers to the metrical nature of a syllable as determined by comparing it specifically and exclusively to the other syllable or syllables of the foot in which it appears. The term is used in relation to and is distinguished from "speech stress," which refers to the relative weight that a syllable has when spoken as part of a larger phrase or clause. Though metrically accented syllables generally have significant speech stress, and though syllables with significant speech stress are usually metrically accented, the two properties do not inevitably coincide. For instance, in Clive Wilmer's pentameter ("Oasis," 6),

> How beauty proper to a watered place

the second, fourth, eighth, and tenth syllables not only are metrically accented, but also have notable speech stress. However, the sixth syllable, "to," although metrically accented, on account of being slightly heavier than the weak syllable that precedes it, does not have prominent speech stress:

```
1    4    1  4    1  2  1  4    1    4
x    /    x  /    x  / x  /    x    /
How beau | ty prop | er to | a wa | tered place
```

Conversely, in Countee Cullen's line ("Yet Do I Marvel," 7),

If merely brute caprice dooms Sisyphus

the first, third, fifth, and ninth syllables are both metrically unaccented and weakly stressed in speech. However, the seventh syllable, "dooms," although metrically unaccented, on account of being slightly weaker than the strong syllable that follows it, has considerable speech stress:

```
1    4    1    4    1  4    3    4    1  4
x    /    x    /    x  /    x    /  x  /
If mere | ly brute | caprice | dooms Sis | yphus
```

The relation and difference between metrical accent and speech stress corresponds to the larger relation and difference between meter (the fixed pattern of the verse line) and rhythm (the variable realization, in actual speech, of the pattern).

Metrics: the study of meter. (See also "Prosody.")

Metrist: a skilled practitioner of meter. The term is also sometimes applied to students of meter.

Middle English: that language (or, alternatively, that stage in the ongoing history of English) characterized by the blending of Old English with Norman French. This process began in the eleventh century; the triumph of William of Normandy at the Battle of Hastings (1066) may be taken as a convenient point of reference. In its entry (written by Tom McArthur and Whitney F. Bolton) for "Middle English," *The Oxford Companion to the English Language* observes: "Three features of M[iddle] E[nglish] contrasted with O[ld] E[nglish]: a greatly reduced system of grammatical inflections; greatly increased lexical borrowing from other languages, in particular French and Latin; and a highly varied and volatile orthography." For most of its existence, Middle English enjoyed little prestige as a literary language, occupying third-class status behind French and Latin. However, the fourteenth century witnessed a wonderful flowering of Middle English verse, and two metrical systems contributed to this efflorescence. In the North and West of England, poets tended to favor a modified version of the old accentual-alliterative versification; in the South, poets tended to favor the emergent accentual-syllabic mode, influenced more by French and Italian models than by the Old English tradition. Scholars place the beginning of Modern English toward the end of the fifteenth century. Middle English can thus be said to occupy a roughly four-hundred-year period from the late eleventh to the late fifteenth century. (See, too, "Old English" and "Modern English.")

Modern English: a language that is descended, via Middle English and Old English, from West Germanic. Today it is the prevailing or official language in some sixty countries throughout the world and is sometimes said (e. g., Crystal, *The Cambridge Encyclopedia of the English Language,* 106–9) to have become a kind of world language.

Modern English emerged circa 1450–1500, mainly from the East Midland dialect of Middle English. No watershed event marks the transition from Middle to Modern English in the way that the Norman Conquest marks the transition from Old to Middle English; however, many have noted the importance of William Caxton's introduction of printing into England in 1476–77. Caxton published mostly English works, as opposed to French and Latin ones, and his editions of such authors as Chaucer, Lydgate, and Thomas Malory helped to extend and build on the revival, begun in the fourteenth century, of English as a literary language. Further, the trade in printed books—the production and national marketing of works in multiple copies with a single standard text free of scribal variations—contributed to a winnowing out of the welter of different and changing forms of English words that had existed previously.

Historians sometimes divide Modern English into Early Modern English (c. 1450–c. 1700) and Later Modern English (c. 1700–present). The earlier phase of this period saw "[t]he development of a single literary and administrative variety of the language that was later to be called 'standard English'" (entry, written by Tom McArthur and Whitney F. Bolton, for "Early Modern English" in *The Oxford Companion to the English Language*). However, at no time during the Modern English period has the language been static. No living language can or should be, since it is important that language always be able to accommodate new experiences, new ideas, and new objects. However, Modern English has acquired a relative stability that Middle English never possessed. This stability has enabled English-language writers to develop a broad range of styles, while remaining intelligible to other English speakers, even those on different parts of the globe or in different centuries. (See, too, "Middle English" and "Old English.")

Morphology: a word comprising two combining forms from Greek, "morpho-" ("shape, structure") and "-logy" ("pertaining to study or science"). In its most comprehensive sense, the word refers to the study of structures of organisms or objects. In connection with linguistics and language, morphology denotes the study of the shapes of words and the patterns of their formation.

Numbers: in prosodic discussion, a term meaning "meters" or "metrical feet." (The term derives from the Latin *numerus,* "a measure.") Though the term is now obsolete, we encounter it in earlier writers, including Pope, who says ("Epistle to Dr. Arbuthnot," 127–28) of his precocity in versifying,

> As yet a child, nor yet a fool to fame,
> I lisped in numbers, for the numbers came.

So, too, when Longfellow begins his "Psalm of Life" with

Tell me not, in mournful numbers,
 Life is but an empty dream!—

he means, "Tell me not, in mournful measures [or 'mournful verses'] . . . ."

Offbeat: in this book, a term indicating a metrically unaccented syllable. (See also "Beat.")

Old English: a language that originated in the dialects of West Germanic spoken by those peoples from northwestern Europe who migrated to Britain in the fifth century A.D., after the Romans left the island. Some linguists regard Old English as a language more or less separate from Middle English and Modern English. Others see Old English more as the first stage in a continuous development that contributed to the formation of Middle and eventually Modern English. Also called "Anglo-Saxon," Old English was "spoken and written in various forms for some eight centuries (5–12c)" (entry, written by Tom McArthur and Whitney F. Bolton, for "Old English" in *The Oxford Companion to the English Language*). Though the development of Old English was little affected by the Celtic languages of the ancient natives of Britain—a circumstance that has puzzled historians and philologists—Latin began to influence Old English as early as the seventh century, when the country was converted to Christianity. And in the eleventh century, the conquest of Britain by the Norman French produced conditions that would transform and transfuse English with Romanic elements. (See, too, "Middle English" and "Modern English.")

Onomatopoeia: a rhetorical device whereby words imitate, in their very sounds, phenomena they describe. Philip Larkin employs onomatopoeia when, at the close of "The Trees," he imagines that their leafy stirrings counsel human beings to "Begin afresh, afresh, afresh." Many words, such as "rasp" and "boom" and "swish," are themselves onomatopoetic. Onomatopoeia (lit., the "making," *poios,* of a "name," *onoma*) also refers to the principle of forming words whose sounds suggest the things they represent. As early as Plato's *Cratylus,* we find the hypothesis that letters of the alphabet suggest natural processes or qualities. Socrates speculates (426C ff.) that lambda, for instance, reminds us of smoothness or liquidity and that this explains why the letter appears in words like *leios* ("level") and *kollôdes* ("gluey").

Ottava Rima: a stanza consisting of eight lines (iambic pentameters in English, hendecasyllabics in Italian) rhyming *abababcc*. Invented by Italian poets in the Middle Ages, it was brilliantly employed by Ludovico Ariosto (1474–1535) in his *Orlando Furioso*. The stanza was popularized in English by John Harington's translation (1591) of this work. English poems in *ottava rima* include Byron's *Beppo, Vision of Judgment,* and *Don Juan*. Yeats uses *ottava rima* (frequently with slant rhymes) in poems like "Sailing to Byzantium," "The Municipal Gallery Revisited," and "The Circus Animals' Desertion." (See, too, "Sesta Rima.")

Pantoum: a verse form in Malay poetry. It consists of a succession of quatrains, the second and fourth lines of each quatrain being repeated as the first and third lines in the quatrain that follows. Though the number of the pantoum's quatrains is not fixed, the final quatrain must have, as its second and fourth lines, lines one and three of the first stanza (i. e., the only lines that, up to that point, will have been spared repetition). In the nineteenth century the pantoum was adapted from Malay into French, most notably by Victor Hugo. Thence the form came into English. An amusing contemporary pantoum is Wendy Cope's "Roger Bear's Philosophical Pantoum." The *OED* reports that "Pantoum" is a French misspelling of the Malay term, which may be more accurately transliterated "Pantun." Some prefer this latter rendering of the word.

Partial Rhyme: also called "off rhyme," "slant rhyme," "near rhyme," or "pararhyme." Rhyme that is, by conventional standards, incomplete. Generally, either the consonants match but not vowels (see "Consonance"), or the vowels match but not the consonants (see "Assonance"). Some authorities use the term with reference to matches between metrically accented syllables and metrically unaccented syllables (e. g., **ríng/búbbling** and prefér/fáther).

Pentameter: a verse line of five feet. In English, poets have generally written pentameters in iambic rhythm, and the iambic pentameter is widely felt to be, in the words of Richard Wilbur, "our fundamental meter" ("Interview with Richard Wilbur," in *Speaking of Frost: Richard Wilbur and William H. Pritchard, Interviewed by Donald G. Sheehy* [Amherst: The Friends of the Amherst College Library, 1997], 13).

Prosody: the study of versification in general, including meter, rhyme, and stanza. Some authorities include, under the heading of "Prosody," other devices of sound such as alliteration and onomatopoeia. (See, too, "Metrics.")

Pyrrhic: a foot in ancient prosody consisting of two short syllables and, in English prosody, a foot said to consist of two metrically unaccented syllables. This study suggests that pyrrhics are rare in English and are, moreover, largely unnecessary and confusing to the metrical analysis of our verse.

Quantity: a term applied to the metrical nature of syllables in ancient verse. In ancient meter, syllables were arranged according to their quantity (i.e., their length). A syllable was long if its vowel was long or if the syllable was "closed" by a consonant; otherwise the syllable was short. In theory a long syllable took twice as long to say as a short one, though such neat proportions did not obtain in practice. As Quintilian remarks (*Institutio Oratoria*, 9.4.84), "[T]here are degrees of length in long syllables and of shortness in short. Consequently, although syllables may be thought never to involve more than two time-beats or less than one, and although for that reason in metre all shorts and all longs are regarded as equal to other shorts and longs, they none the less possess some undefinable and secret quality, which makes some seem longer and others shorter than the normal."

Some scholars suggest that the ancient syllabic quantity can be best discussed in terms not of shortness and length, but rather of lightness and heaviness or unarrestedness and arrestedness. For instance, W. Sidney Allen argues, "[Q]uantity is not concerned so much with the duration of a syllable as a whole (though, in general, heavy syllables will have been of greater duration than light), but rather with the nature of the syllabic ending.... [T]he movement of a light syllable is 'unarrested', whereas that of a heavy syllable is 'arrested' (by the chest-muscles in the case of a long-vowel ending, by the oral constriction in the case of a consonant ending, or by a combination of the two in the case of a diphthongal ending . . .)" (W. Sidney Allen, *Vox Graeca: A Guide to the Pronunciation of Classical Greek,* 3d ed. [Cambridge: Cambridge University Press, 1987], 112).

Quatrain: a stanza of four lines.

Refrain: a line that repeats at regular intervals, usually at the ends of stanzas, throughout a poem. For example, several of the poems in Yeats's sequence, *Words for Music Perhaps,* have refrains. To take the case of "Mad as the Mist and Snow" (poem no. 18 in the sequence), the title line closes each of the three stanzas.

Rhyme Royal: a stanza of seven lines of iambic pentameter, with a rhyme scheme of *ababbcc.* Some believe the adjective "royal" has been applied to the stanza because it was used by James I of Scotland (1394–1437) in his *Kingis Quair* (*The King's Book,* written c. 1424, discovered and published 1783). Others suggest that the term instead arose from the stanza's use, in the later middle ages, for serious subjects or ceremonial occasions.

The latter view is supported by George Gascoigne's having discussed the stanza in 1575, long before James's poem was extant, and having characterized the stanza as "a royal kind of verse, serving best for grave discourse" (*George Gascoigne: The Green Knight, Selected Prose and Poetry,* 143). Though Gascoigne calls the stanza not "Rhyme Royal" but "Rhythm Royal," one meaning of "rhythm," in his day, was "rhyme"; hence his phrase is closer to our "Rhyme Royal" than we might at first think. The view that the term results from James's use of the stanza is supported by the fact that "rhyme royal" is a fairly recent coinage. The date of the *OED*'s first instance of the phrase is 1841. (Gascoigne's remark is the *OED*'s only citation for "Rhythm Royal.")

These two views are not necessarily mutually exclusive. After being one of the staple forms used by English poets from Chaucer to Shakespeare, the stanza fell out of fashion in the seventeenth and eighteenth centuries. In the nineteenth century, the stanza was revived, most notably by Wordsworth in his translations into Modern English of Chaucer and in his own "Resolution and Independence." (In this latter poem, however, Wordsworth made the seventh line a hexameter rather than a pentameter.) When the stanza was resuscitated, the old phrase may have seemed especially apt, on account of the recently discovered *Kingis Quair,* and may have been altered from "Rhythm Royal" to "Rhyme Royal" simply because "Rhythm" no longer had a synonymous association with "Rhyme."

Rhythm: movement (e.g., of musical notes, words, dancers) through time or space or both. The word comes from the Greek *rhythmos*. Most scholars believe this word to derive from *rheô* ("flow"), though some believe it to be related to *eruô* ("draw"). (See Pollitt, *The Ancient View of Greek Art,* 218–28.) For the ancients, *rhythmos* had a variety of meanings, including "temper" or "disposition." In discussions of literature, "rhythm" indicates a general order and movement of speech, as opposed to the more specific patterns of "meter." On this ground, Aristotle associates (*Rhetoric* 1408b30) rhythm with the loose but still perceptible arrangements of artistic prose and meter with the more particular principles of poetry: "[P]rose (*logon*) must be rhythmical (*rhythmon*), but not metrical (*metron*), otherwise it will be a poem (*poiêma*)."

Rising Rhythm: a term sometimes used to describe rhythms, such as iambic or anapestic, that move from lighter to heavier syllables. Some students of meter, however, object to this term, especially when applied to iambic verse. Because iambic lines often are compounded of non-iambic elements of English word shape and phraseology, poets can initiate all sorts of descending countercurrents within the prevailing rising rhythm. An exemplary instance of this occurs in stanza 3 of Frost's "Stopping by Woods on a Snowy Evening":

> He gives his harness bells a shake
> To ask if there is some mistake.
> The only other sound's the sweep
> Of easy wind and downy flake.

In the first two lines, Frost uses mainly monosyllabic words, and of the two disyllabic words, one is rear-stressed. As a result, divisions between feet and those between words largely coincide, and this produces a strong sense of rising rhythm:

> He gives | his har | ness bells | a shake
> To ask | if there | is some | mistake.

In contrast, the remaining two lines feature four fore-stressed disyllabic words. Consequently, words more often cross foot divisions than end at them. Even as the iambic fluctuation continues, the lines have a falling, trochaic character, which in turn suggests the sweeping movement of wind and snow:

> The on | ly oth | er sound's | the sweep
> Of eas | y wind | and down | y flake.

(See, too, "Falling Rhythm.")

Romance-Six Stanza (or "Romance Stanza"): a six-line stanza often used in medieval romances. Its English form consists of a sequence of two iambic tetrameters, an iambic trimeter, two more tetrameters, and another trimeter. The trimeters rhyme. As for the tetrameters, all may rhyme together, thus producing an overall scheme of *aabaab;* or each of the couplets may have its own rhyme, producing a scheme of *aabccb.* Chaucer ridicules the form in "Sir Thopas," but it retains its popularity in later English verse, especially as a vehicle for satirical poems, such as Thomas Hood's "Ode on a Distant Prospect of Clapham Academy":

There I was birch'd! there I was bred!
There like a little Adam fed
    From learning's woeful tree!
The weary tasks I used to con!—
The hopeless leaves I wept upon!—
    Most fruitless leaves to me!—

The summon'd class!—the awful bow!—
I wonder who is master now
    And wholesome anguish sheds!
How many ushers now employs,
How many maids to see the boys
    Have nothing in their heads!

(stanzas 3 and 4)

Auden uses Romance-sixes for one of his finest early poems, "A Summer Night." (See, too, "Tail Rhymes.")

Rondeau: like "rondel," a form which originates in Provençal verse in the thirteenth or fourteenth century and which has a confusing history. Originally, rondeaux included various short poetic forms, the rondel among them; indeed, Grammont (*Petit Traité de Versification Française*, 95) uses the term "Old Rondeaux" for rondels. Toward the end of the fifteenth century, the form we today call the "Rondeau" or "New Rondeau" became established. This consists of fifteen lines divided into three groups: (1) lines 1 through 5; (2) lines 6 through 8; (3) lines 10 through 14. Lines 9 and 15, which are shorter than the other lines, repeat the opening words or phrase of the poem. These two abbreviated lines lie outside of not only the poem's prevailing meter, but also its rhyme scheme, which runs *aabba aabx aabbax*. Clément Marot (1496?–1544) is an early master of this form; one of his most memorable rondeaux is "De la Jeune Dame Qui A Vieil Mari" ("Of the Young Lady Who Has An Old Husband"). Probably the best-known American rondeau is Paul Laurence Dunbar's "We Wear the Mask." "The Hidden Law" by W. H. Auden is another exemplary rondeau. (See, too, "Rondel.")

Rondel: a French form comprising thirteen lines with two rhymes. It falls into three stanzas—the first two being quatrains, the final stanza having five lines. The rhyme scheme runs *abba abab abbaa*. Line 8 repeats line 2; lines 7 and 13 repeat line 1. Charles d'Orléans's "Le temps a laissé son manteau" and Richard Wilbur's translation of it ("The year has cast its cloak away") well illustrate the form. That Charles entitled his rondel "Rondeau" suggests the identity crises that the two forms have historically suffered. (See also "Rondeau.")

Rubáiyát Quatrain (or "Rubáiyát Stanza"): a popular form of medieval Persian verse, practiced by, among others, the astronomer-poet Omar Khayyám (1048–1131). Consisting of four lines, rhyming *aaba* (or, occasionally, *aaaa*), the form was brought into English by Edward Fitzgerald in his translation of *The Rubáiyát of Omar Khayyám*. Excellent twentieth-century poems in English in this form include Robert Frost's "Desert Places" and Dick Davis's "A Letter to Omar."

Run-on: see "Enjambment."

Run-over: see "Enjambment."

Sapphic Stanza: in ancient poetry, a stanza of four lines, the first three of which have eleven syllables (patterned long-short-long-anceps-long-short-short-long-short-long-anceps) and the last of which has five syllables (patterned long-short-short-long-anceps). The stanza is named after its most famous practitioner, Sappho of Lesbos.

Scansion: metrical analysis; the division of verse lines into feet and the recording of the metrical nature of each syllable within each foot.

Sdrucciolo/a: an Italian word meaning "sliding" or "slippery." In prosodic discussion, the word refers to rhymes of three syllables, with the metrical accent on the antepenultimate, as in *sélfishly/élfishly*. Such rhyme is also called "triple rhyme."

Though sdrucciola rhymes in English verse tend toward the comic or the ostentatious, their effect is not so exaggerated in Italian verse. There, sdrucciolo is one of the three general categories of rhyme. The other two are *piana* ("level"), which is disyllabic with stress on the penultimate syllable, like our feminine rhyme, and *tronca* ("cut off, truncated"), which is monosyllabic, like our masculine rhyme. Since piana rhyme is in Italian the conventional type, sdrucciola rhyme produces a line that is only one syllable over the limit, and Italian poets consider this extra syllable as hypermetrical. Hence what is a triple rhyme for us is more like a feminine rhyme for them. (See, too, "Triple Rhyme.")

Sesta Rima: a six-line stanza, rhyming *ababcc*. Sesta rima is thus like ottava rima without the first two lines. First developed by Italian poets, this stanza was popular with English poets during the Renaissance. Shakespeare, for instance, uses it for *Venus and Adonis,* as does William Mure for *Dido and Aeneas;* and Robert Southwell employs it in such lyric poems as "Time Goes by Turns." Later poems in this form include Anne Bradstreet's "Prologue" ("To sing of wars, of captains, and of kings"), Edward Taylor's *Meditations,* and Richard Wilbur's "A Wood." Sesta rima in English is generally written in iambic pentameter, though some poets (e.g., Wordsworth in "I Wandered Lonely as a Cloud") have written tetrametric poems using six-line stanzas with an *ababcc* rhyme scheme. (See also "Ottava Rima.")

Sestina: a fixed form comprised of six stanzas—each having six lines—and a concluding three-line envoy. In the place of rhyme, the same six line-ending words or syllables appear in each stanza, though they appear in shifting order: Stanza 1: *abcdef;* Stanza 2: *faebdc;* Stanza 3: *cfdabe;* Stanza 4: *ecbfad;* Stanza 5: *deacfb;* Stanza 6: *bdfeca.* In the envoy, the customary but not invariable practice is to have the *ace* end-words appear at the ends of the lines and the *bdf* end-words appear in the middle of the lines. With reference to the six six-line stanzas, we can schematized the shifting positions of the end-words thus:

with each successive stanza,

> line 6's end-word becomes line 1's
> line 5's becomes line 3's
> line 4's becomes line 5's
> line 3's becomes line 6's
> line 2's becomes line 4's
> line 1's becomes line 2's

First developed by the Provençal troubadours of the Middle Ages, this form has proved attractive to recent English-language poets. The fascination of what's difficult, to use Yeats's phrase, may account for the interest. Often, however, the form seems more odd and tedious than difficult. Fine modern or contemporary sestinas include Auden's "Paysage Moralisé" and Anthony Hecht's "Book of Yolek." Readers with a taste for elaboration will enjoy the double sestina, "Ye goatherd gods, that love the grassy mountains," that Sidney writes for *The Old Arcadia*. (See, too, "Fixed Forms.")

Shaped Poems: poems that visually on the page represent their subject. Shaped poems have a long history. They were practiced in antiquity, and a group of them appear in book 15 (21–27) of *The Greek Anthology,* that compendium of epigrams in Greek from the seventh century B.C. to the tenth century A.D. Called technopaignia ("art-games"), the most striking of these shaped poems is the one, entitled "Egg" *(Ôion),* by Simias of Rhodes (4th c. B.C.) in the form of an egg. Beginning with a dactylic monometer centered on the page, the poem widens on both sides as it progresses, adding a foot in each line until reaching ten feet in line 10. Line 11 has ten feet, too, and then the count descends, losing one foot per line until, at line twenty, shrinking back at a single foot. And Simias gives the composition another turn of the screw: the poem is designed to be read end-from-end-and-inward. That is, we read line 1, then line 20, line 2, then line 19, line 3, then line 18, and so on. Depending on one's point of view, the poem represents either the heights to which ingenuity can rise or the depths to which it can sink.

The best-known shaped poem in English is George Herbert's "Easter-Wings," a good discussion of which may be found in Fussell, *Poetic Meter and Poetic Form,* 169–70. Herbert's poem consists of two ten-line stanzas, each line being centered on the page. The first line of each stanza is an iambic pentameter; each line thereafter gets shorter by a foot until, at line 5, the line consists of only one foot. Line 6 is a severely indented monometer as well. Thereafter each line grows a foot longer than its predecessor until, with line 10, the line has climbed back up to pentameter. The rhyme scheme runs *ababacdcdc.* If you turn the text ninety degrees, the stanzas resemble the wings of a pair of angels. Form also answers theme in that, as each stanza narrows, the poet describes a process of increasing spiritual attenuation. This progression reverses as the stanzas broaden and the poet speaks of his hope of expanding his spirit and of ascending, as if by wings, to God.

Lord, who createdst man in wealth and store,
Though foolishly he lost the same,
Decaying more and more,
Till he became
Most poor:
With thee
O let me rise
As larks harmoniously,
And sing this day thy victories:
Then shall the fall further the flight in me.

My tender age in sorrow did begin:
And still with sicknesses and shame
Thou didst so punish sin
That I became
Most thin.
With thee
Let me combine
And feel this day thy victory:
For, if I imp my wing on thine,*
Affliction shall advance the flight in me.

*if I engraft on my wing feathers from yours

In Simias's egg poem and Herbert's "Easter-Wings" the metrical-stanzaic form itself suggests the object or idea described, but in other shaped poems, the visual effect submerges the formal structure. "The Mouse's Tale" in chapter 3 of Lewis Carroll's *Alice's Adventures in Wonderland* is a shaped poem of this latter kind. Carroll's poem consists of two six-line stanzas rhyming *aabccb*, with the *a* and *c* lines having two beats each and the *b* lines having four. In Carroll's text, however, the poem is run together within the curving and narrowing outline of a mouse's tail; to see the stanzaic structure, one must copy out the poem, giving the metric units normal lineation. The stanza form Carroll employs is, it is worth noting, a variant of the "Romance-six" stanza. And the kind of rhyme that links the third and sixth lines is "tail rhyme." Hence, in entitling his poem "The Mouse's Tale," Carroll is not only punning on tale/tail, but also is alluding to his tail rhymes. (See also "Romance-Six Stanza" and "Tail Rhymes.")

Short Meter: a quatrain whose first, second, and fourth lines are iambic trimeters, and whose third line is an iambic tetrameter. Its rhyme scheme is *abab* or *abcb*.

Skeltonics: short rhyming lines in irregular rhythm. The term honors John Skelton (c. 1460–1529), author of such poems as "The Commendations of Mistress Jane Scrope" and "To Mistress Margery Wentworth." Skelton's favorite line has three beats; in his longer poems the lines tumble one after another, with no full grammatical stop, for extended stretches. Some of his rhymes look wrenched to us

(e.g., Pállas/**pass** and **new**/vírtue), though it is possible that for Skelton's contemporaries these were exact, due to the persistence of or allowance for French
or Chaucerian pronunciation (Pallás, virtúe).

Sonnet: a poem of fourteen lines, which generally takes one of two forms. The first is
the Italian form (also called "Petrarchan"), which is divided into an octave and
sestet and which has a rhyme scheme of *abbaabba cdecde,* with variation allowed
in the rhyme sequence of the sestet. The second form is the English (also called
"Elizabethan" or "Shakespearean"), which consists of three quatrains and a couplet and has a rhyme scheme of *abab cdcd efef gg.* Additional forms include the
Spenserian sonnet, which rhymes *ababbcbccdcdee.* Further, poets have on occasion introduced heterodox rhyme schemes and divisions. English sonnets are
customarily written in iambic pentameters, though other meters have been used.
Janet Lewis, for instance, has written a sonnet, "Time and Music," in tetrameters.

The sonnet was first practiced in Italy and Sicily in the thirteenth century.
Giacomo di Lentini and Guittone d'Arezzo are considered to be pioneers of the
form. Both are mentioned in canto 24 of Dante's *Purgatory.* On Easter Sunday,
April 6, 1327, in the Church of St. Clare in Avignon, the twenty-two-year-old
Francesco Petrarca saw and immediately fell in love with a flaxen-haired beauty,
whom he was to call Laura, though her real identity has never been conclusively
established. Over the next several decades, Petrarch wrote 317 sonnets inspired by
her. These remarkable poems created an international vogue for sonneteering
that has continued ever since.

Another meaning of "sonnet" is "[a] short poem or piece of verse; in early use
esp. one of a lyrical and amatory character" *(OED).* This meaning persists at least
to the middle of the eighteenth century, as is evident in Samuel Richardson's
Pamela (1740), whose heroine calls a "sonnet" the ten valedictory triplets she writes
for her fellow servants when she believes that she is leaving Mr B's estate forever:

> On God all future good depends:
> Serve him. And so my sonnet ends.
> O may he make you rich amends . . .
>
> (Letter 31, Samuel Richardson, Pamela, ed. by Peter Sabor
with an intro. by Margaret A. Doody [London: Penguin, 1980], 123)

Speech Stress: in this book, a term referring to the weight a syllable has when actually
spoken, usually as part of a comparatively extended phrase or clause. As such,
speech stress is distinguished from "metrical accent," which concerns the prosodic
nature of a syllable, as determined by comparing it solely to the other syllable or
syllables in the foot in which it appears. In English verse, syllables with significant speech stress are generally metrically accented as well, but this is not always
the case. For instance, in this line,

> A snake lies hid beneath the fragrant leaves
>
> (Aphra Behn, "To the Fair Clarinda," 17)

the second, fourth, sixth, eighth, and tenth syllables all carry, in addition to considerable speech stress, a metrical accent. However, the third syllable—the verb

"lies"—is, despite having notable speech stress, metrically unaccented, on account of sharing a foot with and being followed by an even heavier syllable:

```
1   4   3   4   1   4     1   4   1   4
x   /   x   /   x   /     x   /   x   /
A snake | lies hid | beneath | the fra | grant leaves
```

(See, too, "Metrical Accent.")

Spenserian Stanza: a nine-line stanza Edmund Spenser invented for his *Fairie Queene,* with a rhyme scheme of *ababbcbcc.* Lines 1 through 8 are iambic pentameters; line 9 is an iambic hexameter.

Spondee: in ancient prosody, a foot consisting of two long syllables; in English prosody, a foot said to consist of two metrically accented syllables. This study suggests that spondees are rare in English and are, moreover, largely unnecessary and confusing to the metrical analysis of our verse.

Sprung Rhythm: a term that Gerard Manley Hopkins coined to describe accentual verse in general and his own accentual verse in particular. He contrasted sprung rhythm with "Running Rhythm," this latter phrase indicating standard English meter. As Hopkins puts it, "Common English rhythm, called Running Rhythm above, is measured by feet of either two or three syllables . . . never more nor less. . . . Sprung Rhythm . . . is measured by feet of from one to four syllables, regularly, and for particular effects any number of weak or slack syllables may be used" (*The Poems of Gerard Manley Hopkins,* 45, 47).

Stanza: a term defined usually as a group of four or more lines whose metrical and rhyme sequence, established at the beginning of a poem, repeats as long as the poem lasts. Some observers speak of two-line groups and three-line groups as stanzas; others prefer to call these "couplets" and "triplets," respectively.

Stichos: in ancient prosody, a single verse measure that repeats through a long passage or an entire poem. For the ancients, "stichic" verse is one of the two major divisions of poetry, the other being poetry composed in lines of different lengths and arranged according to strophic (i.e., "stanzaic") responsion.

There are four common stichic measures in antiquity: (1) the dactylic hexameter, used most notably in epic; (2) the iambic trimeter, used most notably for dialogue in drama; (3) the elegiac couplet, which though two lines long, is considered a single unit and is used most notably in elegies and epigrams; and (4) the trochaic tetrameter, variously used, including for dialogue in early Greek drama.

Stress: the relative prominence of a syllable when uttered. For some linguists the word is synonymous with "accent"; others distinguish between "stress" and "accent," employing the former to indicate dynamic force, weight, or loudness and employing the latter to denote pitch acuity. This book draws a distinction, for purposes of prosodic description, between "metrical accent" and "speech stress." (See "Accent," "Metrical Accent," and "Speech Stress.")

Strophe: in modern English, a synonym for "stanza." In ancient verse, the word refers either to a group of lines whose structure is repeated throughout a poem or to the first of the three units of the tripartite choral ode. (The second unit is the "antistrophe," which is structurally identical to the "strophe"; the third unit is the "epode," which differs structurally from the strophes and antistrophes, but which corresponds to the other epodes in the ode.)

Substitution: the introduction, into a line of verse, of a foot other than the prevailing one. For instance, when poets place a trochee at the beginning of an iambic pentameter, as in

/ x
Faustus | is gone: regard his hellish fall

(Marlowe, *Doctor Faustus,* "Epilogue," 4)

it is often said that they have "substituted" a trochee for an iamb.

Syllabic Verse: verse in which the number of syllables per line is fixed, but the number of accents varies.

Syllable: In their *Oxford Companion to the English Language* entry for "Syllable" Gerald Knowles and Tom McArthur offer the definition "[t]he smallest unit of speech that normally occurs in isolation"; the *OED* describes a syllable as "[a] vocal sound or set of sounds uttered with a single effort of articulation." A syllable may constitute either a word or a portion of a word. For instance, by itself "but" is a monosyllabic conjunction, whereas in "buttercup" it is the first element of a trisyllabic word. A syllable usually involves a vowel, which either stands alone or is preceded and/or followed by consonants.

The nasal consonants *m* and *n* may serve as vowels and comprise a syllable or the central resonance of a syllable, as in "rhythm" and "isn't." Some linguists feel that the liquid consonants *l* and *r* also function vocalically and syllabically in such words as "cable" and "acre," though in pronunciation guides in dictionaries a reduced vowel often precedes these letters ("ká • bəl" and "á • kər").

Synaeresis: a form of elision involving the slurring together of two adjacent vowels within a word, as in "interior," treated as "in • ter • yor" rather than "in • ter • i • or." (See, too, "Elision.")

Synaloepha: a form of elision involving the slurring together of two adjacent vowels in different words, as in *th'expense* for *the expense* or *th'arch* for *the arch*. Some ancient grammarians (Liddell and Scott's *Greek-English Lexicon* cites the example of Draco Stratonicensis) use the term to refer inclusively to all types of contraction. (See, too, "Elision.")

Syncope (or "syncopation"): a form of elision involving the suppression or omission of a sound from the middle of a word, as in *ta'en* for *taken, o'er* for *over, mem'ry* for *memory,* or *batt'ning* for *battening*. (See, too, "Elision.")

Syntax: the branch of grammar devoted to the study of the ways in which words are arranged to form phrases, clauses, and sentences.

Tail Rhymes: rhymes that answer each other across intervening couplets, triplets, or quatrains and thus form a counterpoint to those structural units. The rhyming of the third and sixth lines of Romance-six stanzas produces tail rhyme, as does the rhyming of the lines that appear after the triplets in Herrick's "The White Island or Place of the Blest":

> There in calm and cooling sleep
> We our eyes shall never steep,
> But eternal watch shall keep,
>   Attending
>
> Pleasures such as shall pursue
> Me immortaliz'd, and you,
> And fresh joys, as never to
>   Have ending.
>
> (stanzas 5 and 6)

Tail rhyme was popular in medieval Latin and French verse. The term itself is a translation of the French *rime couée*. (See, too, "Romance-Six Stanza.")

Tercet: this word and "triplet" (defined below) both refer to a group of three lines which comprise a unit unto themselves. According to common (though by no means universal) usage, all the lines of a triplet rhyme together, whereas the lines of a tercet do not necessarily all rhyme with one another. It is in this latter sense that we call the interlocking *aba bcb* . . . units of Dante's *Divine Comedy* tercets rather than triplets. Indeed, Dante's *terza rima* form suggests the Italian word for tercet, *terzina*. (See also "Triplet.")

Tetrameter: a verse line of four feet. Though English-language poets have written tetrameters chiefly in iambic rhythm, trochaic tetrameters are common as well, whether catalectic or acatalectic, whether used exclusively throughout a poem or mixed together with iambic tetrameters. Further, the anapestic tetrameter has at times proved a popular medium, especially for light verse; and such poets as Byron and Southey have composed interesting work in dactylic tetrameters. Because the four-beat line is relatively emphatic and easy to hear, the tetrameter accommodates different types of rhythm more readily than the pentameter does, even though the pentameter encourages a greater range of tone and modulation within iambic rhythm. (See also "Catalexis.")

Triolet: a fixed-form poem consisting of eight lines rhymed *abaaabab*. The fourth and seventh lines repeat the first line; the eighth line repeats the second. Memorable triolets include Thomas Hardy's "Puzzled Game Birds."

Triple Rhyme: rhymes of three syllables, with the metrical accent on the first syllable, as in **mérited/inhérited**. (See also "Sdrucciolo/a.")

Triplet: three consecutive rhyming lines, whether used as a variant in heroic-couplet verse or as a stanzaic unit that organizes a poem and repeats throughout it. Frost's "Provide, Provide" exemplifies the latter use of the triplet. Frost's poem consists of seven three-line groups of iambic tetrameters, each group rhyming within itself and each set off by white space from its neighbors. (See, too, "Tercet.")

Trochee: a disyllabic foot whose sequence is accented-unaccented.

Tumbling Verse: a term used in 1584 by King James VI of Scotland (later James I of England) in his "Schort Treatise Conteining Some Reulis and Cautelis to Be Obseruit and Eschewit in Scottis Poesie." The term has been variously interpreted; James seems to have meant by it verse that is loose and chiefly anapestic as opposed to regular and iambic: "Ye man obserue that thir *Tumbling* verse flowis not on that fassoun as vtheris dois. For all vtheris keipis the reule quhilk I gaue before, to wit, the first fute short, the secound lang, and sa furth [James uses "foot" here to mean "syllable"]. Quhair as thir hes twa short and ane lang throuch all the lyne, quhen they keip ordour: albeit the maist pairt of thame be out of ordour, and keipis na kynde nor reule of *Flowing*, and for that cause are callit *Tumbling* verse" (Smith, *Elizabethan Critical Essays,* 1:218–19).

Verse: a term with several denotations. It may refer to metrical composition in general, and is sometimes used as a synonym for "poetry," though whether or not poetry should be identified with or limited to verse is a question that has been debated from the ancient Greeks to our day. (The third chapter of my *Missing Measures: Modern Poetry and the Revolt against Meter* surveys the history of this debate.) "Verse" also may signify a line of verse, and in the British Commonwealth especially, "a verse" may mean "a stanza." Our word comes from the Latin *vertere,* "to turn," and *versus,* "a furrow, a turning of the plow"—and, by extension, literary composition in which rows or lines of words turn from one to another.

Villanelle: a poem consisting of five tercets rhymed *aba* and a concluding quatrain rhymed *abaa.* The sixth, twelfth, and eighteenth lines repeat the first line; the ninth, fifteenth, and nineteenth lines repeat the third. Generally, English-language villanelles have been written in iambic pentameter. Memorable poems in this form include Dylan Thomas's "Do Not Go Gentle into That Good Night," Theodore Roethke's "The Waking," Catherine Davis's "After a Time [All Losses Are the Same]," Henri Coulette's "Postscript," Marilyn Hacker's "Ruptured Friendships, or The High Cost of Keys," and Wendy Cope's "Lonely Hearts."

Wrenched Accent: the nonconventional accentuation of a word, out of metrical exigency. This device has been almost universally condemned by English poets and prosodists from Gascoigne forward. In English poetry from Chaucer to Wyatt, some apparent instances of wrenched accent are resolved when we remember that during this period a number of words, especially those derived from French, may have admitted of Romanic as well as Teutonic pronunciation.

Wrenched Rhyme: a rhyme that depends on an unconventional accentuation of a word, as in **sing**/**letting** or **pick**/rhapsod**ic**. In English verse, wrenched rhymes perhaps most frequently appear in song lyrics, as in this, the tenth stanza of the anonymous ballad, "Mary Hamilton":

> When she cam down the Cannongate
> 　The Cannongate sae free,
> Many a lady looked o'er her window
> 　Weeping for this lad́y

The term has also been applied to such comically strained rhymes as **clapperless**/**Indianapolis** (Ogden Nash, "Little Feet," 8–9).

Bibliography of Critical Works Cited and of Several Additional Studies of Verse Form

Abrams, M. H. *A Glossary of Literary Terms.* 6th ed. San Diego: Harcourt Brace, 1993.

Alexander, Michael, ed. *The Earliest English Poems.* 2d ed. Harmondsworth: Penguin, 1977.

Allen, W. Sidney. *Accent and Rhythm: Prosodic Features of Latin and Greek: A Study in Theory and Reconstruction.* Cambridge: Cambridge University Press, 1973.

———. *Vox Graeca: A Guide to the Pronunciation of Classical Greek.* 3d ed. Cambridge: Cambridge University Press, 1987.

Apollodorus. *Apollodorus.* Edited and translated by James G. Frazer. 2 vols. Loeb Classical Library. Cambridge, Mass.: Harvard University Press, 1921.

Aristotle. *The "Art" of Rhetoric.* Edited and translated by John Henry Freese. Loeb Classical Library. Cambridge, Mass.: Harvard University Press, 1926.

———. *The Poetics.* Edited and translated by W. Hamilton Fyfe. Loeb Classical Library. Cambridge, Mass.: Harvard University Press, 1932.

Ascham, Roger. "'Of Imitation': *The Scholemaster* (Book II)." In *Elizabethan Critical Essays,* edited by G. Gregory Smith, 1:1–45. Oxford: Oxford University Press, 1904.

Attridge, Derek. *Poetic Rhythm: An Introduction.* Cambridge: Cambridge University Press, 1995.

———. *The Rhythms of English Poetry.* London: Longman, 1982.

———. *Well-Weighed Syllables: Elizabethan Verse in Classical Metres.* Cambridge: Cambridge University Press, 1974.

Auden, W. H. *The Table Talk of W. H. Auden.* By Alan Ansen. Edited by Nicholas Jenkins, with an introduction by Richard Howard. Princeton: Ontario Review Press, 1990.

Aviram, Amittai F. *Telling Rhythm: Body and Meaning in Poetry.* Ann Arbor: University of Michigan Press, 1994.

Baker, David, ed. *Meter in English: A Critical Engagement.* Fayetteville: University of Arkansas Press, 1996.

Barnet, Sylvan, ed. *The Complete Signet Classic Shakespeare.* New York: Harcourt Brace, 1972.

Bate, W. Jackson, ed. *Criticism: The Major Texts.* San Diego: Harcourt Brace, 1970.

Bate, W. Jackson and David Perkins, eds. *British and American Poets: Chaucer to the Present.* San Diego: Harcourt Brace, 1986.

Baum, Paull F. *Chaucer's Verse.* Durham, N.C.: Duke University Press, 1961.

———. "Sprung Rhythm." *PMLA* 74 (September 1969): 418–25.

Beerbohm, Max. *Savonarola Brown.* In *Max in Verse.* Collected and annotated by J. G. Riewald, with a foreword by S. N. Behrman. Brattleboro, Vt.: Stephen Greene Press, 1963.

Bennett, J. A. W., ed. *Langland: Piers Plowman, The Prologue and Passus I–VII of the B Text as Found in Bodleian MS. Laud Misc. 581.* Oxford: Oxford University Press, 1972.

Benson, Larry D., general ed. *The Riverside Chaucer.* 3d ed., based on *The Works of Geoffrey Chaucer,* edited by F. N. Robinson. Boston: Houghton Mifflin, 1987.

Bessinger, Jess B. Jr., and Stanley J. Kahrl, eds. *Essential Articles for the Study of Old English Poetry.* Hamden, Conn.: Archon, 1968.

Bishop, Morris, ed. *A Treasury of British Humor.* New York: Coward-McCann, 1942.

Bjorklund, Beth. "Iambic and Trochaic Verse—Major and Minor Keys?" In *Meter and Rhythm,* edited by Paul Kiparsky and Gilbert Youmans, 155–81. San Diego: Academic Press [Harcourt Brace], 1989.

———. *A Study in Comparative Prosody: English and German Jambic Pentameter.* Stuttgarter Arbeiten zur Germanistik 35. Stuttgart: Heinz, 1978.

Blair, Hugh. *Lectures on Rhetoric and Belles Lettres.* Edited by Harold F. Harding. Foreword by David Potter. 2 vols. Carbondale: Southern Illinois University Press, 1965.

Bliss, A. J. *The Metre of* Beowulf. Oxford: Basil Blackwell, 1958.

Borroff, Marie. *Sir Gawain and the Green Knight: A Stylistic and Metrical Study.* New Haven: Yale University Press, 1962.

Bridges, Robert. *Milton's Prosody.* Rev. final ed. Oxford: Oxford University Press, 1921.

Brogan, T. V. F. *English Versification, 1570–1980.* Baltimore: Johns Hopkins University Press, 1981.

———. "Spondee." Entry in *The New Princeton Encyclopedia of Poetry and Poetics,* edited by Alex Preminger and T. V. F. Brogan. Princeton: Princeton University Press, 1993.

———. *Verseform: A Comparative Bibliography.* Baltimore: Johns Hopkins University Press, 1989.

Bysshe, Edward. *The Art of English Poetry.* 3d ed. 1708. Edited by A. Dwight Culler. Los Angeles: Augustan Reprint Society, 1953.

Cable, Thomas. *The English Alliterative Tradition.* Philadelphia: University of Pennsylvania Press, 1991.

———. *The Meter and Melody of* Beowulf. Urbana: University of Illinois Press, 1974.

Camden, William. *Remains Concerning Britain.* Edited by R. D. Dunn. Toronto: University of Toronto Press, 1985.

Campbell, Jeremy. *Grammatical Man: Information, Entropy, Language, and Life.* New York: Simon & Schuster, 1982.

Campion, Thomas. "Observations in the Art of English Poesie." In *The Works of Thomas Campion,* edited by Walter R. Davis, 287–317. Garden City, N.Y.: Doubleday, 1967.

Cervantes, Miguel de. *Don Quixote.* Translated by Samuel Putnam. New York: Modern Library, 1949.

Chapman, Raymond. "Iamb." Entry in *The Oxford Companion to the English Language,* edited by Tom McArthur. Oxford: Oxford University Press, 1992.

Chickering, Howell D. Jr., ed. and trans. *Beowulf.* New York: Anchor-Doubleday, 1977.

Chomsky, Noam, and Morris Halle. *The Sound Pattern of English.* New York: Harper & Row, 1968.

Cicero. *De Oratore.* Edited and translated by E. W. Sutton and H. Rackham. 2 vols. Loeb Classical Library. Cambridge, Mass.: Harvard University Press, 1948.

———. *Orator.* Edited and translated by H. M. Hubbell. Loeb Classical Library. Cambridge, Mass.: Harvard University Press, 1962.

Clark, Arthur Melville, and Harold Whitehall. "Rhyme." Entry in *The Princeton Encyclopedia of Poetry and Poetics,* edited by Alex Preminger. Enlarged 1st ed. Princeton: Princeton University Press, 1974.

Coleridge, Samuel Taylor. *Selected Poetry and Prose.* Edited by Elisabeth Schneider. 2d ed. enlarged. San Francisco: Rinehart, 1971.

———. *Notebooks.* Edited by Kathleen Coburn. 4 vols. New York: Pantheon Books, 1957–1990.

The Compact Edition of the Oxford English Dictionary. 2 vols. Oxford: Oxford University Press, 1971.

Congreve, William. "A Discourse on the Pindarique Ode." In *The Complete Works of William Congreve,* edited by Montague Summers, vol. 4, *Congreve's Poems, The Preface to Dryden, The Tatler,* 82–86. New York: Russell & Russell, 1964.

Corn, Alfred. *The Poem's Heartbeat: A Manual of Prosody.* Brownsville, Oreg.: Story Line Press, 1997.

Crystal, David. *The Cambridge Encyclopedia of the English Language.* Cambridge: Cambridge University Press, 1995.

Cunningham, J. V. *The Collected Essays of J. V. Cunningham.* Chicago: Swallow, 1976.

Cushman, Stephen. *William Carlos Williams and the Meanings of Measure.* New Haven: Yale University Press, 1985.

Daryush, Elizabeth. "Appendix." In *Selected Poems by Elizabeth Daryush.* Oxford: Carcanet, 1972.

Davie, Donald. *Articulate Energy: An Inquiry into the Syntax of English Poetry.* 2d ed. London: Routledge & Kegan Paul, 1976.

Davis, Norman. "Versification." In *The Riverside Chaucer,* xlii–xlv.

Demetrius. *On Style.* Edited and translated by W. Rhys Roberts. Loeb Classical Library. Cambridge, Mass.: Harvard University Press, 1932.

Dinesen, Isak. *Out of Africa.* New York: Vintage, 1972.

Drury, John. *The Poetry Dictionary.* Cincinnati: Story Press, 1995.

Dryden, John. *Of Dramatic Poesy and Other Critical Essays.* Edited by George Watson. 2 vols. London: Dent, 1962.

———. *Essays of John Dryden.* Edited by W. P. Ker. 2 vols. London: Russell & Russell, 1961.

Dujardin, Édouard. *Les Premiers Poètes du Vers Libre.* Paris: Mercure de France, 1922.

Duncan, Thomas G. *Medieval English Lyrics, 1200–1400.* Harmondsworth: Penguin, 1995.

Eliot, T. S. "Reflections on *Vers Libre.*" In *To Criticize the Critic,* 183–89. New York: Farrar Straus, 1965.

Elledge, Scott, ed. *John Milton, Paradise Lost.* 2d ed. New York: Norton, 1993.

Evans, Robert O. "Whan That Aprill(e)?" *Notes and Queries* 202 (June 1957): 234–37.

Finch, Annie. *The Ghost of Meter: Culture and Prosody in American Free Verse.* Ann Arbor: University of Michigan Press, 1993.

———. "Metrical Diversity: A Defense of the Non-Iambic Meters." In *Meter in English: A Critical Engagement,* edited by David Baker, 59–74. Fayetteville: University of Arkansas Press, 1996.

Flexner, Stuart Berg, ed. in chief. *The Random House Dictionary of the English Language.* 2d ed. New York: Random House, 1987.

Fowler, H. W. "Meter, Metre." Entry in *A Dictionary of Modern English Usage,* 2d ed., revised by Sir Ernest Gowers. Oxford: Oxford University Press, 1965.

French, Walter Hoyt, and Charles Brockway Hale, eds. *Middle English Metrical Romances.* 2 vols. New York: Russell & Russell, 1964.

Frost, Robert. *Collected Poems, Prose, and Plays.* Edited by Richard Poirier and Mark Richardson. New York: Library of America, 1995.

———. *Robert Frost on Writing.* Edited by Elaine Barry. New Brunswick, N.J.: Rutgers University Press, 1973.

———. *Robert Frost: Poetry and Prose.* Edited by Edward Connery Lathem and Lawrance Thompson. New York: Holt, 1972.

Fussell, Paul. "Poetic Contractions." Entry in *The Princeton Encyclopedia of Poetry and Poetics,* edited by Alex Preminger. Enlarged 1st ed. Princeton: Princeton University Press, 1974.

———. *Poetic Meter and Poetic Form.* Rev. ed. New York: Random House, 1979.

———. *Theory of Prosody in Eighteenth-Century England.* New London: Connecticut College, 1954.

Gascoigne, George. "Certain Notes of Instruction Concerning the Making of Verse or Rhyme in English." In *George Gascoigne: The Green Knight, Selected Poetry and Prose,* edited by Roger Pooley, 137–45. Manchester: Carcanet, 1982.

Getty, Robert J. "Cretic." Entry in *The Princeton Encyclopedia of Poetry and Poetics,* edited by Alex Preminger. Enlarged 1st ed. Princeton: Princeton University Press, 1974.

Gioia, Dana. *Can Poetry Matter? Essays on Poetry and American Culture.* Saint Paul: Graywolf, 1992.

Goldsmith, Oliver. "The State of Literature." In *Collected Works of Oliver Goldsmith,* edited by Arthur Friedman, vol. 3, *Essays and Biographies,* 187–90. Oxford: Oxford University Press, 1966.

———. "Dedication to 'The Traveller.'" In *Collected Works of Oliver Goldsmith,* edited by Arthur Friedman, vol. 4, *The Vicar of Wakefield, Poems, The Mystery Revealed,* 245–47. Oxford: Oxford University Press, 1966.

Grammont, Maurice. *Petit Traité de Versification Française.* Paris: Armond Colin, 1965.

Gray, Thomas. "Observations on English Metre," with "The Measures of Verse." In *The Works of Thomas Gray,* edited by Edmund Gosse, vol. 1, *Poems, Essays, and Journals,* 325–60. 1884. Reprint, New York: AMS, 1968.

Grigson, Geoffrey, ed. *The Faber Book of Epigrams and Epitaphs.* London: Faber & Faber, 1977.

Gross, Harvey, ed. *The Structure of Verse.* Rev. ed. New York: Ecco, 1979.

Guest, Edwin. *History of English Rhythms.* 2 vols. London: William Pickering, 1836–38.

Gunn, Thom. *The Occasions of Poetry: Essays in Criticism and Autobiography.* Edited by Clive Wilmer. London: Faber & Faber, 1982.

Halpern, Martin. "On the Two Chief Metrical Modes in English." *PMLA* 77 (June 1962): 177–86.

Halporn, James W., Martin Ostwald, and Thomas G. Rosenmeyer. *The Meters of Greek and Latin Poetry.* London: Methuen, 1963.

Hamilton, Ian, ed. *The Oxford Companion to Twentieth-Century Poetry.* Oxford: Oxford University Press, 1994.

Hardison, O. B. Jr. *Prosody and Purpose in the English Renaissance.* Baltimore: Johns Hopkins University Press, 1989.

Hartman, Charles O. *Free Verse: An Essay on Prosody.* Princeton: Princeton University Press, 1980.

Harvey, Gabriel. "The Spenser-Harvey Correspondence. 1579–80." In *Elizabethan Critical Essays,* edited by G. Gregory Smith, 1:87–126. Oxford: Oxford University Press, 1904.

Hayes, Bruce. *Metrical Stress Theory: Principles and Case Studies.* Chicago: University of Chicago Press, 1995.

Hemphill, George. "Dryden's Heroic Line." *PMLA* 72 (December 1957): 863–79.

Herford, C. H., and Percy and Evelyn Simpson, eds. *Ben Jonson.* 11 vols. Oxford: Oxford University Press, 1925–52.

Hobsbaum, Philip. *Metre, Rhythm and Verse Form.* London: Routledge, 1996.

Hollander, John. *Rhyme's Reason.* Enlarged ed. New Haven: Yale University Press, 1989.

———. *Vision and Resonance: Two Senses of Poetic Form.* 2d ed. New Haven: Yale University Press, 1985.

Hopkins, Gerard Manley. "Author's Preface." In *The Poems of Gerard Manley Hopkins,* 4th ed., edited by W. H. Gardner and N. H. MacKenzie, 45–49. London: Oxford University Press, 1967.

———. "On the Origin of Beauty" and "Rhythm and the Other Structural Parts of Rhetoric—Verse." In *The Journals and Papers of Gerard Manley Hopkins,* edited by Humphrey House, completed by Graham Story, 86–114, 267–88. London: Oxford University Press, 1959.

Hornsby, Roger A. *Reading Latin Poetry.* Norman: University of Oklahoma Press, 1967.

Housman, A. E. *"Review:* W. J. Stone, *On the Use of Classical Metres in English."* In *The Classical Papers of A.E. Housman,* edited by J. Diggle and F. R. D. Goodyear, 2:484–88. Cambridge: Cambridge University Press, 1972.

Jack, Ian. *Keats and the Mirror of Art.* Oxford: Oxford University Press, 1967.

Jakobson, Roman. "Closing Statement: Linguistics and Poetics." In *Style in Language,* edited by Thomas A. Sebeok, 350–77. Cambridge, Mass.: MIT Press, 1960.

James VI of Scotland. "Ane Schort Treatise Conteining some Reulis and Cautelis to Be Obseruit and Eschewit in Scottis Poesis." In *Elizabethan Critical Essays,* edited by G. Gregory Smith, 1:208–25. Oxford: Oxford University Press, 1904.

Jefferson, Thomas. "Thoughts on English Prosody." In *Writings,* edited by Merrill D. Peterson, 594–622. New York: Library of America, 1984.

Jespersen, Otto. *Linguistica.* Copenhagen: Levin & Munksgaard, 1933.

Johnson, Samuel. *A Dictionary of the English Language.* 8th ed. 2 vols. London, 1799.

———. *Samuel Johnson: Selected Poetry and Prose.* Edited by Frank Brady and W. K. Wimsatt. Berkeley and Los Angeles: University of California Press, 1977.

Jones, Richard Foster. *The Triumph of the English Language.* Stanford: Stanford University Press, 1953.

Jonson, Ben. *Ben Jonson.* Edited by Ian Donaldson. Oxford: Oxford University Press, 1985.

Kellog, George A. "Bridges' *Milton's Prosody* and Renaissance Metrical Theory." *PMLA* 68 (March 1953): 268–85.

Kennedy, X. J., and Dana Gioia. *An Introduction to Poetry.* 8th ed. New York: Harper-Collins, 1994.

Kiparsky, Paul. "The Rhythmic Structure of English Verse." *Linguistic Inquiry* 8 (Spring 1977): 189–247.

Kiparsky, Paul and Gilbert Youmans, eds. *Rhythm and Meter.* Vol. 1 in the Phonetics and Phonology Series. San Diego: Academic Press [Harcourt Brace], 1989.

Kirby-Smith, H. T. *The Origins of Free Verse.* Ann Arbor: University of Michigan Press, 1996.

Knowles, Gerald. "Stress." Entry in *The Oxford Companion to the English Language,* edited by Tom McArthur. Oxford: Oxford University Press, 1992.

Knowles, Gerald and Tom McArthur. "Syllable." Entry in *The Oxford Companion to the English Language,* edited by Tom McArthur. Oxford: Oxford University Press, 1992.

Lanham, Richard A. *A Handlist of Rhetorical Terms: A Guide for Students of English Literature.* Berkeley and Los Angeles: University of California Press, 1968.

Lehmann, Ruth P. M. "Contrasting Rhythms of Old English and New English." In *Linguistic and Literary Studies in Honor of Archibald A. Hill,* edited by Mohammad Ali Jazayery, Edgar C. Polomé, and Werner Winter, 4:121–26. The Hague: Mouton Publishers, 1979.

Leithauser, Brad. "Metrical Illiteracy." *The New Criterion* 1 (January 1983): 41–46.

Lewis, C. S. *Selected Literary Essays.* Edited by Walter Hopper. Cambridge: Cambridge University Press, 1969.

Liddell, Henry George, and Robert Scott. *A Greek-English Lexicon.* 8th ed. Oxford: Oxford University Press, 1897.

Longinus. *On the Sublime.* Edited and translated by W. Hamilton Fyfe. Loeb Classical Library. Cambridge, Mass.: Harvard University Press, 1932.

Maas, Paul. *Greek Metre.* Translated by Hugh Lloyd-Jones. Oxford: Oxford University Press, 1962.

McArthur, Tom, ed. *The Oxford Companion to the English Language.* Oxford: Oxford University Press, 1992.

McArthur, Tom, and Whitney F. Bolton. "Early Modern English," "Middle English," and "Old English." Entries in *The Oxford Companion to the English Language,* edited by Tom McArthur. Oxford: Oxford University Press, 1992.

McAuley, James. *Versification: A Short Introduction.* East Lansing: Michigan State University Press, 1966.

McCord, David, ed. *The Modern Treasury of Humorous Verse.* Garden City, N.Y.: Garden City Books, 1945.

Mack, Maynard. *Alexander Pope: A Life.* New York: Norton, 1985.

Malof, Joseph. *A Manual of English Meters.* Bloomington: Indiana University Press, 1970.

Mayor, Joseph B. *Chapters on English Metre.* 2d ed. Cambridge: Cambridge University Press, 1901.

Moore, Richard. *The Rule That Liberates.* Vermillion: University of South Dakota Press, 1994.

Morris, Jan, ed. *The Oxford Book of Oxford.* Oxford: Oxford University Press, 1978.

Nabokov, Vladimir. *Notes on Prosody.* New York: Pantheon, 1964.

O'Donnell, Brennan. *The Passion of Meter: A Study of Wordsworth's Metrical Art.* Kent, Ohio: Kent State University Press, 1995.

Omond, T. S. *English Metrists.* Oxford: Oxford University Press, 1921.

Partridge, A. C. *A Companion to Old and Middle English Studies.* Totowa, N.J.: Barnes & Noble, 1982.

————. *Orthography in Shakespeare and Elizabethan Drama: A Study of Colloquial Contractions, Elision, Prosody and Punctuation.* London: Edward Arnold, 1964.

Perkins, David. "Wordsworth, Hunt, and Romantic Understanding of Meter," *JEGP* 93 (January 1994): 1–17.

Pinsky, Robert. *The Sounds of Poetry: A Brief Guide.* New York: Farrar, Straus and Giroux, 1998.

Pollitt, J. J. *The Ancient View of Greek Art: Criticism, History, and Terminology.* New Haven: Yale University Press, 1974.

Pope, John C. *The Rhythm of* Beowulf. 2d ed. New Haven: Yale University Press, 1966.

Pound, Ezra. *ABC of Reading.* New York: New Directions, 1960.

Powell, Grosvenor. "The Two Paradigms for Iambic Pentameter and Twentieth-Century Metrical Experimentation." *The Modern Language Review* 91 (July 1996): 561–77.

Preminger, Alex, ed.; Frank J. Warnke and O. B. Hardison, Jr., assoc. eds. *The Princeton Encyclopedia of Poetry and Poetics.* Enlarged 1st ed. Princeton: Princeton University Press, 1974.

Preminger, Alex, and T. V. F. Brogan, eds.; Frank J. Warnke, O. B. Hardison, Jr., and Earl Minor, assoc. eds. *The New Princeton Encyclopedia of Poetry and Poetics.* Princeton: Princeton University Press, 1993.

Puttenham, George. *The Arte of English Poesie.* Edited by Edward Arber. 1906. Reprint, introduced by Baxter Hathaway. Kent, Ohio: Kent State University Press, 1970.

Quintilian. *Institutio Oratoria*. Edited and translated by H. E. Butler. 4 vols. Loeb Classical Library. Cambridge, Mass.: Harvard University Press, 1920.

Ramsey, Paul. *The Fickle Glass: A Study of Shakespeare's Sonnets*. New York: AMS, 1979.

———. "Free Verse: Some Steps Toward Definition." *Studies in Philology* 65 (January, 1968): 98–108.

Ransom, John Crowe. *The World's Body*. Baton Rouge: Louisiana State University Press, 1968.

Rebholz, R. A., ed. *Sir Thomas Wyatt: The Complete Poems*. New Haven: Yale University Press, 1981.

Reynolds, L. D. and N. G. Wilson. *Scribes and Scholars: A Guide to the Transmission of Greek and Latin Literature*. 3d ed. Oxford: Oxford University Press, 1991.

Roberts, Michael, ed. *The Faber Book of Comic Verse*. With a supplement chosen by Janet Adam Smith. London: Faber & Faber, 1974.

Robinson, Ian. *Chaucer's Prosody: A Study of the Middle English Verse Tradition*. Cambridge: Cambridge University Press, 1971.

Rothman, David J. "Ars Doggerel," *Hellas* 1 (Fall 1990): 311–17.

Saintsbury, George. *Historical Manual of English Prosody*. London: MacMillan, 1910.

———. *A History of English Prosody*. 2d ed. 3 vols. New York: Russell & Russell, 1961.

Sambrook, James, ed. *William Cowper: The Task and Selected Other Poems*. London: Longman, 1994.

Schipper, Jakob. *A History of English Versification*. Oxford: Oxford University Press, 1910; reprint, New York: AMS, 1971.

Scott, Clive. *Vers Libre: The Emergence of Free Verse in France, 1886–1914*. Oxford: Oxford University Press, 1990.

Scott, Walter. *The Journal of Sir Walter Scott, 1825–1832*. Edinburgh: David Douglas, 1910.

Scudder, H. E. "Headnote to *Evangeline: A Tale of Acadie*." In Henry Wadsworth Longfellow, *The Poetical Works of Longfellow*, introduced by George Monteiro, based on the Cambridge Edition of 1893, edited by H. E. Scudder, 70–71. Boston: Houghton Mifflin, 1975.

Shapiro, Alan. *In Praise of the Impure: Poetry and the Ethical Imagination: Essays, 1980–1991*. Evanston, Ill.: Northwestern University Press, 1993.

Shawcross, John T. "Orthography and the Text of *Paradise Lost*." In *Language and Style in Milton*, edited by Ronald David Emma and John T. Shawcross, 120–53. New York: Ungar, 1967.

Sheridan, Richard Brinsley. *The Critic*. In *The School for Scandal and Other Plays*, edited by Eric. S. Rump. London: Penguin, 1988.

Sheridan, Thomas. *A General Dictionary of the English Language*. 2 vols. 1780. Reprint, Menston, England: The Scolar Press, 1967.

Sidney, Philip. *The Poems of Sir Philip Sidney*. Edited by William A. Ringler, Jr. Oxford: Oxford University Press, 1962.

———. *Selected Prose and Poetry*. Edited by Robert Kimbrough. New York: Holt, 1969.

Sievers, Eduard. "Old Germanic Metrics and Old English Metrics." Translated by

Gawaina D. Luster. In *Essential Articles for the Study of Old English Poetry,* edited by Jess B. Bessinger, Jr., and Stanley J. Kahrl, 267–88. Hamden, Conn.: Archon, 1968.

Simpson, D. P. *Cassell's Latin Dictionary.* New York: Macmillan, 1977.

Skeat, Walter W., ed. *The Complete Works of Geoffrey Chaucer.* 2d ed. 5 vols. Oxford: Oxford University Press, 1900.

Sledd, James. "Old English Prosody: A Demurrer." *College English* 31 (October 1969): 71–74.

Smith, G. Gregory, ed. *Elizabethan Critical Essays.* 2 vols. Oxford: Oxford University Press, 1904.

Southworth, James G. *The Prosody of Chaucer and His Followers.* Oxford: Basil Blackwell, 1962.

———. *Verses of Cadence: An Introduction to the Prosody of Chaucer and His Followers.* Oxford: Basil Blackwell, 1954.

Spenser, Edmund. "The Spenser-Harvey Correspondence, 1579–80." In *Elizabethan Critical Essays,* edited by G. Gregory Smith, 1:87–126. Oxford: Oxford University Press, 1904.

Steele, Timothy. *Missing Measures: Modern Poetry and the Revolt against Meter.* Fayetteville: University of Arkansas Press, 1990.

———. "Vers Libre." Entry in *The Oxford Companion to Twentieth-Century Poetry,* edited by Ian Hamilton. Oxford: Oxford University Press, 1994.

Stillinger, Jack, ed. *Selected Poems and Prefaces by William Wordsworth.* Boston: Houghton Mifflin, 1965.

Stone, William Johnson. *On the Use of Classical Metres in English.* London: Henry Frowde, 1899.

Swift, Jonathan. "A Proposal for Correcting, Improving, and Ascertaining the English Tongue." In *The Prose Works of Jonathan Swift,* edited by Herbert Davis with Louis Landa, vol. 4, *A Proposal for Correcting the English Tongue, Polite Conversation, Etc.,* 5–21. Oxford: Basil Blackwell, 1957.

Tarlinskaja, Marina. "General and Particular Aspects of Meter." In *Rhythm and Meter,* edited by Paul Kiparsky and Gilbert Youmans, 121–54. San Diego: Academic Press [Harcourt Brace], 1989.

Thompson, John. *The Founding of English Metre.* 1961. Reprint, with an introduction by John Hollander, New York: Columbia University Press, 1989.

Tolkien, J. R. R. "Prefatory Remarks." In *Beowulf and the Finnesburg Fragment,* translated by John R. Clark Hall, 3d ed. revised by C. L. Wrenn, ix–xliii. London: Allen and Unwin, 1950.

Trager, George L., and Henry Lee Smith, Jr. *An Outline of English Structure.* Corrected ed. Washington, D.C.: American Council of Learned Societies, 1957.

Trimpi, Wesley. *Ben Jonson's Poems.* Stanford: Stanford University Press, 1962.

Turco, Lewis. *The New Book of Forms: A Handbook of Poetics.* Hanover: University Press of New England, 1986.

Valéry, Paul. *The Art of Poetry.* Translated by Denise Folliot. Introduction by T. S. Eliot. Princeton: Princeton University Press, 1985.

Watts, Isaac. "'Preface' to *The Psalms of David*" and "The Art of Reading and Writing English." In *The Works of Isaac Watts,* edited by George Burder, 4: 113–24, 679–734. 1810. Reprint, New York: AMS, 1971.

Weismiller, Edward R. "Metrical Treatment of Syllables." Entry in *The New Princeton Encyclopedia of Poetry and Poetics,* edited by Alex Preminger and T. V. F. Brogan. Princeton: Princeton University Press, 1993.

———. "Triple Threats to Duple Rhythm." In *Rhythm and Meter,* edited by Paul Kiparsky and Gilbert Youmans, 261–90. San Diego: Academic Press [Harcourt Brace], 1989.

Werstine, Paul. "Line Division in Shakespeare's Dramatic Verse: An Editorial Problem." *Analytical and Enumerative Bibliography* 8 (1984): 73–125.

West, M. L. *Greek Metre.* Oxford: Oxford University Press, 1982.

———. *Introduction to Greek Metre.* Oxford: Oxford University Press, 1987.

Wilbur, Richard. *The Catbird's Song: Prose Pieces, 1963–1995.* San Diego: Harcourt Brace, 1997.

———. "Interview with Richard Wilbur." In *Speaking of Frost: Richard Wilbur and William H. Pritchard Interviewed by Donald G. Sheehy,* 5–18. Amherst: The Friends of the Amherst College Library, 1997.

———. *Responses: Prose Pieces, 1953–1976.* New York: Harcourt Brace, 1976.

Williams, Miller. *Patterns of Poetry: An Encyclopedia of Forms.* Baton Rouge: Louisiana State University Press, 1986.

Williams, William Carlos. "Free Verse." Entry in *The Princeton Encyclopedia of Poetry and Poetics,* edited by Alex Preminger. Enlarged 1st ed. Princeton: Princeton University Press, 1974.

Wimsatt, W. K., ed. *Versification: Major Language Types.* New York: New York University Press, 1972.

Winters, Yvor. *In Defense of Reason.* Denver: Swallow, 1947.

———. "The Audible Reading of Poetry" and "The Poetry of Gerard Manley Hopkins." In *The Function of Criticism,* 81–100, 103–56. Denver: Swallow, 1957.

Wood, Clement. *The Complete Rhyming Dictionary.* New York: Halcyon House, 1936.

Woods, Susanne. *Natural Emphasis: English Versification from Chaucer to Dryden.* San Marino, Calif.: Huntington Library, 1985.

Wright, George T. *Shakespeare's Metrical Art.* Berkeley and Los Angeles: University of California Press, 1988.

Yeats, William Butler. "A General Introduction for My Work." In *Essays and Introductions,* 509–26. New York: MacMillan, 1961.

Permissions and Copyrights

Index

(This index provides references not only to the text proper, but also to the chapter notes and glossary where they cite works of poets or quote critics and scholars on issues of meter and versification.)

Accent, 19. *See also* Glossary entry for; and *see* Metrical accent; Speech stress

Accentual verse, 140, 246–55; Hopkins's experiments with 253–54; intermediate stresses in, 273–74. *See also* Glossary entry for; and *see* Accentual-alliterative verse; Sprung rhythm

Accentual-alliterative verse, 12, 15, 136, 139; Guest's advocacy of, 140; in Middle English, 250–52; in Old English, 246–49; structurally different from modern iambic pentameter, 161–62; twentieth-century poems in, 247–48, 252–53. *See also* Accentual verse; Alliteration

Accentual-syllabic verse, 20–21, 149–50, 246, 273–74; defined, 14, 54; McAuley on, 306; modulatory capacities of, 27–51, 94–115; monosyllabic words and flexibility of, 42–46; syllabic component of, attitudes toward, 134–41. *See also* Glossary entry for; and *see* Iambic verse; Meter

Addison, Joseph, 152

Aeschylus, 271

Alcaeus, 269

Alcaic stanzas, 202, 269; in Tennyson's "Milton," 276–77

Alexander, Michael, 247

Alexandrine, 65, 142; in English verse, 57–60; in French verse, 15, 57–58, 98, 188–89; Pope's disparagement of, 59; as variant in heroic-couplet poems, 59. *See also* Glossary entry for

Allen, W. Sidney: on quantity, 326

Alliteration, 300; in Austen, 6; Churchill on, 308; in Douglas, 308; in Hopkins, 253–54; in Keats, 4; in Shakespeare,

110–11. *See also* Glossary entry for; and *see* Accentual-alliterative verse

Alliterative Revival, 250–51. *See also* Accentual-alliterative verse

Amis, Kingsley, 163

Amphibrachic rhythm, 55, 236–41; Coleridge on, 240; in Colman's epitaph on Wraxall, 237; Gray on, 239–40; in Hardy's translation of Bembo's epitaph on Raphael, 237; mixed with anapestic rhythm in Gay and Christina Rossetti, 237–38. *See also* Glossary entry for Amphibrach

Amphimacer. *See* Glossary entry for

Anapestic rhythm, 55, 96, 106, 120–21, 153, 155, 193, 213, 234–36; in Byron's "Destruction of Sennacherib," 234; as component of loose iambic verse, 79–84; in Cowper's "Verses Supposed to Be Written by Alexander Selkirk," 235, 244; in Frost's "Blueberries," 235–36; Gray on, 239–40; illusory anapests in Pope, Shakespeare, and Donne when elisions ignored, 141–43; mixed with amphibrachic rhythm in Gay and Christina Rossetti, 237–38; regarded by Samuel Johnson and Jefferson as sole trisyllabic rhythm in English, 230. *See also* Glossary entry for Anapest

Anceps positions/syllables, 13, 39–40, 68, 268, 269. *See also* Glossary entry for Anceps

Aphaeresis, 127–28. *See also* Glossary entry for; and *see* Elision

Apocope, 128–29, 141. *See also* Glossary entry for; and *see* Elision

Apollodorus, 13

233; quarrel with Southey, 230–31; triple rhymes of, 186, 187

Bysshe, Edward: Auden on, 149–50; syllabic interpretation of English meter, 138–39

Caesura, 112–14, 140; in accentual-alliterative verse, 15, 161, 247–54; in ancient dactylic hexameter, 15, 98, 231, 287–88, 312; in Browning's "My Last Duchess," 98–99; in Dryden's *Absalom and Achitophel*, 102–3; in English pentameter, 15–16, 97–98; in French alexandrine, 15, 57–58, 98, 312; in Ben Jonson's "To Penshurst," 103–4; in Lewis's "Days," 102; in Longfellow's dactylic hexameters, 231–32; in Marvell's "Nymph Complaining for the Death of Her Fawn," 101–2; in Seth's "Prandial Plaint," 103. *See also* Glossary entry for; and *see* Feminine caesura

Cage, John, 183

Callimachus, 316

Camden, William, 42–43

Campbell, Jeremy: on grammar, 172

Campion, Thomas, 117, 118, 148, 180, 184, 226; on elision and hiatus, 145–46; imitation of classical quantitative meters, 229, 267–68; on rhyme, 181; on suitability of iambic rhythm to English speech and verse, 282; on unsuitability of English monosyllabic words to dactylic rhythm, 42

Carlyle, Thomas, 20

Carper, Thomas, 87

Carroll, Lewis, 123; shaped verse of "The Mouse's Tale," 331

Cartwright, William, 44

Cassity, Turner, 87

Catalexis, 224–29, 233, 238–41, 268. *See also* Glossary entry for

Catullus: elision in, 117, 120; "Odi et amo," translated by Cunningham, 170–71

Causley, Charles, 314

Cawdrey, Robert, 289

Caxton, William, 323

Cervantes, Miguel de, 94

Chapman, George, 146, 207

Chapman, John ("Johnny Appleseed"), 168

Chapman, Raymond, 283

Charles (duc) d'Orléans, 318, 328

Chaucer, Geoffrey, 12, 16, 21, 30, 35, 41, 50, 65, 88, 92, 118, 134, 136, 140, 141, 179, 180, 218, 250, 266, 281, 296, 308, 310, 319, 323, 326, 336; clipped ("headless") lines in, 85–86, 225–26; dual Romanic-Teutonic pronunciations in, 78–79, 197, 289; elisions in early manuscripts of, 119, 148; feminine caesuras in, 84; final *e* and use of alternative spellings for metrical purposes, 133; fluency in rhyme, 197; on Josephus, 226; meter of, debates about, 288–92; pentameters with only three strong speech stresses, 166; ridicule of Romance-six stanza, 327; "rym dogerel," 314; "*y*-glide" elisions in, 124

Chaucer, Thomas, 85

Chickering, Howell D. Jr., 249

Child, F. J., 206

Chomsky, Noam, 9–10

Choral odes. *See* Pindaric odes

Churchill, Charles, 91, 168; on alliteration, 308–9

Cicero, 103, 183

Clare, John, 9, 33, 34, 205

Clark, Arthur Melville: on rhyme, 300

Clerihew: Auden's on Bysshe and Guest, 149–50; Bentley's on Christopher Wren, 312. *See also* Glossary entry for

Clipped ("headless") lines, 84, 87–88, 102, 112, 157, 238; in Chaucer, 85–86, 225–26. *See also* Glossary entry for Clipped

Clough, Arthur Hugh, 177, 231, 319

Coke, Edward, 212

Coleridge, Mary, 30

Coleridge, Samuel Taylor, 47, 61, 230, 304, 308; on amphibrachs, 240; "Christabel" not entirely accentual, 254–55; definition of poetry, 158, 299; epigram "On a Volunteer Singer," 175; on meter of "Christabel," 140; on puddle in Wordsworth's "Thorn," 292; on trochees, 225

Colie, Rosalie, 157

Colman, George (the Younger): epitaph on Wraxall, 237

Common meter, 14–15, 203–4, 205, 211, 302. *See also* Glossary entry for

Condell, Henry, 92, 292

Congreve, William: management of inverted first foot and feminine ending, 71; on pseudo-Pindaric odes, 272

Eliot, T. S., 275; clipped tetrameters in "Sweeney Erect," 313; free verse of, 264; metrical theory of, 50, 305

Elision, 84, 97–98, 106, 114, 129, 130, 143, 144, 190, 213, 257; ambiguities of, in Bridges's *Testament of Beauty*, 274–75, 297; Beerbohm's parody of, 294–95; Blair's condemnation of, 147; Bridges on, 118, 125, 144; Campion on, 145–46; Cope on, 298; Dick Davis on, 298; decline of metrical apostrophe, 140–41; Dryden and Pope on, 146; in early manuscripts of Chaucer, 119, 148; in early manuscripts of Lydgate, 119; in Egerton manuscript of Wyatt's poems, 126–27, 130; Fussell on, 294; Gill on, 145; in Goldsmith's "Deserted Village," 132; in Herbert, 120; "Jonsonian," 124–25; manipulation of contracted and uncontracted word forms, 130–33; in Milton, 118, 125–26, 148–49; neglect of, by recent editors of earlier poets, 141–43; Puttenham on, 145; Saintsbury's condemnation of, 148; in Shakespeare's *Romeo and Juliet*, 131; Sidney on, 145; Swift's condemnation of, 146–47; Wilbur on, 297–98; Wordsworth's use of, in "Composed upon Westminster Bridge," 149. *See also* Glossary entry for; and *see* Aphaeresis; Apocope; Hiatus; Synaeresis; Synaloepha; Syncope

Elizabeth I, 171

Elledge, Scott, 76

Emerson, Ralph Waldo, 61, 90–91

End-stopped lines, 99. *See also* Glossary entry for End-Stopped

Enjambment, 159–60, 183, 194–95, 207; in Bogan's "Last Hill in a Vista," 112; in Bowers's "Astronomers of Mont Blanc," 316; in Browning's "My Last Duchess," 99–100; in Donne's *Satires*, 257; in Larkin's "Whitsun Weddings," 215–17; in Marvell's "Nymph Complaining for the Death of her Fawn," 101–2; in Milton's *Paradise Lost*, 107–8, and *Samson Agonistes*, 112–13; in Christina Rossetti's "Pause of Thought," 107; in Stevens's "Sunday Morning," 108; in Tuckerman's "As when, down some broad river," 106; in

Wilbur's "Hamlen Brook," 213–15; in Williams's "Yellow Chimney," 262–63. *See also* Glossary entry for English. *See* Glossary entries for Old English; Middle English; Modern English

Envoy, 140, 311, 329. *See also* Glossary entry for

Epigram, 78, 83; Beeching's on Jowett, 221–22, 302; Belloc's on "Lord Finchly," 194–95; Campion's "Kate can fancy," 229; Catullus's "Odi et amo," translated by Cunningham, 170–71; Coleridge's "On a Volunteer Singer," 175; Herrick's "To God," 128; Hoskyns's to son, 111; Landor's on Gibbon, 316–17; Montagu's on Lyttelton's *Advice to a Lady*, 73; Christina Rossetti's on Garrick's "Heart of Oak," 238; Seth's "Prandial Plaint," 103. *See also* Glossary entry for; and *see* Epitaph

Epitaph: Bembo's on Raphael, translated by Hardy, 237; Colman's on Wraxall, 237; Cunningham's "Epitaph for Someone or Other" ("Naked I came"), 70; Jeffrey's on Peter Robinson, 1, 281–82; Lockhart's on Lord Robertson, 281–82. *See also* Epigram

Euripides, 271

Evans, Robert O.: on first line of *Canterbury Tales*, 86

Ewart, Gavin, 83–84

Falling rhythm. *See* Glossary entry for; *see also* Trochaic rhythm; Dactylic rhythm.

Feminine caesura: in ancient verse, 287–88; in English verse, 84, 86–87

Feminine ending, 6, 8, 31, 48, 64–74, 75, 112, 162–63, 166, 227, 228, 229, 238, 270; expressive in Parker, 73–74; more common in blank verse than rhymed verse, 68; origin of term, 63. *See also* Glossary entry for; and *see* Feminine rhyme

Feminine rhyme, 63–64, 153, 187–90, 197, 223–24, 233; alternation of masculine and feminine rhymes in French verse, 188–89; alternation of masculine and feminine rhymes in Hardy's "I Say I'll Seek Her," 189–90; expressive in Montagu's epigram on Lyttelton, 73;

Feminine rhyme *(continued)*
expressive in Weever's sonnet tribute
to Shakespeare, 187–88. *See also* Glossary entry for; and *see* Masculine
rhyme; Rhyme
Fields, Kenneth, 166
Figurative language. *See* Glossary entry for
Finch, Anne (Countess of Winchilsea), 61,
119, 161, 185; iambic tetrameters of
"Song," 56–57
Finch, Annie, 303
Fitzgerald, Edward, 111–12, 168, 328
Fixed forms, 196–98; repeating or refrain
lines in, 197. *See also* Glossary entry
for; and *see* Ballade; French forms;
Rondeau; Sonnet; Sestina; Triolet; Villanelle
Fletcher, John, 128, 129, 316
Foot, 5; ambiguous syllabic boundaries
and foot division, 18–19; divisions between feet not necessarily coincident
with divisions between words and
phrases, 52; principal feet in English
verse, 54–55; unit of rhythm rather
than unit of sense, 16–17, 52. *See also*
Glossary entry for; and *see* Amphibrach; Amphimacer; Anapest; Dactyl;
Iamb; Ionic; Pyrrhic; Scansion;
Spondee; Trochee
Ford, John, 167
Fourteeners (iambic heptameters), 206–7;
in Southwell's "Burning Babe," 206; in
Thayer's "Casey at the Bat," 207. *See
also* Glossary entry for
Free verse, 3, 22, 260–64, 275–76; Stephen
Crane's, 262; Dujardin on "definitive
establishment of *vers libre*," 305;
Eliot's, 264; Valéry on, 260; Whitman's, 261; Williams's, 262–63. *See also*
Glossary entry for; and *see* Vers libre
French forms. *See* Glossary entry for
Frost, Robert, 16, 36, 51, 62, 79, 84, 122, 155,
171, 179, 183, 211, 218, 293, 299, 328, 336;
anapestic rhythm in "Blueberries,"
235–36; blank verse of, compared to
Ben Jonson's, Milton's, and
Wordsworth's, 21; catalexis and
acatalexis in "To the Thawing Wind,"
312; on doggerel, 314; hexameters in
blank verse of, 60; loose iambics of
"Neither Out Far Nor In Deep,"
80–83; management of inverted first
foot and feminine ending, 68–69;

Phalaecean hendecasyllabics of "For
Once, Then, Something," 268–69; on
prevalence of iambic rhythm in English verse, 282, 287; on relationship of
meter to speech rhythm and speech
tone, 284, 287; on rhyme, 196, 301; as
rhymer, 194, 195; on varying sentence
structure in stanzaic verse, 302;
trochaic countercurrents in "Stopping
by Woods," 327; and variable metrical
nature of monosyllabic words, 45–46,
285–86
Furnivall, Frederick J.: and founding of
English Text Society, 169
Fussell, Paul, 169; on poetic contractions
in eighteenth-century verse, 294

Gallus, Cornelius, 105
Gamelyn, 250
Gardner, W. H., 304
Garrick, David: Christina Rossetti's epigram on "Heart of Oak," 238
Gascoigne, George, 19, 98, 276, 336; on
metrical versatility of monosyllabic
words, 43; on origin of term "poulter's
measure," 208; on prevalence of
iambic rhythm in English verse, 282;
on "Rhythm Royal," 326
Gay, John, 121, 239; mixed trisyllabic feet
in *Polly,* 237–38
Giacomo di Lentini, 332
Gibbon, Edward: Landor's epigram on,
316–17
Gifford, William, 141
Gill, Alexander, 145
Gioia, Dana, 166, 300
Goethe, Johann Wolfgang von, 179
Golding, Arthur, 145, 207
Goldsmith, Oliver, 15, 159, 165, 239, 244,
319; on Burke, 245; elisions in "Deserted Village," 132
Gower, John, 12, 136, 250; verse in French,
Latin, and English, 77
Grammar: Campbell on, 172; coordination of meter with, 3, 151–72
Grammont, Maurice, 318; on rondeaux
and rondels, 328
Gray, Thomas, 30, 118, 123, 127, 196, 213,
319; on Chaucer's "Sir Thopas," 314; on
Donne's *Satires,* 256; on trisyllabic
rhythms in Prior, 239–40
Guest, Edwin, 294; advocacy of accentual-
alliterative verse, 139–40; Auden on,

149–50; on organized rhythm of verse and looser rhythm of prose, 282
Guillaume de Machaut, 318
Guittone d'Arezzo, 332
Gullans, Charles, 66
Gunn, Thom, 162, 218, 225, 293, 316; echo poem of, 314–15; internal rhyme in "Pierce Street," 177; syllabic verse of, 258, 259
Gwynn, R. S., 162

H. D. (Hilda Doolittle), 262
Hacker, Marilyn, 336
Haiku. *See* Glossary entry for
Half meter, 204–5. *See also* Glossary entry for
Hallam, Arthur Henry, 109
Halle, Morris, 9–10
Halpern, Martin, 303
Hardy, Thomas, 2, 83, 84, 204, 218, 225, 335; alternation of masculine and feminine rhymes in "I Say I'll Seek Her," 189–90; Corn on rhymes of, 301; on Arthur Henniker, 159; on Keats, 92–93; loose iambics of "The Wound," 80–82; "The Ruined Maid," alternative scansions of, 240–41; translation of Bembo's epitaph for Raphael, 237
Harington, John, 324
Harvey, Gabriel, 127, 265
Harwood, Gwen, 38, 273
Hawes, Stephen, 258
Hawthorne, Nathaniel, 243–44
Headless lines. *See* Clipped lines
Hecht, Anthony, 30, 164, 205, 330
Heminges, John, 92, 292
Hemistich: types of, in Old English verse, 12, 248–49. *See also* Glossary entry for
Henniker, Arthur: Hardy on, 159
Henry VIII, 311
Henryson, Robert, 21, 35, 165
Heraclitus (poet, 3d c. B.C.), 316
Herbert, George, 196, 315; elision in, 120; shaped poetry of "Easter Wings," 330–31; stanzaic complexity in, 210–11, 218
Herford, C. H., 125, 292
Heroic couplets, 21, 203, 207, 213; alexandrine as variant in poems in, 59; Browning's, 95–100; Crabbe's, 59, 319; Ben Jonson's, 103–5. *See also* Glossary entry for Heroic Couplet
Heroic quatrain. *See* Glossary entry for

Herrick, Robert, 63, 316, 335; iambic monometers of "Upon His Departure Hence," 55–56; line lengths in stanzas of "To the Yew and the Cypress," 208–9; rhyme involving elision in "To God," 128, 189
Hexameter (ancient dactylic), 13, 42, 104–5, 117, 135, 137, 231, 333; caesura in, 15, 98, 231, 287–88, 312; fourteener as possible modern equivalent of, 207. *See also* Glossary entry for Hexameter
Hexameter (English iambic). *See* Alexandrine
Hexameter (modern dactylic), 230–32; Clough's, 231; Longfellow on rhythms of *Evangeline*, 243–44; Longfellow's, in *The Courtship of Miles Standish*, 231–32; Southey's, 230. *See also* Glossary entry for Hexameter
Hiatus: Campion, Dryden, and Pope on, 145–46. *See also* Glossary entry for
Hollander, John, 300
Holmes, Oliver Wendell: triple rhymes in, 193
Homer, 121, 130, 144, 182, 207; masculine and feminine caesuras in, 288
Homoeoteuleton, 179
Hood, Thomas, 158, 207; dactylics in "The Bridges of Sighs," 233–34; Romance-six stanzas of, 327–28
Hope, A. D., 273
Hopkins, Gerard Manley, 132, 140, 178, 221, 255, 273–74, 308; on rhyme, 301; theory and practice of accentual verse and "sprung rhythm," 253–54, 333
Horace, 104, 153, 161, 320; on Pindar, 272; Sapphics of, 269–70
Hornsby, Roger A., 312
Hoskyns, John: epigram to son, 111
Housman, A. E., 59, 120, 121, 122, 204, 210; stanzaic structure in "Oh, when I was in love with you," 202–3; on Stone's *On the Use of Classical Metres in English*; 267
Howard, Henry. *See* Surrey
Hugo, Victor, 58, 325
Hulme, T. E., 50
Hypermetrical syllable. *See* Glossary entry for; and *see also* Feminine ending; Feminine rhyme

Iamb: defined, 5; possible origin of term, 13. *See also* Glossary entry for

Iambic rhythm: Aristotle on, 12; Campion, Dryden, Thompson, and Chapman on natural inclination of English to, 282–83; why suited to English, 8–12. *See also* Iambic verse

Iambic verse: degrees of fluctuation between lighter and heavier syllables, 4, 29–34, 37–39, 155, 321–22, 332–33; differences between English and ancient Greek forms of, 12–13; "loose iambics," 79–84; pattern of, enables easy recognition of metrical nature of intermediately stressed syllables, 273; prevalence of, in English, 282–83; principal meters of, in English, 54–60; principal variations in, 61–74. *See also* Accentual-syllabic verse; Iambic rhythm

Ictus. *See* Glossary entry for

Imitation-classical verse, 229, 230, 265–73, 276–77

Indentation: in long poems in blank verse or heroic couplets, 213; in sonnets, 211–13; in stanzaic verse, 208–11

In Memoriam stanza, 209–10

Ionic. *See* Glossary entry for

Isocrates, 179

Isosyllabic. *See* Glossary entry for

Jack and the Beanstalk, 255

Jakobson, Roman, 68, 299

James I of Scotland, 156; and rhyme royal, 326

James VI of Scotland (later James I of England): on "tumbling verse," 336; on variable metrical nature of monosyllabic words, 285

Jefferson, Thomas: regards anapest as sole trisyllabic English foot, 230; on relative stress and different degrees of accent in English verse, 285

Jeffrey, Francis: epitaph on Peter Robinson, 1, 281–82

Jespersen, Otto, 286; criticism of scansion, 17; four-level register to suggest relative stress, 31, 284–85; on effect of pauses within verse lines, 79

Johnson, Samuel, 140, 147, 162, 207, 239, 276; on anapestic meter, 230, 234–35; definition of blank verse, 311; on Milton's views of blank verse and rhyme, 182–83; mixture of acatalectic and catalectic trochaic tetrameters in

"Short Song," 226; on *Paradise Lost,* 182, 184; on "representative meter," 293

Jonson, Ben, 15, 35, 37, 65, 152, 155, 168, 180, 210, 225, 266, 316, 319; blank verse of, compared to Milton's, Wordsworth's, and Frost's, 21; caesural pauses in "To Penshurst," 103–4; on Donne's "not keeping of accent," 256; dual Romanic-Teutonic pronunciation in, 78; elision in, 124–25, 126, 132, 141, 149; indentation in heroic couplets, 104–5; Pindaric odes of, 271–72; satirical attack on rhyme, 181; on Shakespeare's "Caesar did never wrong," 89–90, 292

Josephus: Chaucer on, 226

Jowett, Benjamin: Beeching's epigram on, 221–22, 223, 228

Kalstone, David, 164

Keats, John, 47, 48, 50, 53, 60, 76, 168, 207, 217, 272; Hardy on, 92–93; meter in "To Autumn," 3–6, 14; mixture of iambic and trochaic tetrameters in "Give me women, wine, and snuff," 227–28; "On the Grasshopper and Cricket," 212–13; structural relationship of sonnets of, to odes of, 218

Kemble, John M.: edition of *Beowulf,* 139

Kennedy, X. J., 53–54, 300, 316

Khayyám, Omar. *See* Omar Khayyám

Kimbrough, Robert, 265

King, Henry, 38

Kipling, Rudyard, 167, 270, 316

Klopstock, Friedrich Gottlieb, 230

Knowles, Gerald, 334

Krekel, Tim, 126

La Fontaine, 305

Lancelot, Claude, 138–39

Landor, Walter Savage, 316; epigram on Gibbon, 316–17; triplets in "Little Aglae," 219–20

Lang, Cosmo Gordon, 221

Langland, William, 12, 253, 255, 291; versification of, 161, 251–52, 308

Larkin, Philip, 61, 191, 218–19, 314; broken-backed pentameters of, 87; expressive stanzaic structure in "The Whitsun Weddings," 215–17; iambic dimeters of "New eyes each year," 56; onomatopoeia in "The Trees," 324

Layamon, 250

Metrics: distinguished from prosody, 20.
    See also Glossary entry for; and *see*
    Meter
Meynell, Alice, 129, 171
Middle English: "Alliterative Revival"
    during, 250–52; effect of Norman
    French on vocabulary and pronuncia-
    tion of, 77–78, 289; emergence of ac-
    centual-syllabic verse during, 12,
    20–21, 250; rise of rhyme during, 180.
    See also Glossary entry for
Millay, Edna St. Vincent, 37, 124, 157
Milne, Christian: ballad stanzas of "Sent
    with a Flower-Pot Begging a Slip of
    Geranium," 205
Milton, John, 2, 16, 50, 60, 73, 78–79, 83,
    92, 159–60, 162, 164, 165, 178, 213, 217,
    281, 290, 296, 305, 317, 318, 319; blank
    verse of, compared to Ben Jonson's,
    Wordsworth's, and Frost's, 21; Bridges
    on "Rocks, caves, lakes, fens," 49; criti-
    cism of rhyme, 182; elision in, 118,
    125–26, 129, 140, 141, 143, 144, 148–49;
    use of elision to avoid feminine end-
    ings, 130; enjambment in, 107–8,
    112–13; indentation in "On the Morn-
    ing of Christ's Nativity" and sonnet to
    Cyriack Skinner, 211–12; Samuel John-
    son on blank verse of, 182–83, 184;
    mixture of iambic and trochaic
    tetrameters in "L'Allegro" and "Il
    Penseroso," 227; *Paradise Lost,* appar-
    ently inverted fifth feet in pentameters
    of, 75–76; Tennyson's alcaics on, 269,
    276–77; and variable metrical nature
    of monosyllabic words, 41, 43, 44
Modern English: accentuation in, differ-
    ences from Middle English, 65, 77–78,
    266, 289; iambic rhythm, reasons for
    inclination to, 8–12; meaning con-
    veyed more by word order than word
    ending, 10; monosyllabism in, ten-
    dency toward, 42; multiple rhymes
    harder in, than in Middle English and
    Romanic languages, 196–97; syllabic
    length in, 266–67; syllabic stress in,
    27–29. *See also* Glossary entry for; and
    see Old English; Middle English
Molière, 179, 180
Momaday, N. Scott, 164
Monosyllabic words: attitudes toward in
    Renaissance, 42–43; effective lines

consisting entirely of, 171; Gascoigne
    on, 43; Pope on, 43; Tichbourne's
    "Elegy" composed entirely of, 171–72;
    variable metrical nature of, 40–46,
    285–86
Montagu, Mary Wortley, 165, 239, 244;
    epigram on Lyttelton's *Advice to a
    Lady,* 73, 187
Moore, Marianne: syllabic verse of 258,
    259–60
Moore, Richard, 59
Morphology (word shape and structure):
    and meter, 152, 153–54, 158, 162–72. *See
    also* Glossary entry for
Mother Goose, 320, 321
Muir, John: Winters on, 159
Mure, William, 121, 329

Nabokov, Vladimir, 14, 169
Nash, Ogden, 316; comically wrenched
    rhymes of, 187, 337; iambic monome-
    ters of "Geographical Reflection," 55, 56
Nashe, Thomas: Cunningham on meter
    of "Adieu, farewell, earth's bliss," 309
Near rhyme. *See* Partial rhyme
Nelson, Marilyn, 164
Nightingale, Florence, 221
Nims, John Frederick, 316
Numbers. *See* Glossary entry for

Offbeat. *See* Glossary entry for
Off rhyme. *See* Partial rhyme
Old English: metrical consequences of
    loss of inflections from, 12, 21; metri-
    cal system of, 12, 14, 161, 246–50; po-
    etry of, interest in later centuries in,
    136, 139–40. *See also* Glossary entry for
Oldham, John, 157
Omar Khayyám, 111–12, 168, 328
Onomatopoeia. *See* Glossary entry for
Ottava rima, 186, 187, 218. *See also* Glos-
    sary entry for
Ovid, 105, 145, 207; internal rhyme in, 176
Owen, Wilfred, 34, 192

Pantoum. *See* Glossary entry for
Pararhyme. *See* Partial rhyme
Parker, Dorothy, 316; expressive feminine
    ending, 73–74
Parnell, Thomas, 15
Partial rhyme, 190–94, 259, 260; in Dick-
    inson's "Remorse is memory awake,"

192; in Yeats's *ottava rima* poems, 324.
See also Glossary entry for

Pearl, 250, 251

Peele, George, 128

Pentameter (iambic): caesura in, 15–16, 97–98; Chaucer's, relation to French decasyllabic line and Italian hendecasyllabic line, 250; defined, 5, 14; extra syllables less suitable to, than to shorter lines, 84; flexibility of, 14–16, 154–57; historical importance of, in English verse, 16; metrical variations in, 61–79, 84–93; rhythmical modulations of, 29–37, 97–101; structurally different from Germanic accentual-alliterative line, 161–62; Wilbur on, 325; illustrated by Wilbur's "Transit," 57. See also Glossary entry for; and see Blank verse; Iambic rhythm; Iambic verse; Meter; Metrical accent; Speech stress

Pentameter (trochaic): in Campion's "Kate can fancy," 229

Percy, Thomas, 206

Perkins, David, 303

Petrarch, 145, 179, 212; and the sonnet, 332

Phalaecean hendecasyllabics: in Frost's "For Once, Then, Something," 268–69

Phalaecus, 268

Phillip, Percy, 260

Pindar, 271; Horace on, 272

Pindaric odes (Choral odes), 334; Ben Jonson's, 272; Congreve on, 272; Cowley's, 272–73; structural features of, in antiquity, 271

Pinkerton, Helen, 35–36, 185, 205, 316; expressive use of inverted feet, 74, 75

Plato, 221, 334

Poe, Edgar Allan: nature and effects of internal rhymes in "The Raven," 176–77, 178, 229–30

Poins, John, 218

Pope, Alexander, 16, 30, 41, 47, 50, 52, 98, 140, 148, 161, 167, 179, 196, 213, 256, 281, 319; on the alexandrine, 59; amphimacers of "Lilliputian Ode," 309; elisions in, 121, 122, 127, 128, 130; use of elision to avoid feminine endings, 130–31; facile rhyming, criticism of, 195; hiatus, criticism of, 146; metrical confusions in texts of, as result of editorial failure to register elisions of,

141–42, 144; on monosyllabic words, 43; on own precocity in versing, 323; on relation of sound to sense, 293

Poulter's measure: Gascoigne on origin of term, 208; Surrey's, 208

Pound, Ezra, 36, 50, 207, 262

Praed, Winthrop Makeworth, 38

Prior, Matthew, 244; Gray on trisyllabic meters of, 239–40

Promotion and demotion, 8–9, 10–11, 43–44, 46, 255

Prosody: distinguished from Metrics, 20. See also Glossary entry for; and see Meter

Puttenham, George, 138; on difference between ancient and modern meters, 137; on doggerel, 314; on elision, 145, 149

Pyrrhic, 39–40, 222, 286–87; generally unnecessary and possibly confusing to metrical analysis of English verse, 46–49. See also Glossary entry for; and see Spondee

Quantity (syllabic length), 184–85; Allen on, 326; ancient regulation of syllabic length and modern regulation of syllabic number, 134–39, 256; as basis for meter in ancient Indo-European languages, 12–13; phonetic rather than phonemic in Modern English, 266–67; Quintilian on, 325. See also Glossary entry for; and see Imitation-classical verse

Quatrain. See Glossary entry for

Quiller-Couch, Arthur, 206–7

Quintilian: on quantity, 325

Racine, Jean, 179

Ralegh, Walter, 30, 79, 160

Ransom, John Crowe, 157; on Shakespeare's sonnets, 301

Raphael (Raffaello Santi), 201; Bembo's epitaph on, translated by Hardy, 237

Refrain: in fixed-form poetry, 197. See also Glossary entry for

Rhyme: Burns on, 198–99; Campion on, 181; Clark on, 300; comically strained, 187, 193, 194–95, 337; consonantal and assonantal, 192, 194; Corn on Hardy's use of, 301; couplet, 188; cross, 189; Cunningham on prevalence of, in English verse, 180; Daniel on, 181;

Stanzas, 200–220; basic functions of, 202–3; complex versus simple, 217–18; definition and features of, 201–2; Larkin's expressive use of, in "The Whitsun Weddings," 215–17; terminology of, 201, 203–8, 209–10, 218–20; Wilbur's expressive use of, in "Hamlen Brook," 213–15. *See also* Glossary entry for Stanza; and *see* Ballad meter; Burns stanza; Half meter; Heroic quatrain; Long meter; Ottava rima; Rhyme royal; Romance-six stanza; Sesta rima; Short meter; Spenserian stanza

Stevens, Wallace, 9, 30, 161, 168, 262, 264, 317; blank verse stanzas of, 202; apparently inverted fifth foot in "Sunday Morning," 75; enjambment in "Sunday Morning," 108

Stichos. *See* Glossary entry for

Stone, William Johnson: advocacy of quantitative metric for English, 266; Housman on, 267

Stress: effect of verbal or phrasal environment on, 8–9, 10–11, 43–44; alternating pattern of, in most English words of more than one syllable, 9–10, 10–11; effect of grammatical function on, 10, 11, 28, 45–46; nature and sources of, in English, 28–29; effect of rhetorical context on, 28–29, 44–45, 169–70; different degrees of, 29, 31–32, 284–85; "speech stress" distinguished from "metrical accent," 32–34; variable nature of, in monosyllabic words, 40–46. *See also* Glossary entry for; and *see* Metrical accent; Speech stress

Strophe. *See* Glossary entry for

Substitution. *See* Metrical substitutions

Surrey (Henry Howard, Earl of), 59, 136, 258; introduces blank verse into English, 311; poulter's measure of "When summer took in hand," 208; on Wyatt, 15

Swift, Jonathan, 40, 67, 309; criticism of elision, 146–47; use of elision, 128

Swinburne, Algernon Charles, 76, 221; Sapphics of, 269, 270

Syllabic verse, 7, 256–60; Bridges's, metrical ambiguities of, 274–75; Daryush's, 258–59; Donne's *Satires* interpreted as being in, 256–57; Gunn's, 259; Dylan

Thomas's and Marianne Moore's, 259–60. *See also* Glossary entry for

Syllables: division of, and scansion, 5, 17–19; modern regulation of syllabic number contrasted with ancient regulation of syllabic length, 134–39, 256. *See also* Glossary entry for Syllable

Synaeresis, 118–19. *See also* Glossary entry for; and *see* Elision

Synaloepha, 116. *See also* Glossary entry for; and *see* Elision

Syncope, 121–23. *See also* Glossary entry for; and *see* Elision

Syntax: and meter, 152–53, 158–61, 166–72. *See also* Glossary entry for

Tail rhymes, 331. *See also* Glossary entry for

Tate, Allen, 66

Taylor, Edward, 329

Taylor, William, 230

Tennyson, Alfred, 38, 120, 121, 122, 140, 153, 183, 229, 309; alcaics of "Milton," 269, 276–77; blank verse stanzas of, 202; end-stopped lines in "Tithonus," 315; indentations in *In Memoriam* stanza, 209–10; and Jowett, 221; semi-enjambment in, 109, 110

Tercet, 201, 212, 218, 219, 232–33. *See also* Glossary entry for; and *see* Triplet

Terza rima, 335; Dante's and Shelley's use of, 218–19

Tetrameter (iambic), 8; "clipping" less confusing in, than in iambic pentameter, 88; easier to learn to manage than iambic pentameter, 14–15, 154–56; illustrated by Anne Finch's "Song," 56–57; metrical substitutions in, 66–67; regular form of, mixed with clipped form, in Chaucer, 226, and in Eliot, 313; rhythmical modulations of, 37–38, 101–2, 109, 111, 112; trochaic tetrameters (catalectic and acatalectic) and iambic tetrameters in Milton and Keats, 227–28; as variant in blank-verse poems, 90–91. *See also* Glossary entry for Tetrameter; and *see* Iambic rhythm; Iambic verse; Meter; Metrical accent; Speech stress; Tetrameter (trochaic)

Tetrameter (trochaic): alternation between regular and catalectic forms of, in Samuel Johnson's "Short Song," 226; illustrated by Beeching's epigram on Jowett, 221–22; catalectic form of, illustrated by Elizabeth Barrett Browning's "The Best," 224–25; catalectic and acatalectic forms of, in Frost, 312; catalectic and acatalectic forms of, in Milton and Keats, 227–28; in Longfellow's *Hiawatha*, 222–23. *See also* Glossary entry for Tetrameter; and *see* Tetrameter (iambic); Trochaic rhythm; Trochee

Thayer, Ernest Lawrence: fourteeners of "Casey at the Bat," 207

Theocritus, 202

Thomas, Dylan, 336; syllabic verse of, 258, 259–60

Thomas, Edward, 167

Thompson, John: on natural inclination of English speech to iambic rhythm, 282

Thomson, James, 60, 119

Thorkelin, Grímur Jónsson: and *editio princeps* of *Beowulf*, 139

Tichbourne, Chidiock: "Elegy" of, written entirely in monosyllabic words, 171–72

Tolkien, J. R. R., 248–49

Toomer, Jean, 15

Tottel's Miscellany, 266

Tourneur, Cyril, 128

Trager, George L., 284–85

Traherne, Thomas, 29

Triolet, 196. *See also* Glossary entry for

Triple rhyme, 186, 187, 193, 228, 233, 317. *See also* Glossary entry for; and *see* Sdrucciola rhyme

Triplet, 201, 219; Landor's use of in "Little Aglae," 219–20; as variant in heroic-couplet poems, 59–60. *See also* Glossary entry for; and *see* Tercet

Trisyllabic meters, 230–45. *See also* Amphibrachic rhythm; Anapestic rhythm; Dactylic rhythm

Trochaic rhythm, 221–30; in Beeching, 221–22; in Robert Browning's "Toccata of Galuppi's," 229; in Campion's "Kate can fancy," 229; catalectic and acatalectic forms of, in Frost's "To the Thawing Wind," 312; catalectic and acatalectic forms of, alternating, in Samuel Johnson's "Short Song," 226; catalectic form of, illustrated by Eliza-

beth Barrett Browning's "The Best," 224–25; in Longfellow, 222–24; in Poe, 176–77, 229–30; relative inflexibility of, 241–44, 303. *See also* Glossary entry for Trochee; and *see* Tetrameter (trochaic)

Trochee, 55; Coleridge's characterization of, 225. *See also* Glossary entry for

Tuckerman, Frederick Goddard, 197; enjambment in "As when, down some broad river," 105–6

Tumbling verse. *See* Glossary entry for

Tupper, Martin Farquhar, 261

Turco, Lewis, 300

Tyrwhitt, Thomas, 85

Valéry, Paul, 179, 293; on *vers libre*, 260

Van Doren, Mark, 83, 156

Verse: rhythms of, as opposed to rhythms of prose, 3–8, 282. *See also* Glossary entry for; and *see* Accentual verse; Accentual-alliterative verse; Accentual-syllabic verse; Free verse; Imitation-classical verse; Meter; Syllabic verse

Vers libre, 305; Dujardin on Vielé-Griffin and "definitive establishment" of, 305; Valéry on, 260; and *vers libres*, difference between, 305. *See also* Free verse

Very, Jones, 31, 32, 33

Vielé-Griffin, Francis: and "definitive establishment of *vers libre*," 305

Villanelle, 196; use of refrain lines in, 197. *See also* Glossary entry for

Villiers, George (second duke of Buckingham), 102–3

Villon, François, 311, 318

Virgil, 123, 129, 144, 182, 253, 308, 311, 318

Walker, John, 147

Waller, Edmund, 37

Watts, Isaac, 194, 204; on adjusting pronunciation for rhyme's sake, 190–91; and nomenclature of hymn stanzas, 203

Weever, John: sonnet to Shakespeare, 187–88

Weismiller, Edward R., 294

Werstine, Paul: on lineation of Shakespeare's plays, 292

Wesley, Samuel (the Elder): on prevalence of iambics in English verse, 282

West, Gilbert, 272

West, M. L., 286, 288; on anceps syllables in ancient verse, 310

Wheatley, Phillis, 117, 118

Whitman, Walt: free verse of, 261, 263

Whittier, John Greenleaf: use of metrical grid to point meaning and rhetorical focus in "Abraham Davenport," 169–70

Wilbur, Richard, 21, 33, 34, 35, 61, 83, 168, 205, 217, 293, 316, 328, 329; and accentual-alliterative meter, 252, 308; on elision, 297–98; "Hamlen Brook," expressive use of stanzaic structure in, 213–15; on iambic pentameter, 325; iambic pentameters of "Transit," 57; translations of Molière, 180

Wilde, Oscar, 205

Wilkes, John, 66

William of Normandy, 322

Williams, Miller, 300

Williams, William Carlos: free verse of, 262–63

Wilmer, Clive, 321–22

Wilmot, John. *See* Rochester

Winters, Yvor, 205, 217, 225, 293, 299, 304, 319; on fluidity and sensitivity of English meter, 286; on John Muir, 159

Wood, Clement: on limericks, 320–21

Wordsworth, Dorothy, 90

Wordsworth, William, 43, 60, 63, 164, 167, 206, 207, 272, 291, 329; Arnold on, 72–73; blank verse of, compared to Ben Jonson's, Milton's, and Frost's, 21; divided line in "Tintern Abbey," 90; elision in "Composed upon Westminster Bridge," 149; indentation in "Lucy" poems, 211; revision of "Thorn" in light of Coleridge's criticism, 292; and revival of Rhyme Royal, 326

Wraxall, Nathan: Colman's epitaph on, 237

Wren, Christopher: Bentley's clerihew on, 312

Wrenched accent: possible instance of in Keats, 76. *See also* Glossary entry for

Wrenched rhyme: possible instance of in Keats, 76. *See also* Glossary entry for

Wright, George T., 287, 293

Wyatt, Thomas, 87, 130, 136, 336; contracted spellings of, in Egerton Manuscript, 126–27; Surrey on, 15; terza rima in verse epistles of, 218; versification of, different views on, 257–58

Wylie, Elinor, 156; long meter in "Cold-Blooded Creatures," 204

Yeats, William Butler, 16, 18–19, 47, 48, 83, 119, 217, 326, 330; constituents of iambic meter in "Among School Children," 10–11; iambic hexameters of, 59; and *ottava rima*, 324; trochaic countercurrents in "Second Coming," 73

Young, Edward, 41, 164